THE SUBVERSIVE EVANGELICAL

ADVANCING STUDIES IN RELIGION

Series editor: Christine Mitchell

Advancing Studies in Religion catalyzes and provokes original research in the study of religion with a critical edge. The series advances the study of religion in method and theory, textual interpretation, theological studies, and the understanding of lived religious experience. Rooted in the long and diverse traditions of the study of religion in Canada, the series demonstrates awareness of the complex genealogy of religion as a category and as a discipline. ASR welcomes submissions from authors researching religion in varied contexts and with diverse methodologies.

The series is sponsored by the Canadian Corporation for Studies in Religion whose constituent societies include the Canadian Society of Biblical Studies, Canadian Society for the Study of Religion, Canadian Society of Patristic Studies, Canadian Theological Society, Société canadienne de théologie, and Société québécoise pour l'étude de la religion.

1 *The al-Baqara Crescendo*
   Understanding the Qur'an's Style, Narrative Structure, and Running Themes
   Nevin Reda

2 *Leaving Christianity*
   Changing Allegiances in Canada since 1945
   Brian Clarke and Stuart Macdonald

3 *Everyday Sacred*
   Religion in Contemporary Quebec
   Edited by Hillary Kaell

4 *Convergent Knowing*
   Christianity and Science in Conversation with a Suffering Creation
   Simon Appolloni

5 *Seeding Buddhism with Multiculturalism*
   The Transmission of Sri Lankan Buddhism in Toronto
   D. Mitra Barua

6 *The Subversive Evangelical*
   The Ironic Charisma of an Irreligious Megachurch
   Peter J. Schuurman

The Subversive Evangelical

The Ironic Charisma of an Irreligious Megachurch

PETER J. SCHUURMAN

McGill-Queen's University Press
Montreal & Kingston • London • Chicago

© McGill-Queen's University Press 2019

ISBN 978-0-7735-5732-1 (cloth)
ISBN 978-0-7735-5733-8 (paper)
ISBN 978-0-7735-5834-2 (ePDF)
ISBN 978-0-7735-5835-9 (ePUB)

Legal deposit second quarter 2019
Bibliothèque nationale du Québec

Printed in Canada on acid-free paper that is 100% ancient forest free (100% post-consumer recycled), processed chlorine free

This book has been published with the help of a grant from the Canadian Federation for the Humanities and Social Sciences, through the Awards to Scholarly Publications Program, using funds provided by the Social Sciences and Humanities Research Council of Canada.

Funded by the Government of Canada | Financé par le gouvernement du Canada | Canada | Canada Council for the Arts | Conseil des arts du Canada

We acknowledge the support of the Canada Council for the Arts, which last year invested $153 million to bring the arts to Canadians throughout the country.

Nous remercions le Conseil des arts du Canada de son soutien. L'an dernier, le Conseil a investi 153 millions de dollars pour mettre de l'art dans la vie des Canadiennes et des Canadiens de tout le pays.

Library and Archives Canada Cataloguing in Publication

Title: The subversive evangelical: the ironic charisma of an irreligious megachurch / Peter J. Schuurman.

Names: Schuurman, Peter, author.

Series: Advancing studies in religion; 6.

Description: Series statement: Advancing studies in religion; 6 | Includes bibliographical references and index.

Identifiers: Canadiana (print) 20190054786 | Canadiana (eBOOK) 20190054859 | ISBN 9780773557338 (softcover) | ISBN 9780773557321 (hardcover) | ISBN 9780773558342 (ePDF) | ISBN 9780773558359 (ePUB)

Subjects: LCSH: Evangelicalism—Canada. | LCSH: Big churches—Canada. | LCSH: Irony—Religious aspects—Christianity. | LCSH: Charisma (Personality trait)—Religious aspects—Christianity. | LCSH: Canada—Church history—21st century.

Classification: LCC BR1642.C3 S38 2019 | DDC 277.108/3—dc23

This book was typeset by Marquis Interscript in 10.5/13 Sabon.

For Joseph, Petra, and Grace

Wherever we look, in the present or past, among elites or among ordinary people, among men or women, we find charisma. Charisma may look different, but the phenomenon itself is the same in all places, at all times. Political leaders can be charismatic, and so can neighbors; lecturers and also aunts. Charisma expresses humanity ... a supernatural gift, a gift from God.

Vincent Lloyd, "Ten Theses on Charisma"

Contents

Tables and Figures ix

Preface xi

Acknowledgments xxi

1 Wrecking "Religion" for the Love of Jesus: The Ironic Charisma of a Reflexive Evangelical 3

2 Caught Up in the Dramatic Web: The Sticky Storylines of Ironic Charisma 21

3 From Street Theatre to Silver City: Setting the "Irreligious" Stage 45

4 Irony as Liturgy: Strategic Satire for a Spoiled Identity 71

5 Life Together: Home Church as Romantic Script 94

6 "Irreligious" Teamwork Backstage: The Fly System in the Dramatic Web 125

7 The "Irreligious" Paradox: The Playful Production of Ironic Evangelicalism 156

8 Dramaturgical Trouble and the End of the Show 192

9 Epilogue: Reflecting on Reflexive Evangelicals 223

Appendix: Method: Fieldwork and Posture 245

Notes 251

References 293

Index 353

Tables and Figures

FIGURES

0.1 Bruxy Cavey: Preacher and dance party DJ, November 2016 (credit: Meeting House)   xv
1.1 Teaching Series: "Wrecking Religion: How Jesus Ruins Everything," November 2013 (credit: Meeting House)   9
1.2 The Meeting House Oakville Site: warehouse converted to theatre (credit: Peter Schuurman)   14
2.1 The Kitchener Site: The Meeting House and the Empire Theatre (credit: Peter Schuurman)   24
2.2 A new model of charismatic authority   34
4.1 Promotional flyer: one version of an oft-reproduced "anti-religion" marketing tool   77
4.2 Cavey unveils the new family board game (screen capture from videocast)   85
5.1 Promotional bookmark for seven-week series on Anabaptism and pacifism, 11 April 2010–23 May 2010; a parody of Quentin Tarantino's *Inglourious Basterds* (2009)   103
5.2 The Meeting House's dramatic web   107
5.3 Spin cycle of the dramatic web   123
7.1 *Welcome* DVD 2011: skits, antics, and parodies   164
7.2 Introductory page of TMH 2009 *Spring Report*: glossy final copy spoofs as a draft copy   166
7.3 Organizing a portable church in a rented movie theatre (credit: Peter Schuurman)   175

TABLES

2.1 Three notions of charisma   38
6.1 TMH language training sheet   135

Preface

In face of the opposition between orthodoxy and unbelief, many, and among them the best and most sensitive minds, were cross-pressured, looking for a third way. This cross-pressure is, of course, part of the dynamic which generates the nova effect, as more and more third ways are created.
> Charles Taylor, *A Secular Age*

We don't take ourselves seriously; we just take Jesus seriously.
> The Meeting House *Welcome* DVD

Why are thousands of conservative Christians drawn to a church that meets in movie theatres whose predominant tone could be best characterized as "ironically evangelical"? Within the post-Christian context of central Canada, where an evangelical identity is at best considered a damaged product, and mainline churches' membership numbers continue a steep decline, there is an evangelical church called the Meeting House (TMH) that not only retains a stable attendance, but grew from 100 weekly attenders to 5,000 in ten years and now has nineteen satellite campuses. Most intriguing, it swells with religious vitality while claiming to be "irreligious."[1] How can a church that claims to push away from religion be the source of such religious commitment?

At the centre of this church is a long-haired, overweight hippie-wannabe in a plaid shirt and jeans, sporting earrings and thumb rings. "I've been called the 'blond, beefy, biker-type,'" he will unabashedly tell you. "With the face of Jesus and the body of the Buddha." He's quick-witted, fast-talking, and razor-sharp in his ability to explain an intricate theological issue or offer an insider critique of some evangelical social more. He is Bruxy Cavey (known as "Bruxy" at TMH), the "irreligious" evangelical megachurch pastor preaching within Canada, where the dominant culture is allergic to his extended spiritual family of conservative Christians. The cultural tension that surrounds him is ripe for either a militant apologetic or some disarming good humour. Cavey is a reflexive thinker, however, and chooses the latter option. He can see the incongruities of his situation and take some distance from what's culturally at stake. For him, this tension is most often opportunity for ironic intervention; opportunity to tell the world that Jesus shows a better way than "rules, rituals and religion." For Cavey, church can be irreverently fun – involving the kind of playful antics that might even open people to change.

This ironic play has won him some ardent followers. Said one university professor – a researcher in organizational leadership – who became involved in lay leadership at TMH, "He's one of the most compelling apologists and teachers of the gospel I think the world has ever seen." For some attendees – educated professionals, who, like this man, previously had a tenuous connection to their Christian faith – Cavey has a charisma that binds them to him in a dramatic way. He offers them something precious – a fresh take on Jesus, a way out of a personal crisis, a new identity.

FINDING A THIRD WAY

The faith of Christians in North America comes with a tentativeness, a nervous energy today. Skeptics, likewise, say they are "haunted by faith."[2] "I don't believe in God, but I miss him," writes Julian Barnes in the first sentence in his collection of meditations on death (2008). Fundamentalists, of both religious and atheistic persuasions, shun these uncomfortable, ambivalent feelings. But others can't help but feel fraught and caught: *fraught* because an alternative paradigm shadows their life, and *caught* because in the cross-pressures of hope and doubt, naïveté and cynicism, they seek a third way between the two, one that allows room for both secular and religious sensibilities.

If fundamentalist Christians brook no compromise and retrench themselves, evangelical Christians have historically been more culturally engaged, and they are no exception to these existential tensions. While fundamentalists have not vanished, there is a faction of evangelicals today living within a growing secular context that they hesitate to seal in a compartment apart from their faith life. That post-Christian milieu is especially suspicious of white evangelical Christians, which they associate with manipulative televangelists, the Moral Majority, and the politics of the born-again George W. Bush. In 2016, polls show 81 per cent of white evangelicals voted for Trump, and there was a tidal wave of responses to this surprising statistic, most vociferously from within the evangelical fold.[3] In the spring of 2018, I heard a Latina evangelical pastor from Chicago respond, publicly declaring, "I am incredulous, frustrated and sad that fellow evangelicals would vote for a man who dehumanizes the members of my congregation, calling them 'criminals,' 'thugs,' 'rapists,' and 'animals,'" she declared. "The worst of the matter was this: the church said nothing!" (Schuurman 2018a).

Evangelicals appear to be in the throes of an identity crisis.[4] The *Atlantic* writer and evangelical insider Michael Gerson notes, "Trump's background and beliefs could hardly be more incompatible with traditional Christian models of life and leadership ... 'Evangelical' used to denote people who claimed the high moral ground; now, in popular usage, the word is nearly synonymous with 'hypocrite'" (Gerson 2018). For younger people outside evangelical circles, the image of Christianity was already tarnished with associations of hypocrisy, judgmentalism, right-wing politics, anti-gay sentiments, and a sheltered existence (Kinnaman and Lyons 2007). Especially for Canadians, this morally infected form of Christianity is generally perceived to be *American*, the antithesis of Canadian identity.[5] The urgent task for evangelicals, says Gerson, is "to rescue their faith from its worst leaders." Gerson doesn't even mention #ChurchToo, or the sexual misconduct allegations against megachurch superstar Bill Hybels which had just been made public at that time (March 2018). That scandal was yet to fully detonate on the internet (Crouch 2018; Sanders 2018).

The evangelicals who feel caught between these two competing fields – their own commitment to an evangelical lifestyle and the increasing stigmatization of that identity – I am calling "reflexive evangelicals." They have been called the "new evangelicals" or "emerging evangelicals" (and a smaller group called Red Letter Christians), but I use the term *reflexive* to highlight their approach to their faith with a heightened self-consciousness of their identity as evangelicals. This includes but is broader than the labels above, as post-Trump, evangelicals of many stripes and colours are re-evaluating the label "evangelical" (Campolo and Claiborne 2016). Labberton's *Still Evangelical?* (2018) is a collection of ambivalent responses to the question from prominent American evangelical insiders. One author ironically insists evangelicalism needs to "be born again." These believers are sensitive to the negative stereotype of evangelicals – what sociologist Erving Goffman called a "spoiled identity" – and seek to refashion a more culturally legitimate identity and attitude. This new identity and attitude is more politically detached, more apparently tolerant, and in some cases more ironic. This renovation of identity is less a conversion than a deconversion – from "religion" in general, and from this political evangelicalism in particular.

"A church for people not into church" is their ambivalent, paradoxical motto, and Pastor Cavey's favourite definition of the gospel is that Jesus came to "shut down religion." This is his central theme, his favourite subject, and the face of his church. He wrote on his blog in March 2017 under the title "Wrecking Religion," "Religion is especially destructive when it lays hold of political power to support its own agenda. When religion wields the might of political power, and thereby legislative and military power, to accomplish its ends, truth and love suffer together." Cavey never mentions political figures directly, but he still makes political statements.

Cavey is into parties, but not the political kind. This is perceived as refreshing to many post-conservative evangelicals. "I never wanted to be a pastor," says Cavey when talking about his road to megachurch ministry. "I don't wear suits. I had to borrow one from a friend for my first job interview as pastor. My life's ambition was to be a DJ." Indeed, he still acts as a part-time DJ. "I love dancing and helping people dance. I do weddings and dances. It's funny. Sometimes I DJ the weddings for which I pastor: *all your matrimonial needs ... one stop shopping right there*" (Brierley 2017). Cavey knows evangelicals are stereotyped as dull, serious, angry, or clueless. By contrast, Cavey is cool, playful, gentle, and *in-the-know*, and not just for its own sake, but he would say as a means to "wreck religion" and develop a simpler, more generous, and peace-full community of people who follow Jesus. The Meeting House and its pastor consistently invoke the language of a "third way," claiming to embody "the attitude of acceptance shown by liberals with the Christology of the conservatives." As I heard repeatedly from attendees, "This is the kind of church to which I invite my non-Christian friends." There is something familiar here. Something inviting.

A host at one of the Home Churches (small groups) I attended had come to TMH from another province to do a PhD at an Ontario

Figure 0.1 Bruxy Cavey: Preacher and dance party DJ, November 2016. Cavey's cap reads "Make Christians Christlike Again."

university. Married, with one young child, he and his wife had taken quite quickly to TMH. He recognized the internal tensions of the church, embraced them, and summarized his commitment this way: "I would say that message rings true to me. Like, I like that, I like the structure of that idea that it's not about the structure. It's not about that sort of priestly thing you have to mediate. It's not about all the rules and regulations, it's about relationship. That all makes sense to me."

This is why they come. The "irreligiousness" of this religious group and its leader. The structure of anti-structure rhetoric. An evangelical who is subversive – subversive first and foremost of conventional evangelicalism and its right-wing political stereotype as exhibit "A" of bad religion. Although Canada is technically north of evangelicalism's pulsing centre, to be subversive is to transform from below, or to overturn from underneath. It's the ironic pleasure of a good transgression, for Jesus's sake.

THE MEETING HOUSE'S IRONIC CHARISMA

My project focuses on an ethnographic case study of one particular group of these reflexive evangelicals – the Meeting House in Ontario,

Canada, and specifically its rogue pastor, Bruxy Cavey. Anabaptist in denominational affiliation, they claim to be "Mennonites with electric guitars." They are professed pacifists who watch zombie movies; a self-described "a close-knit family" of about eight thousand people spread across over six hundred kilometres. The playful contradictions abound. Cavey breezily proclaims the dispensability of most Christian staples:

> Jesus is happy to see his followers get organized in order to help spread the message that organizations are not the answer. Christ-followers read the Bible to learn of Jesus' teaching that reading the Bible is not what makes us a Christian. We pray regularly in order to commune with the God who reminds us that praying regularly is not what makes us acceptable to him. We meditate to immerse our souls in the love of God that is already ours, not in order to somehow achieve a state of self-induced enlightenment. And we go to church to collectively celebrate the message that going to church is not what makes us God's children. (2007, 223)

Cavey is constantly reflexive about his Christian practice, approaching it ironically, as contingently sacred.

I argue in this book that Cavey's ironic style embodies a powerful charisma that attracts thousands of conservative middle-class Christians because it offers them a way out of the identity crisis generated by the tainting of their faith in North American dominant culture. This ironic charisma offers them a relief born from ironic distance and the promise of a more legitimate identity within the dominant culture of post-Christian Ontario, Canada. In the end, despite all the protests, Cavey and his church remain in the evangelical camp, but in a hip sort of way that's more palatable to Canadian sensibilities.[6]

The Meeting House is a church for people not into church because its goal, according to Cavey, is to "be in the ministry of busting up people's expectations." So a dishevelled hippie with all the beaded and braided alternative accessories – including sandals or flip-flops – appears on the movie theatre's jumbo screen instead of the clean-cut televangelist in his Sunday suit and tie. Cavey made a comment once during the weekly question-and-answer session after his teaching about "those who are in Christian ministry just so they can make money." He added dryly, "That's why I'm here." The audience laughed, and he continued, raising his arms to show his casual T-shirt and jeans attire, "Please support my expensive taste in clothing."

This ironic subculture is distinguished by more than its style. The style is the signal of a deep desire to be perceived differently. They want to "be Jesus" – a kinder, gentler Jesus, understood as "a religious leader who called for the end of his own religion." Sunday mornings in their large warehouse-theatre and in multiple rented movie theatres across the province offer a consistent satirical engagement with evangelical stereotypes. What I do in this book is unpack through my fieldwork how and why this ironic charisma works for so many middle-class Canadians, investigating how it plays out not just on Sunday morning, but through the various settings of the megachurch. Most significantly, I investigate the energetic teamwork offered by staff and the productive roles played by attendees, especially those who attend their small groups, called "Home Church."

As I examine these different venues, analyzing their video screens and going behind the scenes, I demonstrate how the setting of movie theatres – coupled with the satirical anti-religious narratives, the coordinated stagecraft of staff, and the productive buzz from attendees – all magnify the ironic performance to create a "dramatic web" of meaning and identity for followers. While economics and politics certainly play a role in shaping this community, its vitality is most significantly influenced by its cultural aesthetics, which encourages a suspension of disbelief, captivates attendees' imagination, and engages their emotions like good theatre. The Meeting House's charisma is fundamentally *dramatic*: inspiring, entertaining, and enlivening followers by giving them pleasure, a sense of belonging, and a manageable mission for their lives and families. As a drama, the church is not just a cognitive experience reinforcing beliefs: it's an affective, imaginative, embodied participation in a story they choose to live inside.[7]

My argument culminates in what I am calling "the 'irreligious' paradox," the seeming contradiction in the history of evangelicalism between an emphasis on divine relationship, expressive piety, spontaneity, and family on one hand, and the intensely rationalistic calculus necessary to promote, organize, and control thousands of patrons and manage the accompanying large-scale events. This paradox is intensified with these reflexive evangelicals, as they consistently critique the rigours of institutional "religion" while embracing a "spirituality" contained in the structures of a sprawling centralized bureaucracy – a megachurch. They paradoxically offer not only a church for people not into church, but religion for those not into "religion"; it's the rhetoric of anti-institutionalism housed in a high-tech corporate machine – in effect, an "irreligious" paradox of modern organic counterculture and techno-bureaucratic conformity.

The *Oxford Dictionary* defines *irony* as "a state of affairs or an event that seems deliberately contrary to what one expects and is often wryly amusing as a result." Cavey wants to upend North American expectations for what evangelicals – and more broadly "Jesus followers" – look like, talk like, and act like. He wants to trigger a double take in the mind of those shaped primarily by the dominant academic and mass media stereotypes of conservative Christians by portraying a hippie-like community based in the virtues of pacifism, simplicity, and generosity. And much of this identity labour is done playfully, as church "family." The incongruity of hip urban Mennonite evangelicals led by a DJ pastor functions like a joke – subverting expectations, cultivating a more enjoyable Christian ethic for Jesus's sake.

Do all attendees "get" what I'm identifying as the ironic posture of their church? Do they realize their "irreligious" church *is* a religion, as religion is commonly understood? Certainly attendees do not all perceive the layers of irony to the same degree. Many are intuitively attracted to the church's distance from conventional "religion" that this irony offers. A few others are quite deliberate and articulate about the playfulness and its ambiguities. Most, if they stick with TMH long enough, come to see it as the taken-for-granted style of their pastor and church, which they would describe as consonant with the "way of Jesus." As Bruxy Cavey and former senior pastor Tim Day say in one of their *Welcome* DVDs, "We don't take ourselves seriously; we just take Jesus seriously." Most attendees would accept that at face value, as the core value of the church. What I intend to show is *why* that is attractive, and *how* it is made compelling to so many Ontarians.

Max (pseudonym) was one of the first attendees I met in my first Home Church gathering. It was at a home in a new subdivision not far from my own residence. I asked this young Max, sporting a beard and a ponytail, about the large tattoo of a globe and a young man on his arm. "The Prodigal Son," he tells me, a reference to Jesus's popular parable. We chewed some brie with crackers and sipped herbal tea as he told me he used to work in a tattoo shop. When I ask how he landed at TMH, he tells me he grew up in a "Christmas/Easter" church-going family that was never truly convicted about the faith. He went Pentecostal at age eighteen, but "it didn't fit" him, even though he did not realize it at the time. TMH was like coming home. "I like TMH because even though it's big like Joel Osteen's church, Bruxy doesn't 'sell out' for the crowds," he tells me. "Bruxy tells them if you're just coming for the show and not getting involved, you'd be better to go somewhere else."

Max's face reveals his delight in what I found out was actually a regular ritual of dis-invitation by Cavey, what insiders call "Purge Sunday." I describe this in chapter 4 as a "reverse altar call" intended to shake out the uncommitted and shake up the faithful.

Is Max worried about the culture of Joel Osteen coming north to Canada? "Nope," he replies, smiling. "We're going south. We're making connections across the border, spreading the message. We're on the move."

TMH teems with people like Max – people who left either lukewarm mainline identities (de-churched) or intense conservative/charismatic churches (over-churched). Something in Cavey's presentation resonates in a fresh way, and they leave their childhood traditions behind to pursue the "irreligious" way of Jesus at TMH. People like Max are drawn into TMH and quickly become productive agents in its subculture of "subversive spirituality." But what does the performative contradiction of "irreligious" religion look like in congregational life? How can such paradox provide a stable core for a religious movement?

These are the questions that drove me to enter into the life of this church for the supposedly unchurched. What I found was a high-tech dramatic production offering a new identity for the stigmatized evangelical Christian, a church that had provocative teaching series with playful titles like "Big Buts of the Bible."[8] It promised a high-touch community without "religious" baggage – a spiritual romance of intimate relationships with God and neighbours, always tied back to the person and teachings of a subversive Jesus Christ. This was not your grandmother's religion, they said. No. This would be fun. For a change.

Acknowledgments

Lorne Dawson was one of my graduate professors who was always generous with his time. A Canadian expert on charismatic authority, he once wrote, "The general pattern of need, projection, and identification with the leader is intrinsic to the human condition ... it is a normal part of the life process" (2006, 15). As evidenced in my dedication, Vincent Lloyd (2018) goes even further to suggest charisma is not just an energizing connection with a leader, but to a lesser degree is part of many ordinary relationships. Far from being inherently pathological, as some worry, charismatic bonds can enchant, inspire, and encourage us in our wrestling match with bureaucratic labyrinths and through daily bouts of existential distress.

Such everyday charisma surrounded me during the research and writing of this book, and I would first like to thank the numerous gracious members of the Meeting House who opened their doors to me, answered my endless questions, and shared their brownies and tea. Senior Pastor Tim Day unhesitatingly granted permission for me to explore their megachurch networks, and Bruxy Cavey, whose schedule begged for no further inquirers, was always patient and generous with me and my questions – when I got through his staff to meet him. I was even kindly given permission from staff to use a photograph and a graphic in the last editing moments of 2018. I could mention dozens of other open-hearted Meeting Housers, but as I write I think of one particular regional site pastor, who as my first insider contact was always welcoming to me and my notepad. I hope what follows is taken as a constructively critical engagement with their way of "doing life together."

This book builds on doctoral work in religious studies completed at the University of Waterloo, Ontario. I am grateful to my supervisory committee, including Doug Cowan, Jeff Wilson, Paul Freston, and Jeremy Bergen, who pushed me to read more carefully, think more deeply, and write more precisely.

The circle of those who lent charisma to the project extends much farther, often dependent on electronic connections. James Bielo, Scott Thumma, Warren Bird, and Jim Wellman offered their expertise at moments along my journey. Bill VanGroningen, Peter Erb, Mary Kooy, Norm Klassen, and Paul Joosse offered helpful academic and personal advice. The singular most important voice in turning this dissertation into a more cohesive, more readable, and more marketable book was Gerardo Marti. He walked with me through the PhD and pressed me to reshape, rework, and rewrite the research for a broader audience, always encouraging me, always insisting I had something of scholarly (and publishable) value.

Other colleagues who helped shape my thoughts on Bruxy Cavey and his church include Denis Bekkering, Leah McKeen, Rachel Brown, David Feltmate, Siobhan Chandler, Katie Riddell, Jonathan Vandersteen, David Haskell, Mark Chapman, Adam Stewart, Scott Wall, and Suzanne Armstrong. Brian Carwana was an especially close conversation partner, exceptional in his knowledge of Caveyism and its Canadian evangelical context. I would also like to thank my transcriber, Esther Schletz, who always accommodated me and never failed me.

Key friendships sustained me during the years that lie behind this project. Eric Jensen, Brian Bork, Syd Hielema, and Ben Vandezande shared wise, pastoral support. The group that helped launch me into this new scholarly chapter of life – Glen Soderholm, Jamie VanderBerg, Mark Wallace, and Alex MacLeod – have been a fixed reference point of jocular Cavey-banter in the midst of many personal transitions.

In some ways this was a family project. My wife's illness during the early writing phase brought home to us the inherent precariousness of all our projects. She endured and enthusiastically supported this prolonged academic birthing while pursuing her own obstetrical vocation. Grandparents John and Nellie and John and Jean were a godsend in a time of intense career and family life. And I dedicated this book to Joseph, Petra, and Grace, happy distractions from work, fellow board-game players, who sat in more than one Meeting House cushioned movie chair through the years.

I would like to acknowledge the Ontario Graduate Scholarship program, as their two grants gave fuel to keep the project moving forward. Additionally, I am grateful for the grant that allowed me to participate in Calvin College's Summer Seminar in Christian Scholarship entitled "Congregations and Social Change: Adaptations and Innovations in Religious Communities" for four weeks in the summer of 2011. Finally, I'd like to thank two anonymous reviewers and the team at McGill-Queen's University Press who helped refine the project. Special thanks to Kyla Madden for her key questions and continued guidance along the road to publication.

In sum, like charisma, this book is not the possession of a single individual, but a co-production wrought by the cooperation and generosity of many souls. There are no self-made scholars. Yet I own all the deficiencies, grateful for whatever scholarly charisma might slip on through to curious readers.

THE SUBVERSIVE EVANGELICAL

1

Wrecking "Religion" for the Love of Jesus

The Ironic Charisma of a Reflexive Evangelical

Religion is killing us … At times religion kills through imperceptible strangulation, suffocating us in our sleep. Traditions that have lost their meaning, rituals that have lost their relevance, and rules that have lost their love – all contribute to the numbing of our souls. Until finally, we just … can't … breathe.

Bruxy Cavey

I would say he's certainly one of the most compelling apologists and teachers of the gospel I think the world has ever seen. I don't think that's an understatement. Every preacher needs to be able to speak into his own culture, and Bruxy certainly can do that.

University professor, former male lay leader
at the Meeting House, age fifty-eight

Warming his hands over a small flame in a bowl on his coffee table, Pastor Bruxy Cavey quips from front stage, "Welcome everyone to Hell Sunday. Glad you're here. I'm warm and toasty, how about you? Marshmallow anyone?"

If there is one popularly broadcast teaching that fundamentalists unapologetically espouse but some critically thinking evangelicals and most Canadians find abhorrent, it's the idea of an afterlife for the unrepentant of unending torture in a lake of fire. Bruxy Cavey is one iconoclastic pastor who takes a radically different approach on the subject. In October and November 2017 Cavey taught a series entitled "Bad Ideas: Removing Roadblocks to Knowing God," and he took two services to argue against the "Grand Daddy" of bad ideas – that "God Tortures People Forever."

To problematize the caricature of hell, he showed the clip from *The Wizard of Oz* where the Wicked Witch is doused by water and yells, "I'm melting! I'm melting!" as she crumples and dissolves into a puddle. "Ding dong the witch is dead!" sings Cavey with a mischievous smile, dancing a little jig on the stage. "The wicked witch is dead!"

The audience laughs, but then he quickly shifts his tone: "Is that what hell is going to be like? When we are in heaven and aware that our loved ones are roasting for eternity? Will we be dancing and glad – or sad? And if we're sad, what happens when Revelation says, 'He will wipe all tears from our eyes?' Does he also have to erase our memory or our knowledge of hell? Does it have to be a secret while we're in heaven?"

The humorous quips followed by the serious questioning destabilizes his audience and prepares the way for his critique of the "eternal torment" view of hell, based on his conviction about the overwhelming picture of God in the Bible as merciful, a doctrine he insists is epitomized in the teachings and life of Jesus Christ. Cavey then presents two other theological positions – the annihilationist view (which teaches that the unrepentant simply perish) and the universalist view (which suggests all souls are eventually refined and welcomed to heaven).

By the end of the second Sunday, it wasn't clear which of these two theological views Cavey holds to, so in the regular "Q and Eh?" session after the "teaching" someone must ask him, "So. What's *your* view on hell?" His answer dances around the question, leaving the audience with some ambiguity – a response that frustrates some visitors and delights his followers: "I could be wrong. Depending on which day of the week you catch me, I am a [theological position] two or a three. I just know I'm not a one, and the more I study scripture, the less of a one I become. I'm probably closest to two right now [*smiles*]. I'm a hopeful three. How's that? I'm a two, but if I found out three were true, I would rejoice."

This Pastor Cavey character has no suit, no tie. He does not shout. He is not angry. He offers no promise of fire and brimstone. He never mentions politics. To the contrary: he's unkempt, casual, and cool. His presentation style is a mix of university lecture, fireside chat, stand-up comedy, talk show, and apology for Mennonite theology and lifestyle. When I was attending the church, he confessed he didn't even vote come election time. Five thousand people come to hear him every Sunday, and some just can't get enough of this teaching.

A young English literature PhD student told me it was Cavey's apparent comfort with uncertainty that first drew him to TMH. "Bruxy leaves things up for discussion," he explained. "I associate certainty with arrogance. Even the quotes before the teaching contain contradictory positions, such that you don't know which side he's coming down on." Every service starts with a multimedia presentation – church announcements and an introduction to the current teaching series, which always includes a wide variety of quotes from the disparate sources Cavey has been combing. Consider, too, Cavey has done two summer series interviewing leaders from other Christian denominations (2011, 2013), as well as a teaching series on world religions (July 2000), Islam and ISIS (November 2014), and Jesus and Buddha (April 2018).[1] For some at TMH, the presentation of ambivalence – or at least an acknowledgement of diversity – is considered a necessary virtue.

REFLEXIVE EVANGELICALS: TATTOOED FAITH

Moral Majority icons like Jerry Falwell have died. Billy Graham, having passed 100, died 21 February 2018. Increasingly, however, figures like televangelists and megachurch pastors are being stigmatized as corrupt, and the right-wing religious conservative is routinely discredited in the media. But evangelicals have not become an extinct religious species. They have always been quite adaptable, nimble through changes in the cultural weather. While they have fragmented as a movement (Rah 2009; Worthen 2014), one significant corner of its new mosaic approaches ministry with a distinctively ironic tone. Highly self-conscious, they eschew the stereotypes of uptight, judgmental, politically engaged right-wing evangelicals. This is the irreverent world of leaders like Pastor Bruxy Cavey and his approximately eight thousand followers[2] at the Meeting House in Ontario.

The church is founded upon the paradox of aspiring to be a church for people not "into" church. Cavey, whose long hair, earrings, and thumb rings give him an appearance as strange as his name, professes pacifism while adoring horror films. When he is not teaching with his steel coffee mug in hand, he's jumping up and down as a dance party

DJ. A champion of irony, he tattooed his arm with the reference "Leviticus 19:28," a Bible verse that reads, "Do not ... put tattoo marks on yourselves. I am the LORD."

This brand of evangelicalism acknowledges the stereotype of the right-wing evangelical and plays to deconstruct it. Sometimes called "the new evangelicalism," "the Emerging Church," "emerging evangelicals," or "post-evangelicals," these evangelicals are energized by a highly reflexive, if not ironic charisma ("gift of grace").[3] This new charisma arises out of a deep dissatisfaction by white, middle-class Christians with both the empty horizons of the (post-)secular milieu[4] and the stigmatized caricature of the zealous right-wing evangelical. This creative, persistent, ambivalent evangelicalism seeks to negotiate a new, culturally legitimate identity by distinguishing itself from both the secular left and the religious right to lead its followers into what they call a subversive "third way." Even their architecture, which is neither fully commercial nor substantially sacred space, has been described as a "third place" that is not work, home, or chapel space (Bratton 2016, 10). This church blurs previously taken-for-granted sacred/secular divisions to create a welcoming place for seekers.

These new "reflexive evangelicals"[5] are not only highly self-conscious of their faith and its public perception, but are troubled by the stigmatization the label "evangelical" now attracts and have become ambivalent about the moniker, seeking a fresh liturgy for life, or as I shall suggest in this book, a fresh "dramatic web" for their faith.[6] They don't fall easily into liberal/conservative categories, although some have experienced some socialization in a more conservative and evangelical subculture. They are not confined just to small inner-city churches populated by graduate students and young urban professionals. The Meeting House is a megachurch with thousands of weekly attenders, and I use this case study of reflexive evangelicalism to simultaneously offer a window into the charisma that animates megachurches today. This mega-charisma is not what common sense explanations suggest: it is not simply a religious personality cult, and neither is it simply the crafty manipulation born of business savvy and electronic media. The attraction of the megachurch I argue is best described as a "dramatic web" in which the pastor's visionary charm and the technical expertise around him play a significant role, but a "perfect storm" of factors is necessary to generate the charisma that compels the megachurch crowds, not least of which is the willing suspension of disbelief and active collaboration of audience and staff.

For example, the charisma of any inspired leader requires supporters, carriers, and boosters. So when Cavey tattooed Leviticus 19:28 on his arm, he drew attention to it, as a way of showing they are not a literalistic, legalistic, culturally isolated sect but rather a hip, defiant, and culturally cool "alternative" church. But this act needed to be promulgated to thousands of people, and in-house cameras display the tattoo on screen every Sunday, and his production staff subsequently spread the image to thousands across a variety of wired networks. Additionally, the inking became the introduction to his latest book, *(Re)union* (2017). Cavey's tattoo has become a talking point for followers in casual conversations about the renegade character of their church. Their stories of Cavey and his tattoo create and reinforce his rogue persona and carry his "irreligious" charisma to a broader audience.

I stumbled on a photo of one of their 200 "Home Church" gatherings – small groups that meet during the week to review the Sunday teaching – locally named "Chicory Home Church." Looking at the picture closely, I saw that all eleven people in the group got inked with the same tattoo as their pastor, "Leviticus 19:28." The placement of the tattoo varied from torso to arms, legs, chest, and back; some even had the whole verse written out on their skin. This act of imitation starkly illustrates how the ironic charisma of this megachurch pastor is literally carried by his followers. It began as an ironic image, was electronically reproduced, and then became physically inscribed on his followers' bodies. This new subversive evangelicalism travels with the stories they tell of their altered bodies.

Charisma is a form of branding – self-branding, really. More than a mark, it is an identity inscribed onto bodies and their communal practices. And that embodied identity cannot be understood apart from a larger context: a giant dramatic production that offers inspiration, meaning, hope, and solidarity to followers. In the case of TMH, the drama upends expectations, creates a liminal space for attendees in which they can exchange their spoiled evangelical identity for that of the cool, subversive evangelical.

There are 1,800 megachurches in North America, and they are a diverse group.[7] To fully understand this megachurch, its reflexive evangelicalism, and its self-described subversive ethos, I immersed myself as an ethnographer in this congregation, observing it as a performance.[8] I sought to study it as a deeply cultural, profoundly dramatic religious endeavour in which mostly white, middle-class

Canadian Christians are finding a way out of their angst and distress to connect with something larger that inspires them, motivates them, and changes them. What I found is nothing less than a compelling cultural and religious production uniquely fitted to a secular age.

THE "IRRELIGIOUS" PARADOX

Canada has been known historically as a Christian country. Its Anglican establishment was formally deregulated in 1854 when land was no longer set aside for their denomination's use, although informally the national influence of mainline denominations continued well into the 1960s. For example, up until the 1960s, ten-minute devotions were delivered by mainline clergy on CBC radio, just before the 8 o'clock news. More remarkably, in 1964 a Dutch couple who were landed immigrants in Canada but also atheists were denied citizenship and deported back to the Netherlands. The judge who ruled in the case noted their lack of faith and lack of church involvement: "The things we believe in this country stand for Christianity – being honest and being kind – believing in Christ's teachings ... Not everybody follows this but that is what we try to attain in this country, the Christian way of life" (Miedema 2005, 16). Public institutions gave plausibility to Christian faith and consistent support for the mainline church.

I began this investigation in the Meeting House in the context of a secular religious studies program at a public university in Ontario, Canada, in 2009. By this time, mainline attendance had been in freefall since the 1970s (Clark and MacDonald 2017). Membership rolls in the Anglican Church of Canada and the United Church of Canada had been cut in half between 1968 and 2009. United Church pastor Greta Vosper's *With or without God* (2008) offered Canadians "a way of life ... for those who do not believe in the supernatural elements of religion ... for those who have no need of 'God.'" This was not just a Canadian phenomenon – the New Atheists, hailing from both the United Kingdom and the United States, were on the top of the bestseller lists in much of the West. The fastest growing "religious" demographic in North America continued to be "religious nones" (Putnam and Campbell 2010; Thiessen 2015; Packard and Hope 2015; Drescher 2016). Philosopher Charles Taylor released a tome summarizing the current situation as *A Secular Age* (2007) – characterized as "cross-pressured" between secularism and faith, where religious belief was no longer the default position.

Figure 1.1 Teaching Series: "Wrecking Religion: How Jesus Ruins Everything," November 2013.

I wanted to do a field study, research into the lived religion of people in their community context – as a project in ethnography and congregational studies, a field sorely under-studied in Canada.[9] In this context, I stumbled on the Meeting House, a vibrant, fast-growing church in Ontario, Canada, as a curious case of religious change in North America. While situated in Canada, international boundaries are invisible to some forms of evangelicalism, and reflexive evangelicals are a subculture that resonates in pockets of both countries – particularly in urban places with white, educated, middle-class populations.[10] When I began to study the Meeting House, it was still growing in weekly attendance and in its number of satellite campuses, and it appeared as an anomaly on the Ontario religious landscape. On the surface, its whole vision and mission as a church seemed paradoxically inimical to religion. Cavey's own bestseller had just come out entitled *The End of Religion: Encountering the Subversive Spirituality of Jesus* (2007), and their definition of the gospel proclaimed that Jesus Christ came to "shut down religion." One particular teaching series in 2013 said it best: "Wrecking Religion: How Jesus Ruins Everything." I witnessed people coming by the thousands to hear Cavey elaborate on this theme, week after week. I asked myself, *How does this paradoxical anti-religious church nurture such religious vitality in a secular age?*

Whatever the explanation for the growth and enthusiasm I found there, I knew that scholars considered megachurches[11] to be a microcosm of the prevailing dynamics of evangelical culture and that many of the recent assessments of these institutions have been simplistic and dismissive: they are viewed as religious Walmarts[12] or Elmer Gantry–like personality cults;[13] in other words, the equivalent of consumer crowds or a one-man show. These two assessments are important for their critical perspective, but they are weak when examined from a perspective based on ethnographic fieldwork. Attending a megachurch for several months stimulates a deeper understanding of its dynamics than assessing it from afar through one-dimensional assessments centred on consumerism or celebrity. My personal observation of its worship, interviews with its staff, and sharing small group discussions with its members gave me a sympathetic insight critical for gauging the character of this religious community. Caricatures are easily reproduced from the research space of one's armchair; sustained personal encounters can at least provide nuance to rigid theoretical frames.

This was my preliminary insight: North American evangelicalism is no longer a singular right-wing block, and it suffers from an identity crisis sparked by a cultural backlash in the West against the Religious Right in America. In fact, some new breed of evangelicals have developed a self-reflexive posture cognizant of these evangelical and megachurch critiques. So a new approach to evangelicalism is necessary that takes into account the lived reality of these emergent megachurches and moves our investigation beyond the right-wing stereotypes of evangelical institutions and beyond consumer religion tropes to a more sophisticated evangelical mosaic in North America. Such a nuanced approach allows us to grasp the responsiveness of church leaders to cultural images projected onto them and emphasizes that the ongoing cultivation and reshaping of their self-presentations are enacted and re-enacted with an eye to their assessment of how they are perceived by the general public. Believing their religious truths remain important despite "bad press," evangelicals learn to re-present themselves, reframing their message in order to rescue their core mission: sharing the good news of Jesus Christ.

I draw from Max Weber and Erving Goffman to create what I'm calling "the dramatic web" of an "irreligious paradox." These new evangelical churches capture the imagination of the crowds because of the playful incongruity of an anti-institutional megachurch that vilifies "religion" for the love of Jesus. Being "anti-religious" is not

The Ironic Charisma of a Reflexive Evangelical

entirely new to the evangelical faith, and it's part of our "spiritual but not religious" climate,[14] but I did not start my project with such a paradox in mind. I started with a simple curiosity about Bruxy Cavey and his promise for a "church for people not into church" – a religious ethic that "wrecks religion" in order to save faith and so restore genuine relationship with Jesus Christ and others. It was a story-script I came to understand as satire and romance, a paradox of anti-institutionalism bred within a giant, sprawling religious institution. It was a story with a central dramatic character – a holy fool – that drew people into its plot, a story that plays out in movie theatres,[15] people's private homes, and what is appropriately called the "net." The "irreligious" drama captivates their imagination with its villain of institutional religion and its countercultural hippie hero, and the stated goal was not just to capture an audience, but to transform them into gentle Jesus people for an "irreligious" age.

The "Jesus" they refer to was nicely captured by one young graduate student and new father I interviewed. "Cavey and Tim like to poke fun at themselves. They don't take it too seriously, but it doesn't mean it's not important," he said. "I don't know how to explain it. There's that one poster, or picture, of Jesus laughing. I saw it at a friend's house and they had a picture of Jesus laughing on the wall. And it was like, it just smacked me in the face." He went on to say that pictures of Jesus are always so dramatic and intense, but this was a new image of him. It was startling in its unabashed bliss. It is this image of Jesus that Cavey seeks to disclose through a wide diversity of distribution channels and onward to his imagined wider community of religious "nones."

Pastor Cavey is not always a bundle of witty quips and hilarious stunts. But some of the key identity-shaping moments of the Meeting House certainly are "irreligiously" playful, and play is no stranger to religion, as I shall argue in the chapters ahead.

REFLEXIVE EVANGELICALS:
"A CHURCH FOR PEOPLE NOT INTO CHURCH"

Reflexive evangelicals are first of all reflexive people. After I had written this book I stumbled on an interview of Cavey in late 2017 in which he uses the word *reflexive* to describe himself. The interviewer asks how he became a pastor, and Cavey talks about his career as an undergraduate psychology student at York University in Toronto. He says he questioned whether his faith was just a product of his family and social location, an arbitrary aspect of his life. He went on a quest:

> I tried on every other faith, I tried everything from atheism to Hinduism to Islam. I spent my university years very much trying to be everything else, trying to step into everything other than Christian thought to try it on for size. I've learned that I have what psychologists call a "reflexive mind," which means I'm always questioning and always doubting. I thought that was because Christianity was not answering all my questions and caused so many doubts. But what I realized through this process was that *this is just me*. I carry questions with me everywhere. So if I was an atheist, I would be a doubting atheist, I would be a doubting Muslim. And here I am a questioning Christian.
>
> Eventually I realized that Jesus is not threatened by my questions – he made room for doubting Thomas, for the questions of John the Baptist. I can walk with Jesus, with all of my skepticism, cynicism, and questions and just gather them up and submit them to the life of faith with Christ. (Brierley 2017)

For some evangelicals in multicultural Toronto, who may have attended a secular university, being reflexive about one's faith is a way of life.[16] And not just reflexive about one's faith, but about one's evangelicalism, about which Cavey also has doubts.[17] A "reflexive mind" is the frame of their very consciousness, at least in terms of their faith. Their faith is a precarious vision, shaken by cognitive dissonance, but nevertheless chosen, embraced, and to be shared with friends and neighbours.[18]

Cavey's early biography does not reveal the origins of the Meeting House, however. It began as a church plant of an Anabaptist denomination called the Brethren in Christ in 1986. Started by Craig and Laura Sider, it began with a group of eight people in a Bible study, which slowly grew, with some newcomers joining while still attending another congregation, waiting to see what would become of this new community. It was called Upper Oaks Community Church and never grew much beyond 100 people until Bruxy Cavey became the new pastor in 1996.

Cavey grew up in a large Pentecostal church in Toronto and became a street evangelist as a young adult in the 1980s. He was the lead singer in a band and a key actor in a travelling drama troupe – all part of his expanding evangelical ministry – which evolved even through his time at York University. His name was popular within evangelical networks in southern Ontario, and in 1991 he was asked to pastor a small Fellowship Baptist church. The church immediately grew, but Cavey pulled out a few years later after his separation and divorce. It was 1996, and after he had wandered for a few months in a personal wilderness, the regional bishop of the Brethren in Christ asked him to succeed Sider as the pastor at Upper Oaks Community Church. A name change birthed the Meeting House, and curious crowds began to surge to see the brilliant long-haired preacher with earrings and a disarming sense of humour.

When I began studying the Meeting House in earnest in 2011, Bruxy Cavey had a staff of approximately sixty people (full and part-time). The megachurch had about ten regional sites (which increased to nineteen by 2019) meeting on Sundays in rented movie theatres across southern Ontario, Canada. The headquarters or main "production site" in Oakville features a former automobile plant converted to looked like a giant theatre. This is where the largest proportion of the church gathers Sunday mornings. Growth has started to plateau of late, with about 5,500 people typically attending Sunday services since 2010 (although they say approximately 8,000 people identify with the church as their home congregation, as many do not attend every week). About 45 per cent of these attendees also attend one of two hundred "Home Churches" during the week – a group of ten to thirty people who meet in someone's home to discuss the Sunday teaching, pray together, and plan recreational and service activities together.

My claim in this book, however, is that this story is not just about Bruxy Cavey or even the Meeting House. This church provides a microcosm for understanding the charismatic leadership that fuels the megachurch phenomenon and in this case, specifically, the ironic charisma of a new evangelicalism for mostly white, evangelical Christians who are weary of being caricatured as legalistic, judgmental, and politically motivated. They embrace the pejorative connotations of "religion" and even Christianity in order to carve fresh space for an organic community of more culturally legitimate "Jesus followers." They see their church as a vehicle of religious change, and in turn, personal and social change.

TMH is not just an idiosyncratic Canadian situation, and its key partnerships demonstrate its wider significance. The church has been

Figure 1.2 The Meeting House Oakville Site: warehouse converted to theatre.

part of the Brethren in Christ denomination, which has its centre of gravity in the United States, concentrated in Pennsylvania around Messiah College. During its growing years, the Meeting House made frequent connections with "seeker-sensitive" Willow Creek Community Church in Chicago,[19] and relations have always been warm between Cavey and Greg Boyd at Woodland Hills, a megachurch in Minneapolis (Goodstein 2006). In 2014 Cavey reported an even more collaborative and "theologically and structurally compatible relationship" that has grown between TMH and Ryan Meeks's EastLake Community Church, just outside Seattle, Washington. This church shares a wry religious approach, self-identifying as "a not-so-secret society of average people working together for good." Meeks declares he is determined to "preach what I see as the subversive, counter-cultural, upside-down way and path of Jesus Christ."[20]

Both EastLake and the Meeting House lie within the porous boundaries of what has been called the "Emerging Church" movement.[21] The Emerging Church has been described as a deconstruction of conservative evangelical forms of church – the especially megachurch phenomenon (Bielo 2011; Marti and Ganiel 2014).[22] This critical posture puts TMH in a paradoxical position, a space that they seem quite comfortable to occupy. You might say their vision is to create an incongruity in the mind of its audience – between what visitors anticipate experiencing in church and what they actually encounter when they enter TMH on Sunday. In the fall of 2013 I was at a small gathering of Anabaptist theologians on the campus of the University of Toronto, all of whom were eager to hear Cavey explain the vision of his church. It was a mostly informal evening of conversation, and Cavey, giving reasons for his style of approach, said rather apologetically,

> We are looking for a target market or niche of people who have had a negative church experience, or indirectly, what they've seen on TV is stock Christian characters who just want money, or they've read certain authors that highlight certain [appalling] things in church history. For those who have a negative image of church, we want to create a safe place; for those who are frustrated with religion as a concept, clear away all the rubble. Not everyone will respond, but if they can have a clear vision of Jesus, they'll have that "aha!" moment. So we want to let church get out of the way so they can meet Jesus.[23]

Cavey strategizes a highly reflexive approach to ministry; he makes the assumed prevailing dominant cultural consciousness his starting point and then constructs a church culture that contradicts its assumptions about church. Cavey put it quite concisely that evening: "We are in the ministry of busting up stereotypes, breaking up the line of expectation."

Reflexive evangelicals are highly self-conscious of their public image and how it is perceived by dominant North American popular culture. Their religious work is dedicated to producing a religious drama *about* religion, a reflexive interrogation of their own primary activity, forming a paradoxical orientation: an "irreligious" drama about religion, for religious ends. From a different angle, a paradoxical "irreligious" and anti-institutional drama operated by a large, highly centralized religious institution. Some of these evangelicals see such a critique of religion as serious and prophetic, and often Cavey appears that way. The self-contradictory nature of their project seems to elude them. But as his tattoo suggests, Cavey is often also quite ironic in his approach, and the prophetic mixes with the playful and is intentionally mischievous. Religion, and especially "irreligion," need not be perpetually solemn or severe. The incongruity of the "irreligious" paradox can enliven and energize a crowd, not unlike a good joke. Charisma relies on such foolishness, as signals of transcendence in ordinary life, as I shall argue later.[24]

Cavey seeks to nurture an evangelical community in which faith and fun seamlessly co-exist. One after-sermon question from attendees asked Cavey "Where to draw the line" on fun and parties. Cavey's reply draws no lines:

> Yes, thank you, Jesus cares about us having fun. He turns water into wine. He gets the dance happening. He wants his kids to be happy. If we don't honestly believe he is the source of our joy, rest and fun, and keep fun bits separate on the side, the fun bits are now divorced from Jesus because we have separated them in our mind, which then tends to create fun as an area that is uninformed by the presence and beauty of Jesus. That makes it easier to overdose in things to an unhealthy measure, whether that be that alcohol, whether that be the kinds of relationships we get involved in, etc., and we end up going down a route where fun is just a sinful place. (20 November 2016)

Cavey is a subversive evangelical – subversive of evangelical stereotypes, and more broadly of stereotypes of "religious people." Traditional evangelical moral order exists alongside a faith that is ripe with joy. Joy has always been characteristic of evangelical worship, but with these reflexive evangelicals, it often expresses itself in ironic tones.

BEER STORE ANABAPTISM

There is a story of the beginnings of TMH that is almost legendary. In the 1980s the Brethren In Christ had an unimpressive legacy in urban church plants (churches begun through evangelism in a new neighbourhood); most had failed. In 1985 Craig and Laura Sider moved into the west-end Toronto suburb of Oakville with a vision of creating "a church for people who had given up on church." To begin a church plant, they went door-to-door in Oakville conducting a survey of the neighbourhood, asking people what they needed most in their neighbourhood.

Wendell Murray (pseudonym) worked in a window and door factory for thirty-two years and his was one of the first Oakville doors that Laura Sider knocked upon in December 1985. The story is well known and often told of how Murray's immediate reply to Sider's question about neighbourhood needs was less than ripe for church participation: "We need a beer store."

Murray, however, became involved with the launch of the Upper Oaks Community Church in 1986 and became the first baptized member in the new church.[25] He volunteered for many roles in the church, was then hired part-time in the children's ministry (1998), and is said to have since done "almost every role in TMH," including administrative coordinator, site leadership associate pastor, and now data manager. His journey around various positions resembles the lives of other staff who have been around for a long time; they inconsistently shift their role as the church grows. This rotation keeps people unsettled and constantly challenged while preventing the development of private positional fiefdoms.

In 2011 Murray and his wife were showcased onstage at the "One Roof" twenty-fifth anniversary event as "the first convert" who was enfolded into the church by baptism. Glowing under the spotlights of the giant arena in front of thousands of church attendees, he was introduced as an icon of the church, symbolizing its evangelistic mission and self-deprecating style: their church began with a desire for a beer store. For Anabaptists, whose 1527 *Schleitheim Confession* prohibits the patronage of drinking establishments, this is indeed ironic. But irony is the primary currency at TMH, and many modern Anabaptists would even drink to that today. In one of my interviews in the Cavey home, he offered me a choice of four beers, including some chocolate beer, and a Pumpkinhead beer from Portland Maine's Shipyard Brewing Co. He does not hide his moderate use of some strange brew.

This book elaborates on the ironic culture of this church and its attendees. In a nutshell, my case study offers three fresh ideas to the conversation on evangelicalism and their megachurches. First, I offer a new understanding of megachurches as more than personality cults or religious Walmarts – they are cooperative cultural productions energized by a charismatic bond. Second, this assessment simultaneously depends on a new understanding charismatic leadership – a simple scheme that combines the concepts of Goffman and Weber to create the "dramatic web" of charisma. Finally, I argue that there is a strand of charismatic megachurch leadership today that suggests the evangelical movement has become increasingly diverse and self-conscious, what I am calling "reflexive evangelicalism," manifest in an "irreligious paradox."

The chapters of the book slowly unveil the building blocks of a dramatic megachurch production and culminate in a chapter that brings all the pieces together within the concept of "the 'irreligious' paradox." The second chapter delves into this notion of ironic charisma, unpacking three different meanings assumed in the term *charisma*. Chapter 3 offers some necessary context – the ambivalent religious landscape of Ontario, the biography of Bruxy Cavey, and a short history of the Meeting House.

The next two chapters unfold the key narratives that give the dramatic web its plot, the narratives that enchant followers and carry the "reflexive evangelical" message. Chapter 4 investigates the front stage satirical story of repressive right-wing religion and shows the role distance that Cavey takes from his evangelical colleagues. The Meeting House is *not* your normal evangelical stereotype of church: they are on a mission with Jesus to "shut down religion." The following chapter 5 investigates the romantic hippie-like narrative that promises a way to intimate spiritual community – the offstage world of Home Church. If the front stage is a negative identity, driven by a satirized struggle against "religion," this offstage script offers a positive identity associated with peace, love, and simplicity nurtured in small groups that meet in people's private homes.

Chapter 6 breaks the spell of individual charismatic power by offering a look behind the scenes at the stagecraft and fly system – the coordinated teamwork, discipline, and technology that make the centralized dramatic production possible. The "irreligious" plot requires a common language, media sophistication, grassroots participation and the strategic propagation of the vision and mission of the church. Staff commitment and creativity – including the pastoral work of regional site pastors and the imaginative work of the communications team – are vital to successfully routinizing the dramatic web of charisma. Charismatic authority, like the Wizard of Oz, depends on an invisible apparatus of backstage support to magnify its power.

Chapter 7 sums up "the 'irreligious' paradox" and explains the playful, ironic charisma of the whole production, juxtaposed with the calculated, centralized operations that ensure its efficiency for large-scale audiences. Contrary to the "strictness" theory of church growth, the Meeting House exemplifies what has been discovered in many megachurches: they are a place of celebration, satire, and playfulness. We call dramas a "play," but they also are a form of playful activity, which key sociologists of religion have linked as basic to religion and ritual. At the core of the Meeting House is a paradox, a "church for people not into church," which requires a suspension of disbelief, a willingness to pretend and experiment with a basic incongruity. I examine the church's *Welcome* DVDs, which are saturated with humour and parody, signalling newcomers to bracket their "serious" religious identity. Additionally, the rare "all-site" gatherings of church (called "One Roof") have been a mix of carnival, church ceremony, and dance party. These playful, apolitical events, including the regular activities of Home Churches, engender an attitude amenable to transition and change, while simultaneously giving the church the added cultural legitimacy it so desperately seeks.

In chapter 8 I examine the question so many ask: What if the central actor leaves or dies? I first contend that Cavey's charisma already suffers in some ways, lacking a totalizing control, and these weaknesses have been addressed without significant crises. I then offer a typology of possibilities for the future of the Meeting House and other megachurches, re-emphasizing that charisma is a collective production and not a one-man show. Charisma is carried by multiple actors, audiences, and structures. The complexity of the Meeting House's dramatic web demonstrates that megachurches are precariously poised, but because of the many people and practices that co-produce the scene, it may not be doomed to die with the leader, as many assume.

My concluding chapter analyzes the current dynamics of the church and speculates about its future and that of the "reflexive evangelical" in an increasingly secular society. While their architecture and style of practice may mimic cultural patterns, the world view and politics remain distant and distinct from the (post-)secular milieu. This culturally engaged but distinct approach to congregational life offers a vitality that promises to continue to inspire those looking for a third way amid the cross-pressures of this secular age – skirting the maligned right-wing evangelical stereotype and avoiding the closed, immanent frame of the materialist alternative.[26]

Megachurches are easy to caricature, as are their preachers. This book is not an armchair analysis of these sprawling congregations, but the findings of a participant observer who entered the warp and woof of one particular megachurch.[27] It remains a snapshot – I attended most closely during 2011–14, although I tried to follow the teachings from a distance until 2016 and have used some media clips as late as 2018. Unlike most megachurch studies, I personally interviewed the leading figure (on three occasions). I also attended five House Churches (small groups) for eleven weeks each and interviewed eighty-two people with varying connections to the church. Megachurches are not just sermons, vision statements, and the dramatic scandals reported by mass media: they are people, practising their religious lives alongside their other daily commitments.

To see the depth and quality of religious life, even when presenting as "irreligious," researchers need to study people in their natural, everyday environment, in the cultural context of their congregating. And such context is the focus in chapter 3. Before we explore that, however, the next chapter explains in more detail what I mean by the often overused and misunderstood term *charisma*.

2

Caught Up in the Dramatic Web

The Sticky Storylines of Ironic Charisma

Whether we believe in God or Michel Foucault, we should acknowledge that power works in mysterious ways, especially in all matters that touch upon culture ... either religion keeps up with other cultural aspects of national life, including its commercial forms, or it has no importance.
R. Laurence Moore, *Selling God:
American Religion in the Marketplace of Culture*

I love Bruxy. I really am a huge fan of his. I think he is gifted. He's changed our lives. God's used him to change our attitudes, to get us thinking about issues that we would never have thought about. And so I love him.
From interview with male lay leader, aged sixty-two

The epigraph above comes from "Winston," a former chair of the Overseers board of TMH. He is a professional, having worked decades as a leader in the banking world. Both he and his wife did not grow up Christian, but had conversion experiences in the twelfth year after their marriage. They became increasingly hungry for teaching that would help them grow in faith, and moving from London, England, to the United States, they eventually landed in Toronto and attended an Anglican Church until they heard Cavey speak.

"This guy is good," Winston remembers saying to himself the first time he heard Cavey on a cassette tape in the late 1990s. "He sounds just like John Stott." Stott (1921–2011) was an Anglican priest and a revered leader in the worldwide evangelical movement, a proper British gentleman most often seen in a business suit. "But when I saw Bruxy walk up, I'm like, 'That is the voice. *This* is not John Stott.'"

Enthralled with the hippie-like Cavey, they left their Anglican church and quickly got involved in leadership at TMH. They viewed Cavey as too self-effacing and worked hard to expand his public image. "I would have given him less time off than the board gave him," said Winston. "His teaching grew the church. Without him up there, attendance flagged."

He went on to describe his big dreams for TMH, with Cavey at the helm. "There are few people in this world who can do what he can do," he testified. He noted the lack of enthusiasm for faith in Canada, as opposed to his experience living in the southern United States. But in his mind, with Cavey's charisma, this was just simply greater opportunity: "We still have a community here in Toronto where it's such a minority – the number of people that are actually Christians and actively involved in Christian work. This is like a complete dry field. And so I thought that this Meeting House building would be temporary, that we'd be here for a number of years and then we should be moving on to the next place, and eventually into the SkyDome. This church should continue to grow dramatically."

The Toronto SkyDome (renamed the Rogers Centre) can seat over 50,000 sports fans. Megachurch pastor and TV celebrity Joel Osteen fills the former Houston Rockets' arena, where the seating capacity is 16,800. Cavey's magnetism with crowds looms much larger in this lay leader's imagination.

Not everyone expressed adulation this intense for Cavey, but most of my interviewees agreed that Cavey has a "charismatic personality" – popularly understood as an uncanny ability to mysteriously draw people's attention and loyalty. His capacity to charm crowds was undeniable and formed the centre of many conversations that I witnessed at TMH.

Still, what *is* charisma, and how does it work? More specifically, how does it work with Bruxy Cavey and TMH in Ontario, Canada? My investigation suggests that Cavey may be the star of the show, but his charisma is much more than just an individual effort. Charisma cannot operate on its own; it cannot exist apart from relationships of trust, admiration, and loyalty. And for a population skeptical about institutions and its leaders – especially evangelical ones – nothing is more apt than *ironic* charisma; charisma that recognizes itself with a playful wink. The subversive evangelical Cavey upends secular expectations while modelling a new identity and ethos for conservative Canadian Christians who may feel besieged by the Canadian secular establishment, and internally torn about the recent legacy of their own evangelical identity.

CONSUMERISM, CELEBRITY, AND THE DRAMATIC WEB

Let's step back a moment and look at the larger picture again. How did I get to the point where I identified charisma as the central operating dynamic of this church?

I began by asking, Why is this megachurch thriving in the context of religiously ambivalent Ontario? This is a narrower form of the question: why are megachurches proliferating around the planet?[1]

Scholars have given economic, cultural, geographical, technological, and strategic explanations for the rise of the megachurch, all of which offer some insight into the megachurch phenomenon (Wilkinson and Schuurman 2019). The dominant framework, which I began with in my research, assumed that the main dynamic operating within the church was resonant with *consumer culture*. People came to the church because of the movie theatre atmosphere, the entertaining services with their clever "anti-religion" marketing. It's about the branding, scientific management, and metrics, as well as the familiar big box architecture, the dazzling electronic media, and the post-suburban matrix of life. This assumption fit the readily available "megachurch as Walmart religion" theory and offers a critical view of megachurch life as superficial, passive, and structured by globalized capitalist forces. Many writers go on to say the megachurch is ultimately evidence of secularization – capitulation to an overwhelmingly powerful seduction to be easy, entertaining, and religiously lite for an age of globalized consumption.

This framework has critical import – especially for the prosperity theology megachurches around the globe – and I never dismiss this view. Critical theorists decry church economics from one side while from another side religious economy scholars generally see it as savvy religion.[2] Mainline churches have traditionally sought to tie themselves to the state and citizenship, but the recent multicultural shift in politics has caused those ties to break, and more entrepreneurial evangelical church leaders look to market forces to bolster their institutional weight. Marketing, metrics, and management have become common practice in most churches now, endorsed by what has been called the church growth movement.[3] Still, the warning of Laurence Moore echoed in my mind as I investigated the corners of TMH: "Go slowly

Figure 2.1 The Kitchener Site: The Meeting House and the Empire Theatre.

before assuming that one kind of secularity, the one pronounced in our own times, somehow has a special ability to corrupt or undermine what we call religion. To say that churches are partly secular institutions is as neutral a statement as statements can get. It should astonish or upset no one" (1995, 275). Churches grow in local soils, whatever their variety. Nevertheless, attributing the heart of religious life simply to commercial forces is a reductionism that will miss other, potentially more vital cultural elements that may be at work. Church is cultural labour more than it is economics (Chaves 2004).

I attended the church, joined its small groups, and interviewed its members, and I began to appreciate the central role played by the personality and teaching of Pastor Bruxy Cavey. In fact, he preached against consumerism and passive attendance, and attendees responded by getting involved in their Home Churches and participating in local charity work and social action. There was an ironic approach – or a willingness to live the contradiction – of gathering in a movie theatre around a jumbotron with a Starbucks coffee and protesting the influence of consumerism in North American culture. Attendees do not see themselves primarily as passive consumers but as subversive deconstructive agents and compassionate Christian activists who build community and serve their neighbours. It's an Anabaptist church, after all, where relations with the state, market, and technology are traditionally discerned as a community, and often under the rubric of "separation" or non-conformity to the world. TMH is not Amish; its members are "modern urban Mennonites." But they still cultivate a deliberate "rage against the machine" – resistance to the materialistic and hedonistic vices of modernity.[4]

I began to frame my observations with a different and widely accepted explanation: evangelicalism's central dynamic revolves around celebrity pastors and their personality cult.[5] That megachurch pastors are "holy mavericks" (Lee and Sinitiere 2009) seemed like common sense and was a popular theme among megachurch observers. Additionally, almost everyone I asked at TMH about their reason for attending said first and foremost it was their dynamic lead pastor, Bruxy Cavey, and his extraordinary teaching. He offers them the enchantment of faith, meaning, and purpose in a cosmos sustained by divine love, which contrasts with the drab backdrop of the lowered horizons of secular materialism (Taylor 2007).

Yet Cavey does not spoon feed all the old traditional religious answers. The fact that about 96 per cent of attendees come from another denominational identity indicates that it is not familiarity, heritage, or theology that brings people to this church. Cavey has these people under his "irreligious" spell, and such power comes with the liabilities of manipulation and abuse that after the televangelist scandals of the 1980s – including Jimmy and Tammy Baker, Jimmy Swaggart, and more recently, leaders like Ted Haggard, Bishop Eddie Long, Mark Driscoll, and Bill Hybels – the North American public know too well and instinctively despise. In 2018, #MeToo had its complement of #ChurchToo, and scandals including the superstar megachurch pastor Bill Hybels of Willow Creek heighten suspicion for celebrity pastor power (Bailey 2018; Crouch 2018).

Popular literature adds to the trope of the scandalous megachurch pastor. K.C. Boyd's novel *Being Christian* (2012) presents a vulgar reproduction of Sinclair Lewis's classic novel *Elmer Gantry* (1927). John Christian Hillcox is a violent, alcoholic, crude, philandering megachurch pastor. His followers are equally distorted cartoons, summarized by the phrase "the simple are easily led." Pastor Christian's charisma enables him to rouse these followers into emotional hysterics, and he creates a religious service "perfectly orchestrated to manipulate the human spirit." Boyd describes the Sunday morning services as calculated performances: "This was his show and he was in control – producer, director, writer, star. Entitled to everything, he took it all" (2012, 164). The story goes downhill from there. This grotesque caricature aptly describes the megachurch pastor as part of a show, but mistakenly assumes he is in manipulative, even malicious control.

I did not witness a scandal at the Meeting House, but I did note a heightened *awareness* of such dangers, including the collective concern of being *perceived* as a personality cult. Additionally, there is something passive about Cavey's personality and something limited in his role that requires his staff to work exceptionally hard in building and disseminating his image. In sum, his charisma was not a solo performance based on personality alone, but the product of dedicated teamwork.

What helped me move beyond describing this megachurch simply as a one-man show was the writing of Max Weber (1968) on the notion of charismatic authority. For Weber, charisma is not the singular possession of one person, emanating from the magical power of personality, but rather a dynamic *relationship*, a bond that forms when a leader offers a way out of traditional and bureaucratic social structures. Charisma depends on followers eagerly embracing the leader's revolutionary vision and mission. For the Meeting House, this mission was the "irreligious" message of Jesus preached by Cavey, which promised the "end of religion" and the organic formation of an intimate spiritual community. Within the context of withering religious structures in Ontario and a secular dominant culture, Cavey's hippie-like vision met people's hunger for an anti-institutional Christian faith and practice.

Some scholars have written briefly on charisma and megachurch pastors, and their work makes a fascinating comparative study.[6] Still, I was left with the question, How does this ironic charismatic energy develop, reproduce, and expand to so many people? While I was reviewing my notes on a particular Purge Sunday the answer came to me. Purge Sunday (described in more detail in chapter 4) is the in-house name for the Sundays in which Cavey invites all supposedly passive consumer attendees to leave and find another church to attend. He basically says, "If you're not happy here, it may be time to leave. We'll help you find a church more suited to you." I began to see this ritual as a "reverse altar call" – a *performance* dependent on the history of evangelical practice and yet geared to address cultural critiques of manipulative megachurches. The language of performance pointed me to Erving Goffman's dramaturgical sociology, which frames all social life as performance – as people acting to create impressions and define situations according to their own collective narratives about "what is going on here." This idea of life-as-drama illuminated the charismatic power of Cavey as part of a larger show geared toward the impression management of a "spoiled identity" – in this case, evangelical identity. The central dynamic of the Meeting House's attraction did not lie solely in Cavey or in the consumer culture that permeated the church but in their *collaboration* to create a dramatic religious production intended to "wreck religion" for the love of Jesus. Purge Sunday simultaneously critiqued and played with conventional evangelical ritual, a new variation on an old evangelical practice intended to intensify commitments.

Even Cavey's own language for describing his church follows dramaturgical tropes. When introducing his church's vision, he speaks of the "false impression" of stiff, formal, conservative Christianity and contrasts it with his more casual, accepting, and even remorseful performance of Christianity:

> If there is any community that should be the epitome of honesty and authenticity, that should feel like a come-as-you-are party, it should be the group of people who follow Jesus. But unfortunately, we've often been known as the opposite – the place where I have to be sure I buy new clothes and put on a false face and pretend and then I can finally fit in. We would say *No*, we need to repent, and if we've given that impression, as a pastor now and I'm in a position because of corporate solidarity, to repent on behalf of fellow pastors ... we are sorry, we have given a false impression, and you are welcome just as you are. You may not stay that way, you may be changed, but it will be a change from the inside out. Not cleaning up your externals, not from the outside in but from the inside out. Be open to change, but definitely come as you are. (Brierley 2017)

Cavey pushes off from the negative stereotype of conservative Christians in the media and academy to draw his audience into his own preferred image of church-going Christians: a specific kind of character in a specific kind of drama, like the person who greets you at the door of a party. Not unlike a DJ.

Here's a key point: faith – in anything – is not just a matter of intellectual assent, of cognitive beliefs about the nature of reality.

When I claim that religion involves creating an impression, consciously and subconsciously scripting a dramatic presentation of what life can become, I am suggesting it is an embodied aesthetic, a social imaginary,[7] a set of relationships and roles, a vocabulary and practice of the good life that is caught more than taught. It captures the imagination and trains people in motives, desires, and action. It is not just a script, but an invitation into a play, what I call a dramatic web.

The dramatic web is the cooperative production of a charismatically enchanted narrative that gives compelling direction to an actor's life. Attendees get caught up in the storylines of this dramatic web, which, like any drama, requires a stage, a story, and the teamwork of both actors and technical crew. This last point is crucial, for the general public does not generally recognize just how the "behind the scenes" work generates, reproduces, and expands charismatic leadership. The team works creatively and efficiently together, and a world is constructed in which people suspend their disbelief, empathize with the characters, and enter the story themselves. Evangelical charisma, even when "anti-religious," is a dramatic co-production of leader and people in dialogue with their cultural context. I will discuss this in more detail later in the chapter, but put most succinctly for now, this is the heart of my theory of how charisma works, in a diamond of four elements: (1) a leader and his crew create (2) a "dramatic web" that (3) offers deliverance from a crisis, which (4) resonates with an audience who perceive the leader as extraordinary.

I use the mixed metaphor of dramatic *web* for several reasons. First, it is a reference to anthropologist Clifford Geertz, who wrote with reference to Weber that "man is an animal suspended in webs of significance he himself has spun" (1977, 5). Second, I see the charisma spun by Cavey and his crew as intersecting lines of relationship between Cavey, his crew, his followers, their imagined public, and the identity crisis that constitutes evangelicalism at this moment in history. All these characters and their setting are vital to the dramatic production. Third, this drama is not a neat five-act play with a single storyline and a clear beginning and end; like a web, it's a piecemeal drama that comes in fits and starts, and looks both beautiful and haphazard in its actualization. Finally, the web imagery is apt for an investigation of charisma because it conveys the notion of something attractive, fragile, untidy, sticky, and constantly re-spun. People are voluntarily taken in by charisma, like a drama. They get caught up in the play.[8]

"All the world is a stage" is a metaphor, but this megachurch is literally a movie theatre. So using a dramatic metaphor is apt, and it allows for the recognition that consumer capitalist practices are at work. Theatres are cultural institutions, but they are also places of exchange and economy. I will suggest this dimension of TMH is best understood as part of Weberian *routinization* of charisma – organizing and extending charisma's reach.

Furthermore, this dramaturgical understanding of charisma also incorporates the core idea of the "personality cult" theory: a lead actor is necessary to spin a compelling vision of life beyond the stress of the status quo. Bruxy Cavey promises the ironic "end of religion" and the spirituality of Jesus in an age of stigmatized religion, and on this "irreligious" narrative, his charismatic authority is acted out. He plays a vital role in the dramatic web.

Still, it remains crucial to understand that this mega-enchantment is more than personality or consumerism, and it is only "irreligious" in Cavey's own idiosyncratic way; his vision is a religious mission within a secularized milieu, and his reflexive, ironic contradictions are part of his enchantment. The juxtaposition of rationalized institutional structures and revolutionary religious rhetoric draws people into what I am calling "the 'irreligious' paradox." Certainly evangelists have always combined rigorous organization and dramatic emotional appeal, but with this new evangelicalism the paradox intensifies. Evangelicals are not just critiquing formal religion again, a practice characteristic of their history and identity (Hatch 1989); they are now protesting an image of evangelicalism itself. Key evangelical leaders have become profoundly self-conscious as they distance themselves from right-wing stereotypes and the U.S. Republican leadership while at the same time they reassert their evangelical tradition of Bible-based preaching focused on conversion to the cross of Jesus Christ (Bebbington 1989). In other words, megachurches use critiques of megachurches to bolster their own evangelical charismatic appeal. The Meeting House demonstrates the playful precariousness of this approach: they run a giant, efficient, professionally operated organization that promises the flexibility, spontaneity, fulfillment, and pastoral approach of an intimately personal spiritual community.

Why do people come to the Meeting House? Because it's a megachurch for people not into megachurches, offering evangelicalism for people not into evangelicalism, led by a charismatic religious personality for people not into charismatic religious personalities. TMH's central animating drive is a creative, ironic, dramatic production that (mostly) white, middle-class Christians enter with enthusiasm because it offers them a way out of tired traditions and religious institutions that have lost their cultural legitimacy in the dominant culture's secular milieu. It's a savvy new evangelicalism, self-aware and self-critical, carving cultural legitimacy where their legacy, if not rotten, has gone stale.

THREE MEANINGS OF *CHARISMA*

Charismatic authority and energy draws the crowds to megachurches, and a specifically ironic charisma animates a new sector of the evangelical fold, a group I am calling "reflexive evangelicals." People use the term *charisma* in at least three different ways today, however, and I want to be clear about these overlapping meanings and my own specific use of the term.[9] The word has a long history and varied usage, some of it quite sloppy or dismissively pejorative.[10]

Charis is an ancient Greek term that was used to describe the favour of the gods falling on someone, bestowing them with an attractiveness, beauty, or charm, which in turn made the recipient beholden to the god (Potts 2009, 13). A form of this word appears in the Septuagint version of the Hebrew scriptures (Zechariah 12:10) where God says he will pour out a spirit of grace (*pneuma charitos*) on the house of David. This concept of charisma is analogous to moments in the Hebrew scriptures when the "Spirit of God" falls or rests on a prophet or a judge such as Samson in Judges 14:19 (Sanders 2000; Potts 2009, 15). Literally translated, *charisma* is usually rendered as "gift of grace."

This first and oldest meaning of the word I refer to as "spiritual charisma," which corresponds to how the word is used in Pentecostal and similar circles today. It is really from St Paul in his letters gathered in the New Testament, however, that the word *charisma* receives more definitive meaning. The term *charisma* appears sixteen times in New Testament texts (such as Romans 1:11, 5:15–16, 12:6–8, 1 Timothy 4:14, 2 Timothy 1:6), and the most frequent and extended discussion comes in the first letter to the Corinthians. Chapter 12:1–11 is a key text in the letter, where Paul explains the democratic distribution and diverse character of spiritual charisma (charisma$_1$):

> Now about the [*charisma*] of the Spirit, brothers and sisters, I do not want you to be uninformed ... 4 There are different kinds of

charisma, but the same Spirit distributes them ... 7 Now to each one the manifestation of the Spirit is given for the common good. 8 To one there is given through the Spirit a message of wisdom, to another ... knowledge ... 9 to another faith ... to another *charisma* of healing ... 10 to another miraculous powers, to another prophecy, to another distinguishing between spirits, to another speaking in different kinds of tongues ... and to still another the interpretation of tongues ... 11 All these are the work of one and the same Spirit, and he distributes them to each one, just as he determines (NIV with Greek term *charisma* in italics).

Charisma in this passage refers to spiritual gifts or talents not innate to the person but perceived to come from the Spirit of God in Jesus Christ. These charismata (plural) are given not to one particular leader but to everyone in the spiritual community – as interdependent gifts in a "pneumatocracy" (Joosse 2014, 269). Finally, the charismata are characterized not as attractiveness or charm – or even leadership per se – but as different "gifts of grace," including faith, wisdom, healing, and miraculous powers.[11]

After the time of the early church, as Christianity spread and developed institutionally, the terminology of charisma (understood as a spiritual charisma I call "charisma$_1$") finds marginal use in the church (Potts 2009, 51–84). Almost two millennia pass before the word resurfaces in a significant way, partly because of the wave of charismatic movements begun in the early twentieth century but spreading most visibly in the 1960s and 1970s (Cox 2001). Since then, use of the word *charismatic* in discussion of megachurch leaders in some cases means both "spiritually gifted" and potentially "member of the charismatic movement." I would argue this is not actually Paul's broader meaning of the many charismata but specific reference to just *one* charisma: the charisma of leadership mentioned in Romans 12:8.

Because charisma$_1$ refers to a diversity of spiritual gifts distributed through the church and intended for harmonious interdependence within the church, it lies on the periphery of my analysis of megachurch charismatic leadership. It is important, however, in understanding the history of the word *charisma*, and it also informs the perceptions of many of those who follow megachurch leaders: they perceive their pastor as having the spiritual gifts of teaching, administration, and leadership.

My investigation lies more firmly in the sociological tradition of Max Weber, who is another reason for the popularization of the word *charisma*, as his works were translated into English by the mid-twentieth century. Weber borrowed the word from the theological writings of Rudolf Sohm and transposed the meaning into a universally applicable secular political key and "value-neutral" typology (D. Smith 1998; Weber 1968, 19). The Christian term describing the gifts of grace to all believers was both broadened and narrowed by Weber: broadened to apply to all extraordinary leaders but narrowed insofar as it referred only to leadership ability, not other talents or graces such as those named in the New Testament epistles. Weber defines charisma (charisma$_2$) as a form of authority, "a certain quality of an individual personality, by virtue of which he is set apart from ordinary men and treated as endowed with supernatural, superhuman, or at least specifically exceptional powers or qualities. These are not accessible to the ordinary person, but are regarded as of divine origin or as exemplary, and on the basis of them, the individual concerned is treated as a leader" (Weber 1968, 48). Charisma is a perception, a hunger aroused within a follower for someone larger than life.

Weber contrasted this charismatic authority with two other kinds of legitimate authority: bureaucratic authority (also called rational/legal), which is based on rules and efficient procedures such as those found in modern governments; and traditional authority – customary ways of doing things as seen in families, religious groups, and monarchies (Weber 1968, 46). Charismatic leadership challenges these other two stable, if not sterile, authorities with revolutionary force, upsetting the "iron cage" of bureaucracy and legalistic tradition and ushering in a new social order. Whether prophets, shamans, warlords, or heroes, charismatic leaders disrupt the given rules and rituals to emancipate people into a creatively inspired future. They have both a perceived extraordinary mission and extraordinary powers by which to complete their mission (S. Turner 2011). Weber said charisma$_2$ always proceeds from the declaration "It is written ... but I say unto you ..." (Weber 1968, 24).[12]

If we stop our analysis of Weber here, charisma$_2$ appears as a spellbinding personality trait that elicits deep devotion in people, and it comes with a Romantic (anti-modern) bias.[13] This is too simplistic for Weber, who elaborates immediately after the above definition of charisma: "What is alone important is how the individual is actually regarded by those subject to charismatic authority, by his 'followers' or 'disciples'" (Weber 1968, 48). Charisma$_2$ is thus not as much a *personality trait* as it is a *bond*, a strong emotional tie between leader and followers that obligates followers to obey the leader, whom they see connecting them more directly with the fundamental order of the cosmos (Shils 1965). In other words, there are no charismatic leaders apart from the recognition and submission of followers. Not a gift of grace, "the locus of power is in the led, who actively (if perhaps unconsciously) invest their leaders with social authority" (Joosse 2014, 271).

For Weber, this relational understanding of charisma$_2$ is more accurately understood by what I am calling "situational" charisma, for the charismatic bond is strongest in the context of *social crises* – "times of psychic, physical, economic, ethical, religious, political distress" (Weber 1968, 18). When social tensions rise and people feel anxious or uncertain, they look for someone who can connect them to the core of reality and empower them with a vision of a hopeful future. The charismatic leader is a hero with extraordinary gifts who compels people to follow and obey as part of a journey towards a new social order.[14] In the case of the Meeting House, disillusioned white Christians are offered a vision of a life with Jesus amid the "cross-pressures" of the age (Taylor 2007) – between faith and unbelief, beyond both the empty horizons of the secular elite and the culturally stigmatized right-wing evangelical stereotype.

My analysis here suggests a new model of charismatic authority. Not unlike Griswold's (2008) "cultural diamond," I see charisma as the cultural product of three elements: producers, receivers, and a social world. In effect, "charismatization" involves not just one person's spellbinding presence, but rather four variables: a talented leader and his staff, followers who recognize the leader as extraordinary, and a social context, more specifically, a situation of crisis or distress. The fourth point in the diamond is the "dramatic web" of charisma, and it is the product of the first three elements in dynamic synergy. In a sentence, charisma is an elaborate performance generated by a star and his stagecraft that resonates with an audience caught in some cultural predicament, offering them a way out.[15]

To illustrate, consider Rick Warren, who began as an enterprising young man with some exceptional leadership skills and an ambition to lead a megachurch. He grew a following of enthusiastic disciples who saw him as a man with exemplary vision that addressed the malaise of post-suburban middle-class life in southern California

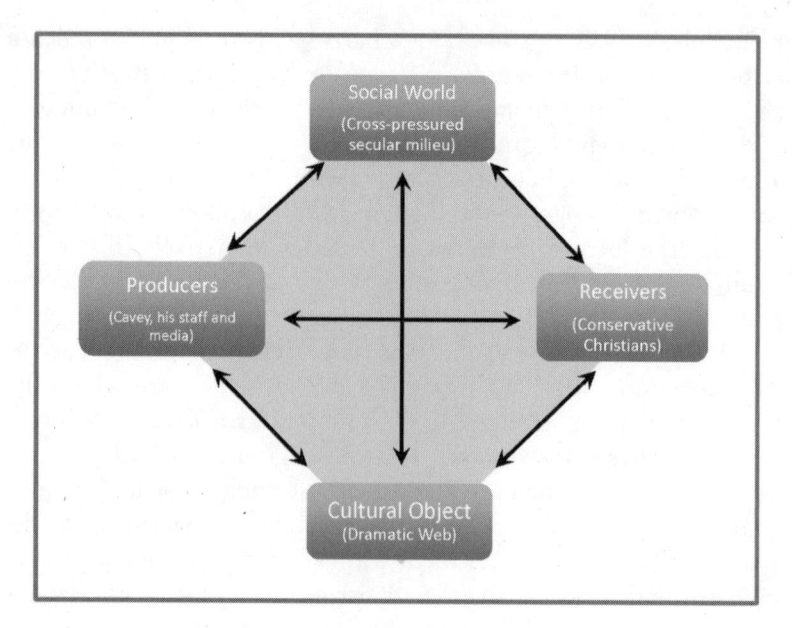

Figure 2.2 A new model of charismatic authority.

(Wilford 2012). He offered a life of purpose – including a personal Christian spirituality and a global Christian mission – to what sociologists have called the "homeless minds" of modern urban America (Berger, Berger, and Kellner 1973). His charisma lay in the dramatic presentation of what he called the "purpose-driven life." Cavey is similar, but his drama is characteristically about "the irreligious life."

This leads to my third meaning for *charisma* (charisma$_3$) – one derived originally from Daniel Boorstin but elaborated through much of the growing discipline of celebrity and fandom studies.[16] Boorstin's lament, *The Image: A Guide to Pseudo-Events in America* (1961), is an original and seminal text in celebrity studies and serves here as a paradigmatic model and prototypical expression of a late-modern form of charisma. The book elaborates on a series of contrasts – between illusion and reality, images and ideals, and, most significantly here, celebrities and heroes. Heroes, argues Boorstin, have charisma, understood as "divine favour, a grace or talent granted them by God" (50). The historical presence of such "greatness" has been recently levelled by democracy, cynically undermined by the social sciences, forgotten by literature, and, most importantly, "lost in the congested traffic of pseudo-events" (54).[17] Pseudo-events are social happenings manufactured by public relations engineers to meet the extravagant expectations of the modern public, says Boorstin, and their main character is the celebrity, defined vacuously as "a person who is known for his well-knownness" (57). As "human pseudo-events," these moments are creations of press agents and mass media for an age of contrivance.[18] Summarizes Boorstin, "The hero was distinguished by his achievement; the celebrity by his image or trademark. The hero created himself; the celebrity is created by the media. The hero was a big man; the celebrity is a big name ... While heroes are assimilated to one another by the great simple virtues of their character, celebrities are differentiated mainly by trivia of personality. To be known for your personality actually proves you a celebrity. Thus a synonym for 'a celebrity' is 'a personality'" (1961, 61, 65).

Boorstin does not use the term *charisma* to describe celebrities, for celebrities' charisma is at best contrived, or pseudo-charisma, the illusion of divine gifting.[19] Spiritual charisma is a gift, and situational charisma precariously rests on follower recognition, but contrived charisma arises from calculated marketing and manipulation.[20]

One need not accept all the sharp binaries of Boorstin's critique or its normative assumptions about heroism in order to agree that there is another meaning to the word *charisma* that has flourished in the last few decades, one that is related but distinctly different from Weber's heroic notion (Friedman 1990; Furedi 2010). I call this "contrived" charisma because, in the words of the *Oxford English Dictionary*, it means "ingeniously or artfully devised or planned." There is an aesthetic dimension to charisma$_3$, carried by media and marketing but primarily popularized through narratives that provide existential reference points for people's lives (Gabler 2001, 2009; Tataru 2012), an argument critical to my notion of charisma as a dramatic web fleshed out in subsequent chapters. Lloyd (2018) argues that normatively good charisma should operate to unveil and critique its own mediation, and to the extent that it does not, it leans towards an authoritarian character. Lloyd, along with Boorstin, see something cheap, inauthentic, and even dangerous in this contrived dimension of charisma.

To return to the example of Rick Warren, he easily had thousands of followers in California. But when he published *The Purpose Driven Church* (1995) and then the outrageously popular *The Purpose Driven Life* (2002) his charismatic authority exploded to international range, making him and his trademark Hawaiian shirt a household image.

The role of media – books, magazines, and all electronic forms – reinforces, magnifies, and extends local celebrity charisma. It is a form of routinization beyond Weber's early twentieth-century imagination, and the heroism of charisma$_2$ begins to be layered with the propaganda machine of charisma$_3$.

As Boorstin makes clear, celebrities are not merely media constructions – they are a response to the "extravagant expectations" of the American public. Celebrities exist because they fulfill a popular demand for glamour and spectacle. Moreover, the term *contrived* carries some of the critical tone found in Boorstin, which is appropriate not only as a contrast with the positive connotations found in Paul and in Weber, but because writers in megachurch literature can often use the terms *charisma* and *celebrity* in pejorative ways. Charisma$_3$ may seem benign in its public manifestation, but it can be construed as a pathology such as narcissism (Pinsky and Young 2009), political oppression that supports the capitalist status quo (Marshall 1997), a screen for hidden interests (Bensman and Givant 1975), or a manipulative, degrading performance (Schickel 2000). Lawler simply states, "Celebrity is the lowest form of fame. Being a celebrity is a sort of gift of public opinion, which is formed by no one in particular" (2010, 419).

Philip Rieff (2008) pejoratively labelled this sort of contrived charisma as "spray-on charisma," and its synthetic nature derives from the fact that, unlike Pauline or Weberian charisma, it is generated through instrumental design. In fact, authors of popular self-help resources promise that charisma can be learned if readers practise specific techniques of communication as well as certain virtues of other-centredness.[21] Charisma$_3$ in this context is not a spiritual gift of grace intended for the common good, nor is it necessarily about heroic leadership towards social transformation in the midst of crisis. Rather, it is about self-development for personal advancement or even a form of rationalized politics (Bensman and Givant 1975).[22] This variation of charisma$_3$ reflects what Boorstin called superficial "charm" (1961, 44). *Charm*, coming from Latin, meaning "song or verse" developed into the Middle English meaning of "spell or incantation" and, significantly, has no etymological relation to the Greek word *charisma*. Yet charm harkens back to the ancient Greek meaning of charisma as an attractiveness or beauty. Our analysis of the meanings of charisma thus comes full circle.

MacNair's (2009) exposition of the megachurch as an ideal type focuses on this last understanding of charisma. The megachurch, argues MacNair, arises from the confluence of three cultural streams: frontier evangelism, commercial civilization, and celebrity culture. Celebrity culture surfaces in the megachurch insofar as the leaders are first of all star performers whose "most distinctive attribute is that they are *known* ... Fame is the beginning point, not a result or a reward for being worthy" (6). In the one instance where MacNair uses the term *charisma*, he pairs it with *personality* in a way reminiscent of Boorstin: "The personality and the *charisma* of a person are the centre of the church's life" (12). MacNair omits any mention of either Pauline and Weberian notions of charisma throughout the book because his unambiguous disdain for the megachurch runs deep, and he concludes that although "the term *Christian* properly spreads a wide net," a megachurch "is *not* a Christian church" but rather a false assertion of church, in effect, a pseudo-church (my term) subject to the vagaries of the market (224; all emphases are in original). If MacNair observes any charisma in the megachurch, it is neither a divine gift nor even heroic, but rather simply contrived and shallow, the result of power personalities exerting control over unreflective, if not manipulated audiences.

Note that while these three types of charisma follow a general historical progression – from Paul to Weber to Boorstin – the categories are not entirely mutually exclusive. Charisma$_1$ is most distinctively in its own category, as it is a theological term; writers and followers continue to use it to assert that divine grace has given spiritual gifts to a particular leader. My dramatic web idea controversially suggests the blending of charisma$_2$ and charisma$_3$ – contending that the pervasiveness of electronic media has blurred Weberian heroes with celebrities, and likewise politics and religion with performance and artifice. Boorstin himself writes at length about how heroes degenerate into celebrities (his main example is Charles Lindbergh, the first pilot to make a solo flight across the Atlantic Ocean). So the purpose of my investigation of usage regarding charisma was to uncover the multiple meanings that lie within the term as writers use it in the megachurch literature (see table 2.1), note some normative ambivalences, and set my own trajectory in a synthesis of Weberian and celebrity studies.

The three uses of the word *charisma* are also three dimensions of charisma, as evident in Bruxy Cavey's role at the Meeting House and in rogue evangelicals like him. Most of my interviewees spoke admiringly of Cavey's "gift of teaching" (charisma$_1$), demonstrating the

Table 2.1
Three notions of charisma

Type	Charisma$_1$	Charisma$_2$	Charisma$_3$
Description	Spiritual	Situational	Contrived
Author	Paul (as interpreted by Potts)	Max Weber	Daniel Boorstin
Source	Gift of grace/God	Confluence of social factors	Media and marketing
Embodiment	Church community	Heroic leader	Celebrities
Meaning	Diversity of talents	Revolutionary leadership	Manufactured fame

New Testament understanding that informs the perceptions of attendees. Cavey's "irreligious" message and mission resonate with people who seek an evangelical spirituality that rises above the stigmatized Moral Majority, and they develop an emotional bond with him (charisma$_2$). His hippie costume, however, and the extensive apparatus of cameras, podcasts, and television appearances facilitated by a marketing and communications staff of seven people implies a layer of celebrity (charisma$_3$). My approach is at heart a Weberian framework, as Weber's interpretation of charisma can encompass elements from the other two meanings: he included the perception of the gift of grace as described in charisma$_1$; and when I add the role of media into his sociology of charismatic authority, I open investigation into the influence of charisma$_3$, which can be seen as an intensification and routinization of charisma$_2$. As a hero, a person acts as a leader of a movement; as a celebrity, that person is an object to an audience, a media product. Media shape, magnify, and distribute charismatic authority for wider exposure; this, however, simultaneously makes the persona more vulnerable to critique, parody, and cynicism. Overall, a leader's charisma needs to be evaluated case by case, in order to assess where it is empowering and emancipatory and where it is manipulative and despotic (Lloyd 2018).

All three meanings of *charisma* are important to understanding the success of the megachurch: charismatic authority is at heart a religious appeal in a secularized society; it offers a liberating vision for troubled populations; and it depends on media to be enhanced, magnified, and propagated to a large audience. For a new evangelicalism, that means offering a legitimate identity that frees them from stigmatization while continuing to connect them with God and their innovative conservative tradition in a secularized milieu. Such charisma can empower evangelicals for life in a busy, disenchanted, and often alienating electronic urban matrix. At best, it includes their recognition of the status of religious celebrity and critiquing it, while simultaneously using that celebrity to extend the very same critical message to more people. This is the ironic, tongue-in-cheek charisma of the emerging evangelical, best seen from the vantage point of ethnography – from the place where people live their faith. Field study, too, allows one to feel the dramatic web at work in oneself and recognize its multilayered, and in many ways mysterious pull.[23]

A THIRD WAY WITH SAME-SEX MARRIAGE

One dramatic example of Cavey's charisma operating on these three levels is evident in his approach to same-sex marriage since the turn of the millennium. This is one public issue, like abortion, that pits evangelical Christians (and many other conservative religious traditions) against the dominant culture in Canada. Legal action against the morality codes of Trinity Western University and its proposed law school (Rhodes 2015) and human rights complaints against Christian Horizons, a publicly funded Christian group home network for the developmentally disabled (*Ontario Human Rights Commission v Christian Horizons*, 2010) have both been high profile and centred on the nexus of religious freedom and the rights of LGBT students and employees. Closer to TMH, the Pride Toronto event is said to be "one of the largest organized gay pride festivals in the world" (Wikipedia n.d.).

Canadian evangelicals know this is a highly contentious issue in which their conservative views will be publicly and legally repudiated. For example, journalist Marci MacDonald's bestseller *Armageddon Factor: The Rise of Christian Nationalism in Canada* (2010) feeds the worst fears of some Canadians regarding evangelicals, who,

> aggressive and insistent ... are driven by a fierce imperative to reconstruct Canada in a biblical mould ... where non-believers – atheists, non-Christians, and even Christian secularists – have no place, and those in violation of biblical law, notably homosexuals and adulterers, would merit severe punishment and the sort of shunning that once characterized a society where suspected

witches were burned. Theirs is a dark and dangerous vision, one that brooks no dissent and requires the dismantling of key democratic institutions. A preview is on display south of the border, where decades of religious-right triumphs have left a nation bitterly splintered along lines of faith and ideology, trapped in the hysteria of overcharged rhetoric and resentment. (2010, 359)

Published by the self-described "world's most global trade publisher," Penguin Random House Canada, MacDonald sounds the alarm that the Canadian equivalent of American right-wing theocrats threatens the operations of Canadian Parliament. While she cannot see the irony of her use of the phrase "hysteria of overcharged rhetoric and resentment," evangelicals get the signal from such distorted views in Canadian media that they are disliked and even "un-Canadian." MacDonald asserts that Canadian evangelicals are especially hazardous for the gay community, fellow citizens whom evangelicals seek to punish like witches executed in the sixteenth to eighteenth centuries of Europe and America.[24]

Into this cultural context Cavey carries some immediate social capital, as his face and teachings on the topic litter the internet. The manufactured image I have called charisma$_3$ is the first and most constant connection evangelical attendees have with Bruxy Cavey. He has directly addressed the ethics of homosexual orientation and same-sex marriage in numerous teaching videos on YouTube (1999, 2002, 2005, 2013, 2014, 2016), while on tour through the conference circuit, in multiple podcasts, and as part of a panel of pastoral experts in the New Directions DVD *Bridging the Gap: Conversations on Engaging Our Gay Neighbours* (2009). News media have reported that he speaks on the subject at conferences,[25] universities, and regularly at Messiah College, the BIC denominational college in Pennsylvania.[26] Media presence offers celebrity, and celebrity is a form of cultural authority.

Cavey's central influence comes in the form of charisma$_2$, however, because Cavey is an extraordinary pastor with a vision that offers evangelical Canadians a way to be evangelical without feeling like the gay-haters that journalists like MacDonald describe. Cavey is highly reflexive about his position as an evangelical, and he is intensely intentional about how this issue gets played out at TMH. When I was investigating TMH he had two central documents explaining his views on the topic on an easily accessible webpage entitled "The Meeting

House: Resources." They are two of only eight documents on issues of curiosity (including documents on dancing, divorce, and biblical authority) and are entitled "Gay-Friendly Statement" and "Same-Sex Marriage: A 'Third Way' Approach."[27]

In summary, as in all his teachings on the subject, Cavey leads the reader through scripture emphasizing that Christians should be as open, accepting, and embracing as they can be, asking questions, listening, and leaving disapproval as a secondary option. He explains that "acceptance does not mean approval or agreement," but leaders at TMH are seeking as a church to be a "third way" that is "theologically conservative but emotionally liberal." Put differently, they are taking a stance that is theologically clear, but they are resistant to condemn others and desire to be profoundly gracious to those with other opinions.

One key teaching Sunday on this topic entitled "Being a Third Way Family" came in a series in October 2013 entitled "Modern Family: Living Like Jesus Intended." Cavey begins with a humorous video clip from the TV series *Modern Family*. He then explains that TMH is a family of brothers and sisters in Christ that seeks to be a safe place where people get to know each other's hearts, and where the diversity of a spiritual family is celebrated. "We can learn from one another, argue with one another, and challenge one another – as family." Because of this unique approach, and the way TMH has navigated the gay marriage issue, the Evangelical Fellowship of Canada asked for consultation with Cavey at its annual national roundtable with member denominational representatives.

Having just returned from this meeting, Cavey explained to his audience, "We are a little further down the path than other evangelical churches. If we can put the thought and the theological work into doing this well, if we can be true to scriptures and the vision of Christ, we can not only experience a healthier dynamic as a church but offer that as a gift to other churches in Canada." Cavey sees his "third way" teaching on this matter as a model for evangelical churches across Canada. He explains that BIC members' Anabaptist ancestors have been living the "third way" for hundreds of years already – between the warring Roman Catholics and Protestants.

Next Cavey briefly summarizes TMH position on gay marriage: "We believe that God does not affirm gay marriage and that people with same-sex attractions are called to singleness and celibacy as 'eunuchs of the kingdom' – and we think that's another version of awesome.[28] So we don't affirm or support this. At the same time, we are willing to admit that there are good and godly Christians who have come to a different conclusion. And we don't automatically treat them as heretics or outside of family to us, and so we create that space to be challenged and work it out together."

Cavey then shows a video of himself, squished on a small couch between "two of his favourite people" named "Stace" and "Tams" – a lesbian couple who had come to Cavey a few years ago for counselling about their relationship. Cavey had urged these Meeting House attendees not to couple but instead to split up. But he "failed miserably" with his pastoral advice. The two women did their own study of scripture and went ahead anyway, moving to Vancouver.

In the short video, the three friends express their differences while affirming their relationship with Jesus and their love for each other. Stace recalls Cavey's role in their pastoral encounter: "You were super honest to me and you said, 'I love you first,' which I felt – which was so important to me." They sensed genuine welcome but acknowledged Cavey was on a different trajectory. Cavey explains, "Our disagreements are the differences not of enemies, but of family."

"I'm so thankful for the community of TMH to welcome us in the questions, in the journey, whatever that looks like," says Stace. "I love you buddy."

"And I love you guys," says Cavey. "Group hug." The video ends with Cavey's arms around them both as they lean into him and affectionately murmur, "Awwwwww."

Cavey ends the teaching time by saying, "We want to be a conservative mind with a liberal heart." He then promises attendees three things: it will take work, they will make mistakes, and it will all be worth it.

I was attending the Oakville site on the Sunday morning of this teaching, and as I was filing out of the auditorium I ventured a random conversation with a white, middle-aged man standing by the doors. He was excited: "This guy is an incredible speaker, eh, like you would have to pay big money to hear a speaker like this somewhere, and he's right here close by, for free. I'll tell you there is nothing I'd rather fill my brain with on the weekend than what this guy says, and it sticks with me into the week, and it gives me direction for my life."

If $charisma_3$ encapsulates Cavey's evangelical celebrity authority that arises from his habitually mediated image, and $charisma_2$ arises from a heroic rescue he is perceived to offer beleaguered evangelicals, the sense of wonder and awe this male attendee has for his teaching ability on faith and life suggests both kinds of charisma, with a hint of charisma$_1$ – that he is "anointed" to preach to this generation in a divinely inspired way. Cavey offers a creative way out for stigmatized Canadian evangelicals – a more socially acceptable conservative Christian social ethic in the milieu of Pride Toronto.

Significantly, Cavey has said on a few occasions, "I could be wrong about this," and I was told that in this case the remark had upset a few attendees. But I met and spoke with more attendees who were inspired by this humility. One thirty-something-year-old male told me, "It's challenging. I, you know, I come from a background where I'd been pretty hard-nosed about that – that I don't care if you're gay, there's no reason you should get married. But I would take a more softer view now, that we shouldn't hold someone to a standard that, if they don't adhere to the Christian standard of marriage, then we have no right to tell them what to do."

Charisma, even ironic, ambivalent charisma, has the power to unsettle people and give them opportunity to change. Cavey models a way that attendees value because it allows them to hold to their convictions while claiming the identity of mainstream, multicultural, tolerant Toronto.[29] Cavey is a subversive evangelical because he subverts dominant secular expectations of what evangelical Christians should be like. Cavey's views will remain abhorrent to much of the LGBT community; nevertheless, it shows his persistently reflexive approach to ministry, and attendees *perceive* themselves as more loving and accepting. He constructs his vision in contradistinction to the stereotype of the offensive evangelical who judges the intimate acts of sexual minorities as an "abomination before the Lord."

"We're glad you're here at Heresy Central," said Bruxy from the stage on 15 July 2018, after being labelled a false teacher in some online blogs by a local Harvest Bible Chapel pastor for Cavey's views on sexual ethics, among other things. Cavey attempts to disarm critics by embracing their critique and enjoying the image of being rebellious. Again, there are multiple layers to what Cavey is doing. He is happy to be a heretic to contentious Calvinists. Yet everyone knows his whole ministry has been dedicated to upholding an orthodox form of Christianity – a particular conservative tradition of Anabaptism. He's playing with the heretical image to distance himself from other forms of evangelicalism. "We are just too nice to gay people ... and Catholics," he adds wryly, and his audience laughs, interrupting his speech. "And if you're Catholic *and* gay, well ... you're not welcome at some churches." More laughter.

This chapter has sought to offer a deeper, more theoretically precise account of the nature of charisma. Charisma, as understood here, is not the individual property of uniquely powerful human beings, and few can develop substantial charisma by merely learning a few techniques. Charismatic authority is a relationship between leader and followers based on the perception – magnified by media – that the leader is exemplary, even divinely gifted, and able to rescue them from a distressing situation. In this scenario above, the distress of evangelical Ontarians is caused by stigmatization as "American" right-wing evangelicals who are a threat to the LGBT+ community and to Canadian democracy itself. In Cavey's terms, any anti-gay, aggressive, destructive public activism would be fuelled by "religion" and its bad ideas, and so he models how to be cool, culturally legit, tolerant Canadian Christians. This new identity and ethic offers enormous relief. In what follows I will provide some historical and sociological context for this interpretation of what has drawn so many Ontarians to TMH.

3

From Street Theatre to Silver City

Setting the "Irreligious" Stage

> [Canadian Protestants] are habitually overlooked. In spite of their historical dominance, they welcome invisibility, present an image of embarrassment, tolerate their belittlement by others, and quietly suffer neglect by scholars of religion.
> C.T. McIntire, "Protestant Christians"

> Christianity has an image problem. If you've lived in America for very long, I doubt this surprises you.
> David Kinnaman and Gabe Lyons, *unChristian*

Before he has even uttered a word, Cavey's hippie style reveals his mission, and the stage – a dark movie theatre or in the Oakville Production Site warehouse converted into a theatre – suggests a white, middle-class, de-churched audience. He is known as a leader in Canadian evangelical subcultures, but his grungy, dishevelled look makes him seem out of place at church conferences. Cavey has fashioned himself as an icon, model, and visionary for a "church for people not into church," and more specifically, as an evangelical for those not into evangelicalism. This is the heart of his genius: he models a way to be normal by offering a behavioural and linguistic code for other evangelicals to follow.

Cavey is a charismatic leader in three basic ways: in the Weberian sense, sociologically, because core members recognize extraordinary abilities in him, and they feel obligated to follow his challenge against the rules and rituals of institutional religion. Attendees themselves would insist in line with St Paul that Cavey's teaching abilities are not just exemplary – they are a divine gift intended for service in the church community. Spiritually speaking, they perceive him to have the charisma of teaching. Finally, in a more contrived way, a dimension of Cavey's charismatic authority overlaps with his role as an evangelical celebrity: he is a person who is also a media commodity, packaged and broadcast transnationally, and has "intimate strangers" who are his fans (Schickel 2000). These three layers of charismatic presence reinforce each other as long as people continue to be devoted to Cavey and his message.

All these layers of charisma combine to offer a vision for a new kind of evangelical church member[1] – one particularly suited to the Canadian context. I asked an American pastor after one of Cavey's conference speeches what appeared Canadian about Cavey. She replied, "He's not slick, but embracing his dufosity, not picture perfect, but unique, unusual." I asked the same of a former Meeting House leader who now worked for a New York City church. He said, "What's Canadian about TMH? In a healthy way, it's not that ambitious to be known outside of its own context. They don't show up at places and don't make themselves out like Willow to have the secrets to the next best thing ... Canadians are less self-consumed than Americans, less self-promoting and more self-effacing. In a sense, 'What's the big deal?' they say, not realizing we can learn lots from them."

Cavey is a model of the successfully transitioned new evangelical for a Canadian public. His formative years were spent mixing in the multicultural Toronto crowds and in the ironic popular culture of the 1990s. He has brought that training to the heart of his megachurch, sharing in broader culture's skepticism towards authority, institutions, and the American right-wing evangelical establishment of the Moral Majority years while strategically embracing the promise of a digital age. Before I elaborate on his ironic vision in detail, however, I want to introduce you to his context – his Canadian culture, his personal history, and his people. Each of these three factors is critical in the development of his ironic charisma: in fact, there would be little enthusiasm for his person and message apart from their vital biographical contribution. Charisma, I argue, arises from the dynamic interaction of these three elements with a fourth factor – what I call the *dramatic web* – to form a "charismatic diamond." But first I want to introduce the other three factors, to set the stage for the narrative that carries the ironic drama that lies at the heart of TMH.

Irony has prophetic power, and it is used often to undermine established authority. For the average middle-class North American who is suspicious of institutions, it resonates. It contains a jaded distance from cultural life and develops its power from a negative identification, which leaves an open space for some new positive identification to take place. For many at the Meeting House, Cavey acts as a model of that positive identity in contemporary Canada.

THE STIGMATIZATION OF EVANGELICALISM IN CANADA AS AN IDENTITY CRISIS

Jen Pollock Michel is an American evangelical, a writer, and a mother of five. Before writing her *Christianity Today* award-winning book, she moved from Chicago to Toronto. She describes Toronto as welcoming to immigrants, but not to Christianity or Christians. Her impressions of urban Ontario culture give a picture that I will flesh out in more detail. "Toronto is a city where the historical Christian faith is excluded from public discourse on the basis that it is backward and boorish," she writes. "Toronto, characteristically polite, is politely hostile to orthodox faith: even the mention of attending church can be cause for dreaded awkwardness in friendly conversation" (Michel 2014, 71–2).

Apparently Toronto has this reputation in some evangelical circles. Michel's friends were concerned for her, not only because Toronto is "relentlessly secular," but because instead of home-schooling her children she was going to send them to a French immersion school. "What will it matter in heaven if your children speak French?" one of her friends challenged her. Michel sees this comment as short-sighted, and mostly for theological reasons, but her friend's question indicates a kind of environmental sensitivity in evangelical circles. Spiritual vitality is paramount, and the ecology of your life – the places, institutions, and atmosphere – matter. Especially if they are perceived to be hostile to faith.

The scene of every drama includes a front stage and backstage. Surrounding both is the cultural context in which the performance takes place. This cultural context can resonate and affirm the performance or undermine its legitimacy. Jeffrey Alexander argues that effective cultural action fuses all the aspects of a performance together – actors, scene, audience, and background culture – but when the background culture does not support the local performance, a "de-fusion" occurs that weakens the performance (Alexander 2004, 2006; Cordero 2008, 532; Wilford 2012; see also Zilber, Tuval-Mashiach, and Lieblich 2008). The goal then is to "re-fuse" local performances to larger cultural meanings in order to give them the character of authenticity and ensure their broad success.

This fracture in the performance directly affects the charismatic power of the show. Weber explained that charisma is strongest in the context of social crises – "times of psychic, physical, economic, ethical, religious, political distress" (Weber 1968, 18). When social tensions rise and people feel anxious or uncertain, they look for someone who can empower them with a vision of a hopeful future, ideally fused with the wider cultural horizon. The charismatic leader becomes the hero with extraordinary gifts who compels people to follow and obey as part of a journey towards a new social order.[2] My argument here is that evangelicals suffer an identity crisis in Ontario due to their stigmatization by the dominant secular culture, and this context creates an opportunity for charismatic leadership, which Cavey has ingeniously capitalized on with his ironic vision for evangelical church life. The charisma of a dramatic web is both attractive and invisible to those caught up in its performance.

For attendees in the urban centres of southern Ontario, one significant part of the cultural context includes the fragmentation of post-suburban life – the mobility, the disconnection from the land and extended family, and the cosmic sense of "homelessness" (Berger, Berger, and Kellner 1973; Taylor 2007; Wilford 2012). Identity is considered to be as mobile as one's body and as flexible as one's imagination, but identity is necessarily a social construction, a project for which the raw material and resources for reshaping are largely culturally predetermined – or one might say, come as a gift, depending on one's hermeneutic.

Evangelicals in Ontario have what Goffman called a "spoiled identity." They have been stigmatized, meaning they have a social identity marked by a perceived undesirable attribute, a shortcoming or failing that taints them, discounts them, and discredits them if discovered (Goffman 1963, 3). This "spoiled identity" causes constant tension for those in stigmatized environments as they must manage information about themselves or be exposed as lacking credibility. In what follows I will briefly lay out some historical shifts and cultural commentaries that suggest evangelical marginalization and disparagement in Canada, and Ontario specifically.

On the broadest historical landscape, Charles Taylor (2007) has said Canadians are part of a larger shift into a "secular age" – meaning not only differentiation of religious authority from many social institutions or a general decline in belief but also the problematizing of belief itself. That is to say, the conditions of the age are such that belief not only becomes difficult, but disbelief for many becomes the default option (14). Taylor writes as an academic in Quebec, and this social location conditions his conclusion that belief has become problematic; but it is an assessment applicable to the world of the white, educated professionals who form the core of TMH in Ontario. It is the same constituency of Peter Emberley's 350 interviewees in his qualitative study of Canadian spirituality who, Emberley contends, are jaded by the church's legacy with regards to women, gays and lesbians, and children under its care, and are left with "a staggering erosion of confidence in institutionalized religion" (Emberley 2002, 12).

Surveys of religious belief and church attendance confirm the trend. Reginald Bibby, after years of documenting the "fragmenting gods" (1987) and increasingly "unknown gods" of Canadians (1993), suggested a "renaissance" in the making (2004); but he withdrew that thesis in a later publication in favour of postulating increased polarization in Canada instead (2011, 837).[3] One indicator of this polarization would be the popularity of the "new atheist" bestsellers in Canada (Dawkins 2008; Hitchens 2009), that have not been shy in their declaration of faith as delusional and poisonous to "everything." The trend includes the younger generation as well: while 12 per cent of teens in 1984 described themselves as "religious nones," in 2008 the number jumped to 32 per cent (Bibby 2009, 32). As a more recent paper published by McMaster Divinity School professors summarizes it: "The prospects for Christianity in Canada, and more broadly in the West, are bleak" (Studebaker and Beach 2012). The director of the Flourishing Congregations Institute in Alberta agrees: "Simply put," he summarizes, "individualism, respect, and tolerance – not religion – are the common social bonds that bind the majority of Canadians." Even more succinctly, "In Canada religion has [been], is, and will be on the decline" (Thiessen 2015, 176).

For evangelicals in Canada specifically, the last hundred years have radically shifted their status on the national landscape. Mark Noll (2006) notes a "great reversal" in North American religious history: while Canada in the eighteenth century displayed a "more radical, more anarchistic, and more populist" evangelicalism than the United States (Rawlyk 1996, 11; see also Gauvreau 1991), it now lags behind its southern neighbour in church attendance and general Christian cultural influence. Similarly, over the last century, Canadian evangelicals in particular have lost much of the confidence and appeal experienced by their religious cousins in the United States. For one thing, the majority religion has been Roman Catholicism in Canada, which counterbalances any Protestant or evangelical hegemony. Additionally, since the sixties and the subsequent shift to an officially multicultural country, the Christian religion as a whole has suffered a loss of "power, popularity, and prestige" (Bruce 2002) that effectively moves the nation into a post-Christian era (Miedema 2005). The Quiet Revolution in Quebec, which emptied the cathedral pews and effectively secularized government, media, and public education in the sixties, found a milder and more gradual complement in English-speaking Canadian institutions.

While the residue of Christian privilege can still be found in some national institutional symbols, a process of "de-Christianization" in Canadian institutions continues to disentangle Christian tradition from public institutions (Bramadat and Seljak 2008, 13). In a comparative study of US and Canadian congregations, Lydia Bean concludes Canadian evangelicals are embattled like their US evangelical neighbours (see Smith 1998), but "embattled as a *religious minority*, in tension with Canadian society as a whole" (Bean 2014, 110, emphasis in original). Reimer and Wilkinson (2015, 37) elaborate on tensions evangelicals cope with in everyday life, and they compare evangelical congregations with both a linguistic minority (citing theologian Jonathan Wilson 2007) and a cognitive minority (Berger 1970) – both of which suggest the need to continually maintain boundaries and socialize members regarding insider rules and values.

To be clear, this does not mean I hold to the full-scale "secularization theory" (Bruce 2002). My sympathies lie more with Casanova (1994), who sees differentiation operating at the national level – not assuming that religiosity itself is waning across the modern world. My point more narrowly contends that the Christian faith has lost its previous institutional privilege in Canada – especially in politics, media, and the academy. Not only has such faith lost privilege, young evangelicals experience a prejudice they describe as stigma.[4]

American televangelist scandals and the political manoeuvrings of the religious right influence the perceptions of evangelicals in Canada

(Thiessen 2015, 99, 139). General public perceptions of "fundamentalists" (the same term often used to refer to Muslim extremists) can extend to evangelicals. One poll reports that Canadians are slightly more likely for vote for a Muslim prime minister than an evangelical one (Todd 2008b). Canadian evangelical religious studies professor John Stackhouse Jr says evangelicals are viewed in Canada as "fast-talking, money-hustling television preachers. Pushy, simplistic proselytizers. Dogmatic, narrow-minded know-it-alls. Straight-laced, thin-lipped kill-joys." That is not the worst of it, either; evangelicals are perceived as "right-wing, and ... American" (Stackhouse 2005). Evangelical convictions regarding public issues such as abortion and homosexuality foster a "chilly climate" for them (Stackhouse 2011), as demonstrated by ongoing legal action against Trinity Western University (Rhodes 2015).[5]

Canadian evangelicals and their congregations remain vital institutions – more so than mainline equivalents (Reimer and Wilkinson 2015; Haskell, Flatt, and Burgoyne 2016). Modest estimates put evangelicals at a stable 8 per cent of the Canadian population (Bibby 2004), but if one includes Catholics and mainline Protestants with evangelical attitudes in the statistics, the number rises to 16 per cent (Rawlyk 1996, 224) and more generously by another poll up to 19 per cent of the population – almost one in five Canadians (Todd 2005).[6] Additionally, some scholars voice concern about the vestiges of Christian privilege in public institutions, which they labour to expunge (Beaman 2003; Beyer 2013).

Despite such lingering advantage, Canadian evangelicals generally know they are not a celebrated presence in the Canadian media (Haskell 2009) or internationally (Marshall, Gilbert, and Green-Ahmanson 2008; Olasky and Smith 2013). An indication of this posture towards evangelicals on the political level includes the failure of the Christian Heritage Party since its founding in 1987 to gain significant public recognition and support, let alone a single seat in the Canadian Parliament (McKeen 2015). Telling as well was the ridicule and political failure of Stockwell Day as an "out of the closet" evangelical when he was elected leader of the Canadian Alliance Party in 2000. Public commentators heavily criticized his beliefs concerning gay marriage and mocked his young earth creationism; within a year he was ousted as leader of the party (Haskell 2009, 28).

North American evangelicals remain intensely scrutinized in the secular academy as well. Bramadat (2000) and Zawadzki (2008) both studied evangelical student groups on public university campuses in Ontario. Bramadat noted both "bridge" and "fortress" strategies employed by the InterVarsity Christian Fellowship group at McMaster University. While their faith led them to make bridges to those outside their group, the secular context of the university left them feeling besieged. Eight years later, Zawadzki noticed more of the latter in her study and characterized evangelical student experience as "strain" and stigmatization, using the conceptual framework of Agnew (1992) and Goffman (1963) respectively. Zawadzki says student lifestyle issues pertaining to alcohol consumption and sexual activity are part of the experience of strain, but the academic bias against conservative Christians is more foundational to their university experience.[7] Anthropologist Susan Harding writes of the "otherness" put on fundamentalists (a term often conflated with evangelicals in popular media), whom some academics parody, characterizing them as "aberrant, usually backwards, hoodwinked versions of modern subjects" (1991, 373; see also Ault Jr 2004; Lee and Sinitiere 2009, 6; Fletcher 2013). Paul Bramadat concurs in his ethnography of Canadian evangelical students, adding that one might alternately view evangelicals as "religious and cultural innovators" – as bricoleurs who are working in the midst of dynamic tension with the dominant secular milieu to forge, piecemeal, something new (2000, 147). Such tinkering is not unique to evangelicals, but that is precisely the point; rather than failed agents, they are as much modern subjects as many other religious groups.

Now evangelicals can overstate their feelings of being discredited; Canadian Muslims, atheists, and religious nones can feel stigmatized as well (Thiessen 2015, 97). Douglas Todd, religion writer for the *Vancouver Sun*, has said, "There is even some truth to it, in terms of Evangelicals being somewhat stigmatized. But sometimes I think it's overdone" (Todd 2008a); in fact, he has elsewhere called it a "persecution complex" (Todd 2011). Having a long-standing prime minister associated with evangelicalism could be viewed as one symbolic challenge to an argument for their marginalization; but similar to Zawadzki's Christian student subjects at a public university, Stephen Harper knew very well to keep his faith private, even if evangelicalism forms the heart of his tradition (Todd 2008b). In sum, evangelical stigmatization carries some ambiguity; it is not as severe as evangelicals perceive it to be, but perception directs the negotiation of their identity and the impression management displayed in their public communications. In fact, what I am calling a crisis of evangelical identity is, in part at least, a social construction that evangelicals co-produce and that pastors such as Cavey highlight in their vision for revolutionary change (Ellingson 2007).

Bibby summarizes the Canadian scene in words that act as an appropriate preface to Bruxy Cavey's message and mission: "While religion has been scorned and stigmatized and rejected by many, spirituality has known something of celebrity status" (2011, 118). Canadian ambivalence about religion, and evangelicalism in particular, provides the cultural context for Cavey's "irreligious" vision.[8] Goffman (1963) maintained that the experience of stigmatization draws the stigmatized into small solidarity groups, which often designate someone who is a little more vocal, a little better known, or a little more connected to become the group representative. Such a professional spokesperson will advocate for the group among outsiders by trying, among other things, to soften the social labelling and model for the group how to "pass" for a "normal person" (24, 134). He or she provides them with a "code" – instructions on how to manage tensions and impressions when among others (109–11). This representative leader for some Ontario Christians is Bruxy Cavey, who is well aware that outsiders easily associate conservative churches with stereotypes of angry, judgmental, politically ambitious, right-wing fundamentalist Christians. In order to cultivate legitimacy in the cultural context of the Greater Toronto Area, his religious performance needs to manage the stigma not only of being religious in Canada, but specifically of being a conservative evangelical Christian group centred upon a single charismatic leader.

Significantly, as mentioned at the beginning of this book, there is also profound insider ambivalence about being evangelical in North America, especially since polls showed overwhelming white evangelical support for Trump as U.S. president. One African-American female pastor publicly declared that "2016 was a response to 2008" (referring to Obama's election to the presidency). "Eighty-one percent was almost a deal breaker for me" – in terms of her evangelical identity (Schuurman 2018a). Other evangelicals are voicing their own disillusionment with the right-wing faction of their movement (Labberton 2018).[9] Inside and outside of evangelicalism, the movement and its label are under heavy scrutiny.

IDENTITY CRISIS AT TMH?

Do Meeting House attendees feel this stigmatization? Ambiguity about one's identity has been considered a significant source of stress that is conducive to "charismaticization" (Ingram 2014, 50–62). My interviewees consistently avoided not only the identity of "evangelical" but also "Christian" and most certainly "religious." One young female attendee said she used to call herself an evangelical, but then the term "apparently got a bad connotation" so she's warming to the label *Christ follower*. Another young couple suggested the term *Jesus follower* fit them best. A young male Home Church leader skirted the question of labels altogether; he said whenever he is asked about his faith, he asks inquirers how they understand Jesus and then he describes himself in relation to their answer.

When asked if they were "religious," an older wealthy couple responded that they were instead "full of grace." They explained they had lived in the United States for a while and they had since distanced themselves from their evangelical Republican associations. Time with Cavey at TMH had transformed them. "We're more interested in politicians and governments that take care of the poor," they explained. "Christ talked far more about the poor than he did about abortions … and I'm upset with evangelical Christians because they of all people should know better that Christ wants us to take care of the poor."

One final intimation of some shame associated with a conservative Christian identity came from a young real estate agent. She explained to me why it was such a relief to walk into a movie theatre Sunday morning rather than a church building where people would be speaking "Christianese." "It kinda keeps you normal if there is a kid sweeping up popcorn beside you," she said. "You aren't going to say weird stuff you don't even know the meaning of." Her husband then spoke of the trappings of "the Christian subculture, especially in the States," and how it distracts them from more important things. The casual attitude fostered by TMH, the young woman repeated, "keeps you normal," echoing Goffman's idea that the stigmatized long to pass for a normal person.

Cavey himself may not name this crisis directly as I have stated it here. Cavey takes a broader and more theological approach that resonates with this social context but allows attendees to project their own experiences onto his definition of the situation. The crisis Cavey proclaims is that of "religion" – the taming of the scandalous message of Jesus into a conservative system, a "treadmill of legislated performances powered by guilt and fear" (2007, 13). Cavey defines religion as "any reliance on systems or institutions, rules or rituals as our conduit to God," and he attaches it to legalism, judgmentalism, and violence, contrasting it with the celebration, love, and generosity of Jesus (37). Religion is always baggage for Cavey, and TMH home web page has often introduced TMH with the opening line "Are you burnt out on religion?" Religion is construed as a burden, tiresome or odd, and the church itself is complicit in losing the core message of joy and love in Jesus.

Nevertheless, the vagueness of this spectre of "religion" is significant for its widespread appeal, as it could apply to many different groups in the consciousness of the audience. Cavey wisely does not name some sociologically definable "other" – like some charismatic leaders in radical Islamicist groups do (Ingram 2014). Rather, he keeps the enemy broad and amorphous, doing with "religion" what some conservative women's groups have done with the term *feminism* (L. Smith 2014). Having an unnamed villain also keeps communications more polite, more civil.

Yet Cavey's theological critiques are most consistently directed at American right-wing evangelicalism, a group with a clear stereotyped identity and a sufficiently broad influence to connect with the religious career of most conservative Christians – whether through their own church or their experience with parachurch organizations. Again, the televangelist scandals of the last thirty years cannot be underestimated in their shaping of cultural consciousness; they have not just spoiled but seared the image of evangelicals of Cavey's generation. They are what Joosse (2018) calls "unworthy challengers" – one of various counter-roles in a charismatic performance. In sum, when Cavey speaks of the nefarious influence of legalistic, angry religion, he is signalling a crisis that conservative Christians recognize personally or from mass media. The promise to "wreck religion" (the title of a 2013 teaching series) asserts charismatic authority against traditional authority, and the hippie-like "subversive spirituality of Jesus" (the subtitle of his 2007 book) provides the remedy to the crisis of "religion." This is in fact the whole unspoken but ubiquitous mission of TMH: to exacerbate the "religious" identity crisis of Ontarians in order to ameliorate it with a "countercultural" Anabaptist spirituality of Jesus.

Note that Cavey's vision is not for a return of Christian privilege in Canada. He displays no nostalgia for an earlier "Christian Canada."

In fact, as an Anabaptist he explicitly decries the presence of Christians in politics and public service, saying they should have "no interest in running the country." Even civil servants are implicated in the state's monopoly on violence – which pacifists like Cavey would rather avoid. This may explain why Cavey generally moves under the radar in Ontario. His church is no challenge to the secular establishment in the public institutions of government, media, and academy. His drive is for a legitimate cultural identity, and for evangelicals that explicitly means ignoring a prophetic stance towards public institutions. The one public institution he delves into full force is popular culture, a socially acceptable – even habitualized – Canadian cultural diversion. In this light, Cavey's touted "subversive spirituality" seems less subversive and more quietist. His views of gay marriage may be conservative and challenge the dominant Canadian perspective, but Cavey systematically avoids all politics and social policy. Compared with American bête noire pastor Mark Driscoll or the lingering shadow of Jerry Falwell's Moral Majority, Cavey is utterly innocuous to the political establishment and is thus ignored by mainstream media. His subversion is selectively directed towards his own Christian subculture.

THE CREATOR AND STAR: BRUXY CAVEY'S MYTHOLOGICAL RISE, FALL, AND REDEMPTION

Having set the cultural scene, the script writer, director, and lead performer now enters – Bruxy Cavey. He is just a man, a small man at that (he stands at about 5'7"). But his presence is large, his vision is global, and his audience is vast. In the imagination of many attendees, he is extraordinary. In this section I focus less on Cavey's connection to Canadian culture and instead give background to his role as creator of the drama, laying the foundation for his charismatic performance.

Charismatic authority is a performance, and drama is driven by story. Because the stage or the screen mediates most people's first encounter with Cavey, it is vital that celebrity studies shed light on understanding Cavey's charisma. Neal Gabler (2009) has argued that national celebrities, as shallow and salacious as some of their lives may be, provide narratives that bring meaning to life, distract people from their difficulties, and unite a politically and socially fragmented populace. While Gabler's contention that celebrity is the "great new art form" claims more than necessary for his thesis, the more modest assertion that celebrity functions as the social glue that crosses all lines of stratification, world view, and geography – giving diverse citizen groups something in common to talk about – holds more promise. The hookups and breakups, the scandals and suicides, the fame, frauds, and fortune provide stories that people voyeuristically enjoy, vicariously live out, or disdain with self-righteous zeal. "Celebrities don't have narratives," he maintains, "celebrity is narrative ... The size of the celebrity is in direct proportion to the novelty and excitement of the narrative." Fiction has always laboured to give the impression of credibility to be "believable." Celebrity does not require such work; celebrities have the immediacy of real life action in which something is always at stake, and fans are often left waiting for the next installment of the celebrity saga. "That is how celebrity works – as a kind of endless daisy chain that amuses us, unifies us, and even occasionally educates us" (2009, 30).

Gabler argues that celebrity has become "cultural kudzu," and the best of celebrity stories provide us with life lessons, capture the cultural moment, give us a glimpse of transcendence, or inspire us. Cavey is a far cry from the inanities of Paris Hilton; but even as a subcultural celebrity (Ferris 2010) who is reticent to talk too much about himself, Cavey is carried along by media events that highlight his latest teaching or commentary, and he is subject to the dynamics of the stagecraft that accompanies the production of a transnationally broadcast performance. Less salacious and nobler celebrities such as Cavey can have their marketers focus the main story on their message, talent, example, and success. Celebrity can elevate others in its best moments – as Mother Teresa, Barack Obama, or Bono are examples of more socially responsible celebrities who challenge the derogatory meanings of celebrity with their social activism and heroism.[10] The boundaries are blurry.

In what follows I will recount a few of the stories about Bruxy Cavey as they come from a variety of sources: from Cavey in his teachings, in interviews with me, and from attendees who share the stories and become carriers of the charismatic narrative. While there are many stories to choose from, I have documented the ones that approximate the cultural mythology of celebrity: discovery and rise, tragic fall, comeback and redemption (Goodman 2010; see also Alexander 2010b; Carroll 2010). The mystique of this narrative structure intensifies charisma as it spreads through the ranks of followers.

This section also serves as an introduction to the life of Cavey and demonstrates his grooming as a performer and his ironic account of his own biography.

Discovery and Rise

Cavey's birth story is certainly worthy of a prophet. It begins with his brother Stephen, a sibling he never met. Stephen was six years old and playing outside one day when his mother, Lois, noticed a small lump under his arm. Investigation proved that he had cancer spreading through his still developing body. He underwent numerous cancer tests and treatments for the next six years until he finally and tragically died at age twelve. "Half his life he battled cancer," reflects Cavey, when telling the story on a Sunday morning.

Fred and Lois Cavey were done with raising infants – they had their last daughter in 1956 and it was now 1963. They were in their forties by then with three daughters. One day after Stephen's heartbreaking death, Cavey describes how his family met around the kitchen table – to vote about having another baby in the family. They all voted yes except his sister Cathy, who "wanted to stay the youngest in the family." "I've never forgiven her," jokes Cavey. She would be overruled, and as Cavey himself puts it, "Baby Bruxy won the vote." Within the next year, Timothy Bruce ("Bruxy") was born to the family in the city of Montreal, 1965.

"I wouldn't be alive today if someone didn't die," asserts Cavey in a teaching given at a Christian leadership conference in Columbus, Ohio, 2013. "I am living my life for two boys. I was [my mother's] miracle child." He will from time to time refer to the fact that so many people in his family have had cancer – including his siblings, parents, and other relatives – and he is nervously poised to receive the same diagnosis someday. "We've had the conversation with our daughters," he explained to attendees in a 2010 teaching on suffering, emphasizing how the threat of pain and death is a constant companion in his life.

Such a dramatic story adds to the special status of Cavey as the charismatic community leader. He is charmed with a remarkable birth story, one bathed in the terminology of sacrifice and substitution, and thus a particular precariousness surrounds his continued existence. These stories function to reinforce his charismatic status, even if he appears to be casually sharing a poignant personal illustration. The dramatic web need not be consistently deliberately spun. But Cavey has learned to spin his story with flair.

Cavey grew up showered with attention from his three elder sisters, though Cavey will often add with his characteristic self-deprecating humour, "getting hand-me-downs was a drag." Cavey soon moved with the family to Scarborough, where he would attend the People's Church Christian Academy – the school associated with the large and prominent People's Church. The church has a long history in Toronto, stretching back to its founder, the charismatic Oswald J. Smith in 1928 and continuing successfully under his son, Paul B. Smith, and now under the popular preacher Charles Price (Stackhouse 1993). On Sundays the Caveys attended Agincourt Pentecostal Church, another growing megachurch a few kilometres from People's Church.[11]

Cavey thrived at church and school. He won numerous speaking contests at school, switched to a public high school and started a Christian student club, became a leader in his youth group, and participated in street evangelism in Toronto. His street evangelism including preaching, but more often than not it included some performance art, such as a skit or break-dancing. Cavey embraced the role of emcee, and he would introduce their performances, but not without some trepidation. "I remember the moment before I would grab the attention of the crowds," he said in one interview. "I thought, *Right now I'm just one of the crowd, but in a second I'll be disturbing the scene with talk about Jesus*. It was weird."

Agincourt Pentecostal was not unlike many Pentecostal churches in the eighties – a place where prophetic talk was common, warnings of the end times punctuated evangelistic messages, and speaking in tongues was integral to Sunday worship. When I asked Cavey whether he had personally experienced any miraculous encounters – such as healings, visions, or speaking in tongues, he said no. In fact, he explained how many in his church tried to facilitate a second baptism in the Holy Spirit for him without success. One well-meaning lady prayed intensely over him, switching from tongues to pleading for his reception of the gift and back again to tongues, and then finally directly urging him to just speak in tongues. He told her he knew quite well how to mimic the sounds he heard in church, but a real filling of the Spirit should be more than mimicking. So he gave in to her request, repeating sounds he had heard before and the lady became ecstatic and called a small crowd over, and they all rejoiced that Bruxy had received the second baptism. Cavey himself was unconvinced and went to the youth pastor for some advice. The youth pastor was not sure what to say, and Cavey was left skeptical about the whole experience.

This was a significant moment in Cavey's life – the beginnings of his deconversion (Harrold 2006; Bielo 2009). While the story of a conversion experience in a leader's biography, especially a dramatic narrative, has been known to reinforce charismatic authority (Storr 1996; Hong 2000a), deconversion can function similarly for a sympathetic audience. Without a definable second baptism in his biography, Cavey was lacking an experience central to the Pentecostal understanding of the Christian life. He thus understood himself to be disqualified from leadership in the Pentecostal denomination. He was determined to focus his life on telling others about Jesus, and he was resigned that it would not be in the role of preacher. Some pressed him to consider it in spite of his lacking the gift of tongues, but to Cavey this would be making a lie the foundation of his ordination.

Cavey went on from high school to York University, obtaining a BA in psychology. He avoided student life at York, as the large concrete commuter campus seems hardly an invitation to community and faith. After that he completed a master's in theological studies at Ontario Theological Seminary (now Tyndale Theological Seminary), but he bypassed the master of divinity degree, which is the expected degree for future preachers, as he had no ambition for the pastoral role. He also evaded taking Greek, which was not required for the MTS as it was for the MDiv. Curiously, he reports an intense love affair with Calvinism at this time, as he admired the professors' introduction to the teachings of the Reformation and Calvin's own "beautiful theological system" (as he calls it). He would soon repudiate Calvinism and all religious "systems."

His passion was performance. Cavey continued to participate in different forms of Christian ministry, working part-time as a leader with "4 CRYING OUT LOUD!" – a performance art troupe that specialized in drama, dance, and mime. He also was the lead singer, songwriter, and eventually bass player for a band that also took on the same name. "I don't know much about music," he confessed, "but I would hum out the various parts I saw for the various instruments, and we would go from there. The others were real musicians."

Cavey did some promotion work for World Vision at this time, helping schools and groups organize a thirty-hour famine, a fundraiser for World Vision's international work in poverty relief. He became known through evangelical networks in Ontario, and both churches and parachurch organizations invited him to speak at various venues. He spoke at Heritage Fellowship Baptist Church in Ancaster one day in 1991, and some elders afterwards approached him, saying they had been looking for new preacher for a few years and they would like to interview him. There were 100–150 people attending there at the time, and they had just survived the scandal of a pastor who left his wife for another woman, so they were recovering and looking for a new leader.

In my interview with Cavey, he once again emphasized how his trajectory was set away from the career of pastor, suggesting both divine intervention and his own delight at the irony of his current life's vocation. This is a story that some of the longstanding Meeting Housers know well. So in conversation with the elders of this church Cavey explained this was not his goal, and how he didn't own a suit and had never taken a single course in homiletics.

"Well," they persisted, "buying a suit is not a difficult thing."

"Furthermore," one elder pressed home to him, "we will only hire you on the condition you promise to never take a course in homiletics."

"OK," replied Cavey. "But I'm too young" (he was twenty-six at the time).

"You're wise beyond your years," replied an elder.

Cavey was reluctant, but he remained open to the possibility because his integrity was not at stake, as it would be if it were a Pentecostal church. Speaking in tongues was not expected in Baptist theology. His conscience was free to accept. Cavey took the job in 1991 with a one-year probationary period, and the church immediately started growing. News of the intelligent and humorous hippie preacher in Ancaster soon spread around the region through word of mouth, and within a few years, attendance rose from over 100 to 1,000, and the church shifted Sunday services over to the 970-seat auditorium at Redeemer University College a kilometre down the road. In a typically modest Canadian way, Cavey was an evangelical celebrity on the rise.

Tragic Fall

The mystique offered in the romance of rising fame is paradoxically often intensified with a fall from grace. Goodman (2010) says celebrities may succumb to the illusion of invincibility, impervious to the precariousness of their status; stars must fall, he adds, and "supernova means explosion."

It was late 1995 and his burgeoning Sunday congregation was full of excitement and promise. The attendance numbers were growing monthly. Behind the scenes, however, Cavey suffered marital breakdown. As he tells it, his wife Sharon had been unfaithful; the first time, her affair was handled internally with elders, and both reparative and preventative measures put in place. Nevertheless, a second affair followed, and on this occasion she insisted she wanted out of the marriage. The church leadership offered a full-year paid sabbatical for Cavey, during which he might heal and recalibrate his ministry. He was devastated and felt he could no longer remain as pastor at the Baptist church – or any church, for that matter. The divorce went against his own biblical ethics; he felt disgraced and so left the ministry altogether in early 1996. Unemployed and unmarried, Cavey now anticipated work in some profession outside church boundaries.

Within a few short weeks of his exit, Sunday attendance numbers were back down to their pre-Cavey levels, and the congregation returned to its original church building down the road with about a hundred people. Many followers were disillusioned, so suddenly bereft of their charismatic leader and the excitement that surrounded his burgeoning congregation. I sent emails to Heritage Baptist Church in 2014, hoping to hear the story from an insider at the time of Cavey's resignation. I did talk with one elder who verified the gist of Cavey's story, described the pain that still surrounded the event, and recommended I not contact other witnesses of that part of their history. He said the memories still caused hurt.

This disruption in Cavey's ministry forms an important part of the congregational lore at TMH. Although personal testimonies – especially narratives of pain or struggle – are endemic to evangelical faith (Meigs 1995; Harding 2001; Hindmarsh 2005), Cavey rarely speaks of his divorce. If Cavey does mention it publicly, it is with few details, lurid or otherwise, and he talks quite matter-of-factly about it as part of some larger theological point he wants to make. I attended a Home Church where the majority of attendees were divorced and had come as refugees from the churches in which their divorce took place. My inquiries confirmed they were fully aware of Cavey's marital history. Additionally, there are a few select teaching documents on specific theological issues available on their main website, namely gay marriage, dancing, biblical interpretation, and divorce. In this short online document Cavey names his own divorced status but tells only the story of his theological shift to accept divorce as a Christian option, not the circumstances of his divorce. The fact that this information is available on the website – and is so readily available as part of the gossip in the church – makes it a vital moment in the biography of the church's main figure.

Recovery and Redemption

Cavey's fortunes soon changed after he left Heritage Baptist Church. He was approached in the spring of 1996 by the regional bishop of the Brethren in Christ denomination (BIC, as of 2016 was renamed "Be in Christ" in Canada) and asked if he would consider a pastoral position at a decade-old church plant in Oakville. From the way Cavey tells it, when the hiring committee interviewed him for the job they offered him the position of senior pastor. He knew enough about his organizational skills and interests to request that he be hired only for teaching and that another leader be hired to cover the administrative tasks of running a church. The board resisted and declared that Cavey should take all the roles that church leadership requires. The conversation went back and forth until Cavey finally relented.

Cavey then explains what happened next with a mischievous grin: his first goal in the role of senior pastor was to find another person to take up the role of senior pastor so he could focus on the teaching. This begins his return to local celebrity status, and attendance at the church plant quickly began a steep incline. One long-time member said he was like a one-man band, with all the accessories, drawing crowds with teaching times up to an hour as well as skits, contemporary music, and clever marketing ideas. Within years, overflow, then closed-circuit television, building renovations, and multiple moves were necessary to accommodate the burgeoning crowds.

They changed the name to "The Meeting House" in 2000, and in February 2001 they passed the 1,000 Sunday attendance mark. Tim Day, born and bred BIC, former intern with Craig Sider at TMH in 1989–90, and now ordained pastor with an MDiv from Tyndale Seminary, joined the staff team as mission pastor in July 2001. He later officially became senior pastor – to fulfill Cavey's original dream of passing on operational duties to a co-leader. In December 2001 they moved into a former Cineplex Odeon Theatre on Speers Road. Soon after, satellite sites began to be added in cities across southern

Ontario,[12] and in 2007 the large warehouse on Bristol Circle was purchased and converted into a theatre-like auditorium with 1,200 seats. His book *The End of Religion* was published by Navigator Press in 2007 as well, and the book hit the Amazon bestseller list in Canada soon after. These days were busy, full of change, growth, excitement, and promise – a wild roller coaster ride that parallels the experience of other young megachurches (Kuykendall 2011). The staff grew to over sixty and has become one of the largest Protestant churches in Canada and one of the largest Anabaptist congregations in the world.

Cavey's redemption reflects not only in the numerical success of his new church, but also in his personal life, which is often public news for congregation members. The story of his second engagement has become part of the in-house lore of the church, and since it was captured on video camera, it was screened at the twenty-fifth anniversary of TMH in 2011 (see also Cavey 2017, 15). The story itself is unusual, as Nina, now his wife, proposed to him during the Sunday morning service in the regular question-and-answer session after Cavey's teaching (called "Q and Eh?"). The reversal of traditional gender roles in this plucky proposal reinforces the growing lore around Cavey's character as a self-confessed "beta male." Friends stood up in the crowd with signs that read "Make an honest woman out of her!" and "It's about time!" When he said, "Yes," he cried, she cheered, and a raft of balloons fell from the ceiling. People find the whole proposal story unique and winsome, and it simultaneously buttresses his egalitarian teachings on gender roles.

Cavey consistently characterizes himself as uncomfortable in the limelight. I asked him what fuels his ambition for ministry and he immediately said, "Boy, it really sounds cliché, but it's Jesus and the gospel ... [I]t would have to be some kind of cosmic payoff to get me to do that each week." When I probed further, asking what got him out of bed on Sunday morning, he said, "Yeah, if I don't show up, that's not nice. That would just be a mean thing to do ... People are counting on me to communicate clearly ... if I don't show up, I'm failing my teammates." This reveals deep religious convictions, a strong allegiance to community, and an impulse for approval. It also suggests the psyche of a performer – someone who does not want to disappoint his team or audience. Cavey has lived much of his life on the stage, and performing has become a way of life. The show must go on.

I have argued for four variables as being necessary for charismatic leadership, but the central and most visible element is obviously the charismatic leader. Cavey's appearance, teaching, and background story add significantly to his charismatic performance, forming its foundation, its mythology, and its appeal. Cavey's dramatic birth story, his deconversion from Pentecostalism, and his soaring success on the religiously skeptical Canadian landscape form the fabric of his popular appeal. Growing up in the shadows of two megachurches positions him as a second-generation megachurch leader (Hey 2013, 275), and his numerous experiences in performance have prepared him well for the role. An in-depth analysis of his psychology, arising from his birth situation, birth order, and divorce are beyond the scope of this project, although similarities can be found with famous preachers such as Jonathan Edwards and Henry Ward Beecher, who also grew up with an audience of older sisters and basked in their attentions (Applegate 2007; Marsden 2008).

Cavey's sense of loss after leaving his Pentecostal roots seems negligible; in interviews with him, I sensed his marital divorce harboured a deeper psychic wound, as he said shuttling his children back and forth with their birth mother each weekend was a constant reminder of his personal fallibility. He was suggesting to me this humbling experience kept his celebrity in check, even as groupies fawn over him. Nevertheless, his biography extends beyond his own subjective rendering of it, and it follows the three-fold typology common to celebrity – discovery and rise, tragic fall and recovery, and redemption. The circumstances of his birth, his consistent rejection of the pastoral role, and his public divorce and remarriage – all give his story an extra mythological aura. If a megachurch is a dramatic web of human pathos and victory, the main character requires a storyline of archetypal stature. He needs to appear larger than life to his followers, and it is such stories that make the leader.

AUDIENCE: WHITE, CONSERVATIVE, CULTURAL CREATIVES

So far, I have described the cultural scene and the star of the charismatic performance that together shape the crisscrossing storylines in TMH's dramatic web. Every performance, however, requires a third element: an audience. Sociologically, the problem with the concept of audience is that it can be too quickly imagined as passive receivers of a centrally produced drama, and this gives a false impression. At TMH, some people come as genuine spectators, curious about the Cavey phenomenon, or seek anonymity for a season as they heal from some hurt or sort out some personal issue. But belonging at TMH is rarely a matter of ascribed identity, since so few followers have BIC background; belonging must be achieved, and such achievement best comes through participation. In fact, to be completely frank, there is no charisma without followers. There is no dramatic web without the creative labour of followers: they co-produce the threads of their own captivation.

The culture of TMH therefore is better compared to experimental theatre than to a movie theatre. Experimental theatre intends to include audience participation – in Bertolt Brecht's language, to take down the invisible "fourth wall" between performers and audience (McTeague 1994; Thomson and Sacks 2007, 56). In some ways, audience members can be directly involved in the Sunday performance, as when Cavey interviews Meeting Housers, fields questions, or asks for volunteers to come on stage and help illustrate a point through an improvised drama. Attendees are active participants in another way as well; almost all attendees who join were not members of TMH's denomination, Brethren in Christ. They have deliberately chosen to come to TMH because they embrace it as a resource for their own spiritual journey. They are mobile believers, bricoleurs (Roof 2001), cobblers (James 2006), tinkerers (Wuthnow 2007), or syncretists (Harrison 2014), picking and choosing from Cavey's teachings, and when they no longer feel nourished by Cavey, they move on to other spiritual resources and personal projects. Attendees can be intensely loyal, but they can also be fickle. This reflects what Marti and Ganiel (2014) have said about the Emerging Church movement more generally – they function as "pluralist congregations" that "permit, and even foster, direct interaction between people with religiously contradictory perspectives and value systems" (2014, 34). In a town hall meeting in June 2018, Cavey announced a shift in vision, from "one church in many locations" to "one family with many expressions." Internal pluralism will be not simply a sociological reality, it will become an institutional goal.

The Meeting House can be best imagined not as a static group of people, but as a subway train, with many different cars in which people get on and off at different stops. Not only is it made of over sixteen different sites, but people stay for varied lengths of times and often have cross-cutting commitments beyond their relations with the people in TMH. Internally conducted surveys twice a year (2012–14) show approximately 70 per cent of attendees have joined within the last five years, including about one-third who have joined within the last year. Of those who attend, only 40 per cent attend every Sunday gathering – radically different statistics from other BIC churches in Canada, where 85 per cent attend every week, in addition to another 10 per cent who attend more than once a week (Burwell 2006).[13]

The general demographic and socio-cultural context of the central MH sites reveals a population of well-educated mainline affiliates and religious nones drawing on income from a cognitive-cultural economy and living middle-class and upper-middle class lives.[14] These figures do not necessarily reflect all who attend TMH, but they do reflect their target audience. Oakville and Mississauga citizens are mobile, connected to a global economy, and surrounded by a major multicultural urban centre. The Greater Toronto Area (GTA) is the home to many of Canada's influential entrepreneurs, especially in the "cognitive-culture economy" (Davis and Mills 2014), which includes a high concentration of "cultural creatives" (Leslie, Hunt, and Brail 2014; Florida 2014). I found the writing on "bobos" (bohemian bourgeois) and "crunchy conservatives" bore some resemblance to the people I observed and met during my fieldwork (Brooks 2000, 2004; Dreher 2006), although the descriptions would need to be adjusted for a Canadian cultural context.

This description mirrors what Thumma and Bird (2014) have said about the global megachurch being a product of large, dense, urban populations and their aspirations for upward mobility. Rather than being simply innovative institutions, they are extensions of fragmented post-suburban structures (Wilford 2012) and, more critically, detention basins for "displaced folk" in a time of significant social change (VanGronigen 2013). Von der Ruhr and Daniels (2012) have called these mobile people both seekers and religious refugees, but they can also be described as free riders, free agents, and bricoleurs who use religious institutions as a resource for their own spiritual collage. They hitch a ride with TMH because they see something of value for them in their spiritual journey. To switch metaphors, they take what they need from it and weave it into the evolving tapestry of their own life.

Going through my interview data, besides those with little faith background, I found that followers could be separated into two large categories: the refugees and those who empathize with the refugees. The first group consisted of those burnt out on church – either they were tired of the culture of legalism, authoritarianism, or sectarianism (interviewees mentioned rules about drinking, dancing, Sunday dress, gay marriage, or women in leadership that exasperated them), or they had specific experiences such as divorce that distanced them from their original congregation. One young couple were recovering from a congregational conflict, describing themselves as "victims of spiritual abuse that were lied to ... We thought we might never step in a church again ... we needed time to heal." The complementary group of followers consists of individuals who did not have this negative experience but seemed to understand it vicariously. One Home Church leader explained the "irreligious" themes of TMH this way: "I can think of a lot of people who had some sort of baggage, or issue, when they were in their sort of young adult phase, that they totally turned away from the church and then ended coming back. And TMH might have been the first church they came back to."

At the town hall in 2018 Cavey summarizes this target audience as the religious "nones" (while labelling himself as SBNR, spiritual-but-not-religious). He breaks down the nones into two further groups: the "dones" who are the wounded attendees with a Christian history and had become disgruntled with their faith; and the "nevers" who are children of the dones or anyone who has no Christian memory.

TMH in-house surveys from 2011 to 2014 show 5–14 per cent of those who attend the Meeting House have little or no previous Christian identity. If the statistics are broken down to individual sites, it appears Brampton, Burlington, and Kitchener have mostly transfers from other churches, while Ottawa and the two Toronto sites drive the unchurched statistics up overall. Oakville seems to be about average. Brethren in Christ denominational statistics from 2008 for TMH record 41 conversions and 93 baptisms, while in 2010 they report 32 and 105, and in 2011, 49 and 135 respectively. These numbers are quite small if 5,000 people weekly attend and approximately 8,000 would call it their church home; less than 1 per cent of attendees are converts each year. While the number of converts ought to accumulate in the more than twenty-seven-year history of the church, the high turnover rates prevent it. The conversion rates especially appear small if one compares with another megachurch, such as Steve Furtick's Elevation church in Atlanta, which boasted over 3,500 baptisms in 2012. Elevation, however, has been under severe scrutiny for emotionally manipulating people towards baptism and manufacturing a "Disneyfied" assembly line–style baptism ceremony that includes hundreds of baptisms at a time (Watson 2014). At TMH, they happen with three to six people at a time and often in small ceremonies outside the Sunday service time. In sum, although a small but significant percentage of attendees may self-identify as coming from a non-religious background, and many have experienced a form of conversion or deconversion, most of the people who attend TMH come with some church experience. Generally, such experience rests in their recent past, but a few attendees come from nominal Christian backgrounds.

In sum, megachurch attendees are not a monolithic group of submissive fans or passive consumers – they are patrons who take in the parts of the performance that suit their predilections and become supporting actors and producers of the performance, insofar as they participate and extend conversations about it with others, inside and outside of TMH. The Meeting House leadership recognize this variety of commitment and even welcome some of the theological diversity. Cavey, for example, brought a long-time Meeting Houser up for an interview on stage because he was an Ontario Provincial Police officer – in order to demonstrate how people need not agree in order to be siblings in the officially pacifist Meeting House family.[15] Again, there is no charisma without followers to generate the sticky appeal of a dramatic web.

In this chapter I establish that Cavey's charisma is not merely personality: it requires a cultural crisis for followers to be rescued from, a dramatic story to inspire followers, and extraordinary talents and feats for followers to enthusiastically broadcast. Similarly, charisma is not just technical manipulation: it is a concert of elements working together in creative harmony. There is an ingenuity to Cavey's vision at this time in Canadian history, but without people to recognize Cavey for this ingenuity and passionately disseminate his ideas, he would not have a megachurch. And as we shall see in a later chapter, his staff play a key role in helping generate the perception of ingenuity and extending it across international networks.

In the next chapter, however, we shall see the front stage of the church – the new, ironic evangelicalism up close. This includes my investigation of a leadership strategy that encourages people to move deeper into the culture of the church – or else suggests they find another church to attend. This Purge Sunday strategy plays with the evangelical tradition of the altar call by reversing the social pressure: instead of calling people to the front stage for Jesus and church membership, Cavey asks people to leave the building for Jesus and participate in another church – if their current default would only be as a spectator at TMH. This both playful and daring ritual causes a stir in the ranks – an emotional reaction of mirth, guilt, self-justification, or disdain. But more importantly, it reinforces the culture of the church as a megachurch for people not into megachurches. At least, people not into the kind of megachurches that pressure people to come up to the front and desperately cling to every potential tithe-paying member. It's a subversive strategy of the new, reflexive evangelical.

4

Irony as Liturgy

Strategic Satire for a Spoiled Identity

Irony has become our marker of worldliness and maturity. The ironic individual practices a style of speech and behaviour that avoids all appearance of naïveté – of naïve devotion, belief, or hope. He subtly protests the inadequacy of the things he says, the gestures he makes, the acts he performs. By the inflection of his voice, the expression of his face, and the motion of his body, he signals that he is aware of all the ways he may be thought silly or jejune, and that he might even think so himself.

Jedidiah Purdy, For Common Things

Religion is horse-hooey when compared to knowing Jesus. It's not about the system or symbology that God invented: once you turn to the system as a source of salvation, you've missed the point.

Bruxy Cavey teaching on Philippians 3:8

The last chapter introduced the three elements of the charismatic diamond – the cultural setting, the star, and the participants – of the drama of "a church for people not into church." What that chapter analytically separates, this chapter dramatically integrates. This chapter offers a window into the public performance of TMH: its Sunday services as centrally constructed and distributed at the Oakville Production Site through the leadership and teaching of Pastor Bruxy Cavey.

This performance is the first that most people encounter when investigating TMH – it is the public face of the church and the part most centred on the personality and appeal of Bruxy Cavey. I argue that the tone and content of these productions consist of a satirical deconstruction of religion in general, and of right-wing evangelicalism in particular. It successfully brings the four elements of the charismatic diamond together: Cavey satirizes his role as evangelical megachurch pastor in a society skeptical about evangelicals, with the help of his evangelical staff and followers, creating a dramatic web of ironic charisma. In effect, Cavey first offers his audience a negative identity through the Sunday service, promising them what they will *not be* if they commit to participation in TMH. This is a precursor to a positive identity, that of being an "irreligious" revolutionary connected with an Anabaptist denomination that champions Home Church – the subject of chapter 5.

This performance gets to the heart of what charisma accomplishes sociologically – it involves followers recognizing their leader has an intense "connection with (including possession by or embodiment of) some *very central* feature of man's existence and the cosmos in which he lives" (Shils 1965, 201). In his satirizing of institutional religion, Cavey names a problem that resonates with conservative Christians in Ontario – that religion is a barrier between the individual and his or her intimate connection with God. Cavey naming the problem is not enough, however, for the sealing of a charismatic bond; he has to provide a credible solution, and for many, this is found in "doing life together" in their Home Church communities so that they find an unimpeded relationship with the Jesus of the Beatitudes.

The opening act of this drama requires an intentional negotiation of the stigmatized identity of an evangelical church – what Goffman (1959) called "impression management" and what I would call more broadly identity management. Goffman explained that impression management involves both verbal and non-verbal gestures intended to over-communicate messages that buttress their preferred self-image while under-communicating any signals that may undermine that image. These messages define the situation and shape the behaviour of other people. Although Goffman's focus was the structures of the "interaction order" that exists between people in face-to-face encounters or in teams within a micro-setting, his conceptual framework can also apply at the level of institutions and even the macro level of society (Hughes 2000). The goal, however, is not just to manage impressions, but to negotiate one's own subjective and social identity.

The identity management done at TMH, I argue, although an attempt to mitigate the perception of Cavey's central celebrity role, simultaneously intensifies the emotional bond attendees have with him. The previous chapter revealed how Cavey's "extraordinary" character was recognized by attendees through stories by Cavey, and stories of Cavey's life, which extended his charismatic authority through the distributed structures of the megachurch. This chapter demonstrates how Cavey's charismatic authority intensifies through dramatic scenes that *unsettle* his audience. In one sense, this appears to undermine the dramatic web; but for the audience members who continue to attend, the over-all effect, in fact, strengthens an emotional connection with Cavey and thus reinforces the strands of the web.

TMH is a highly reflexive religious project. Reflexive performances are typical of what has been called the Emerging Church Movement (Marti and Ganiel 2014). Emerging Churches deliberately rather than customarily construct their faith – a form of what Marti and Ganiel have called a "strategic religiosity" (60). This means they approach their religious identity as a project of seeking out certain legitimized forms of religiosity while shunning undesirable – and I would add stigmatized – forms of religious identity. This means critiquing right-wing megachurch practices and embracing more individualized and pluralistic subcultures. Such deconversion strategies orient by what they are against or what they wish to leave behind – an "escape from standardized agency" socialized in their evangelical past (76). I put strategic religiosity into dramaturgical terms, suggesting TMH cultivates a "*satirical* strategic religious counter-performance" – an intentional production directed against their own broader religious identity in the big tent of evangelicalism.

By characterizing much of this primary performance as satire, I am arguing the dramatic life of TMH embraces irony, parody, and even transgression to paradoxically expose and denounce the folly of institutions – and specifically religious institutions. Cavey is shaped by what David Foster Wallace (1993) calls "postmodern irony" – which he calls cynical, irreverent, rebellious, and iconoclastic, with a heightened sensitivity towards hypocrisy, developed through the increasing self-referential culture of television. While Cavey was deeply socialized in the popular culture of the 1990s, irony and satire have a longer history.

Satire is a larger category than irony, understood theologically as prophetic criticism made funny (Jemielity 2006, 21) or "the art of diminishing or derogating a subject by making it ridiculous and evoking toward it attitudes of amusement, contempt, scorn, or indignation" (Abrams and Harpham 2008, 320). Irony is often an instance of satirical critique, a form of critique common to Emerging Churches, who seek a "third way" beyond liberal and conservative categories (McKnight 2008; Bielo 2009). The first words on TMH website in 2014 were "Everything we read about Jesus in the Bible paints a clear picture of a revolutionary and radical who intended on turning our ways of thinking upside down and inside out. He wasn't interested in creating a new religious system of dos and do nots, wrongs and rights, rites and rules. Rather, he had a completely irreligious agenda." Satire is a prime instrument of prophetic challenge, which seeks to upend the business-as-usual mindset.[1]

In this chapter I investigate several instances in which such strategic, satirical counter-performances demonstrate their management of evangelical stigma. This spoiled identity is managed by rituals like Purge Sunday, a fetish for zombies, and a constant parodying of fundamentalist or charismatic American evangelicals. These polemical performances essentially signal a *negative identity*: TMH is not a cult of personality, it is not a sentimental culture, it does not promote a prosperity theology, and it is not an angry, judgmental place. The word *not* is key to their brand slogan and overall rhetoric; its usage has been postulated as a common practice of charismatic leaders (House, Spangler, and Woycke 1991; Fiol, Harris, and House 1999). TMH conveys the over-all paradoxical impression, I argue, that they are an "evangelical church for people *not* into evangelicalism" and a "megachurch for people *not* into megachurches."[2]

Much of what I examine in this chapter could have been investigated under the primary rubric of brand management and brand differentiation rather than identity management. Although such a frame places TMH into larger discussions of consumer religion, it also limits the analysis to the rational choices and calculus that characteristically motivate such economic activity and tends to configure religion as a mirror of economic life. By using theatrical terms, I can still discuss branding practices (as every theatre needs marketing) while including broader notions of religious meaning, motivation, and identity constructed through performance. So I draw insight in this chapter from theatre studies, performance theory, and Emerging Church research to offer a more inclusive cultural analysis of TMH. People join TMH not merely because of clever marketing design but also because they have been drawn into a web of religious drama that gives their life meaning, excitement, hope, and joy.

REFLEXIVITY, ROLE DISTANCE, AND THE ALIENATION EFFECT

Before investigating Cavey's reflexivity in his pastoral role, I will examine the significance of reflexivity for modern religiosity and its emergence in "role distance" and the "alienation effect" in an audience. The Emergent Church Movement displays a radical reflectivity towards its belief and practice, what has been called "a religious orientation built on a continual practice of deconstruction" (Marti and Ganiel 2014, 25). Marti and Ganiel see the Emerging Church Movement as an institutionalizing structure constantly deconstructed and reframed by "religious institutional entrepreneurs" who paradoxically seek to resist the institutionalization of their movement (see also Packard 2012). To deconstruct means to irritate and problematize conventional practices and paradigms by drawing attention to their contingent – if not arbitrary – status. Put differently, Emerging Church leaders' posture towards ministry can be characterized as "the intentional provocation of reflexivity" (81).

This reflexivity has an equivalent in performance studies. Goffman's notion of "role distance" offers one enduring example, defined as "actions which effectively convey some disdainful detachment of the performer from a role he is performing" (Goffman 1961b, 110). Goffman presents the example of a five-year-old child on the merry-go-round, who, unlike the younger children around him, takes an irreverent stance on the wooden horse, demonstrating to all that he is not caught up in the activity; this posture forms a psychosocial "wedge between the individual and his role, between doing and being" (107–8). Role distance makes an appearance in the surgeon who sings off-colour tunes during the operation and the waitress who speaks of her music career – any instance where people suggest to their audience "I am not only what I appear to be" (Cohen 2004, 117). Cavey dresses down to convey he is not a starched-collar evangelical pastor, and his DJ role liberates him from his sacred vocation altogether.

Although the discussion of acting roles turns attention towards the actor on stage, I want to include analysis of the audience's response to this reflexivity, specifically a theatrical term called *the alienation effect*.[3] The notion of the alienation effect is attributed to playwright Bertolt Brecht (1898–1956), who developed the concept from Chinese theatre, defining it as "playing in such a way that the audience was hindered from simply identifying itself with the characters in the play"

(Brecht 1964, 91).⁴ While the goal of conventional theatre performances was to draw the audience into a *suspension of disbelief*, such that they would be caught up in the play, Brecht's goal was to *disrupt* the performance and prevent any such escape into illusion. He wanted to historicize the performance on stage, alert the audience to the political urgencies of the day, and, as such, empower people with critical thought and political action (Brecht 1964, 96; Sargisson 2007; Bissonette 2010). The goal is "stripping the event of its self-evident, familiar, obvious quality and creating a sense of astonishment and curiosity about them" (Thomson and Sacks 2007, 191).

By turning the familiar and ordinary into the strange and unexpected, the audience becomes alienated from the character portrayed. The actor takes on a "double role" – as the character and himself/herself-as-actor at the same time, with both roles being accessible to the audience (Brecht 1964, 143, 194). Brecht gives one everyday life example of the child whose mother has remarried, revealing the mother in a second role of another man's wife. The taken-for-granted expectation is disappointed and made odd. Significantly for my analysis of charisma, Brecht admitted the alienation effect did not motivate as much political action as he hoped; the audience continued to emotionally attach and personally identify with the actor and the actor's role (Gassner 1966; McTeague 1994).

Always reflexive about its beliefs and practices, a post-evangelical drama strives for a performance that generates an alienation effect. The practices I examine here are not the equivalent of backstage sightings that reveal the hypocrisy of the leader (Joosse 2012), nor the legendary scandalous antics of American televangelists (Buddenbaum 2013). They are, however, the opposite of charismatic performances intended to suspend disbelief and cultivate naïve faith (Luhrmann 2012). The events and rituals described here are intended to unsettle, but they unsettle in order to disabuse the audience of participation in a conventional evangelical performance, not with the intention of completely estranging their followers. They cultivate just enough alienation to disturb the evangelical visitor by establishing distance from right-wing evangelical stereotypes and cultivate the reflexivity Cavey desires. In the process, the audience bonds with the charismatic leadership of Cavey.

How does a satirical counter-performance reinforce the charismatic bond? If it does not prompt attendees to leave, the disruption of the evangelical performance suggests something new and revolutionary

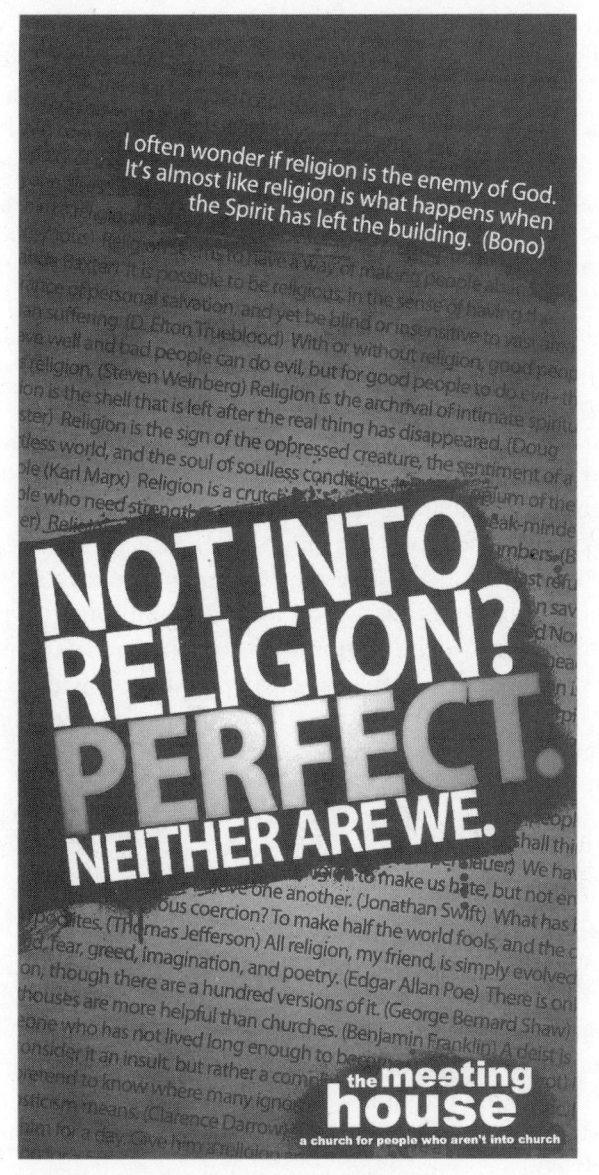

Figure 4.1 Promotional flyer: one version of an oft-reproduced "anti-religion" marketing tool.[5]

that resonates with the already disaffected attendees and validates their disillusionment with religious institutions. Cavey narrates a crisis in Christian religion and offers a way out that engenders a sense of self-efficacy in participants' lives (Madsen and Snow 1991). He effectively promises people they can be saved from the cultish, violence-endorsing, angry, legalistic, judgmental liabilities of right-wing evangelicalism and reinvent themselves in his gentle pacifist, "irreligious" image – echoing themes of irenic Canadian evangelicalism (Reimer 2003) in his nostalgic hippie attire. He calls them not to a conversion as much as a deconversion (Harrold 2006; Bielo 2011), in the name of Jesus, who came to "shut down religion."

Like other Emerging Churches, this aspect of TMH reflects the "underlife" of institutional evangelicalism today (Goffman 1961a; Marti and Ganiel 2014, 27). Attendees do not truly escape institutional life, but they form their identity over against evangelical beliefs and practices because "selfhood can arise through the little ways in which we resist the pull" of socialization (Goffman 1961a, 320). Persons are "stance-taking entities," says Goffman, who take up positions somewhere between identification with and opposition to institutions – a form of reflexivity. In this case, people identify with Cavey and develop bonds of affection and loyalty to him while distancing themselves from the wider evangelical subculture.

PURGE SUNDAY: NOT YOUR EXPECTED ALTAR CALL

Megachurches are defined by their large size and often characterized by an ideology of expansion. Rick Warren scouted out famous megachurches and then set himself the goal of building a church of twenty thousand members. His training in McGavran's Institute of Church Growth at Fuller Theological Seminary gave him the rationale to pursue quantitative growth as a sign of faithfulness to God and taught him the strategy to accomplish it: targeting the felt needs of middle-class "Saddleback Sam" and "Saddleback Samantha." When a group of his early converts expressed a preference for a smaller community church, Warren simply told them, "Well, then, goodbye" (Sheler 2009, 136).

Various scholars have critiqued this kind of entrepreneurial vision. MacNair argues that megachurch leaders are determined their church will "grow fast and furiously," and they "jettison unnecessary theological, ecclesiastical and liturgical baggage" in pursuit of expansion to the point where their organization can no longer be identified as a Christian church (2009, 46, 224). Maddox (2012) defines megachurches – especially those with prosperity theology leanings – as "growth churches" and even "capitalism's cathedrals" because of their "overriding commitment to growth" and their "gospel of growth." "Growth is elevated to the highest organizational and religious value," argues Ellingson (2007, 184) in his critique of megachurch networks; megachurch expansion for Ellingson includes the "colonization" of other churches and their traditions through the distribution of megachurch growth strategies and resources.

In contrast, although not without ambiguities, TMH presents as a growing church for people not into church growth. There is a Sunday morning ritual I have mentioned earlier that Meeting Housers internally refer to (with ironic tones) as "Purge Sunday." This is an occasional Sunday disinvitation, a sort of evangelical "anxious bench" counter-performance or reverse altar call, and it demonstrates clearly the ambivalence of TMH leadership towards megachurch growth pressures while at the same time reinforcing aspects of it. It is an act performed to reinforce the central story of its drama, to further secure its "irreligious" identity. Purge Sunday is a signal to their audience communicating their distance from high-pressure evangelical churches and cults as well as from the stereotype of megachurches as greedy for members.[6] Paradoxically, it signals that they are "a megachurch for people not into megachurches."

On Purge Sunday, which typically happens unannounced in September, and at times in January, Cavey issues a challenge to his audience just before his teaching time. In September 2008, he said, "If you feel this church is not where you can serve your best, we'll help you find another place. We're not a cult. If it's not a good fit – if you need something more liturgical, expressive, conservative, emotional, charismatic, etc., you may move onwards. If you left TMH and got more passionately involved in another church, that would be a success story for the broader kingdom of Christ. That's better than a limbo half-commitment here."

Then Cavey turns to a slide that has appeared on the screen and says, "We have a riotous diversity of people here":

1 New visitors
2 Spiritual seekers
3 Supporters of seekers

4 Healing from trauma (temporary season of healing)
5 A Christ-follower enthusiastically engaged in our mission
6 A Christian who has come from another church and really likes TMH but doesn't completely consider it your church "home" and is taking a long time to belong because of some lingering issues or simply because you have slowly become comfortable hiding in the shadows.

This is an important moment. Cavey knows that not all free-riders are opportunists or free-loaders. Some are genuinely in process towards a commitment, and the cost of accommodating them is worth the investment if they are indeed potential recruits. But the "bad" free-riders he wants to sift out. In September 2007 he addressed them directly: "There are some who just kinda come who are like barnacles on a boat ... And every so often you have to scrape the boat. You're just slowing us down. We do believe we have a mission and a calling and we want you to participate. If you are #6 we want to lift you up into category #5. If not, we just need to scrape the boat and say you best not come back next week. There are great churches we want to commend to you. Our site pastors will be happy to help you."

He apologizes to visitors, saying this doesn't happen every week. He then adds, "Someone came up to me after the last service [this morning] and said they were a barnacle and they need to make a commitment. We chatted a bit and then I said, 'Well, goodbye.'" His tone is matter-of-fact, not one of pastoral concern.

This purging ritual deserves close attention. As mentioned earlier, Goffman (1963) explains that stigmatized groups will mobilize around a savvy representative who can teach them some "code" that instructs them on how to manage tensions and pass for a normal person. Cavey often gives his attendees instructions on how to share their faith with others – sometimes even dedicating a whole series on the topic.[7] Purge Sunday suggests another "code" instruction moment at TMH – where Cavey explains expectations for membership and distinguishes TMH from consumer religion, possessive cults, and "sheep stealers" (churches that draw transfer growth from other congregations). I will briefly discuss the ritual in light of what Goffman says about use of narratives, the role of humour in impression management, and identity ambivalence among the stigmatized.

First of all, Goffman discusses the function of publications and public presentations in formulating the ideology of the group through narrative – including both success stories and atrocity tales (1963, 25). Cavey's Purge Sunday has become a more broadly discussed identifier of this church. The ritual was briefly featured in an article in the evangelical magazine *Leadership Journal* that critiqued passive "Magic Kingdom" amusement culture in the North American church (Stearns 2012); it also was the focus of an article in the Canadian news magazine *Christian Week* in which Cavey describes the ritual as a way to tell those who won't "get in" to church volunteering to "get out" of the church (Paddey 2005).[8] The *Leadership Journal* article quotes Cavey as saying that 10–15 per cent of the church leave after Purge Sunday, only to have the loss regained over the months that follow. The percentage seems remarkably steep to me; yet it certainly adds to the performance of a purported "radical church." The article helps to manage the church's identity by contrasting the Purge Sunday ritual with the icon of consumer culture, Disneyland, and analogous megachurches.

Similarly, when Cavey has spoken at Christian conferences across the continent, he has translated this event to other audiences under the title of "How to Attract Seekers, Not Shoppers." He explains that at TMH, Purge Sunday is "not some cheap manipulative trick" but the goal is to confront "Christian tourists" – often those from other churches who came to TMH after their own morning service was over – with their hypocrisy (that is, their play-acting Christian identity) and through pastoral relationships in the local settings, help these people move one step further in faith. He will tell a story, for example, of someone who left after a Purge Sunday and returned to thank Cavey ten years later for his timely rebuke. The choice-making ritual takes on a mythological power as it is publicized and discussed across the continent and becomes sacralized in its mimicry of an altar call, except the rhetorical emphasis rests on *leaving*, not coming forward. The underlying purpose, however, is to draw people *deeper* into their church participation.

A second focus of Goffman is how humour and jokes are used to manage the tension that arises between a stigmatized person and a normal person in everyday encounters (1963, 108, 116–20, 133–7). Cavey, as the spokesman for his church, uses humour to address the assumed consumer behaviour of his audience and demonstrate his own distance from such superficial cultural practices. You can imagine the chuckling on Purge Sunday, 2008, where he runs through a string of dating break-up clichés: "Maybe we need to go through a bit of a break-up. I'd love to do it with a candle over dinner, but why don't we just do it right here. Could be better fits for you out there. Maybe it's not you, it's me. It's not your fault. You're not meeting your full potential and maybe I'm holding you back. There are better people out there for you. I just want to release you. I'll pay for your first-year subscription to eHarmony.... We can still be friends."

This performance of dating break-up clichés provokes congregational laughter. The particular Purge Sundays I relate here were generally more elaborate than others, with the 2007 performance becoming affectionately known to insiders as "Barnacle Sunday." The majority of responses I received from attendees when I asked about this ritual were variations of enthusiastic mirth mixed with pride and a simultaneous acknowledgement of the practical necessity of purging spectators (e.g., "Brilliant!" "Shocking!" "I love it! Every church should have one!"). One female interviewee was spurred on by a Purge Sunday to start volunteering the following week, and she eventually became a Meeting House staff member. The ritual disturbed her to action, a positive example of the alienation effect.

With such humour, Cavey not only signals TMH's self-identity in contradistinction to a spectator sport, but at the same time conveys the risqué and playful character of the congregation – characteristics that contrast with the stereotype of the eager and serious proselytizing televangelist. Rick Warren, for example, performs a ritual similar to Purge Sunday in his megachurch, but this one has no comic element. Warren says, "Let me just be honest with you as somebody who loves you. If you passively just want to sit around in the next ten years and waste your life on things that won't last, you probably want to find another church, because you're not going to really feel comfortable here. Because if you're in this church, I'm coming after you to be mobilized" (Kwon 2010).

Warren's approach is both more sentimental and more threatening, and it lacks the playfulness that Cavey brings to it. Cavey, more so than Warren, wants to distance himself from the hard-sell evangelical subculture.

A third concern in Goffman is the deep ambivalence that the stigmatized feel towards their fellow-stigmatized, as they are both attracted and repelled by this group that they cannot fully embrace or let go (1963, 106–7). Cavey aims to eliminate ambivalence in attendees on Purge Sunday, but he unintentionally simultaneously creates it. This is to say, impressions can be managed but not comprehensively controlled. At TMH, people share an experience of Cavey and their disdain for conventional evangelical religion; but they have little else that binds them to each other in ethnicity, traditional affiliations, or even geographic location. TMH thrives on a *negative identity*, which fosters ambivalence from the start. Besides, as Cavey emphasizes, there are so many other options from which to choose for church.

The ambivalence that surfaced in one particular attendee interview was not ambivalence for the evangelical identity from which Cavey seeks to distance himself but ambivalence for Cavey's purposes in the purge ritual, based in a deep conscientiousness the interviewee had about his own spiritual performance. An older man involved in various aspects of Christian ministry, he explained to me, "What happened was after I hit about the third Purge Sunday, you know what? I find that too hard. I don't want to get purged again." He felt guilty about not coming every Sunday to the movie theatre, and although he was a regular at the Home Church, he felt he was charged with hypocrisy for going only occasionally on Sundays. "OK," he says, "I'm going to go when I'm 100 per cent committed to it." He is disgusted by the image of being vomited out (purged) and chafes against the assumption that the level of his participation in Meeting House activities is the measure of his Christian discipleship. "I don't want to commit to an institution and all it does; I want to commit to people." As he spoke to me his body nervously shifted as he wrestled with the experience. The alienation effect was operating; two years later I found he had left TMH for a more local church plant.

The Purge Sunday ritual suggests some performative contradictions. Intended to be a display that purges the church of consumeristic members, it relies on a *market logic* – that people should choose the church that attracts them most. Similarly, a ritual that Cavey uses to demarcate TMH from high-pressure evangelistic megachurches in the equivalent of a reverse altar call simultaneously demands 100 per cent commitment from attendees. In a case study of Hillsong Church in Australia, Wade (2010) draws on revised understanding of Goffman's (1961a) concept of the "total institution" as well as Lewis Coser's (1974) investigation of "greedy institutions." Unlike the coercive and draconian asylum that Goffman studied, the new kind of total institution Wade suggests is voluntary and seeks not to obliterate the self as much as promise self-actualization through complete commitment. Thus, the megachurch can be a "greedy institution" that seeks "exclusive and undivided loyalty ... [T]heir demands on the person are omnivorous" (4).

Although TMH deliberately limits its main programs to Sunday services, Home Church and more intimate "Huddles," numerous activities are attached to each venue that can consume large portions of an individual's and family's week. That TMH doesn't have AA and divorce recovery groups, a recreation centre and hair styling salon (like many other megachurches) does not necessarily mean it demands less of an individual's commitment. Regardless, many other congregations and religious groups make time-intensive demands on their members. TMH is not unique in its demands of its membership.

The difference with TMH is their constant drive to be distinguished from other churches. Cavey differentiates his Emerging Church–type congregation from the stereotype of megachurches greedy for growth and distinguishes his church as one for the committed rather than spiritual consumers. While the ritual does indicate the character of "a megachurch for those not into megachurches," it also reinforces what it rejects. Ironically, Cavey calls members to deeper commitment while acknowledging the priority of their preferences and their freedom to choose. He assumes the ecclesiastical mobility of the individuals in his audience – that information on what churches might be a "better fit" is readily available, and that attendees would be in a position to switch, apart from the needs and feelings of their friends, spouse, or children.

In sum, if an open range of choices defines consumerism, megachurches are well suited to providing numerous options to their pool of free-riders. This, however, does not mean that commitment is weak or that megachurches are somehow secularized. Consumerism has affected every religious community to some degree, but megachurches can capitalize on the consumer's desire for options and sacralize that cultural impulse as a path to authenticity. In the long term, it may draw deeper commitments from its core community than other religious institutions because its participants feel their commitments were freely and personally tested and chosen. In effect, it nurtures a consumer-oriented church for people not into consumerism.[9]

ZOMBIE FANDOM: NOT FOCUS ON THE FAMILY

Former senior pastor Tim Day explained to me in one interview, "We have special value as the leadership here for trying to be a place where

Strategic Satire for a Spoiled Identity

Figure 4.2 Cavey unveils the new family board game.

the reverse of what you think will happen, happens." Meeting House staff have told me that this was much more the modus operandi during the years of rapid growth in the early 2000s, but once in a while Cavey still gives his audience a jolt. He is the subversive evangelical – subversive less of popular culture than of conventional evangelicalism.

During one service before Christmas in 2012, Cavey was teaching about the importance of family time and the distraction of electronic devices. He said for the month of December his family had agreed to put their devices in a basket by the door and commit to playing board games together. Cavey, who often highlights his love for his Blackberry, remarked, "[This idea] is practically Amish, and it's practically going to kill me. I hate board games. No laser beams, car chases, or explosions."

He then drew the audience's attention to a small table beside him, with a blanket draped over a mysterious object. He told his viewers, "My [teenage] daughter Chelsea isn't here today, so I'm going to show you what she's getting for Christmas." He then pulled the blanket off the table to reveal *The Walking Dead* board game, based on the popular post-apocalyptic horror TV series about groups of survivors trying to protect themselves from ravenous zombies – and from other nefarious survivors.

"Gotta start in familiar territory," he quipped. Cavey's zombie fanaticism is one of the first things people are told about him. In introductions on interviews or at conference presentations or in short bios online, he is named as the teaching pastor at TMH and a fan of zombie films (his favourite film being *Dawn of the Dead,* 1978). Cavey's old Myspace site has photos he took of his daughters at a Toronto zombie walk in 2006 ("A nice way to spend a relaxing Sunday afternoon," he posted).[10] He revels in these moments of role distance, in which he alienates sections of his audience. Zombie references during his teachings may soften the juxtaposition, since they occur in a movie theatre, but he seldom explains to his audience why, as a pastor (and more ironically, an ardent pacifist pastor),[11] he so flagrantly promotes his fondness for horror films.[12] This is a significant part of his public persona, a key piece in his strategic evangelical counter-performance.

One qualitative study of four American churches that regularly use film clips concludes that only conventional Hollywood genres are used in churches, except for two genres: documentaries and horror films (Moore 2013). Zombie films are not the recommended genre from Focus on the Family, and such gory violence would repel many Sunday worshippers. At the very least, zombie references are risky in an evangelical church because there is a stark contrast between *The Walking Dead* and taken-for-granted evangelical mores around movies and violence.[13] "The emotionality at the core of modern evangelicalism," writes Todd Brenneman, "is a specific type of emotionality, one best labeled sentimentalism." He defines sentimentality as "tender feelings" expressed in nostalgia for the nuclear family[14] and a romanticized understanding of divine love for individuals, who are often conceptualized in infantilized terms (Brenneman 2014, 4). Evangelicals typically prefer stories that are clean and wholesome, and have happy endings. "Christian readers are too easily satisfied with sentimental tales that don't descend into the valley of the shadow of death," says one evangelical professor, alluding to Psalm 23. "Our own literature often lacks the bite and angst our worldview ought to embrace" (Harris 2015).

Yet Cavey's use of zombie films is not without evangelical zeal, and I would add evangelical shallowness. While plenty has been written on zombies as symbols of social anxiety, rampant consumerism, and repressed thoughts of death (Giroux 2011; McNally 2012; Paffenroth and Morehead 2012; Cowan 2008; Platts 2013), Cavey offers little cultural analysis to ease the cognitive dissonance,[15] except the occasional one-liner, such as a 2011 tweet about his purchase of the new season of *The Walking Dead*: "As a Christ-follower I feel the burden 2 support any show about death & resurrection." In September 2012 he used a clip from *Shaun of the Dead* and made passing reference to a scene in *The Walking Dead* to illustrate "zombie faith" – faith without following Jesus, going through the religious motions but being dead inside. Such use of zombie films stops short of cultural criticism; zombies are merely analogies for nominal Christians.[16] Unlike evangelicals who have been historically ambivalent about film and have written moralistic critiques, Cavey embraces all genres, including the most sensationally violent. In traditional evangelical fashion, however, his use of media during a Sunday service remains mostly *instrumental* – as a means to connect with the unchurched (Moore 2013; Christians 2013) and, as I argue here, to distinguish TMH from other evangelical churches. "When we're starting to make religious conservatives uneasy," said Cavey in a 2015 interview, "we're probably starting to live like Jesus."

In this light, Cavey's celebration of zombie films will jolt most visitors, especially when couched in the context of a sermon on "family time." Still, many attendees I interviewed were entertained or inspired by Cavey's love for the horror genre. "Like Bruxy, I have the whole set of *Walking Dead* comic book volumes," said one attendee, gesturing at his bookshelf. Another attendee more ambivalently concluded, "It's just one of his idiosyncrasies." Regardless, whether viewed as inspiring, endearing, or shocking, Cavey's zombie fandom cultivates emotional ties between himself and attendees and signals an effort to distance the church from right-wing evangelical mores.

SIMPLICITY: NOT THE PROSPERITY GOSPEL

Coming into the mall or auditorium on Sunday morning, a visitor can be excused for thinking that a feel-good message of God's love and material blessing awaits at TMH. Anyone familiar with the TV shows of televangelists such as Joel Osteen or T.D. Jakes may expect similar prosperity theology to be the standard fare at a megachurch such as TMH.[17] As mentioned in the first chapter, globally speaking, most megachurches lean in varying degrees towards a health-and-wealth message. Brian Houston, the celebrity pastor at Hillsong megachurch in Australia, unabashedly sells a spirituality of upward mobility, exemplified in his book *You Need More Money* (2000). Wade (2010, 20) summarizes the book and the church, saying, "Hillsong's consumer ethic is therefore not just a rationalization for wealth, but indeed a call to aspire to greater wealth and consumption."[18]

Cavey's theology is characterized more by austerity than prosperity. He persistently critiques the synthetic, insulated, and comfortable life of most Canadians. He knows his audience, as most are middle to upper class, and Oakville's site – by far the largest and central – sits in one of Canada's wealthiest exurbs. With constant themes of self-sacrifice and a tempered Anabaptist asceticism, teaching series carry titles such as "Cruciformity," "Can't Buy Me Love," and "Get Over Yourself: Rebelling against Our Culture of Narcissism." A June 2007 teaching series entitled "The Secret Revealed," directly critiques positive thinking in general and Rhonda Byrne's book/film *The Secret* (2006) and its purported "law of attraction" in particular. Its magical-formula world view is "completely incompatible" with the relational world view of Jesus, argues Cavey, even if it mimics some "Christian" practices.[19] Its prosperity teaching, says Cavey, echoes what he heard in his Pentecostal church growing up and from televangelists; if you give, God will give back more, because "You can't out-give God." This is a lie about what Jesus really taught, says Cavey, for Jesus declared wealth puts people at a spiritual disadvantage. Christians should never value money and possessions enough to seek them.[20] True treasure is God's kingdom community, where rich and poor hang out "soul to soul, naked and unashamed, just relating."

Cavey seeks to unsettle privilege; he will contrast the North American cushioned life with the persecution of Anabaptist communities throughout history – their simple living, and their martyrdom; he will address terminal illness such as cancer, describing how it has afflicted his family of origin and signals the fragility and precariousness of human life; or he will remark on horrific news such as the Newtown school shootings in December 2012 and declare such violence the common fare for many people worldwide from which North Americans have been sheltered. He suggests his audience lives in a "fantasy land where we think that we can buffer ourselves against it. So we react in the West as if it is the oddest thing. We are out of tune with suffering" (16 February 2013). Cavey will then mention that 30,000 children die every day from malnutrition, but such news does not grab the attention of North Americans to the same degree as smaller, more local tragedies carried by the mass media. When suffering does come close, he says, we cry, "Why me?"

Cavey insists that the true altar call for disciples of Christ invites people to come and suffer – more precisely, to follow Jesus and go where love takes you, which will be towards those who suffer. "Suffering is the great world view switcher," he says; it brings non-Christians to seek Jesus and it turns Christians away from Jesus. For Cavey, our expectations drive our reactions, and he insists the Bible promises suffering, not protection from it. "This is Jesus' pitch, his invitation to be spiritual," says Cavey in a 2010 teaching entitled "The Spirituality of Suffering." "You're going to suffer; it's going to suck. Follow me ... This is not the Jesus of prosperity gospel, but the Jesus of Scripture."[21]

Unlike prosperity theology, the theology of downward mobility has less popular appeal, and for Meeting Housers in the upper echelons of professional work, it is more difficult to put into practice. Most attendees I interviewed could speak of modest changes they have made to simplify their life, and some deliberately live below their means in order to give more generously to the church and other causes. My focus here, though, is the contrast between scene and script; attending a celebrated, growing church with a celebrity pastor and hearing a call to sacrifice without the accompanying promise of mirrored personal success can be jarring. The counter-performance alienates and can appear like a sudden change of script. It is a successful church for people not into success.

"I love being in the ministry of busting up people's expectations," said Bruxy in a 2014 interview at Unseminary.com (Birch 2014). "It keeps them kind of unsettled, 'What is going on here?' I think it then prepares us to say, 'Let's take a fresh look at Jesus together.'"

PACIFISM: NOT THE ANGRY PREACHER

One of Cavey's signature teachings, which he wrote in his book (2007, 65) and often uses when on tour and in interviews, critiques the religious affections of evangelicals. Often he begins this talk with the subject of religion, which he defines in pejorative terms as something people typically use to defend themselves or offend others. At the heart of this teaching is a parody of evangelical preachers, who he claims end their words with an extra syllable. He mimics the tone: "The wrath-uh of God-uh is coming upon you in the name of Je-*sus*."

He then tells the story of how when listening to a radio preacher one day in the car, his wife Nina suddenly asks why he listens to angry Christians. Cavey expresses surprise and plays up his incomprehension at her remark. He then relates how his wife, who was not socialized in a Christian family, explained to him, "If this preacher was talking that way about any other topic, you would think him dysfunctional and in need of therapy." Cavey then imitates the preacher's voice again, but attaches the voice to mattress sales, a university math lecture, and then a lover's talk, the last of which he says should most resemble Christian speech. The incongruity between the tone and content humorously displays the assumed dysfunctional behaviour and distinguishes Cavey from those other evangelicals while training his followers in the code, so that they, too, may pass as Goffman's "normals."

This is how it dawned on him, testifies Cavey; evangelicals were angry people. Evangelicals will rationalize such anger as holiness or passion, Cavey goes on to explain, but that holiness functions as a euphemism for a judgmental spirit, and judgment properly belongs only to God. Anger is one of the seven deadly sins and is frequently mentioned in the lists of vices in the Bible, argues Cavey – not in the list of the fruit of the Spirit (Galatians 5:22). In a 2014 online interview, Cavey explains that "absent from the list [of spiritual virtues] at any time is anger, or even just those generic terms of, 'I'm passionate, I'm excited, I'm on point, I'm on fire,' which we sometimes use as euphemisms for 'I'm a bully'" (Birch 2014).

Cavey models gentleness, humour, and a conversational style in his teaching, what some journalists have described as a combination of lecture, stand-up comedy, and talk-show host (St Philip 2006). The casual and jocular tone, especially during controversial teachings or onstage interviews with contentious others such as a Muslim guest (November 2014) can cause indignation in some of his audience. Cavey explains, "For religious people who have lived within a tradition of *anger equals holiness equals truth*, it throws them off, but they need to be thrown off" (Birch 2014). Through such emotional labour, Cavey creates role distance from the "passionate" evangelical preacher and generates alienation in sections of his audience.

Sometimes Cavey connects this teaching with Anabaptist pacifism, charging that non-Anabaptist Christians have killed in the name of holiness and righteous anger. At a Xenos conference talk he gave in the United States in 2013, he offered a sweeping historical judgment; the mainstream Christian authorities stopped killing only when the Enlightenment came and robbed the Church of its power to kill. That is to say, the Church never repented of its violent ways on its own but only by the force of secularization, which disestablished its cultural dominance. Today, religious people, Cavey added, "can only murder people with attitudes and judgments."

This teaching often includes commentary on the "wrath" of God. Only God can be wrathful, says Cavey, because he is the ultimate judge. His wrath is always under the direction of his love, as love is fundamental to God's essence, while wrath is accidental.[22] Jesus, who turned over tables and brought out a whip in the temple one day, was expressing his judgment against the "den of robbers" who occupied its court. Jesus did not recruit his disciples to such action, emphasizes Cavey. Christians need to distinguish when to imitate Jesus and when to stand back and worship. Such disapproving emotion is properly exclusive to the divine, and Cavey insists Christians should "have a reputation on the street for being gentle, graceful, merciful, and very embracing" (Birch 2014).

At one point in the 2014 Unseminary interview Cavey concluded, "I think that's one of the key lessons that we as Evangelical Christians in the West need to unlearn, is that anger is not the emotion that will help us display our holiness." Such declarations put Cavey outside the evangelical mainstream. For example, one prominent evangelical professor of human emotions has written that "anger expresses a sense of justice and a sense of being in the presence of responsible agents. A person who cannot get angry is seriously defective" (Roberts 2014).[23]

Cavey's contentious claim here, like most criticisms of evangelicalism directly or indirectly assumed in this chapter, beg some critical comment. It is ironic that English literature scholar Ian Gordon (2002) describes satire as the "fusion of laughter and contempt," as satire's chief weapons of ridicule, parody, and mockery use laughter for aggressive purposes, "vexing the reader's complacency and provoking his or her anger." That Cavey connects his theology of anger with his Anabaptist pacifism draws out a similar irony; James Davison Hunter detects a passive-aggressive streak in the neo-Anabaptist camp, contending their criticism of state, market, and mainstream church create a public tone that is "overwhelmingly a message of anger, disparagement, and negation. Christianity in America, as it is believed and lived by most believers, is just not Christian enough" (Hunter 2010, 165). "Theirs is a world-hating theology," argues Hunter, which affirms neither social world nor creation but only the pacifist church and its God (174). Some Nietzschean *ressentiment* – a psychology of entitlement endemic to politics at large today[24] – also creeps into the Anabaptist narrative, as Anabaptist scholars and pastors recite the history of injuries against Anabaptists and intimate their position is on the "right side of history" (175). Ironically, proponents use the language of politics (and for Cavey, this includes terms such as *revolution* and *subversion*) to frame a selectively sectarian identity (Ellingson 2010) forged primarily against the state while making instrumental use of markets and electronic technologies.

Hunter overstates his case here, and some have called his characterization of the neo-Anabaptist approach unfair and uncharitable (Thiessen 2011). The irony, however subtle, remains; Cavey's demeanour is consistently gentle, casual, and jocular, and his satirical tone is more the witty Horatian than the serious Juvenal (Abrams and Harpham 2008); but he is also contentious and passionate, vigilant about theological boundaries, as he was in his series on pacifism, the series against Calvinism, and in his series exploring other denominations (April 2010). Coincidentally, this discussion can turn attention back to the beginning of this chapter and Brecht's alienation effect. Brecht argued that the aim of the alienation effect was to nurture a critical attitude that evoked "justified anger" in the audience that "cannot be passionate enough" (McTeague 1994, 26). If Cavey instills a critical stance on religion (and evangelicalism in particular), he may not avoid arousing negative emotions in his already disaffected crowd.

Yet Cavey models his teaching well in his approach and tone; he is consistently gentle, civil, and witty, even when being critical. His shunning of anger, if unintentionally ironic, proved to be of therapeutic value for some of the Meeting Housers I met in Home Churches. I was in one prayer group during a Home Church meeting that had recurring discussions and prayers about anger management – one father was concerned about his daughter's temper, and another father was struggling persistently with his uncontrollable rage. Not everyone at TMH may theologically agree with Cavey on the ethics of the emotion, but therapeutically speaking, controlling anger seemed an unquestioned good.

In sum, Cavey's teaching on anger highlights his polemical relationship with evangelicalism as well as the foundationally paradoxical nature of TMH, a religion for people not into "religion," a megachurch for people not into megachurches, a satirical performance for those not into anger. I point out these performative paradoxes not to suggest their community has failed as a religious experiment but to emphasize that its charisma rests in these playful and provocative tensions that amuse, unsettle, and intensify loyalty and affection for Cavey.

I have suggested that a dramatic web enchants Cavey's charismatic authority, and in this chapter I demonstrated ways in which TMH deliberately satirizes and critiques the stereotypes of the right-wing evangelical church. TMH is intensely aware of the stigmatized identity of religion in Canada, and of evangelicalism especially, and awareness of this context directs their post-evangelical drama, characterized by strategic, satirical counter-performances. However, such counter-performances suggest a reflexivity towards religiosity that has its own charms, and a playful irony helps manage audience expectations of conservative religion. By creating role distance from the evangelical celebrity pastor, they alienate the audience from evangelical assumptions, and if it does not turn them away from Cavey, it binds them more closely to him.

I have now covered the deconstructive performance that forms the unsettling and provocative opening act of Bruxy Cavey's dramatic web. This satire is not fully satisfying on its own, however – it names the problem that begs for a solution. Beneath much satire lies an ideal, a romantic notion of social life that informs the satirical critique, and at TMH this romance comes in the script that is given for their Home Church life – what is said to be the true centre of the church. The combination of satirical critique and utopian alternative complete the charismatic connection offered by Cavey to his followers. This taps into deeper mythologies of North American history and the early Christian Church, giving Cavey's charisma enough novelty to be attractive and enough familiarity to be credible.

5

Life Together

Home Church as Romantic Script

At any given moment, all over the world, hundreds of millions of people will be engaged in what is one of the most familiar of all forms of human activity. In one way or another they will have their attention focused on one of those strange sequences of mental images which we call a story ... They are far and away one of the most important features of our everyday existence.

Christopher Booker

I get the benefit from [Cavey] doing all the work [*chuckle*]. And yet, in order for me to take it from head knowledge to heart and action, that's where I come home, I do my study, I go to Home Church and we talk about it. And that has been one of the most helpful areas of being able to grow. Because I can see how I'd be talking about an issue that I'm struggling with, in terms of, for example, a co-worker, at work, just came on board and she's a nasty, nasty person. I'm just astounded that anybody could be so mean. So, this is where the rubber hits the road. We're learning to love our enemies; we're learning.

Middle-aged female, hospital clerk,
co-leader of Home Church

The most sacred place on the planet is the space between you and me when we love one another as Jesus does.

Bruxy Cavey

Cavey's signature teaching declares the gospel is that Jesus came to "shut down religion." The welcome page of the TMH website in 2015 explained that they seek to "reject the lens given to us by religion, even the Christian religion, and become a community who opens our Bibles regularly with fresh eyes and re-live the accounts of those who first followed Jesus." They spurn history and institution to recreate a primitivist ideal – the original community of Jesus, a shift they describe as being from *religion* to *relationship*: "Our real focus (our hidden agenda) is on what we call Home Church. These are small groups that meet in individual homes each week to talk, become friends and to reach out to their local communities. This is the core of who we are because we feel that only when people connect relationally with people, discuss ideas, serve together, and learn to get along, that they truly function spiritually as God intended. We feel that if there is any one thing a person should focus on, it's this – even at the expense of our Sunday morning services." Sunday morning, says Cavey, is merely their "public preaching point." Their Home Churches *are the church*.

The previous chapter focused on Cavey's satirical critique of religion, and evangelicalism in particular, as communicated from the front stage Sunday mornings. While satire may descend into disengaged cynicism, it can also harbour a deeper romantic vision (Guhin 2013). This chapter shifts from the Sunday show towards the small group drama that takes place during the week, what I am characterizing as the revolutionary romance narrative – with its nostalgic promise of adventure, fighting against monsters, and finding love (Frye 1957). I first examine Cavey's articulation of this script in two forms – as a revolutionary community and then as a Mennonite restorationist program, and then I investigate how this script is performed in the Home Churches I visited. Megachurch research needs to move from the preacher's words to the lived religion of his followers.

As in the previous chapter, the analytical separation of the four points of the charismatic diamond in earlier chapters is now integrated into an investigation of the dramatic web of the church. Cavey offers a message and mission that is shaped and distributed onto people's screens across Ontario – at home and in rented movie theatres. This message of relationship rather than institutional religion resonates with social and cultural conditions that have nurtured skepticism towards institutions and fragmented human communities, leaving people longing for more meaningful relationships, what Giddens (1991) has called "pure relationships." Attendees recognize Cavey's talent and vision and live out his script for them while sharing it with others through word-of-mouth and social media. The charismatic diamond makes explicit what is implicit in my unfolding of TMH's dramatic web, just as analyzing the setting, star, stagecraft, and spectators of a performance does not illustrate the play.

THE BIG STORY: OVERCOMING THE MONSTER

Christopher Booker (2004) suggested that stories can be generally grouped into seven basic plots. The majority of megachurches worldwide fall into some version of a "prosperity gospel" subculture, often as part of the neo-Pentecostal or charismatic network.[1] The narrative plot championed in these churches comes closest to Booker's second plot description, entitled "rags-to-riches," exemplified in T.D. Jakes's biography and in his message to his followers (Lee 2005). This plot follows a trajectory to similar the American Dream and other globalization narratives in which the main character "who has seemed to the world quite commonplace is dramatically shown to have been hiding the potential for a second, much more exceptional self within" (Booker 2004, 52). In theological terms, health and wealth are rewards for faith in God.

TMH, however, eschews the prosperity gospel church, and in their script the forces that threaten are grander and more terrifying than the personal struggles in a rags-to-riches plot (Booker 2004, 244). The first of Booker's plots, entitled "overcoming the monster," fits best with the driving narrative of TMH where "the existence of some superhuman embodiment of evil power" threatens a community and must be fought to the death by the hero (23). The monster, which can also be a force or machine in some other renditions of this archetypal romantic narrative, takes the shape of institutional religion in the Meeting House narrative.[2] It is ironic that religion would be what threatens a church, but it is not surprising, given the perennial struggle that evangelicalism has had with "formal religion" (Hatch 1989). The story of religion, as a system of rules and rituals, is scripted as a fall into sin and decay, a tragedy. But there is hope beyond the fate of religion. Cavey's version of this plot is best compared to its revolutionary renditions, in which radical social transformation ushers in communitarian ideals (Booker 2004, 578). Close, organic, church-based relationships defeat the spectre of aggressive, rigid, arid religion.

These stories give meaning, order, and mystery to people's lives, and in the context of organizations, these narratives are not merely texts but embodied local performances. By storytelling, leaders conjure a world in which followers can think, imagine, and feel in a new way, and thus be drawn into protest, mobilized for action or enticed deeper into community participation. Beyond straight logical rationales for action, narratives have an openness and fluidity that allows people to "imaginatively organize their agency" and develop a vision for an alternative social order (Reed 2014). Storytelling gives people a sense of power and possibility; stories arouse hope and fear, admiration and envy, curiosity and excitement that solidify a charismatic bond with their source, overturning conventional patterns of life, and drawing people into transformational social movements. In sum, stories are scripts for life.

THE 1960S REVOLUTIONARY COMMUNITY

Cavey's negative story – "relationship, not religion" – catches the wave of suspicion towards institutions that has become part of the dominant culture of the West. When combined with his pacifist position, denominational connections, and polite approach to ecumenical encounter, Cavey has created a Christian community well-tailored to Canadian sensibilities.[3] The core *positive* story that Cavey tells borrows from two cultural wells, narratives I have dubbed "the 1960s revolutionary community" and "the Mennonite restorationist dream." Both plot a struggle to overcome the monster of established institutions – and especially religion – and carve space for a revolutionary, restored modern community of what Giddens (1991) calls "pure relationships."

The first core narrative performance includes Cavey's hippie costume, including the long hair, T-shirt, and jeans, and has been articulated most coherently in two related teaching series entitled "The Way: Teachings from the Original Hippie from Nazareth" (April 2004, October 2009) and echoes the rhetoric of the hippies and the Jesus People Movement with Sunday teaching titles such as "Make Love, Not War" and "Give Peace a Chance" (employing the image of multi-coloured flowers). The history of the Jesus People in North America includes some pockets in Toronto that Cavey connected with as a teen, and it forms the backdrop for much of TMH subculture and the ethos of the Emerging Church Movement.[4]

In this series Cavey starts by saying he wants to give the audience a sense for the context of the sixties. He explains:

> It was a crazy time, far out time. Tremendous upheaval. Old institutions were being questioned, and radical ideas were being investigated. The nation was at war and divided over whether to fight, but this radical subversive group said maybe freedom and peace are not just goals to be pursued but a way to live. They refused to see war as the answer and instead headed in the other direction, fostering intentional communities of peace, love, and togetherness. They rebelled against the war and lots of things acceptable in society like capitalist ideals, rejecting materialism that ensnared so many in it, and with radical simplicity and sharing everything, living communally and saying what is mine is yours; and so they were a countercultural movement not only as far as war and peace issues were concerned but also as far as economics and material possessions were concerned, but going so far as to go against the flow by going against some of society's most cherished institutions, like religion itself.
>
> They were very spiritual people and spiritually questing in a variety of ways, creating all kinds of issues but they shunned organized religion basically with the idea that it had had its day and quite frankly it had failed. It was the great failed experiment of humanity, religion was, and instead they pursued spirituality and faith. They said we are moving on from a time of law to a time of love, because all you need is love and love is all you need.

After some more detail Cavey pulls the rhetorical twist: "Everything I've just said is about the 60s. Not the 1960s." He then explains that thirty years after the death and resurrection of Jesus Christ in the first century, the original sixties, his movement, the Way, was calling for love and peace formed in radical community.

Glimpses of a dramatic web become more evident now. Cavey puts layers of stories together, creating a web of overlapping storylines, including the early Church, the 1960s, the spiritual but not religious subculture, and as this sermon ends, he plays a clip from *The Matrix: Revolutions* where the female rebel character, Niobe, declares regarding the hero, Neo, "I believe in him." Pop culture and a remixed tradition reinforce each other to emphasize the all-encompassing imperative of overcoming the monster and trusting the champion to rescue the imperilled community.

Cavey consistently associates his narrative with the rhetoric and symbolism of radicalism and revolution. A teaching series entitled "R*evol*ution" (a word within which they highlight the backwards-spelled word *love*) uses a parody logo of the Che Guevara silhouette with a crown of thorns on his head. The pacifist Cavey delights in the irony of using a symbol of revolutionary violence to promote his rendering of the peace-pursuing community of Jesus. Such iconography also deliberately appeals to the "rebel consumers" who associate Guevara's image with "a challenge to authority in any guise, a 'cry for freedom' that no longer has any specific meaning in it" (Caistor 2010, xi, 134).

The Jesus figure at the centre of Cavey's grand narrative is not the meek and mild pastel-coloured portrait of Sunday school; nor is it the muscular evangelical Jesus of the early twentieth century (Putney 2003; Kee 2006); neither is Cavey's Jesus primarily the king who sits on the throne as the ruler of all creation in conservative Christian theology (N.T. Wright 2012; Keller 2013). First and foremost, Cavey's Jesus is the prophetic Jesus of the Sermon on the Mount, who stands up to teach the crowds a countercultural ethic; this Jesus challenges the status quo of violence with a promise of peace, and eschews riches to comfort the poor, and follows a path to suffering rather than personal security. In middle-class urban Toronto culture, Cavey's faux Guevara/Jesus may carry the intensity and urgency of socialist revolution, but it does so apart from the context of murderous political struggle, apart from the radical sacrifices that such revolutions demand, and apart from the social transformation of the political economy.

Comparatively speaking, Cavey's "revolution" entails convictions that often remain open-ended, nurtures relations that are respectful and tolerant of others, and as a conservative Anabaptist, negates the possibility of political protest or political involvement of any kind. "The only way we 'bear arms,'" writes Cavey with regards to his pacifism, "is by wearing T-shirts" (2017, 128). In effect, his "revolutionary" language does not refer to overcoming the current political-economic system to reconstruct a new society but rather to develop a society parallel to the current configuration, centrally based in church community and its intermittent forays into broader society through "compassion" activities. A Jesus who avoids violence, riches, and institutions remains modestly at the margins, in the tradition of "separation" from the world, which has been the characteristic social ethic of the Radical Reformation, epitomized by the Amish. Cavey's use of the word *revolution*, similar to his use of the word *religion*, is idiosyncratic and requires the context of his larger oral and theological tradition to be properly understood.

Cavey's social ethics share with liberation theology a concern for praxis – an emphasis on what participants can do to make a difference in their everyday lives rather than simply interpreting texts. This focus on discipleship is also characteristic of his theological tradition. All his teachings end with practical suggestions for action that most busy professionals could incorporate into their lives. "Compassion" initiatives stretch beyond the private sphere through collective action in concert with other Christian mission agencies: TMH concentrates attention and millions of dollars toward the poor, especially in 2009–14 to those communities affected by AIDS in southern Africa (through the global BIC, World Vision, and Mennonite Central Committee networks). According to spring reports, "compassion" ministries, which does not include any ministries to their own members, account for about 14 per cent of their total budget (in 2011 the budget total was $8 million).[5] To be clear, Cavey does not hold to the preferential option for the poor, nor does he seek any structural change in the political economy in Canada or beyond. His notion of the "kingdom of God" is much narrower and much more spiritualistic than the liberation theologians (Gutierrez 1988) – or many emergent church pastors, for that matter (Bielo 2011).[6]

The revolution Cavey describes champions authentic relationship, community, and living simply and generously, and while that may involve scaling down one's purchases and assets, it has little to do with structurally transforming society as a whole or pursuing the common good. The Meeting House's entire "Transform" mission – their five-year plan for ministry begun in 2012 – has no strategy for change in the culture or political economy of their municipalities, let alone the nation. In traditional Anabaptist fashion, they interpret Jesus's words "My kingdom is not of this world," to be a rationale for political quietism.[7] Cavey provides well-circumscribed boundaries for the "revolution"; in one 2008 "Drive Home" podcast on gender differences, Cavey explains that "the gospel is not a social reform movement but a 'heart reform' movement, not transforming society and institutional structures such as patriarchy and slavery but about the transforming freedom from slavery to our sin, selfishness, attitudes." Cavey does not deny the significance of some social reform movements, but the gospel for him is something spiritual and of transcendent importance. It is ultimately a revolution of the heart; or to borrow the title from a book from one of Cavey's favourite thinkers, a "revolution of character" (Willard and Simpson 2005).

THE MENNONITE RESTORATIONIST DREAM

This leads directly into the second core storyline, which, contrary to American trends towards non-denominationalism, follows the megachurch's denominational identity – Be in Christ (BIC), historically known as Brethren in Christ.

Arguing historically that the sixteenth-century Protestant Reformers were not radical enough in their reforms, Anabaptists like Cavey claim the core of faith rests in discipleship with Jesus and that the first-century Church is the prototype of Jesus's original vision: meeting in people's houses, active in evangelism, and at odds with its surrounding culture. The turning point in the plot – the central conflict or complicating action of this story – is the "fall" of the Christian Church in the fourth century, when the Christian movement calcified into an established institution linked with the state through Constantine. Jesus's message became obscured in rules, rites, and religion, and the violence of Christendom – the storyline's monster – was occasionally meted out against the Anabaptists in the sixteenth century and beyond.[8] In sum, teaching pacifism, simplicity, and revolutionary community, TMH promotes itself as "urban-dwelling Amish" or "Mennonites with electric guitars."

Anabaptism, the lesser-known underdog of Protestantism, offers resonance with current countercultural trends among the middle class that romanticize the local, authentic, green, and organic.[9] The Anabaptists were persecuted by the Christian establishment in centuries past, became known in Canadian literature for their controversial pacifist position in wartime through Rudy Wiebe in his *Peace Shall Destroy Many* (Wiebe 2002). More recently they became the object of nostalgia, as one memoir recounts an almost fanatic pilgrimage to the culture of quilts (Bender 1991), another attests to the happiness that lies off the grid (Brende 2009), and more popularly, superstar Harrison Ford brought their plain-dressed but charming lifestyle to the big movie screen (*Witness* 1985). Of late, Anabaptist life has been commercialized not only through tourist attractions such as St Jacob's Market, just north of TMH's Waterloo site, but also through such authors as American Beverly Lewis and her two-dozen bestselling Amish romance novels. One of her books, *The Shunning* (2008), has been made into a film of the same name (by Hallmark 2011), and it complements other recent Amish films (*The Devil's Playground* 2002; *Amish Grace* 2010) and the more popular TV shows such as *Amish in the City* (Stick Figure Productions, 2004), *Amish Mafia* (Discovery Channel 2012), and *Breaking Amish* (TLC 2012) with its sequel *Return to Amish* (2014). While I did not notice any direct references to such popular culture in TMH, their Anabaptist heritage resonates with these popular culture productions. "We're Mennonites without the horse and buggy," explain Meeting House leaders. Significantly, there are no Calvinist equivalents in popular culture – Cavey's nemesis.

Regardless, the Amish are not the full embodiment of Anabaptism. Anabaptists are also known for addressing global poverty, hunger, and sustainability, notably through the advocacy of BIC-affiliated writers Shane Claiborne (2006) and Ron Sider (Swartz 2014), the latter of whom penned the controversial bestseller *Rich Christians in an Age of Hunger* (1978). Anabaptists are also known through the developmental work of the Mennonite Central Committee, and its ethics are popularly expressed in *The More with Less Cookbook* by Doris Janzen Longacre (1976) and its various sequels. In sum, while Anabaptism remains on the sidelines of establishment Protestantism, it has elements with "allure" that "enchant" and challenge mainstream culture (Kraybill 2003; Weaver-Zercher 2013).

The Anabaptist character of TMH stimulates the *restorationist* or *primitivist* impulses that reverberate through TMH. This is a notoriously controversial concept, and Anabaptist theologians prefer to dance with it at arm's length (Yoder 1995; Schlabach 1995). It can be defined as "attempts to cut back through the corruption built up over centuries in order to recover the pristine purity of Christian faith and practice on the model of the church's early period" (Noll 1988). One significant part of this primitivist impulse is a sense of the "fall of the Church" and an understanding that Church tradition, rather than an authority from which to glean, becomes a barrier to radical discipleship. One clear indication at the Meeting House was their seven-Sunday "Inglorious Pastors" series, which emphasized a "fall of the Church" under Constantine and began with this promotional statement: "The Meeting House is a church trying to push back through 2000 years

Figure 5.1 Promotional bookmark for seven-week series on Anabaptism and pacifism, 11 April 2010–23 May 2010; a parody of Quentin Tarantino's *Inglourious Basterds* (2009).

of religious tradition to learn from the biblical Jesus." In effect, history and its evolving Church institutions contaminate the original charismatic body and so TMH's teaching often leans back towards the first century, seeking more fluid community relationships.

For Cavey, his restorationist impulse is most prominently ecclesiastical: decoupling the Church and state establishment initiated by Constantine and returning to New Testament networks of house churches that intentionally build community, or as they say at the Meeting House, "do life together." Yet similar to many evangelical churches and revivalist movements, this restorationist impulse also seeks to push through the perceived cold formalism of mainline churches and foster a more casual, energetic atmosphere (Hatch 1989). Church rituals, routines, and roles, especially when rhetorically coupled with legalism, hypocrisy, and judgmentalism are spun in a negative, pejorative frame, which mirrors many evangelical writings today.[10] In effect, Cavey's "irreligious" ethos can be linked to his new Anabaptist lineage as well as to his biographically more long-standing evangelical faith.

HOME CHURCH AS PURE RELATIONSHIP

The Meeting House leaders describe themselves not as a megachurch but as "a network of about 200 house churches." Their logo encapsulates this contrarian narrative; TMH in blue letters, except the two *e* letters in the word *meeting* are facing each other, in this manner: eɘ – because "real church happens when we turn our chairs and face one another." Cavey elaborates on the cliché, saying that Sunday morning features their *teaching program* or "public preaching point," intended to meet with cultural norms for gathering spaces but is not the church. Church is Home Church.

At this point, I want to emphasize the similarity of Cavey's narrative with Giddens's notion of "the pure relationship," which he defines as "one in which external criteria have become dissolved: the relationship exists solely for whatever rewards that relationship can deliver. In the context of the pure relationship, trust can be mobilized only by a process of *mutual disclosure*" (1991, 6). Modern people gravitate to relationships without ascriptive ties, pursuing them for their own sake, and they endure as long as their satisfaction lasts (Giddens 1992, 58). While Giddens refers primarily to sexual relationships and their "purification" through the compartmentalization of sexuality from reproduction, the concept can translate to a megachurch small group, purified from the dynamics of ethnicity, family, nation, tradition, and shared memory – (recall that 99 per cent of attendees at TMH are not from BIC background). They are voluntary relations, entered into for their own sake and for self-development, democratically structured, reliable "until further notice." Both contemporary sexual relationships and megachurch attendee interactions are modern relations that rely less on history or nature for their bond, and rest more on precarious and fluid social agreements. They are risky, always in danger of dissolution or codependence. In Giddens's sociological understanding, these relations must be constantly resolidified and renegotiated in a disembedded, "runaway world" of globalizing forces, which sweep away traditional markers by enhancing risk and relying on experts and abstract systems. Without inheriting pre-existent patterns for life, individuals must continually choose in matters of lifestyle and identity in a perpetually reflexive way.

Cavey's romantic script echoes with some of Giddens's social analysis. In a question-and-answer session one Sunday night in the summer of 2014, in what Cavey called a "Theology After-Party" for those interested in further discussion on the morning's teaching, Cavey compares Home Church with professional counselling, suggesting that the relationships forged in Home Church may obviate the need for professional therapeutic help:

> What we do in the West is take one element that should be part of our personal lives in the church and professionalize it, because it makes us comfortable. We love professional versions of personal things. So as friends, we should be a lot more open about how our lives are doing, how our marriages are doing, how our relationships with our kids are doing, what it's like being single, what my personal struggles are. We should be much more open about our personal emotional life. We should probably have those people we are much more open with and regularly meeting with for ongoing mentorship and wisdom – we tend to be more private, those things get bottled up, we say, "I need to get a therapist" – that's the secular version. Now I pay a person money, so they can look into my life and I can catch up on this whole process of intimacy and give me wisdom.

Cavey does recognize a place for professional therapeutic intervention, but he suggests more regular self-disclosure (the word *open* appears three times in three sentences) in our everyday relations could replace therapeutic help. He goes on to explain the value of the Meeting House's smaller and more intense configuration, called Huddles, where two to four people "are going to be more intentional, more intimate" than they would be with "the average brother or sister" in Home Church and "confess their sins to each other," "lay bare their lives before one another and work through things together." Cavey expects accountability in their faith journey, as participants whose lives may be "off in left field" in some unhealthy way would be effectively requesting an intervention. He takes on the voice of his ideal Huddle member: "Oh, please, make it your business; my life *is* your business, actually, and *your* life is *my* business."[11]

Cavey explains that Sunday services, Home Church, and Huddles form three concentric circles that encompass TMH, the Huddles forming the innermost ring of the church's social structure. These concentric rings I compare with the concentric threads on a spider's web, with the radiating lines as the narratives that hold the diverse social circles together. The centre of the web is not Cavey or Jesus, but the utopian goal of "pure relationship" – where all storylines converge, and where the radical community demonstrates it has overcome the monster (see figure 5.2). Mobile urbanites are caught up in this dramatic web, a symbolic "web of significance" (Geertz 1977) that brings meaning, purpose, excitement, and a strategic religiosity to their disembedded lives. When Cavey writes "The most sacred space on the planet is the space between you and me when we love one another as Jesus does," he's touching a soft spot in some lonely lives (Cavey 2017, 149).[12]

At times Cavey calls this intimate cloister "friendship"; other times he calls it "discipleship" or "mentorship." However, the most common metaphor he uses for his megachurch community is "family." But these relations are often not as proximate or sustained as a biological family; they are transitory and often last as long as personal satisfaction and work schedules last. The Huddle epitomizes more typically a therapeutic community not unlike other religious small groups in which people seek voluntary, provisional, fluid connections based in intimate self-disclosure of their personal struggles (Wuthnow 2001). In a sense, these Huddles are "purer" than Giddens's pure relationships, for Giddens has been criticized for ignoring the power differentials inherent in opposite-sex relations (Hay, O'Brien, and Penna 1997). Home

Home Church as Romantic Script

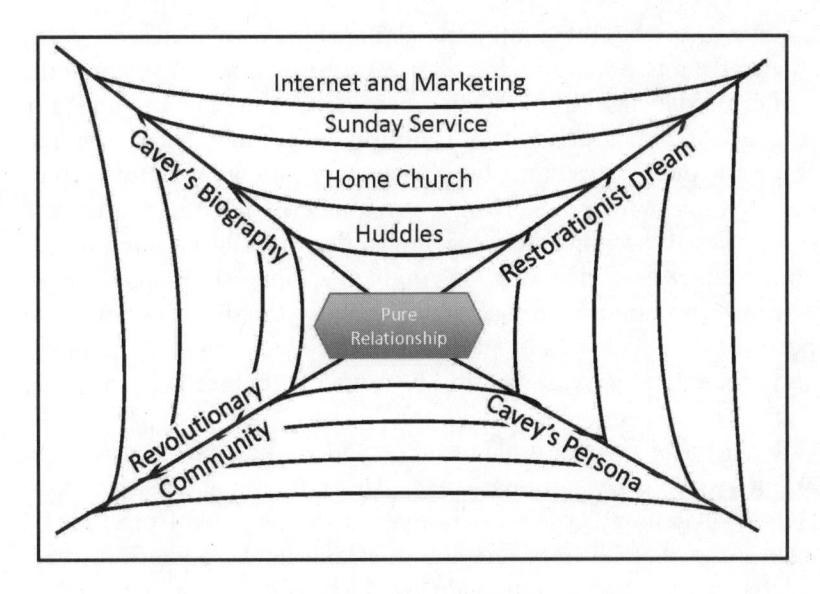

Figure 5.2 The Meeting House's dramatic web.

Church prayer times and Huddles, by contrast, are almost always gender segregated. While there remains some homogeneity in faith that binds people together, the diversity of past religious affiliations present in one group can be vast, ranging from Roman Catholic to Pentecostal. The charisma of Cavey and these narrative performances hold the group together in their quest to overcome the monster – their negative experiences of institutional religion.

These narratives are not only foundational to TMH discourse; they are to be performed as part of their post-evangelical drama. I participated in five Home Churches and attended each for eleven weeks. While I did participate in one intense Huddle group, there was too much turnover, transition, and interrupted meeting routines for stable long-term relationships to form for the vast majority of attendees. People switch groups, groups split, and they usually break for the summer season. The core script, however, with its promise of pure relationship in contrast to the legalistic, self-justifying, and historically violent institutional church, charismatically functions to engender increased self-efficacy for deconverted evangelical attendees (Madsen and Snow 1991). The narrative functions to cultivate a charismatic bond with the long-haired, fast-talking, and jocular Cavey, all bathed in the irony of being "a megachurch for people not into megachurches."

Cavey describes these intimate relationships in biblical terms with Anabaptist interpretations, but they resonate with the modern, mobile, white, middle-class urban-dweller because they are not *too radically* Anabaptist. Anabaptists have traditionally emphasized communal living and decision-making, but this was a more comprehensive community project, including living in proximity to each other and enforcing ecclesial discipline. Most significantly, the "mutual interactivity among diverse participants" in Anabaptist understanding is "most evident in economic sharing," which included the sharing of material possessions, which was "regarded favourably by the lower classes" and authentically expressed in Hutterite communes (Finger 2004, 242, 254).

Readily available cultural narratives about religion demonstrate an affinity with Cavey's dramatic web. This intimate understanding of *church* suggests a depoliticized organization removed from the tarnished legacy of Christendom and its establishment powers. Instead, it offers a privatized and individualized form of religion that puts the choices, struggles, and needs of the attendee at the centre. While a strong communal discourse and practice still surrounds the Home Church, it appears in the form of "cooperative egoism," which "involves the management and assertion of one's individuated self" while simultaneously pursuing empathy and connection with others (Marti and Ganiels 2014, 166).

Additionally, an evangelical mythology and the broader Christian narrative of the biography of Jesus Christ most fundamentally enchant the performance (Falco 2011, 27). Cavey would have much more work to do in order to connect with his de-churched and over-churched audience if he could not immediately make the connection with strangers already socialized to varying degrees within the drama of Jesus Christ and such staples as the Bible, Sunday worship, prayer, and forgiveness. This forms the subcultural base from which Cavey builds, and his romantic script rests upon it, as he gives it his own interpretive spin within a wider dramatic web, and the "irreligious" quality of the story comes across as fresh and innovative to his followers.

Like most narratives, this story is by no means uncontested (Phelan 2008). Culturally available alternatives that promote more traditional church practices or more individualistic consumeristic themes surround Meeting House participants, not only in their everyday urban lifestyle, but TMH itself plays with consumer themes and even deliberately puts itself in the context of the movie theatre and mall. There are ironic associations on many different levels of this church. These ironies will keep a certain kind of more serious or literalistic personality type away from TMH, while others will feel inherently drawn to the pastiche of paradoxical messages that TMH engenders by its pop culture marketing, theatre and mall locations, and idealized vision of pure relationship.

HOME CHURCH PERFORMANCE: THE AMBIVALENT ROMANCE

In this section I report on my observations while attending five Home Churches for eleven weeks each. I elaborate on three levels of engagement with the dramatic web, what I am calling on-script performances, off-script performances, and "failed script" narratives.[13] The first on-script performance I relate took place in a Home Church connected to the Oakville site led by an overseer and her spouse; it was attended by some MH staff and others who were quite committed to the Sunday services and regular Home Church participation. My experience demonstrates the permission that Home Churches have in structuring their meetings and their freedom to practise a "sacrament" that is normally the privilege of clergy in mainline churches.

We were convening in the living room discussing Bruxy Cavey's latest teaching on prayer. It was a weekday evening in March 2012, and there were fifteen people present, white professionals of both genders mostly in their thirties. One leader announced we would have "communion" together and invited everyone to go in the kitchen, help themselves to a wine or juice, and enjoy it with some pita bread and snacks. They added that no one had to do it if they did not feel comfortable with the ritual. Those from traditional Christian backgrounds would have noticed there was no scripture reading, no prayer, no ordained clergy, and no theological introduction to the ritual. They said this was more a "celebratory" style of communion. Less formal. Less religious.

I poured myself a glass of wine, and one of the leaders said "Cheers" to me, then "To Jesus," and many of participants clinked glasses. There were also home-baked cookies there, so I took one along with some pita bread. It felt like we were playing "church" and that that was OK.

I asked if they always did communion like this. One leader replied they have done it many times before in Home Church, but usually they read some of the intent of the ceremony beforehand. "Things are always different around here," she said.

I was at another Home Church in a different town that had a whole meal together, marked by the celebration of communion before the meal with bread and wine. As Cavey contends, Home Church is not an optional program in their church, like a small group Bible study would be in another church setting, but the heart of their ecclesiology. This scene testifies to the possibilities for forming local communities of diverse Meeting Housers, as most members came from different ecclesiastical and geographical backgrounds, although all members were white, white-collar workers in their thirties.

The focus of a typical evening was usually Cavey's teaching from the previous Sunday, and we usually reviewed questions that Cavey had prepared for Home Churches – some of which were on the Sunday bulletin, and some of which were given only to the Home Church leaders by email from Cavey. After discussion of an hour or so, we divided into gendered groups and spent time sharing and praying about our personal joys and struggles. The group I was with usually consisted of about four or five young men, and our times together resembled Cavey's description of what a Huddle should be.

Here men shared about their disagreements with their wives, their struggles with supervisors at work, and their problems with time or anger management. The level of disclosure was quite intense for a group of males, and I found it both embracing and uncomfortable. Some newcomers never came back, as the group developed a depth of intimacy that made it awkward to join in without being committed to do so over the long term. Nevertheless, I considered the group to be genuinely motivated to live out Cavey's vision for focusing on building intimate relationships through their weekly gatherings in people's homes.

Special gatherings of the Home Churches break from the discussion of Cavey's sermon and focus on a different agenda. I attended progressive dinners, helped out at the local Salvation Army food bank, played football and soccer with the young men, and went bowling. One particular night in January 2011 was a "games night" for a Home Church connected to the Kitchener site. Modest amounts of beer and wine flowed along with cheese, crackers, chocolates, chips, and dip. We were at the Home Church leaders' house with about ten people, mostly all under age thirty-five, playing the Mattel party game Apples to Apples. Everyone begins with seven cards, each with a descriptive noun or activity on it. The "judge" flips over a random adjective card, and players must put down their noun card that they believe best corresponds to that adjective. The judge then determines the noun card that best fits his or her adjective card, and the person who originally presented that card wins the round and becomes the next judge.

Joanne, a biology major who now works for the Ontario Conservation Authority, was the judge and turned over the adjective card "Selfish." With ten nouns to choose from, she gradually eliminated all of them but two: "George W. Bush" and "Saddam Hussein." She hesitated a moment and then made her decision: "selfish" was best paired with George Bush, the forty-third president of the United States.

Here again, the scene follows Cavey's script quite closely. Attendees are spending their leisure time "doing life together" and enjoying food and drink. Even the way people play the game mirrors Cavey's convictions, in this case the shunning of right-wing evangelical politicians and showing some degree of leniency towards enemies, although in an inconsequential way. These moments of Home Church life, where people share sacraments without clergy and where a game night flows naturally alongside Cavey's own politics, demonstrate that the dramatic web of TMH is more than a shared story; it is a shared dramatization, a story in action. These Home Church leaders have been cultivated by Cavey's teaching for over a decade, and they are firmly caught in the dramatic web.

OFF-SCRIPT PERFORMANCES OF "IRRELIGIOUS" LIFE

Other experiences I had in the Home Churches revealed attendees less caught up in the dramatic web, and the beliefs and practices seemed "off-script" from Cavey's vision. These examples are not necessarily "off-script" because they demonstrate participants' disagreement with Cavey's theology. This is something Cavey recognizes and even invites, acknowledging that there is high turnover in his church, and people come from a wide diversity of ecclesial and non-ecclesial backgrounds. As long as disagreement is done in a healthy way – not by harsh arguments or silent resistance – Cavey calls this part of being a "modern family" (also a reference to the TV show *Modern Family*). The off-script aspect is revealed as Home Churches ignore the directions and questions given by Cavey for the Home Church and embrace more conventional evangelical or charismatic practices and mores.

For example, a third Home Church I observed was also linked to the Kitchener site and one particular evening they were serving "Scripture Tea" – with tags containing Bible verses. It was April 2011 and we were discussing the questions given about Cavey's teaching series "Licence to Sin: When Christians Push the Boundaries of God's Grace" (a study of 1 Corinthians). The group was a mix of university students and older couples, and no one was enamoured with Cavey's interpretation of Paul's command for the unmarried to "remain as you are" (7:20). Cavey said that means "staying single is best" for a young Christian, and it should be the default status for believers rather than marriage.

"My single life was miserable," said an accountant who married later in life.

"Ever since I've been married I've been sleeping much better," added his wife. "My pets used to sleep in my bed."

The conversation then left the direction given in the questions, and people began to discuss faith and divorce, and how to help those struggling in their marriage to keep their vows. Then the question was asked how Home Church could help couples, and some tips were shared. Someone mentioned that Home Church can be a great place to meet a future spouse. We then circulated a card printed by DaySpring Christian card company (a subsidiary of Hallmark). A couple was struggling with cancer and a death in the family, and this was intended to encourage them. In the end, the bachelor life ideal was long forgotten.

A comparable "off-script" scene took place at another Home Church I attended in Guelph. We were gathered together in the living room discussing Cavey's latest Sunday message on "the spirituality of suffering." It was a Monday evening, 6 December 2010, and there were fifteen people present, white professionals of both genders mostly in their thirties.

Rodney, in particular, was not following Cavey's line of argument – that Christians who follow a cruciform Christ will find themselves close to those who suffer and inevitably bear some of that suffering.

"I just don't get it," said Rodney, referring to Cavey's example of the Meeting House couple who gave up their middle-class life in Ontario to serve in Haiti for the indefinite future. "I'm not going to give up everything and go to Haiti," he insisted.

Members of the group helpfully offered less extreme examples, such as befriending neighbours who might be going through a difficult time by having them over for dinner. Rodney seemed open to that.

"Like not buying sweatshop clothes, or drinking fair-trade coffee," he added. "That makes more sense."

People were eager to distinguish Cavey's message from some form of masochism. "Think of those televangelist preachers who teach the prosperity gospel," said someone. "Bruxy is resisting that. The point is: don't insulate yourself from the suffering of the world by pursuing a protected comfort and then get surprised by hurt. Share in the sufferings of others." This does echo Cavey's theology, but it also subtly takes his self-declared radical message and effectively filters and reshapes it to manageable, ordinary, middle-class decency.

I visited a fifth Home Church (connected to the Waterloo site) in October 2011, during a teaching series by Cavey entitled "Chosen and Choosing: How God's Life Becomes Ours." This series was a direct polemic against the five points of Calvinism, and each Sunday Cavey critiqued the Calvinist position while extolling the Arminian alternative. The group consisted of mostly older people, the majority being over fifty-five years old.[14] They began with a review of the dinner they served for the homeless the previous week and made plans for next month's dinner. Then a short discussion of the Home Church's involvement in the TMH's annual "AIDS Care Kit" campaign followed. This was very much on-script.

One middle-aged women was slated to lead the discussion of Cavey's teaching, and she had her outline for the evening printed out in front of her. It became immediately evident that all members of the group were ambivalent about this series. The women appeared disinterested: "Makes me uneasy," said one. "This is the 'religion' I wanted to get away from," muttered another. "It makes me agitated," admitted a fourth, while a fifth woman said, "I'm not following this [series] at all." These women contributed little to the discussion that evening, staying mostly quiet and appearing bored.

Two men said they do not have any strong feelings on the Calvin/Arminius debate, although the evening demonstrated they do have opinions. A former pastor in the group said quite openly he's a Calvinist. A night-shift worker who was taking courses in Russian literature as a mature student said he used to be Arminian, but after studying the Bible with a learned mentor, he became ardently Calvinist.

"Bruxy is setting up more of a straw man here," he authoritatively explained. "Calvinists do believe in free will. Bruxy is simply misrepresenting the other side." He then launched into a summary of the difference between supra- and infra-lapsarianism (a debate about the logical order in which God makes his salvific decrees). The discussion leader for the evening and the Home Church leader both seemed uncertain how to proceed.

The leader then informed the group that I belong to a Calvinist church, and people asked me about my feelings on the series. I said that I would try not to be too defensive and keep an open mind, but I wished Cavey would give opportunity for a Calvinist theologian to respond in person. They nodded approvingly of the idea. I felt more conspicuous than usual that evening and tried to refocus people's attention elsewhere.

One mother then exclaimed that she sends her daughter to a Christian Reformed congregation because of its wonderful girls' program called "GEMS." She was one of a number of group members who had allegiances to other congregations from other denominations.

The Calvinist/Arminian debate then heated up in the group, as members argued whether Calvin denies the image of God in human beings and whether faith is a gift or a work. Suddenly, one of the men interrupted the discussion, breaking into spontaneous prayer and weeping for an acquaintance who had joined the Jehovah's Witnesses. His prayer transitioned into expressions of gratitude to God for his wife, who saved him from so much "crap." Group members whispered, "Thank you Jesus" and "Yes, Jesus" and "Hallelujah!" A few other people prayed too, including someone who prayed for another family member who had left the church. Reflection on Cavey's teaching was left to the side as prayers drew the evening to a close. To me, the emotional intensity and prayer practices felt more typical of a Pentecostal setting, and the "irreligious" mission of Jesus was obscured by more conventional evangelical practises.

Later that month, I attended the final Home Church gathering for this series, which Cavey designed as a wrap-up for the previous six Sunday teachings. This evening completely ignored the teaching and questions from Cavey. The leader read through the letter of 1 John instead, "as preparation for our next teaching series." The conversation bounced from Christmas preparations to false prophets, world religions, and demons. I noted three books mentioned that evening: Stephen King's *Under the Dome*, purported to be about a "horrible man" who thought he was called by God; David Augsberger's *Caring Enough to Confront: How to Understand and Express Your Deepest Feelings toward Others* (2009), which allegedly shows that we should be like Jesus, "soft on people but hard on the issues"; and Todd Burpo's *Heaven Is for Real: A Little Boy's Astounding Story of His Trip to*

Heaven and Back (2010), which prompted stories from the group about people who had seen apparitions of dead relatives. Calvinism and Arminianism were never mentioned.

While the first two Home Church meetings I mentioned above were operating closely to Cavey's general script of "doing life together" and reflect his own creative flair and theological style, these latter three Home Churches were less caught up in their pastor's expectations for their group. These three groups were linked to regional sites – not the Oakville site – and thus there was some additional social distance from Cavey and his staff. These people never see Cavey teaching live, and his personal residence is located farther away from them. I noticed these groups were more often free to disagree with Cavey's teaching and to stray from the slated questions. Mainstream evangelical language, merchandise, and charismatic practices contributed to the subculture of the groups. While Cavey invites differences of opinion and welcomes dialogue in the Home Churches, these groups seemed less cohesive than the other two, lacking Huddle groups, and appeared further from the vulnerable "pure relationships" that Cavey envisioned in which all "do life together." This is not to say they are illegitimate or deviant – they could just as well be making progress towards socialization in the language and practices of Cavey's dramatic web. Time will tell.

The leader of one of the "off-script" Home Churches was also a worship leader at one of the regional sites. "They give us a list of 100 songs from which we can choose," he told me. "But there are local favourites here, and I sometimes sneak in some of the more familiar Christian songs that people like around here." At one point in 2014 the Oakville leadership tried to direct which four songs would be sung in all sites on a given Sunday. But a strong backlash from the regional sites reversed that initiative. The dramatic web of Cavey's charisma inspires and unites all Meeting Housers but it does not homogenize all practices or coalesce all opinions.

LEAVING CAVEY: BECOMING AN EX-MEETING HOUSER

Some participants live closely by the script, others energetically engage it, and a significant number of people leave it altogether. In 2014, in-house surveys showed *one-third of attendees at Sunday teachings had joined in the last year*. When the total number of attendees is relatively stable (since 2010) at around five thousand, that means a significant number are exiting the back door as new potentials walk in the front door. Many may leave because they relocate to other cities, but many also leave because they have become dissatisfied, and they pull free of the dramatic web to find a new script by which to live.

I formally interviewed six ex-members of TMH and casually met many more. One young female teacher with a background in the Associated Gospel Church said she and her husband met while volunteering at TMH. They enjoyed Cavey's teaching and the worship, but after a six-month stint overseas their feelings changed. When they returned to Ontario, she explained that TMH seemed "too big and too impersonal," adding, "We just didn't feel that we fit there anymore. And it became … I didn't want my church experience to be coming in, listening to the sermon and music, and leaving, without ever talking to anyone besides who I'm sitting beside, my husband and my family. I think church needs to be more about community. And I think TMH tries to push for House Churches, and that sort of thing, but it's way too easy to come in, have your own little secluded church experience, and then leave. So we weren't getting that community aspect that we wanted."

At this point she admits she had a falling out with a friend who attended the same site, and it contributed to their decision to find a new congregation. She insists, however, that although TMH offers Home Church, the experience for most attendees – at least the 55 per cent that attend only on Sundays – is a sense of disconnection with the organization. Note she did not mention disillusionment with Cavey and his "irreligious" message.

Similarly, I interviewed two married couples on separate occasions who both had evangelical backgrounds and who both left TMH after painful life experiences. One woman struggled with depression, which led to marital trouble, and the other couple had their baby diagnosed as autistic. The first couple said turnover was too high in the church and in their Home Church, and "then when you need help there's nothing there for you … They were more worried about getting the seekers in." The second couple echoed the first couple's complaint, saying they had been in three different Home Churches in three years, and when their crisis came they "didn't get any phone calls or anything, or any offers of help … the accountability was lacking." Both couples shifted to the more conservative neighbouring megachurch, Harvest Bible Chapel.

Lack of pastoral care was a common reason for leaving, and it also includes those close to the centre of operations. One professor of leadership studies was an MH overseer (their board of trustees equivalent). He had mainline church experience and started attending TMH after seeing Cavey in the newspaper after moving to Toronto. He was enamoured by Cavey's adaptive approach to leadership and became deeply involved during the years of tremendous growth in the early 2000s. He described his growing disillusionment with the church: "Everything became so focused on growth ... people weren't comfortable with the size, they weren't comfortable with the showmanship, they weren't comfortable with the professionalism of it." He seemed to be describing his own critique here, but it was a sense of being abandoned that hurt him the most and caused his exit from TMH:

> A whole series of things in my life just came off the rails. My wife of twenty-three years had an affair and left ... My daughters were in university at the time ... [In] the middle of that, my mother passed away ... I left multiple [voice mail] messages, saying, "I need help." I mean spiritual help. I needed relationship. I needed someone to walk with me. Never got a return phone call.... Never got a message.
> I was sick with cancer, too. And by then I had left TMH, I had had enough ... and my daughters – for me the *coup de grâce* – my daughters, seeing what was happening to us as a family, and seeing the lack of support from the church ... said, "That's it. If that's what church is all about I don't want to be part of it ..." They are still so bitter about that.

He admits it was a difficult time for many of the leaders, as Day was going through a tumultuous period of leadership and Cavey was distracted, writing his book. He has since met with Cavey and Day and come to an understanding. But this man attends a large, seeker-styled Plymouth Brethren church now.

A final example includes dissatisfaction with pastoral care again, but it builds on the leadership professor's critique of the corporate "growth" culture of TMH. Ironically, he was a single young man working in the financial services industry. Multi-talented, he was deeply involved in TMH for nine years, leading in Home Churches and the worship music at various sites. He came from a strict Plymouth Brethren background, where he had experienced some church conflicts, and felt "a lot of guilt and legalism ... 'You will never be good enough' [messages]." He became alienated from this faith.

When he left for university, he had some friends invite him to TMH, and the energy, the music, the spirit of freedom seduced him back to regular church attendance. "They are showing movie clips and this kind of thing ... *The Matrix* was up [on the screen] all the time ... it was cool and hip ... a new thing for me ... and lots of provocative quotes!" He would note the books that Cavey quoted from and eagerly purchased and read them; it reawakened his faith.

Over the years, however, he became disenchanted with the slick branding, the "hero worship" of Cavey, and the growing corporate structure of the church. He was caring pastorally for many different people in the church who he felt were unattended by the leadership. "Institutionally, they weren't set up to deal with the tough stuff where people were being hurt," he explained, naming people who were going through divorce, church conflict, or burning out. Sadly, he reports, "There was no one to catch them." He also may have been referring to himself here, as it was during this time he broke up an intense relationship with a girlfriend.

His exit from TMH was finally articulated as a need for *relationship within religion* – his personal need for ecclesial roots, communal practice, and a stable, caring community, which he could not find at TMH. "I want something with roots – a sense of history and tradition. And I actually want *ritual*, and I want *religion* ... I want my imagination formed, and I want to mend some connection with the past." He said he will "forever be grateful to Cavey and TMH," but the church was a "gateway drug" for him, and now he was attending an Anglican church and looking towards the Roman Catholic community. The dramatic web of Cavey's "irreligion" no longer had any appeal to him. Anabaptist heritage included, he did not perceive the BIC as sufficiently "rooted."

Pastoral neglect is obviously not everyone's experience at TMH. A young couple in one of the Home Churches I attended gave birth to twins, and for weeks they were surrounded by their Home Church members who brought meals and helped care for both the parents and babies. This was a tighter group of young couples, and they shared many different aspects of their lives over a number of years as their families grew at a similar pace. But the story of people feeling pastorally neglected is not unusual, and the younger age of some Home Church leaders presents one possible reason why. Except for "roundtable" podcasts from Cavey and a few meetings a year, they are inexperienced and untrained and can be confronted with significant personal crises among their membership that they are ill-equipped to engage. They have the script but don't have the skills to play their role well yet.

It is noteworthy that the reasons for exiting TMH are like the reasons I heard for first *joining* TMH. That is to say, times of crisis or transition preceded many attendees' entrance to TMH in their chronicles of their spiritual journey, and as described above, times of crisis or transition are also the catalysts for leaving TMH. This echoes the long-standing research into conversion by Lofland and Stark (1965), who concluded after studying a new religious movement that new converts, besides defining themselves as seekers and developing more relational attachments with those in the new group than with people outside it, were significantly preconditioned for conversion by the experience of general tension or strain in their personal life (such as frustrated marital relations or unmet ambitions), and their transformation was triggered by a "turning point" in their life circumstance (such as illness, migration, loss of employment, or graduation).

My research, however, more accurately describes a process of *deconversion* rather than conversion – or more accurately, the stimulus to switch to a new church. Nevertheless, the literature on deconversion focuses less on the triggers in one's life circumstance than the intellectual and emotional process of disillusionment leading to disaffiliation (Davidman and Greil 2007; Streib et al. 2009; Gooren 2010, 2011; Wright et al. 2011). An additional piece of the exit process for those who strongly identified with Cavey's charismatic leadership is their disaffection with him, the "severing of the socio-emotional bond" that charisma cultivates (Jacobs 1987). I suspect the articulated critique of Cavey and his message more often follows after a personal crisis in the process of leaving. It never loomed large as the primary reason for exiting the TMH scene.

Since Emerging Churches such as TMH are said to be places the deconverted move *towards* (Harrold 2006; Bielo 2011), it is noteworthy that all of the ex-members I interviewed shifted to more conservative Christian congregations or a more conservative liturgical style. This suggests either that the dramatic web at TMH was not compelling or convincing in an enduring way or they associated their personal crisis with Cavey's script and returned to a more familiar conventional conservative script to stabilize their life. Wright et al.

(2011) identify primarily "push" rather than a "pull" factors in deconversion from Christianity, and that may suggest the latter explanation for disaffiliation. Grief isolates people and sends them on a journey.

In sum, the charismatic authority of a megachurch leader can seem monolithically spellbinding as multitudes come to hear him speak every week. It is easy to overlook the diversity of commitment present in a large crowd. My observations from spending time among numerous Home Churches, which are purported to be the centre of TMH, is that there is a continuum of identification with Cavey's vision for "doing life together" in an "irreligious" way. The concepts of core and periphery may be helpful here, as there is a stable core of faithful, longstanding Meeting Housers who are caught up in Cavey's vision for intimate, local, cell group life. But around this core are people with varying degrees of attachment to Cavey and his vision, and they may be potential future core members or temporary participants who are in transition to another Christian community. The megachurch, because of its size and fragmented, multiple venues, is conducive to exacerbating "the circulation of the saints" (Bibby 2003). People orbit the megachurch like objects around a planet – they either land on the surface and stay for a longer period, or they get whipped around and out into space towards a different heavenly body (VanGronigen 2013). Once grounded on the planet of a dramatic web, to transcend the force of its gravity takes extra energy – often some mounting tension ignited by a significant trauma or turning point.

Cavey claims Home Church is the centre of his church and represents a local Christian community that "does life together." This is, in many ways, a fiction: by far the vast majority of resources, staff labour, and Cavey's own energy is poured into the Sunday morning event. Home Churches turn over constantly, transition to new venues and leadership, and split to form new groups. People switch groups, attend sporadically, and most significantly, in-house surveys show 55 per cent of attendees on Sunday do not attend Home Church at all. Moreover, all the Home Churches I attended broke for the summer season.

My use of the word *fiction* is not a critique, however; I mean it as part of the dramatic web that Cavey spins for his followers, who are at varying stages of being caught up in the performance. The fiction is really an organizational vision that is not descriptive, but prescriptive, and nurtures imagination for a new way of being "church." Attendees who are captured by this fiction see it realized more concretely in their own lives, and Cavey's promise of organic Christian community displacing rigid institutionalized rituals and structures increases in plausibility (Berger and Luckmann 1967). That TMH is in fact itself an institution with its own structures, rituals, rules, and roles does not completely escape the notice of Cavey and some attendees, and they live the incongruity, seeing the contradictions reconciled in the unity of their own biographical narrative. Their personal story stretches to reflect the big story: overcoming the monster of religion and following the subversive Jesus.

DRAMA AS STORIES SCRIPTED FOR EVERYDAY LIFE

Human beings are storytelling creatures, and everything they imagine and do is shaped by the stories they inhabit (Roof 1993).[15] Paying attention to people's stories highlights the role of culture in determining the moral structure of everyday life. People use stories to enter "symbolic made-up worlds of meaning" held together by "webs of significance" (Geertz 1977). Plot brings disparate moments of action together, suggesting an order, meaning, and purpose, but also mystery, nuance, and the comfortable cohabitation of contradictions – such as the paradox of caring individualists and untraditional conservatives (Roof 1993). Especially in the West, where people's lives have been disembedded from tradition, their stories have become piecemeal, temporary, therapeutic, and characterized by disorientation.

Stories are the structure of drama; dramas are story in action. Story, like a script, is what drives drama and what primarily forms the dramatic web of TMH with its charismatic character embodied in Cavey. Management scholars have used Goffman's ideas to show how business leaders can be studied dramaturgically (Gardner and Avolio 1998; Sharma and Grant 2011). For example, CEOs like Steve Jobs create and manage a persona and company story that forms a charismatic bond with their employees as they identify with the leader, the product, and the brand. Their self-esteem and self-efficacy grows as their positive perception of their leader grows. The key, however, is the story, which in the example of Jobs is a grand narrative that "is itself an absorbing, perhaps heroic story of learning, growth and redemption" (Sharma and Grant 2011, 20).

In figure 5.3 I conceptualize this dramatic process as a "spin cycle." The performance team at the core of an organization like TMH offers a stable set of meanings and practices that create and disseminate charismatic authority primarily by spinning a narrative – a script that guides action in the form of a dramatic web. The stories, language, symbols, and practices of this web are framed, scripted, staged, and performed by leadership (Gardner and Avolio 1998), but they are necessarily received by followers, interpreted by them in various ways, and acted out to varying degrees. In fact, the script is often neglected, critiqued, or outright rejected. Like a spider web, the dramatic web of charisma is sticky but also fragile, with gaps. Its hold is imperfect and at times temporary.

By taking on the language, rehearsing the inner folklore, and by participating in Sunday and Home Church events, attendees appropriate and routinize charismatic authority – what Barker (1993) describes as the "charismatizing" experience of participating in the group, and Schrauwers (2002) calls developing a "vocabulary of motives" that derive from the vision of the charismatic leader. Aspects of the drama are then marketed by the leadership team and by followers themselves through word-of-mouth and social media. Finally, staff measure the quality and quantity of their reception among followers and the public, which in turn guides a reframing of the narrative and its images, language, and associated practices.

If management scholars see narrative as a key component of business organizations for its power to make meaning, encourage devotion, and define new worlds for people, how much more should religion researchers value the role of story. This certainly applies to evangelicals, for whom the Bible is an anthology of stories, the central character Jesus is himself a storyteller, and for whom personal testimonies are a primary ritual in their religious performance (Harding 2001; Hindmarsh 2005). I would venture that storytelling is especially important for religious actors in a megachurch without a taken-for-granted denominational history, for storytelling of the megachurch becomes a primary way to create solidarity among people from vastly disparate backgrounds and potentially draw them into a new tradition. *Story becomes the script that captures the imagination and drives the drama* – the drama onstage performed by the charismatic leader but also improvised in the daily lives of followers.

This chapter has shown the romantic vision that lies beneath the satirical front of TMH: overcoming the monster of "religion." These highly mobile urbanites, situated in a cultural context where conservative religion has become a pariah, resonate with Cavey's stories of a rebellious Jesus movement that overcomes tyrannical religious systems

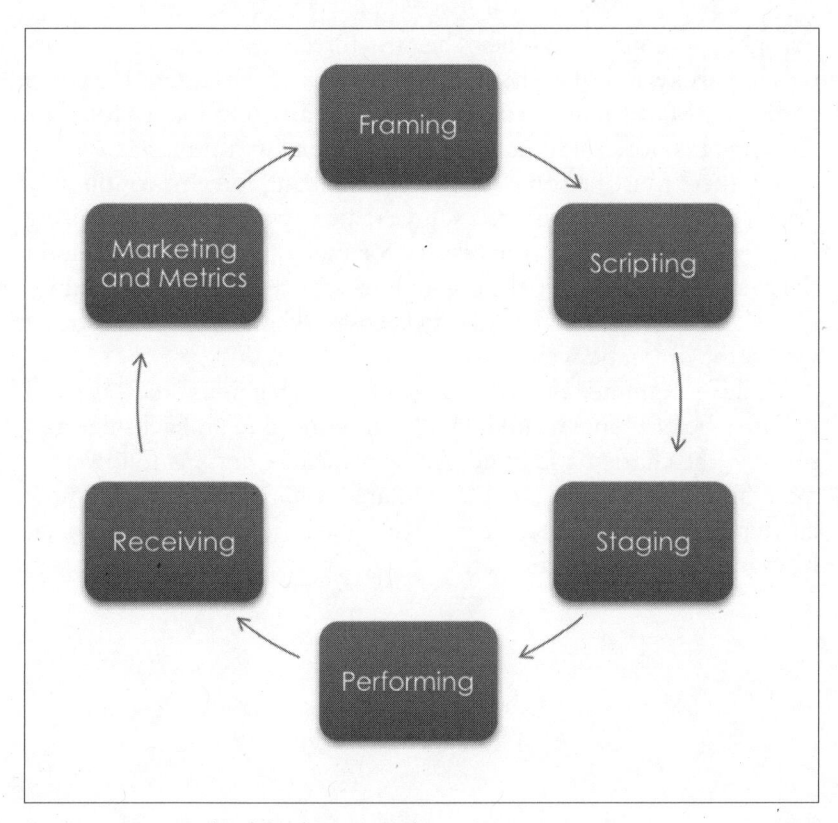

Figure 5.3 Spin cycle of the dramatic web.

to move towards a utopian future characterized by therapeutic "pure relationships." This draws crowds to Sunday services, congregates about half of them in Home Churches, and motivates a significantly smaller number of them to form exclusive Huddle groups of deeper intimacy. The alternative world constructed by Cavey's narratives enables followers to think, imagine, and feel in a new way, and thus be drawn into a form of religious protest that is arranged into loose communities of mutual identification, and mobilized for occasional forays of compassionate action in their neighbourhoods.

Home Church epitomizes the positive productive performance that animates TMH underneath the image of its negative identity as a place dedicated to ending "religion." The two kinds of performance – deconstructive and constructive, satirical and romantic – at times complement each other and at times exist in tension with each other or even outright contradict each other. This structured tension and precariousness in part keeps the charismatic component of the church attractive and alive. Charismatic authority begins as a revolutionary force by disrupting routines and conventions; while new routines are established, there must be some regular destabilizing force to continually draw people to the charismatic source (Falco 2011, 3). The routinizing and disrupting rhythm is necessary for the community to maintain the excitement that gave the community its original start and subsequent solidarity, and that solidarity keeps the charismatic bond strong within the dramatic web.

We have examined the front stage of the "irreligious" message and the offstage of Home Church life. Next we need to go backstage and see how the charismatic bond between a leader and his followers is maintained, intensified, and disseminated. Charisma does not simply emanate from a superstar; it is carried, cultivated, and championed by many supporting teammates.

6

"Irreligious" Teamwork Backstage

The Fly System in the Dramatic Web

> Those who participate in the activity that occurs in a social establishment become members of a team when they cooperate together to present their activity in a particular light.
> – Erving Goffman, *The Presentation of Self in Everyday Life*

> There's something about the amounts of volunteers that we actually really do need to pull things off on a Sunday morning, that I think creates a quicker, or more cohesive community because it has to exist ... That's been a really, really neat thing to see. A really neat thing to be a part of. You really do get the sense that people want to see, want to see it happen, you know. They'll do what it takes.
> MH youth pastor, 2014

Many Meeting Housers do not realize that behind the celebrity image of Cavey lies a group of hard-working staff promoters – the intermediaries of his renown. In the world of theatre such creative labour is called *stagecraft* – the backstage technical work that includes everything from preparing stage scenery, sound, and lighting, to costumes, make-up, and props. The mechanisms such as ropes, pulleys, and counterweights that make stage sets, props, and actors fly quickly offstage or above the stage is called the *fly system*. Stage managers and designers use their professional skills to enhance the audience's experience of the performance onstage and by working the fly system, they add a touch of magic to the show.

Ever since Max Weber, commentators have theorized about the role of supporters and staff in the development of a charismatic leader, different commentators giving various weight to the role of the followers in the routinization of charisma. What is needed, however, is research that actually shows *how* charisma is a joint production of staff and followers. Charisma undoubtedly involves some mysteries, a certain *je ne sais quoi,* but its success very much depends on teamwork or it falters and fails.

Cavey is the star of the show, but he does not run the show, and his charm depends on staff and followers enhancing, magnifying, and distributing various lines of the dramatic web. Goffman (1959) conceptualized performances in terms of colleagues and teams, which he defined as "a set of individuals whose intimate cooperation is required if a given projected definition of the situation is to be maintained" (104). Although one team member may be the "star, lead, or centre," power can be distributed differentially to directive, dramatic, and ceremonial roles, and all members depend on each other to maintain a common front. In fact, says Goffman, teams rather than individuals are the basic unit of performances (85). Charisma, in effect, takes the work of a troupe and not just a lone star performer to successfully pull it off.

Goffman suggests that the effectiveness of teamwork depends on keeping the extent and character of teamwork concealed and secret (1959, 108). This is true for much of the Sunday performance, especially when one is thoroughly caught up in the show. But there is also a transparent discourse of "team" at TMH that performs important ideological work. Unlike many other churches, they have no "committees." Instead, they have "teams": the teaching team, executive team, the multimedia team, start-up teams, set-up teams, student leadership teams, and worship teams. The leaders want people to understand TMH as a team production, not the work of a single personality. In fact, since they do not own most of the facilities they use, they depend on dozens of behind-the-scenes volunteers to pull off a Sunday service. All church furniture, welcome tables, free-standing signs, education materials, toddler mats, and pack-and-plays must be taken out of a truck, set up, and afterwards torn down and reloaded into the trailer. This includes sound mixers, speakers, and I even noticed some sites using their own DVD projection equipment. A site cannot start up until dozens of volunteers are assured.

One schoolteacher attendee presciently said, "I wouldn't say Bruxy is the leader of the Meeting House, although he is the public face of the Meeting House." This testifies to the general recognition that as much as the church is dependent on Cavey, Cavey is dependent on assistant pastors and his staff of about sixty-five persons. Cavey openly acknowledges this regularly; he once introduced the chair of the overseers board with the quip, "If the Meeting House had a pope, he would be it." Additionally, there have been attempts to hire a second teaching pastor, but so far those efforts have come up short.

The relationship between the discourse of teamwork and the reality of charisma is complex. Critics and some scholars insist on the vital role of a personality.[1] Insiders, however, plead that teamwork should get the credit, as they are wary of "cult" or "celebrity" critique. In fact, the discourse of team leadership in megachurches is a symbol of what they wish and value. But the teamwork centres on the development and maintenance of the dramatic web of charisma, which is centralized in one heroic character and the story he lives inside and narrates.

Some staff members will bluntly acknowledge Cavey's vital connection to the church's success, while others are noticeably shy about it. "The leadership are weaning people off Cavey over time," they will say, and point out that Cavey is preaching fewer Sundays per year.[2] They will add that he left on a sabbatical over the summer of 2012 and attendance did not drastically plummet, which shows that leaders like Tim Day and former executive team member Christa Hesselink were capable teachers. Yet the attempt to mitigate Cavey's celebrity status can simultaneously exacerbate it, by drawing more attention to him through the effort to downplay his role. Furthermore, in my judgment, the contrast between his theological acumen, public speaking skills, and onstage persona with that of substitute teachers often heightens his exceptional ability. They may be good, but Cavey is great. The team doesn't dilute his greatness; they sharpen and intensify it.

So there is a danger of overemphasizing the centrality of Cavey and missing the strength of the dramatic web that has been spun; but it's necessarily spun around Cavey's "irreligious" persona. I have argued that charisma is a dramatic web formed at the junction of multiple elements: a leader, followers, and a context of crisis. The leader has no charisma without the cooperation and hard work of followers. The goal of this chapter is to show how teamwork, as both a concealed operation and a discourse, works to create and magnify the dramatic web of charisma that surrounds a leader like Cavey.

One needs to imagine this chapter exploring the teamwork around Cavey in a set of concentric circles around him. Closest to the centre is his executive teammate, Tim Day. Their co-leadership extends through the array of site pastors and other staff and their volunteers.

Next I suggest that the architecture of the movie theatres, the protocols, and language instruction for Sunday volunteers are vital as scene, prop, and scripts that carry and extend "irreligious" charisma. Then I explain how powerful word-of-mouth can be, creating a buzz of testimony and story that extend the mythology of Cavey's gift of grace. Finally, on the last ring of concentric circles that routinize Cavey's charisma is the disciplined work of TMH communications department as they create in-house marketing and prompt a sprawling matrix of Meeting House videos, tweets, websites, and virtual friends that crosses denominational lines, oceans, and borders. Everyone may have some gift of grace, but some people like Cavey have their gifts displayed on a large stage, refined by a vast support team, and shared with a transnational public.

LEADERSHIP TEAM: THE ROLE OF EXECUTIVE PASTORS

Joosse (2017) elaborates on Weber's notion of "the charismatic aristocracy – trusted disciples who help build the confidence of the leader, help refine the mission, and serve as models for other followers. Drawing on Weber, Toth (1972) posits the notion of "double charisma," whereby a charismatic leader is often paired with a second leader who "borrows or shares" the charisma of the first in order to routinize it. While the original leader receives the "outer call" and appears "strange, fascinating, unusual, unearthly," the second leader consolidates the movement's vision and presents as "more conventional, mundane, practical." Toth offers a long list of historical examples including Jesus and Peter, Joseph Smith and Brigham Young, Lenin and Stalin, Guevara and Castro, and Kennedy and Johnson. Although Toth's argument is brief, it echoes what Weber suggested about the role of administrators with respect to the charisma of the monarch (1968, 40) and bears some resemblance to the scene at TMH.

By both strategy and necessity TMH tries to undermine its celebrity fulcrum and mitigate the structural and psychological dangers of being completely dependent on one person by implementing a deliberate structure of team leadership. Thumma and Travis (2007, 71) have said dual leader models or leadership teams are becoming an increasing trend in megachurch leadership because organizational management and teaching are "two distinct tasks seldom found in the same person, even among megachurch pastors" (68).

The Meeting House is a case in point. From the day of his hiring, Cavey reports he began building a leadership team and specifically began looking for someone to fill the role of senior pastor so he could focus on his strength: teaching. "Team leadership is biblical," he will say, and its primary virtue is "mutual submission." "I am submitted to, and listening to, and learning from our other leaders," he explained to me. Besides, he will add, "It makes me feel more secure ... warm and fuzzy. I know my place." A deliberate chain of feedback structures the relationship between site pastors and the executive leadership, which Cavey says conditions his choice of topics for Sunday teachings and the direction of church vision. "If I'm the primary communicator, I need to represent some of the spice that is out there in leadership. If they think something is important, then it is important. There is a lot of groupthink that might be behind some aspect of the sermon." Groupthink in this context is a positive practice. Every elder in the church (there are over two hundred) has his phone number and can text him at any time, although few take advantage of the opportunity. Realistically, while the feedback mechanisms may be in place, the elders are not always engaged, and the decisions ultimately rest with the executive leadership.

The executive leadership team has consisted of three to six people over the years, and Tim Day was hired in 2001, eventually becoming senior pastor for almost fifteen years. He oversaw much of the day-to-day operations of the church, functioning like a chief operating officer. Born and bred Brethren in Christ, he had worked at its denomination's summer camp, Camp Kaquah, for many summers. He has an MDiv from Tyndale Theological Seminary and, before coming to TMH, he worked as a congregational ministry pastor at Maranatha Christian Reformed Church in Bowmanville.

Similar to Cavey, Tim Day is physically short – even a little shorter than Cavey, an attribute Cavey publicly enjoys. Unlike Cavey, he is clean-cut and appears physically fit. He dresses casually but neatly. His language is more conventionally evangelical, and his tweets tend to be more moralistic and therapeutic than Cavey's more playful and punchy quips. He is not a Goffmanian "sidekick," however, simply there to give the comfort of a teammate in the performance (1959, 133, 189, 206). His organizational management skills receive praise from attendees, as does his pastoral demeanour. More than a few spoke of Day's calm presence and "Jesus eyes" (apparently Day has a compassionate way of listening that attendees and staff have affectionately described as the eyes of Jesus). As I said in my acknowledgements, everyone has some charisma, but it is Cavey's charisma that is routinized here, and Day is one of its carriers.

For one thing, Day often publicly extols Cavey, at times with extended hyperbole. In a teaching called "Explosion" in October 2011, Day was the featured speaker on Sunday morning summarizing the mission and potential of TMH. He first recommended attendees go back and listen to a previous series Cavey did on non-invasive personal evangelism strategies (called "Say What?" June/July 2010). He added that sharing faith was "not just the job of elite communicators like Billy Graham or Bruxy Cavey" – they had to spread word about their church. "I want to be upfront and clear. I believe we have one of North America's best communicators as our teaching pastor," he testified. "I believe Bruxy is one of the best communicators of the message of Jesus that exists in North America." The audience applauded. "I don't say that for pride's sake, I say that's reality; I have people outside TMH tell me that all the time: church leaders from the United States and Canada say that all the time, Bruxy is clearly one of the best communicators out there. We are stewarding that as a church family. Do we realize that? Do we get behind it? Or do we get used to eating gourmet food all the time?" He adds that Meeting Housers are themselves also very talented and gracious. He ends this section by saying, "Because we are so blessed, we forget what God has given us."

Many followers will swear that Day played a vital role in the Meeting House, including the meaningful way he taught when Cavey was absent. But he was always in the supporting role. One attendee intuitively suggested that Tim Day was the "wizard behind the curtains" who held up the structures of the church, and the church was most dependent on his organizational acumen. "Tim is really the brains behind the operation," one site pastor told me. "He's the little man behind the curtain pulling the levers." Day has now released his own book, *Plot Twist: God Enters Stage Left* (2014), an introduction to the biblical narrative he seeks to use in transnational missionary efforts. But it is self-published, and depended on the network and brand of TMH to find its readers.

My interview data showed that no one joined the Meeting House to hear Tim Day, and when Day left, he was replaceable as an executive leader.[3] Day worked to help the operation run smoothly, but it is Cavey who draws the crowds and gives them reason to stay. Other executive leaders through the years have worked hard to carry the charisma of Cavey and his vision to a wider group of people, and their action behind the scenes has provided both stability and growth to the whole operation.

The "wizard behind the curtains" comment above is, of course, a reference to the ending scene in *The Wizard of Oz*, where the impressive giant wizard of fire and smoke is revealed to be generated by a little old man manipulating the levers of a machine. "Pay no attention to the man behind the curtain," he shouts into the microphone when his control room curtains are suddenly drawn open by the dog, Toto, and his ruse is exposed. What is helpful in this analogy is the notion that charisma is manufactured by mechanisms that generate a spectacle. But this dramatic web is no deliberately malicious ruse: it is a religious vision for personal and social change. And it's not just one man – either Cavey or Tim Day – who works the smoke-and-mirrors machine – or more accurately what I have called the fly system. It is an entire team, including followers, working together in a dramatic production of an ironic "irreligious church" for a jaded or stigmatized audience – an audience that includes themselves as subjects of transformation.

DISCIPLINING TEAMWORK

As already explained, TMH is a megachurch for people not into megachurches. It is for people not into bombastic megachurch leaders, and for people not into mega-organizational bureaucratic culture. TMH leaders promote their community as a place of intimate connections in a house church atmosphere, a place they call "family." Still, it remains a vast organization spread over hundreds of kilometres and requires administrative acumen in order to function smoothly. You cannot effectively run a 5,000-member church without setting up routines, protocols, and policies. And to prevent confusion and disintegration of the brand across the nineteen sites, you need to enforce some consistency in image and practice. Teamwork needs to be coordinated, if not disciplined in order to be efficient teamwork.

Developing protocols for regular tasks and potential incidents coordinates teams while providing brand and operational consistency across sites. Even before a geographical location is deemed site-worthy, it must prove that it can manifest a minimum number of volunteers – the number was something like one hundred pairs of hands when I was investigating. This is not just for the practical purpose of getting all the equipment set up in the movie theatre; it is also the magic glue of an enthusiastic, growing community.

I opened this chapter with a quote from a female youth pastor. This extended quote highlights the group dynamics that galvanize volunteers and intensifies their connection to TMH:

> There's something about the amounts of volunteers that we actually really do need to pull things off on a Sunday morning that I think creates a quicker or more cohesive community, because it has to exist. And so for the last five years my husband was the weekend service producer at our site. So he was the one kind of coordinating the volunteer set-up, tear-down, tech ... music set-up, classroom set-up, and all that kind of thing. There's a really unique challenge to that, but I think a lot of wins in it, and it requires ownership and investment from the community. You know, you can't just have a passive church, people sitting on their hands. You have to have people involved. That's been a really, really neat thing to see, a really neat thing to be a part of. You really do get the sense that people want to see, want to see it happen, you know. They'll do what it takes.

Teamwork aids in the development of the dramatic web of charisma, but it simultaneously bonds people to each other. Bonds of affection and loyalty to Cavey's persona also spin threads of attachment to their site, their small group, and their Huddles, if they attend all levels of the church. Protocols for start-up, set-up, tear-down, and any emergency give the dramatic web structure and consistency, which enables it to stretch out to a wider population of potential attendees.

The dramatic web is also carefully monitored: the Oakville office keeps rigorous statistics on all its sites. This includes data on Sunday attendance, visitors, baptisms, conversions, giving, and Home Church attendance. They also conduct regular in-house surveys that gather additional information on their demographics, including age, gender, infant/adult baptism, church background, beliefs about Jesus, and self-assessment of their spiritual growth. The data are rather extensive and are valued by the executive leadership, as the numbers are used in reporting, decision-making, and promotional presentations on TMH. They want to be responsive to the perceptions, needs, and demographic shifts in their community.

What relates to the teamwork theme of this chapter is not only that the dramatic web of charisma can be measured in limited ways by the rational calculus of mathematical tallying. What is significant is that this accounting labour requires a variety of personnel: volunteers to do the counting every Sunday morning, Home Church leaders to keep statistics on their members, and centralyzd staff to operationalize surveys, code them, and analyze them for the executive leadership and overseer board. Assessment takes teamwork.

One Sunday morning I bumped into the person who was doing the counting and I photographed the duty sheet. It was a "Kitchener – Attendance Tally Sheet" template in which all the heads in the two movie theatres were counted, all the kidmax and Junior High groups, as well as all the leaders and those milling about in the foyer who were not counted in other spaces. The total at the bottom was 312, which was passed on to the Oakville office.

Teamwork itself is measured. Sites are compared in their attendance, baptisms, and giving. This knowledge is not shared publicly or in-house, but it does become a part of performance reviews; and low, declining, or static numbers in the perceived key areas of health and growth can mean a poor performance evaluation for a site pastor. Furthermore, these statistics have been used to discipline site pastors, who can be given growth goals for their site.

A similar picture develops when one examines the work of music teams across the sites. A list of 100 approved contemporary worship songs was circulated, and worship leaders were expected to choose songs from that list. As mentioned in an earlier chapter, there was also a moment when the central office tried to predetermine exactly which songs would be sung at all sites each Sunday morning. This met with resistance and central leadership backed off. To be sure, the degree of centralized control and freedom for ministry at the various sites has changed through the decades, and it changes as the executive leader in charge of site management changes.

What is significant here is that the dramatic web of charisma does not come without the aid of bureaucratic tools and centralized control. If I saw this in Foucauldian terms, it would be framed as biopower and carry dystopian connotations (Schuurman 1995; Lyon 2007). In Weberian terms, this is part of the routinization of charisma, which I would argue is a blend of control and care, both authoritarian and empowering structures (Lloyd 2018). Routinization requires coordinated labour, oversight, and discipline, and in a word, teamwork – if it is to capture people's loyalty and transform lives and communities.

ARCHITECTURE AND LANGUAGE AS DRAMATIC PROPS

While Cavey describes their Sunday services as a "dietary supplement" to local Home Church gatherings, my observation is that Sunday actually functions as the centrepiece of TMH staff and volunteer activity. The majority of resources and personnel work are dedicated to making these professional and entertaining events for the thousands who attend or watch from remote locations. Identity management receives the most deliberate attention in this venue, and I will provide a brief description of its structure by giving a tour of a Sunday morning service.

The physical setting itself predetermines the definition of the situation. It is the stage that sets the scene for the team and configures its imagination and limits. Whether it's the rented movie theatres or the central warehouse location, which looks like a movie theatre on the inside, there are no spires or cathedral domes that loom before pilgrims, greeting them with bells as a call to prayer. No catechetical iconography fills the facade of the church; no columns, mosaics, or statues of biblical figures intended to "evoke a profound sense of goodness, beauty, and truth" (Rose 2009, 44).[4] All sites are located within or near malls and plazas, surrounded by franchises such as Starbucks and East Side Mario's. The scene is smattered with logos, including the giant Empire theatre sign that stares down on visitors as they pass the oversized outdoor movie posters – icons promising romance, adventure, titillation, and escape. Theatres are modern doors into fantasy worlds. Twitchell comments on such a scene: "Yes, the megachurch is the religious version of the gated community. And yes, it is religious Disneyland, but it is also the ineluctable result of combining powerful narrative with human yearning and plenty of free parking" (2004, 280). It has been said that architecture always gets the last word. In Goffman's (1959) language, the scene and its props "give off" impressions to visitors that give the performance extra credibility. Ironic charisma wouldn't fit as well in a traditional cathedral.

More subtle, but equally powerful is the discourse used by leaders, staff, and volunteers. The texts and language people use are significant performances more directly "given" to visitors. Signage with

Table 6.1
TMH language training sheet

Hot	Not
Teaching	Preaching
Teachings	Sermons
Music	Worship
Program	Bulletin
Theatre	Sanctuary
Kidmax	Children's/Kids' program
The Underground	Youth/teens program
Home Church	Small groups
Team	Committee
Invite	Recruit
Opportunity	Need
Experience	Service
Core community	Membership
Compassion	Missions/outreach
Community	Congregation
Reflection and teaching theatre	Overflow Theatre or Theatre B
Oakville production site (or "the Office")	Oakville

TMH-brand fonts and colours mark the setting and offer directions to visitors. Whether one attends the main site or distance sites, there are always volunteers and a welcome table ready to greet people. Generally, volunteers wait to be approached, as they have been trained to give visitors the degree of anonymity they choose for themselves.

Volunteers have strict instructions on the language they use in conversation with attendees. I was given a copy of a training sheet used with volunteers in 2013. Under the church logo at the top, the title "Communication 101" prefaced this paragraph: "We want our communication to help people take their next step toward Christ and toward being a part of our community. We want to keep everything our audience sees, listens to, or touches simple and that every aspect of their engagement with the Meeting House clear and meaningful."

This was followed by the subtitle: "VERBIAGE – What's Hot ... What's Not," then two columns, giving instructions on the language volunteers are to use when on duty (table 6.1).

Clearly, by the very language they are instructed to use, TMH volunteers are giving and giving off impressions that promote their desired image of a "church for people not into church." The term *Underground* – the name of the youth program – is especially resonant with a church that construes itself as a revolutionary force, subverting the church establishment. One might wonder, How would youth rebel against a rebellious adult church?

Many pet phrases that circulate through TMH networks are caught more than taught. I kept a record of some key sayings, like "One church, many locations," "Relationship, not religion," "It's all about Jesus," "Press the reset button on church," "Become the best version of ourselves we can be," and "You need to separate the principle from the precept." Most of these originate with Cavey, or at least are promulgated by him through his Sunday morning platform. Some of his teachings, like on gay marriage, come with a memorable and thus portable proverb, like "There can be acceptance without agreement." In many ways, TMH is its own oral culture, and its dramatic web of charisma is spread orally, through the silk threads of spoken words.

These language rules, as well as the scene and other props, are not unlike many other seeker-friendly churches. What is significant is the extent to which the language training is so structured, even didactic. For a church that promotes itself as being beyond religious rule-keeping, there are a new set of "irreligious" rules. These disciplined ways of talking demonstrate some role distance from traditional ways of doing church, and they may cause alienation in some attendees who expect language and practices that are more conventional. Leadership were fond of telling me the story of some young men who came to TMH for a Sunday morning, all dressed in their Sunday finest, only to feel utterly conspicuous among the casually dressed Meeting House crowd. Rendered awkward, out of place – it was a subtle form of church discipline. In sum, all props, volunteers, and even the habitual attendees milling about on Sunday morning function as supporting actors in the post-evangelical drama whose star is yet to perform.

Attendees make their way through the dim theatre light and past the cash registers and popcorn machines, drop off their children for kidmax, grab a coffee or tea on offer for a voluntary donation, and then move through the gallery of Hollywood celebrities, superheroes, and monsters. The service in the dark theatre begins with singing led by a small band at the front, typically consisting of a guitar, keyboard, bass, drums, and a vocalist or two. The music essentially serves as a warm-up band for the main event of Cavey's teaching. People continue to enter the theatre during the music; a number of stragglers come after the band has completed its twelve-minute set and the site pastor has begun with the six minutes of weekly announcements and prayer. An offering is taken as in-house MH commercials project onto the large screen, and people put their coffees into the cup holders and rock back on their plush seats. Anticipation thickens.

The video portion of the service always excites with the professionally produced church announcements followed by the week's teaching series title sequence. It includes dramatic imagery, arresting music, and quotes that pertain to the day's teaching. Again, language plays an important role, and some visitors may even find the titles of the teaching series rather scandalous, such as "Big Buts of the Bible," "ISIS, Islam, and Jesus," or "Don't Drink the Kool-Aid." Titles often play off popular culture titles: "Inglorious Pastors" (*Inglourious Basterds*), "Grace Anatomy" (*Grey's Anatomy*) "Earn, Save, Give" (*Eat, Pray, Love*) and "Licence to Sin" (James Bond's *Licence to Kill*). Cavey regularly includes a video clip from some aspect of popular culture – not as an opportunity for nurturing media literacy, but to develop a theme, segue to his teaching, or just create an entertainment break. Cavey's approach is more like a television host than a preacher; his tone is casual, he sips his coffee and smiles at the cameras as he guides the audience through the teaching notes they received at the entrance.

In sum, the architecture, language, and style all associate first with popular culture, distancing the visitor from conventional evangelical language and church architecture. This is not perceived by TMH people as a bait-and-switch, but as a generous accommodation to their target audience's tastes, needs, and desires. In Cavey's language, it's removing unnecessary barriers. In the language of my dramaturgical analysis, it's part of the teamwork on the front stage, using the script and props to intensify the dramatic web of charisma for people who are not "into" church, but may be compelled by an active community that looks fresh, different, yet familiar in an "irreligiously" hip sort of way.

THE PRODUCTIVE BUZZ OF AN ACTIVE AUDIENCE

Bramadat (2000, 26) has written that one of the vulnerabilities of ethnography is the complex webs of different biographies that form the fabric of one's case study become flattened by analysis – a necessary distillation that distinguishes patterns and generally makes idiosyncratic data more manageable. In effect, much of the thickness and richness of my eighty-three interviewees and the roughly eight thousand Meeting House attendees may be obscured in broad sociological reflection. Bramadat ameliorates the problem by offering a whole chapter with four detailed subject profiles from his study group.[5] I instead reveal the different attachments attendees have to Cavey's charismatic authority and simultaneously show how an audience – by sharing opinions about their charismatic leader – can become co-producers of his charisma.

In fact, I would argue that few things are more productive of charisma than the stories audience members pass on to their friends and family. Marketers call this "word-of-mouth" (WOM) and contend it is the most powerful of communication devices, extending to eWOM in an electronic age.[6] Similarly, some scholars refer to "celebrity gossip" as one key means of producing celebrity (Gamson 1994; Turner 2004; Van Krieken 2012), but this is also less crudely described as testimony or witness. I have chosen to use the term *buzz*, however, to avoid the pejorative connotations of *gossip* and the too lofty label of *testimony* and rather emphasize the excitement generated around Cavey's personality and character. Buzz denotes not only enthusiastic chatter considered to be a form of marketing (Hughes 2008) but also, more colloquially, the mild flush of pleasure from alcohol or drug use, which has been used as an analogy for the emotional energy or collective effervescence released in the crowds of a megachurch (Wellman 2012).[7] These mobile stories of Cavey's identity perform numerous functions: they give pleasure, provoke curiosity, arouse admiration and envy, inspire emulation, and develop a faux sense of intimacy with Cavey. As has been said of other celebrities, these emotions can be "coloured by a subconscious feeling of wistful regret" in the fans – regret that they, too, might have become famous if they had been dealt a slightly different hand of cards (Friedman 1990, 115). The emotions stirred up by these stories both create and intensify the charismatic bond.

The buzz I disclose about Cavey investigates not so much full narrative plots as little stories told about Cavey's persona – not only stories told by Cavey but stories shared by attendees with each other and with me as interviewer. They are more the "bits and pieces" (Boje 2001, 18, 137) of a larger narrative about Cavey's extraordinary gifts and character, which form a significant storyline in the dramatic web of Cavey's charisma. Most of the quotes below were selected from a host of similar opinions in my interview transcriptions, which I have grouped into buzz about his teaching, his lifestyle, and his appearance.

The singularly most common answer attendees give for joining the Meeting House is the appeal of Cavey's teaching. In this sense, celebrity charisma need not be separated from talent and accomplishment, even if in our current context of reality TV and stars like Paris Hilton one can achieve celebrity status without any admirable talent (Gabler 2001; Hellmueller and Aeschbacher 2010). Talent may not be necessary for celebrity status, but the perception of it can enable more consistent, enduring publicity. Talent functions as one way of establishing a foundational narrative that can entertain or enlighten fans.

Attendees remark with enthusiasm about Cavey's ability to stimulate theological reflection, make difficult concepts clear without being dogmatic, engage controversial topics with graciousness, provoke extended spiritual conversations with their families on Sunday afternoon, and always "focus everything back on Jesus." Interviewees characterized the Sunday teachings as forty-five-minute university lectures, with lecture outlines handed out at the door, live question and answer afterwards, and guided tutorials to review the material during the week (Home Church). "It was like a continuation of the university experience," said one lapsed Catholic who married into the Meeting House community. "Similar style."

As lectures, however, they are anything but pedantic or boring for the audience. Attendees extol Cavey's delightful speaking talents, describing in rapturous terms how time stands still when he teaches. "Forty-five minutes had gone by," said one attendee, "and I was disappointed it was over. My friend beside me, who was my guest and a skeptic, yelled, 'Don't stop! Keep preaching!'" Others have testified that every time they hear him speak they go home talking about the teaching all the way home in the car. "We never used to talk about sermons," explained one young adult spouse to me. "He just gets you thinking."

One young married teacher maintained, "He always did his research. Some of these pastors give you a sermon and they don't really back up why they say something. 'Don't just take it as you see it' [says Cavey]. 'Go research it. Go look.'"

One university professor in history remarked with appreciation, "Bruxy knows what he is doing. He is obviously extremely well-educated, well-versed when he talks about the historical context of events that are described in the Bible; he's done his homework." A philosophy PhD student said, "They take the scriptures seriously and recognize the care we have to take in interpreting it, and mistakes have been made and we're not going to get it right. There is a respect for the intelligence of the congregation ... and we are free to disagree with one another."

A banking executive talked about catching a few sermons from Cavey while he and his wife were members of an Anglican congregation: "We were being fed by Bruxy, right? We both sort of felt alive again, and like we were growing, and we were being challenged." And so they switched loyalties to the Meeting House. "He's uniquely gifted by God to speak to this generation ... I would have no problem listening to his sermon for the second time, I do even for the third, fourth, and fifth time. You always get something out of it." He then added, "When Bruxy went on sabbatical for a number of months, we just stopped going [to TMH]. You can tell the difference in attendance when Bruxy isn't speaking."

Another young couple said something similar during a Home Church gathering I attended: "We groan whenever we hear the speaker isn't Bruxy." There were nods of general agreement. Even the frequent guest pastor from a megachurch in Minneapolis, Gregory Boyd, falls short of Cavey. "He yells too much, repeats himself, and is not as funny as Bruxy," they concluded.

Other attendees admire Cavey as much for his modest lifestyle as his impressive teaching skills. Here the presumed shallow entertainment of celebrity merges with a moral discourse (Gabler 2001; Inglis 2010) that suggests more the revolutionary mission of Weber's charismatic hero. Celebrity narrative and charismatic authority blend to become a model of and for behaviour, and the drama's script provides plot lines for attendees to follow and improvise in their own lives.

"Why do I come? It's less dogmatic, they teach different points of view, and there is an emphasis on community," reported one young adult attendee I casually engaged after a morning service. "And Bruxy lives what he preaches. I know because I've had lunch with him."

Attendees testified about Cavey's singular focus on Jesus, his modest lifestyle, his humble spirit, and how he "walks the talk." A few I met were aware Cavey asked for a salary cut; many knew that he drives a Honda Civic and scaled down on his house. One older engineer who volunteers as a Home Church leader explained, showing how insider language is picked up and disseminated: "It used to be called 'The Cavey Castle,' but now it's the 'Cavey Cottage': he made the change when he wanted to simplify his life."

Attendees admire Cavey's open-door policy at his house, and how the Caveys welcome almost anyone who stops by. Cavey makes it clear that guests may be given special attention the first time they visit, but soon after that they are considered part of the family and expected to blend in with family activities and chores. During the five-part teaching series entitled "Modern Family," Cavey interviewed numerous attendees who have been part of the Cavey household in some way – either as regular dinner guests, as frequent visitors (one called Cavey her substitute father after her biological father died), or as people seeking temporary accommodations in a time of personal crisis. Cavey intended the showcasing of his household as a model for attendees of the kind of generous hospitality expected of those who follow Jesus through the Meeting House. It also very clearly included some attendees in the production side of Meeting House Sunday services and in reinforcing a "family-like" congregational culture.

Some attendees are quick to point out that Cavey stresses practical application of his messages, as each teaching outline has a "To Take Out" section at the end, where Cavey suggests "homework." A school portable mover I chatted with after a service said he's been following Cavey for over a decade while attending another church because of Cavey's "ability to teach about how to live and not just how to think." The questions at the very end of the teaching outline are reserved for Home Church and consistently stress practical ways of living out the message of the week, an emphasis that comes in part from Anabaptist tradition and Cavey's deep immersion in the writings of Dallas Willard (Black 2013).

Cavey's appearance, however, is the first aspect of his performance that attendees encounter, and it meets with a mixed reception. Lofton says of Oprah, "The show is her show, this show is her biography, and her biography is largely her body on display. No aspect of Winfrey's particularity receives more press, or more of her own self-appraisal, than her body" (2011, 100). In a similar way, Cavey's body is the central icon of his church and the symbol of his vision for the Christian life. Unlike Oprah, Cavey's body is not a therapeutic example of how the self can improve and become whole; it signals his vulnerable humanity as well as the nonconformity and foolishness of his "irreligious" gospel.

Cavey's appearance is certainly striking as a clergy uniform. His casual dress and hippie appearance signal an ethic of resistance to convention and religious formalism.[8] Cavey indicates from his dress that he is not abiding by the cultural mores around male beauty. His clothes are often ragged, and his jeans faded, and he wears either sandals or even flip-flops. In 2016 he shaved off his moustache and lengthened his beard, in order to mimic the old photos of Mennonite elders. But he retains his giant watch, pinkie rings and earrings, as well as his long hair. The colourfulness of the terms I heard used to characterize him is revealing: "long-haired schmuck," "thug," "Joe Schmo," "bearded hippie," "clown," "downright ugly," "slob," "obese." One person said she mistook him for the cleaning staff when she first came, and another said he looked as if he was a homeless person. These stories enhance the perception of his radical character and add to his charisma.

A story I have heard from multiple sources involves a grandmother who is brought to the Meeting House to hear Cavey speak. Disgusted by his appearance, she asks to be brought home. Her son convinces her to stay, asking her to just close her eyes and listen. Sure enough, after a few minutes of Cavey's speaking, she is won over, and afterwards she concludes with enthusiasm, "He's a great teacher!"

Drawing attention to his body is not always cute or instructive, however. I attended a pastors' conference in March 2012 that featured Cavey and the current senior pastor, Tim Day, as the plenary speakers. In the morning session, while Day was teaching, Cavey walked in a little late, looking tired, with bags under his eyes. He sat down to wait his turn in the front row, and while a belt held up his jeans, his intergluteal cleft was clearly showing through the gap in the folding chair. I could see it from halfway to the back of the room of some two hundred pastors, but the gentleman who sat behind Cavey was shocked. He told me after, "Every time he leaned over to get up to speak, I could see his crack. I have never seen a keynote speaker's butt before.... [I]t was like some plumber ... it really threw me off."

Although Cavey's appearance acts as the icon of the church, his hippie/hipster look is not imitated by anyone but a few site pastors in the church. Members do not imitate Cavey's appearance, even if they vicariously experience some countercultural rebellion through identification with him.[9] The vast majority of attendees at the Meeting House may dress from casual to trendy, but almost none of the males groom for the long-haired hippie look. Gabler (2001, 14) maintains vicarious living through celebrity is endemic to celebrityhood, and thus attendees need not change their appearance to feel an association with a Christian counterculture.

This is a short summary of an immeasurable amount of buzz around Cavey's teaching, lifestyle, and appearance. There was similar buzz around his remarriage, his bestselling book, and his being publicly declared a "false teacher" by a neighbouring pastor (online, see more details on this in chapter 8). These bits and pieces of story are testimony to charisma, for good or ill, and are productive of the dramatic web that captivates attendee loyalty.

NOT A CULT: TEAMWORK IN NARRATIVE CONSTRUCTION

Stagecraft – including working the fly system above the stage – is the invisible teamwork that enables the performance to be seen and appreciated by a wider audience. The stage enables better viewing and amplifies sound for a wider audience. In the twenty-first-century megachurch, stagecraft includes not only what is needed for the Sunday morning onstage performance, but the teamwork necessary for the performances that are created and distributed through all its media channels. Cavey's persona and message is carried by multiple transnational networks that spin his dramatic web faster and farther to more people than previously possible. Charisma today can have an electronic engine and a wired infrastructure that creates flows of information, products, and people that spread across the globe like an invisible net.

At TMH up to seven staff people (full- and part-time) have formed the marketing and communications department with the mandate to promote the identity and programs of TMH, with Cavey as its icon and key spokesman. This includes a website coordinator, video production manager, video storyteller, graphics designer, social media coordinator, marketing manager, and administrator. Their creativity, technical decisions, scriptwriting choices, and attitude, including their sense of humour, significantly shape the Cavey persona that most Meeting House attendees recognize. While Cavey used to have much more input into the marketing of the church, his preferences and personality still shape the language and tone of their media work. They shape his image, select the key moments of sermons for highlights, and at times write blogs using his name and selected transcriptions of his teaching. This clearly demonstrates that contrived charisma

– in the form of celebrity – is as much socially constructed by a team of people as it is some innate personality trait. Although some scholars criticize such creative work as crass manipulation or even conspiratorial obfuscation (Boorstin 1961; Bensman and Givant 1975), impression management happens on every level of human encounter, including face-to-face (Goffman 1959), and the media that magnify and deceive may also diminish and expose if downloaded into unauthorized hands (Bekkering 2015).

Drawing attention to electronic media and their stagehand crews is a move that directly connects charismatic authority with notions of celebrity.[10] It is through media that charismatic leadership is generated, packaged, and disseminated, and not just as a neutral tool of distribution but as a medium that intensifies and reshapes the image of the charismatic leader. It places leaders outside their local milieus and into the context of a wider marketplace, alongside other celebrities with differing shades of notoriety and infamy. It puts the leader on a screen, associating him with all other personalities on a screen. Additionally, once commodified and distributed, the images and stories become part of a public electronic canon from which attendees and seekers can choose what they want to engage. In an age of interactive media, this allows viewers to be co-producers, creating and posting videos of Cavey that extol him, or less frequently criticize him, satirize him, and potentially undermine his charismatic authority.[11]

For example, North Americans have become especially wary of "cult" leaders since the 1960s. A friend of a Meeting House attendee said to me, "I can't believe they all sit in a theatre to watch a recording of him speaking. It makes Cavey seem like some creepy cult leader. He even looks like one. You listen to him and you know he's not. But still ..."

Meeting House communications are in conversation with mass media and its stereotypes – especially the clichés about "cults." As a result of mass media attention, such groups as Jimmy Jones's People's Temple, David Koresh's Branch Davidians, and the Krishna Consciousness (ISKCON) are to varying degrees popularly associated with the nebulous and foreboding notion of "cults."[12] Their ability to "brainwash" is a mythological part of public consciousness of "cults" – more objectively categorized as "new religious movements" (Dawson 2006). A "personality cult" carries less negative stereotypes but is nevertheless often a matter of public disapproval (Corsi 2008; Plamper 2012).

"Celebrity," by contrast, can have cultural acceptance and may be something to even aspire toward.

As already established, irony, in the form of self-deprecation, characterizes reflexive evangelicals who critique the conservative side of their evangelical community and themselves. This reveals their discomfort with some aspects of their own religiosity, and they shape their Christian identity to publicly demonstrate that self-critique. Because of this intense self-consciousness, identity management becomes a very deliberate part of their religious performance. They need to avoid the impression – and allay any fears – of being rightwing evangelical, but also suspicions that they are a Bruxy Cavey (personality) cult. This is especially important in busy, liberal, multicultural, secular Toronto.

One deliberate way to manage the optics of MH leadership roles and allay fears of a personality cult involves the use of satirical in-house videos. When the congregation's size started increasing by the hundreds per month, there was a consciousness of Cavey's celebrity status, and various in-house videos were produced, making sport of Cavey in some way. Cavey encourages such playfulness around his pivotal role, as I elaborate below. But the impression management around the perception of his role takes considerable teamwork – considerable creative talent and technical skill, and Cavey is only a small part of this communications labour. It takes a whole village to raise a persona.

A two-minute video created by their communications staff in 2007 entitled "What's the Worst That Could Happen? Power Trip Pastor?" was still on TMH YouTube channel with 17,000 views in 2017.[13] It features a couple in a TMH parking lot on a cold fall day, the woman with a scarf and the man with a toque. "Oh, I feel so nervous about this," says the woman.

"What is there to be nervous about?" asks the man.

"Well, what if the pastor is on one of those power trips? You know, I heard about this church one time where once you were part of it, you just couldn't leave."

The man assures her, "I'm sure the pastor is a regular down-to-earth guy."

But his companion is not convinced: "How do you know it isn't some sort of cult or something?"

The man then puts his arm around her and leads her towards TMH: "Honey, come on. What is the worst that can happen?"

They enter the new building in Oakville. Electronic dance music is playing. They work their way through the crowd to find their seats. The lights go down and it's quiet. Suddenly trumpets blare, and the lights flash back on, and a bare-chested man jumps down onstage shouting in a strange language. In a mock primitive island festival, bongo drums begin to beat, torches alight, birds squawk in the background, and the audience jumps up, screaming and waving their arms. The camera pans across more bare-chested men with paintmarks on their faces.

Then suddenly the crowd hushes again as Bruxy Cavey appears onstage in a bright golden robe arrayed with multiple giant necklaces. Incence burns around him. He suddenly opens his arms up wide and shouts, "My people! Can you dig it?"

The crowd screams hysterically, wildly jumping up and down.

Cavey continues, "People! Meeting House! Erupt in praise to me!"

Surrounded by a frenzy of excitement, the camera shows the couple looking at each other, worried. Then the words appear across the screen, ending the video: "What's the WORST that could happen?"

Especially when all the main actors are white, the cultural cliché of the primitive tribe subservient to the whims of a self-indulgent leader could be viewed, as they were by one academic observer, as "uncomfortably white." But the fear being addressed in the skit is directly stated to be of the "pastor on a power trip." This would be an allusion to megachurch pastors of the likes of Mark Driscoll (formerly pastor at Mars Hill in Seattle) or televangelists like Pat Robertson (*700 Club*). The concern behind the skit, however, is wider than authoritarian leaders. I asked one of their communications staff why such videos were featured on a public site meant to promote their church and its teaching pastor (Youtube.com and Bruxy.com). He explained the MH community's concern about public perception:

> So it's kind of like, OK, the anti-cult leader, right? To put people at ease, we're not some kind of cult. So, by making fun of it, you know, some people may not get it, but I don't care [*chuckles*]. But it's fun because, you know, we want to be the anti-cult, the anti-authoritarian, the anti, you know, screaming pastor. In this sense I'm kind of making fun of that as well, right? The yelling, aggressive, screaming pastor who's a control freak. Where we want to be the antithesis of that, right? And I think Bruxy is like he is. He's a gentle – if anybody knows him, he's the total

opposite. He's gentle, doesn't get mad, you know, totally like that. Not a control freak. Not an authoritarian. He doesn't even run this place, right? It's other people that do it. He's studying.

In other words, this video appears to be self-aggrandizing, but the humour – for anyone who knows the Meeting House and Cavey – develops from the juxtaposition of Cavey with a primitive cult leader. Communications staff intend the satire to function prophetically – to ridicule their celebrity pastor and indirectly communicate his harmlessness. Staff seek to assuage the fears that the Meeting House is covertly operating as a personality cult, while at the same time signalling that this church is indeed different from fundamentalist churches; it values an irreverent, campy style and comic relief. The MH leadership are "in the know" about evangelical authoritarianism. In a double irony, the video can simultaneously reinforce his celebrity status, as only a confidently humble leader with some growing notoriety would both need and allow such self-satire. It's a bold communications risk.[14]

Meeting Housers I interviewed generally adore these in-house commercials, revelling in the humour and expressing pride about the production quality and the acting talents of their fellow church members. An awareness of the potential idolatry and corruption of their celebrity leader will surface, but they view such as a matter of managing outsider perceptions rather than a significant spiritual danger to Cavey or the congregation. Significantly, attendees and staff repeat this anti-cult and anti-celebrity message to newcomers. I sat in what was the equivalent of a new members introductory meeting and witnessed site pastors carefully explaining how Cavey is de-centred in the leadership of TMH and how humble and democratic – and at times outright oblivious – he can be to everyday church operations. Such commercials reflect the insider discourse.

It is important to note that these commercials do not feature Bruxy Cavey per se but rather a persona that is carefully created by staff who write scripts and do highly technical video editing. The "Pastor Bruxy" on marketing videos is a construction of a team of behind-the-scenes cultural creatives. For a church, TMH has a rather large communications (or "marketing") staff. They fulfill the promotional and educational purposes of the church, including invitation cards for special events, PowerPoint ads to be played before and during the service, and special videos that emphasize the importance of volunteering, Home Church, or baptism – or explain the church's work in "compassion," mostly in Africa. Additionally, they produce a fun Christmas video every year, which receives some of the largest numbers of hits on YouTube.

The annual budget for all communications work, including salaries and website maintenance, would be in the hundreds of thousands of dollars. These funds resource the staff at the Oakville Production Site, which true to its name, is the centralized location where the inspiration and distribution of marketing material originates. Marketing is vital to TMH because it is a church that wants to grow, and growth requires drawing in those from outside the church and outside their Anabaptist tradition.

Marketing is not only vital for reaching those outside the church, it is essential for informing those who are already attending. Many new attendees are just floating through the Sunday morning service, and many prefer to remain anonymous at first. Because staff are reticent to engage visitors too assertively, in-house marketing is their only connection to casual attenders. These "free-riders" need to be socialized in the MH subculture in order to learn the "irreligious" language, the style of dress and humour, and how to present MH to the broader secular public, who will be wary of any charismatic religious leader.

ELECTRONIC MEDIA AS STAGECRAFT

Media are as old as human civilization. One of the traditionally seminal ways in which Christian leaders have developed renown is through the writing of gospels, letters, and more recently, books. Bestselling books are seminal in the formation of Protestant celebrities, as they develop a "para-church Christian identity" through the networks of Christian bookstores, magazines, and newspapers that supersede denominational boundaries into transnational arenas (Bartholomew 2006). "Print and Christian celebrity have gone together since the very beginning of the medium," as books disseminate not only ideas, but names of their authors as well (11). Megachurch pastors, because their congregations number in the thousands, have a better chance than most to have their book achieve the status of bestseller and boost their sales to levels that get recognition and then feedback again on further sales (Walker 2015). Books, websites, television shows, and podcasts effectively become an informal tradition or "secondary scripture" for megachurch attendees, as they routinize the charisma of the leader through diverse media and as intermediaries, such as site pastors and small group leaders, further promote their use and interpretation.

Cavey is a case in point, and books were his first significant leap onto a transnational stage. His Canadian (Amazon) bestseller *The End of Religion: Encountering the Subversive Spirituality of Jesus* (2007) was successful enough to be published in Urdu and find distribution in India. It was number five on a list of non-fiction bestsellers in Canada, coincidentally just behind Christopher Hitchens, Richard Dawkins, and Rhonda Byrne's books – all authors whom he has directly engaged as topics in teaching series in July 2007 (entitled "The God Debate" and "The Secret Revealed"). In fact, Cavey was the number one bestselling non-fiction Canadian author on the Amazon bestseller list that year. In 2017 he released his second book *(Re)Union: The Good News of Jesus for Seekers, Saints, and Sinners*, which made the *Globe and Mail* bestseller list in January 2018.

News media have spread Cavey's "irreligious" net wider. He has been featured in Canadian evangelical media such as *Christian Week* and *Faith Today*, and *The Christian Courier*. His book launched him beyond the boundaries of his church and Canadian evangelical networks, as I noticed a Jesuit priest in Guelph, Ontario, reading Cavey's book, and numerous book reviews online from around North America. All the major newspapers from the *Vancouver Sun* to the *Ottawa Citizen* in Canada have run a story or two on Cavey and his church, and even the *Herald Sun* (Melbourne, Australia) ran an editorial featuring an extended discussion of his book. Such exposure does not merely expand Cavey's renown; it shapes his persona as an evangelical celebrity and, by his appearance and book title, as a theological rogue.

Electronic media enable these global flows of information and connection, and TMH is wired for transnational connection. Beyond their website and podcasts, Cavey has appeared on television, mostly on programs coming out of the Crossroads Television System (CTS), headquartered in Burlington, Ontario. Shows such as *Listenuptv* and *Context with Lorna Dueck*, *100 Huntley Street*, *Real Life*, as well as other media such as GraceTV and Peaceworkstv have featured segments with Cavey. He also is one of the theological figures interviewed in the New Directions DVD *Bridging the Gap: Conversations on Engaging Our Gay Neighbours* (2009), and similarly in Canadian journalist John Campea's DVD on pacifism and Christianity entitled *Prince of Peace – God of War* (2007). Cavey has flown across Canada on a number tours; for example, one tour was with a band, geared evangelistically to a general audience, and another in 2014 was with World Vision and their national "church ambassador" Don Moore. He has also spoken at numerous conferences and universities across the continent, giving general talks on Christian apologetics or promoting the "irreligious" theme of his church and bestselling book. Cavey is always accompanied by a "handler" – someone to be his guide through foreign territory and his buffer against inquisitive crowds. He is both producer and product, prophet and persona in his team's expanding transnational web.

THE OTHER WEB AND ITS VOLUNTEER MARKETERS

The worldwide web of media further expands the possibilities of exposure, visibility, and shaping of Cavey's persona and its dramatic web. It widens the stage, offering faster, farther, and more persistent public attention to his message and mission. For example, the Meeting House app was downloaded by 11,000 people, and the website had over a million page views (by May 2014). Cavey regularly contributes to his Twitter (17,400 followers) and Facebook (10,384 likes) accounts, and he previously had a Myspace page (November 2018 totals). He attempts to answer genuine questions from inquirers and even dropped a tweet once that said, "Hanging out on Queen St downtown Toronto. Any Meeting Housers in the area wanna grab a drink & a chat? Text or call me" (21 July 2013). In the face of critiques that he is a distant and inaccessible pastor, Cavey claims to be at least electronically available.

Videos of his teaching are uploaded weekly to YouTube and iTunes. Since 2007, his iTunes podcasts have been consistently in the top ten (spoken word) Religion and Spirituality podcasts every year in Canada and often are the number one Canadian voice. In November 2013 he was the top Canadian religious podcast after CBC *Tapestry*, and sixth overall after Joel Osteen, Oprah, Mark Driscoll, and an Alcoholic Anonymous podcast. On 17 June 2014 the iTunes store reported the week's Meeting House podcast ranked seventh in Religion and Spirituality, and of the Canadian podcasts, only third after CBC *Tapestry* and Christian apologist Ravi Zacharias. Staff reported that there are 400,000 downloads of audio and video clips per year from various sources, including iTunes, YouTube, and their website. A staff member maintains www.bruxy.com, a site "for all things Bruxy"; this includes marketing for his book, short blogs, excerpts extracted from sermons, or highlight clips from sermons themselves.

Of singular importance to the electronic routinization of Cavey's charisma is the main website, www.meetinghouse.com, a virtual powerhouse of promotion and a vast storeroom of teaching, resources, and everything necessary to connect with the life of TMH. It is run by an international business based in Ottawa, Ontario, called Radiant, "a creative agency that produces world-class design, communications strategies and technology platforms." This site functions as a hub for all aspects of the Meeting House, including a "teaching archive" that provides downloads for Cavey's teachings dating back almost fifteen years. It comes with a versatile search engine that will scan all archived teachings by key word, scripture text, teaching title, or teacher. In effect, this online material has become an electronic oral tradition that functions like a catechism or congregational Midrash – it offers reference material for followers to draw from so they can learn the official position of the church on a diverse array of topics. Often in his teachings or in answering questions from the audience, Cavey will recommend past teaching series. This not only is a convenient way to answer difficult questions, it simultaneously extends Cavey's charismatic authority through electronic means and disseminates it as far as internet access is available. Cavey does not need to be physically present at all sites or all Home Churches, as his virtual presence is available at the click of a mouse.

The line between production and consumption of celebrity blurs with the new development of social media, as audiences themselves participate in the production and promotion of celebrity content (Hellmueller and Aeschbacher 2010).[15] Any Facebook entry about Cavey can essentially make an attendee a member of the team that spreads the dramatic web. Earlier I explained the role of "buzz" around Cavey and the stories that are repeated about his antics and character. With social media this buzz is exaggerated. For example, there are websites maintained by regional site pastors, including the local site Facebook pages and site pastor blogs. There are numerous attendee blogs that refer to Cavey, and Facebook pages that draw attention to the Meeting House and "like" it. Leaders are regularly asking attendees to post ads for events or help a playful Meeting House video "go viral" through attendees' social media. Yet so far no upload on YouTube has really been a big hit (only about twenty had crested 10,000 hits as of November 2017).[16] This network of social media, websites, podcasts, and videos combines to form a sprawling matrix of Caveyism – a vast web of wired connections that seemingly knows no boundaries other than public interest and accessibility.

As already discussed, Home Churches are the weekly small group gatherings that TMH describes as the centre of their church. They, too, function as media of Cavey's charismatic authority, as they focus each week on discussion questions on Cavey's teaching. The number of total Home Church groups varies, growing, for example, to upwards of 184 in 2014 and 161 in 2018. There are also small "distance groups" that gather around Cavey's podcasts surfacing in cities across Canada that are not affiliated with a regional site, including (in 2015) Dawson Creek, British Columbia; Calgary, Alberta; Saskatoon, Saskatchewan; Quebec City, Quebec; Bell Island, Newfoundland; and ironically for a pacifist church, the Canadian Forces Base in Petawawa, Ontario. Further afield, a Facebook page offers contacts for groups meeting in American locations such as Orange County, Indianapolis, and Nashville, as well as countries such as Belize, Dominican Republic, Qatar, Rwanda, South Africa, Sweden, Hong Kong, Indonesia, Japan, Kenya, Australia, and other international locations. While many of these people are Canadian expatriates who attended the Meeting House and are now working internationally, they gather friends and co-workers to form local small groups that study Cavey's teachings. In September 2011 Tim Day announced while teaching that they have home groups meeting around their teachings in fifteen countries and podcasters from at least twenty-four different countries. These global flows increase as TMH matures, although in 2018 the numbers of distance groups on the FaceBook page were waning.

Extensive mass media exposure adds celebrityhood to charismatic authority. Some audiences worry about Cavey's celebrity status and occasionally ask him how he manages the fame. Cavey quickly reminds people that all pastors are in positions where people may bestow on them unhealthy expectations. Although megachurch pastors are viewed as uniquely powerful, investing messianic hopes in a pastor can happen with any size church, he explains. Still, Cavey did concede in interview that being on a screen in a movie theatre does bestow an extra aura on one's person and thus his position is more likely to be projected with unrealistic expectations. Furthermore, any abuse of his position and power would have consequences on a far grander scale than from a small country clapboard church vicar. Scandalous events always receive the headlines and thus the widest exposure, and so a study that looks beyond moments of disgrace is of increased importance.

FESTIVE FLAIR

I end this chapter with an example of a video produced by a Meeting House that exaggerates the staff's veneration of Cavey while offering an analogy to the argument of this chapter: charisma is the product of a team.

For numerous years, the Meeting House staff released a short, humorous video in December to wish their congregation a Merry Christmas. Judging by YouTube hits, one of the more popular ones is a skit entitled "The Meeting House Christmas Festive Flair Competition." This video shows how staff create a mythology of their leader and model enthusiasm for him, while at the same time take an ironic stance on his charismatic power.

The storyline begins with the announcement of a MH staff competition to see who can decorate his or her office space with the most spectacular Christmas decor. A small crowd of festively dressed staff follows the camera through the Oakville headquarters, revealing increasingly creative and elaborate Christmas office decorations as they proceed down a main hallway. Finally, the growing crowd approaches Cavey's office.

Cavey, wearing his customary jeans and terra cotta hoodie with a green "Jesus Plus Nothing" T-shirt barely visible beneath, is just leaving his office, shutting the door, with his usual mug of coffee in hand. The crowd clamours to see his decorated office.

"Whoa. No, no, it's nothing," he modestly protests. "You guys are amazing. This little thing? It's really nothing."

"Do it! Do it!" the crowd chants.

Finally, he relents. "All right, OK, I don't know if you're going to like it. C'mon take a peek."

As he opens his office door, the camera shifts 180 degrees to the faces of the office staff as they gaze past the camera into his decorated office. Their mouths agape and their eyes wide, multiple coloured lights stream across their bodies, and the sound of fireworks exploding combines with the eruption of Handel's "Hallelujah Chorus." They squeal and cheer with delight, then clap enthusiastically as dry ice swirls around them. The viewer can only guess what miraculous spectacle the awe-struck staff are witnessing.

In the final shot Cavey closes his door and says nonchalantly, "Ah! Now that's how you do 'Festive Flair.'"

That Cavey's creative charm should outshine all other staff and his office explode with angelic choruses and fireworks offers a metaphor for his place in the matrix of the Meeting House. Yet the slapstick is intentionally laced with irreverence and irony – to satirize the idea that Cavey is supernaturally gifted, worthy of Handel's *Messiah*. Attendees testify in interviews that Cavey is just an ordinary human being, and Cavey himself dresses in an ordinary way, referring to himself as merely "the paid teaching staff" or "Uncle Brux"; and while the messianic symbols are spoofs, they simultaneously reinforce Cavey's central charismatic role in the culture of the church. This blurred boundary between the ordinary and extraordinary has been a key ingredient in celebrity; celebrities are familiar enough to be identified with but admirable enough to be adored (Gabler 2009; Furedi 2010). In effect, the video ironically offers a charismatic hero for those not into charismatic heroes. Being viewed by thousands of people – in theatres on Sunday morning and through Facebook and YouTube – becomes a productive link in the dramatic web of his charisma.

Cavey protests his glorified central role at times, gesturing to his team: "You guys are amazing." It's a refrain he sings often when interviewed about his megachurch success in the cold winds of secular Canada. "I've got an incredible team around me," he will modestly say, and it's the sociological truth. No charismatic leader spins a dramatic web without a team. In fact, the team make the leader as much as the leader makes the team. Some sociologists even contend that the followers are the *more important* variable. Nothing attracts a crowd like a crowd. But within the crowd must be true believers and skilled administrators, communicators, and lay leaders who set the stage, prepare the props, work the fly system, and act as supporting actors. No team, no charisma. Know team, and you may know the dramatic web of charisma.

Looking back on the concentric circles of routinized charisma in this chapter, it becomes evident that much of this labour is a mix of discipline and play. It also is quite significant to note how much of TMH is dependent on an oral and image-based culture rather than a text-based culture. I interviewed many Meeting Housers who owned Cavey's book but either had not read it or had read only portions of it. "I've heard most of that material already," they would say. So what

I have called their online "electronic oral tradition" functions as a secondary scripture or Midrash on scripture. Cavey's charismatic authority is mediated and thus shaped by electronic orality and image rather than printed text. Moore (1995) contends that oral culture, unlike print, "is bound up with fun." He quotes Walter Ong (1967, 30, 128): "Verbalized learning takes place quite normally in an atmosphere of celebration and play." The medium is the message and the "massage," and oral communication carries the impression of energy and immediacy, not the depth and distance of print (McLuhan 1964; McLuhan and Fiore 1968). It is into this playful word of immediacy and energy that we venture next.

7

The "Irreligious" Paradox

The Playful Production of Ironic Evangelicalism

Q: What do we do with those who believe in God but not in the Trinity?
A: Label them heretics and slay them.
Question to Cavey from Sunday morning audience

Our car was stolen in the night. I wanted to catch the guy, but I'm a pacifist and what would I do – stare at the person and try to make them feel guilty?
Bruxy Cavey, Sunday morning teaching

It was "Appetizer and Games Night" at a Waterloo Home Church. As I stepped in with my cheese and cracker offering, I beheld a magnificent buffet. Two different plates of sushi, grilled shrimp with fresh lime, Swedish meatballs in a slowcooker surrounded by veggie trays, doughnuts, brownies, and chips with humus. I made it just in time for the prayer.

"Darren" was leading the prayer, and he spoke quickly and enthusiastically. He joked in his prayer, anticipating a time of intense competition, asking the Lord that it would be "an evening of triumph for all." Instead of chorus of "Amen" at the end, there was laughter.

There must have been about twenty people present, and we divided into groups to play different games. I joined a group to play cards around a large crate that substituted for a coffee table.

"What's in there?" someone asked.

"Bodies," answered the host.

The dealer looked across the crate to the Home Church leader, who was visibly pregnant. He held out a card and asked, "Are you playing for two?"

I thought that was witty, and much of the night included more of the same. I realized it wasn't just Cavey who was clever. He seemed to attract some real cards. The evening proceeded in further silliness but ended in some serious conversations over food and drink about dating and marriage and their connection to faith.

This chapter brings all the previously discussed building blocks of the drama together into the ironic production of an "irreligious" paradox. Cavey's plucky "irreligion" presents itself as centred in personal relationships, family, and organic community meetings, and as a divinely driven movement in opposition to institutions, systems, rules, regulations, and rituals. He summarizes his vision as "relationship, not religion" and the fiction inspires people with its playful irony, its distance from conservative right-wing politics, and its promise of intimacy with others and the divine. It is a fiction many Ontarians find worth pursuing, even if it is never fully manifest in their life or church. And that's OK, because it is reflexive, and it feels liberating. It is often fun.

I chose the framework of drama because of the theatrical setting and style of TMH, but it is significant that drama is both "a play" and "play." Drama is a primary aspect of ritual and religion, and key sociologists of religion (discussed below) have linked play or recreation as basic to religion and ritual, as they refresh people for the ordinary work of their lives and help them transcend the mundane world into a space where spiritual powers offer consolation and inspiration. Play is a voluntary, imaginative, all-absorbing experience that is separate from the everyday taken-for-granted world. Evangelical faith in particular, I argue, has a history of playfulness within its revivalist sector – a part of the tradition geared towards personal transformation. In the case of TMH, however, such transformation is more often deconversion than conversion – deconversion from "religion" as well as from political affiliation and avowedly from a distracted consumer lifestyle.

In what follows I challenge aspects of the "strictness" theory of church growth and point to the opposite: a playful attitude that cultivates large, growing churches. This suggests a larger "seriousness fallacy" when it comes to understanding religion: real religion must be sombre, reverent, earnest. The Meeting House exemplifies something more nuanced – something observed in many megachurches: they are often places of celebration, enjoyment, and, with reflexive evangelicals, even satire. The ironic charisma of TMH creates a liminal space that transports followers from a spoiled identity to a more culturally legitimate identity, from the serious, angry, ambitious evangelical stereotype to a "kinder, gentler" personality. Charisma, drama, play – they are all part of a charm that entices people to suspend their disbelief and enjoy the show. I am suggesting further that such play accomplishes work – both affective and identity work (Hynes and Wade 2013; Johnson 2018). Evangelical megachurches, like human action itself, are less centrally about beliefs than they are about emotions, practices, embodiment, and identity (Smith 2009). Says Christian philosopher Robert C. Roberts, "Whatever else Christianity may be, it is a set of emotions. It is love of God and neighbour, grief about one's own waywardness, joy in the merciful salvation of our God, gratitude, hope, and peace" (1983, 1).

Granted, some playfulness is mere entertainment – an escape into fiction that distracts one from the things that matter most, such as one's personal growth and the flourishing of one's community. Such cheap amusement undoubtedly is blended into the play I uncover in the communal life of TMH. At best, it is a holiday from trouble. At worst, it is superficial and disempowering, replicating the alienation of consumer capitalism. The charge of "entertainment" in church life, however, is well covered in the literature, and my focus is a redemption of the concept of play in congregational research – the kind of play that can be transformative and restorative. The Meeting House claims to seek to deconvert people not just from religion, but from materialistic consumer culture as well.

Paradox, too, is play – a play with words, an incongruity that holds some mysterious truth in its tension. At the core of the Meeting House is a paradox, a "church for people not into church," which requires a suspension of disbelief, a willingness to pretend and experiment with an incongruity. This chapter delves into some of the satirical communications of TMH, its recreational play, musical parodies, "love feasts," and most symbolically significant, its all-sites "One Roof" dance parties. These events reveal their blurring of sacred/secular boundaries in order to eschew a "serious" Christian identity. These playful, purportedly apolitical activities have a liminal quality to them, and they engender an attitude amenable to transition and change, while simultaneously giving the church added cultural legitimacy. TMH is a cool church for people not into a strict, serious, sombre church.

The irony of what I am calling the "irreligious" paradox consists in this: a performative contradiction that has become the sacred ethos at the heart of the dramatic web of their charismatic community. More specifically, the "irreligious" paradox describes the situation in which intense, professional organizational management, with corresponding efficiencies and disciplines resembling consumer capitalism, creates an environment that TMH claims to be anti-institutional, offering spontaneous, playful, intimate, spiritual experiences for attendees. In other words, the rationalized scaffolding of corporate techniques are overlooked in a thick rhetoric of divine encounter, spiritual family, and recreational community. Revivals have always had this dynamic, and the incongruities are intensified in the new reflexive evangelical milieu: they resist and rebel not only against formal religion, but against their mass mediated evangelical stereotype. Their Christianity has become even more sharply "irreligious" than their revivalist predecessors; their institutionalization, rhetorically more anti-institutional.

TMH is a large, efficient institution for people not into large, efficient institutions that offers religion for people not into "religion." Cavey may be aware of the first paradox and boldly champions the second, always insisting TMH is a "spiritual community" rather than a "religion." The irony is thick and intentional. When Cavey declares the goal of his church is to "bust up people's expectations" about church, he is suggesting an effect not unlike that of a *joke*: an incongruity that may elicit laughter. If we want to understand the attraction – and the charisma – of a megachurch, our analysis cannot miss the enjoyment that people feel in its crowded theatres. I would venture that this connects with Durkheim's notion of *effervescence*, but with a distinctly evangelical flavour: it is casual, irreverent, and intentionally pleasant in a way consistent with evangelical and charismatic history. It is the faithful at play. Not always, and not always successfully, but the comic fiction of this Christian drama intrigues thousands of people every week.

HISTORY OF EVANGELICAL JOY

The megachurch has a historical progenitor in the camp meetings and revivals of previous centuries for two basic reasons: because of the crowds and the entertaining nature of the Christian gathering (Loveland and Wheeler 2003). In fact, evangelical enjoyment may be a historically persistent example of the natural connection between recreation and religion.

American history is rife with examples of entertaining evangelicalism. One progenitor of evangelicalism in North America, George Whitfield, took his former acting skills to the revival circuit and both inspired and entertained thousands with his dramatic sermons (Stout 1991). The "divine dramatist" would enthrall crowds in the countryside or at camp meetings, and people would travel from miles around to witness his evangelical fervour. It was a leisure activity as much as Christian spirituality. Former baseball star turned evangelist Billy Sunday entertained and inspired thousands as he challenged the crowds under the revival tents while dramatizing the running of the bases or the passionate call of an umpire (Martin 2002). Sports, games, and faith mixed freely. And Aimee Semple McPherson, whose auditorium church Angelus Temple in Los Angeles featured regular evangelistic spectacles, brought in people from around the entire country to see and hear her (Sutton 2007). She would bring a horse or a motorcycle onstage – or do something like fly an airplane offstage – to attract the attention of the American public.

McPherson, few realize, was from mild-mannered Canada. And even in more modest Canadian style, a number of evangelists in the last century and a half were as much entrepreneurs as preachers (Kee 2006). They brought faith into the marketplace, competing with secular leisure activities and using forms of popular entertainment to compete for crowds. Roving evangelists Hugh Crossley and John Hunter marketed themselves at the turn of the twentieth century as "actor preachers," and Crossley sang and preached while Hunter played the comedian. Oswald J. Smith wrote songs and poetry and brought the crowds into his Toronto People's Church by offering free movies and concerts. Frank Buchman's itinerant evangelist group targeting the elite attracted the upper classes with celebrities in swanky hotels. Finally, Charles Templeton, at one time an influential colleague of Billy Graham, was known to bring acrobats, jive-talking preachers, attractive female singers, choirs, and jazz to his revivals. For these evangelists, the mixing of sacred and secular for the sake of Christian mission was a God-given vocation. Kee offers a quote from Graham's partner, Charles Templeton, that might apply just as well to megachurches today: "There's something about the stadium-sized audience that impresses people and makes them receptive – and the anonymity of individuals in a big crowd allows them to drop their poses and be their natural selves. Their guard is down, and they are ready to listen to something that may be out of their usual way of thinking" (2007, 180). This was not just entertainment; the goal was personal change.

Templeton's personal success did not ensure a life-long career in evangelistic rallies, as he later in life renounced his faith and turned to journalism and politics. But few were more clever than he in their skill at making a revival meeting an enjoyable event geared to transforming lives.

While there is certainly considerable continuity between the entertaining nature of the megachurch today and the longer history of evangelicalism in North America (Balmer 1999, 2014), there is a significant difference with today's megachurches. All of the above evangelical examples existed on the margins of the church and society: like Whitefield, they gathered the crowds outside the official parameters of the church, or like Oswald Smith and Aimee Semple McPherson they had their own church, but it was marginalized on the mainline denominational landscape. Smith was shunned by the press, "respectable society," and even his home denomination. McPherson set up in Los Angeles and was both a spectacle and a scandal.

In contrast, the megachurch is not only an integral part of the established Christian landscape today; these 1,800 Christian behemoths dotting the highways of North America are arguably the central figures on the national Christian scene. Their churches are disseminating resources to thousands of other churches on how to "do church," and their leaders are the figures invited to lead inaugural prayers for the US president. What is new is that recreational Christian ministry is no longer isolated to camp meetings and city revivals; it is part of the everyday life of the largest and most influential congregations in North America.

Christian faith has undergone a shift: from a religiosity shaped by national boundaries and culture to a new situation shaped primarily by an open market. When Christianity takes the mould of a nation as most older denominations have done, with membership understood as inherited citizenship, with democratic procedures and large bureaucratic structures, church comes with a certain seriousness, even defensiveness, and an ethic of loyalty and obligation. Christian groups that stand outside the establishment have more agility to break the mould.

When the national frame for Christianity dissolves, however, and an open market becomes the primary reference point for Christian institutions, a sense of free choice and creative entrepreneurship replace the ethos of citizenship, loyalty, and obligation. This is the main exogenous stimulus of social change that has allowed the creative and entertaining evangelical culture of the margins to shift closer to the core of Christian activity in North America. Church attendance is not culturally required anymore; and if it cannot be coercive, it must become attractive (Hatch 1989; Moore 1995).

Yet it must also become calculated. From Charles Finney's revival *method* (Hambrick-Stowe 1996) to D.L. Moody's genius with the press (Evensen 2003) to Billy Graham's networked operations that built momentum for his rallies (Wacker 2014), evangelical revivals and crusades have been the nexus of extensive organization and apparent serendipitous divine encounter. The second can be reduced sociologically to the first as Durkheimian *effervescence*, yet the two phenomena also hold in tension a certain paradox. The more intensive the human management and control in a marketplace revival, often the more grandiose the rhetoric against "formalism" or institutions and the more daring the claim of divine presence and power. It's an irony not many charismatic preachers would recognize, let alone publicly acknowledge. Yet I suggest it is a tension that energizes many preachers, naively or not.

In what follows I will elaborate on the playfulness of TMH to further deconstruct what I call the seriousness fallacy. At the same time, I will demonstrate from several angles the function of *religious ludism* in creating a liminal space that refashions identity. The broad vision of the Meeting House is to create a "church for people not into church" – a rebranding endeavour that requires a leader, spaces, events, and material culture that signal such a reconfiguration of Christian identity. Some of this is passive entertainment, mimicking the consumer playland of America. But some elements betray something more than contextualization or accommodation: they are a means to loosen categories, unsettle old patterns, and potentially at least, ease the route to personal transformation shaped by the virtues of joy, love, and peace. In other words, it is a site for deconversion of the "religious" imagination.

ANTICS IN COMMUNICATIONS

The ironic charisma of TMH and its consistent brand of satirical humour has been investigated in previous chapters. What I want to do next is offer more of a window into the everyday playful life of this reflexively evangelical church – in its communications, but also in its regular programming. This is the gift of ethnography: it describes a people as they practise their religion in their habitual environments. It offers artefact, practice, and story to support the theory.

The Playful Production of Ironic Evangelicalism

The first artefact that epitomizes TMH and its ironic charisma is the gift of a *Welcome* DVD. It is promoted from the front by the site pastor during announcement time on Sunday mornings as a DVD for all visitors to introduce them to "the family" of the Meeting House. Volunteers walk through the auditorium handing them out to all those who raise their hands. The cover of the DVD they used in 2011 displays humorous still frames taken out of a diversity of their marketing videos (see photo). Several of these videos are available on the DVD as bonus features. The photo of Cavey and Day in angelic light beneath the logo of TMH is satirical, conveying the habitual "tongue-in-cheek" posture of the church.

The main video on the DVD features pastors Bruxy Cavey and Tim Day in their usual casual attire lounging in the church theatre seats offering a simple welcome to people and briefly stating the vision of the church. Another scene takes place in the church nursery as they sit on miniature chairs and play with the toy Noah's ark, again simply describing the mission and vision of the church. What is unusual is that the quality of the film is less than crisp, the digital metrics of the film are all still present on the screen, and Cavey and Day are flubbing all their lines, laughing at each other's mistakes, and sometimes just being silly. The video clip is cast as out-takes or bloopers without any corresponding final polished cut. One of the last things they say in this clip aptly summarizes the video and the church: "We don't take ourselves seriously; we just take Jesus seriously."

I was told by Day later that Cavey and he were not told about the "blooper" theme, so all the flubbed lines and laughing was genuine. So the appearance of the clip is deliberately emphasizing authenticity – gritty, unrehearsed video footage. Ironically, the viewer might well assume that the authenticity is manufactured, since the blooper approach seems to be the intentional design of the product. Regardless, the subculture of the church is well represented: seeking an image of authenticity communicated through a casual style and the pastor's buffoonery. They take their marketing seriously, but it's not serious marketing.

The previous *Welcome* DVD came in the form of a parody of Hollywood film DVDs. A young female actor introduces the church and seems to be the central communication in the DVD; but really the viewer needs to navigate to the dubbed "director's comments" where Cavey and Day talk about how they hired the actor because, as they explain, she was better looking than they were. This honesty

Figure 7.1 *Welcome* DVD 2011: skits, antics, and parodies.

is humorous and simultaneously carries the aura of authenticity, as it suggests a "behind the scenes" revelation from the directors. The two pastors proceed to give their own version of what the Meeting House is all about, and it carries greater authority than the paid actor, who is more of a distraction.

A similar approach was taken with the *Spring Report* in 2009. This was used for the Annual General Meeting that year and contains program, mission, and budget reports. What is distinct about this report is that it has the word "DRAFT" stamped on the front and has critiques scribbled in black marker on most pages. So an arrow points to the title "Spring Report" and the hand-written words beneath it say, "Is that the catchiest title we could come up with?" On another page where they talk of building expansion plans, a blueprint graphic has black marker comments over it: "Nice touch ... nothing gets people excited about a building campaign like fake blueprints in the background." Even the opening letter from the two pastors is headed by mugshots of Cavey and Day that have been tampered with. Cavey has glasses sketched over his photo and Day has a moustache scrawled under his nose. In effect, it's a church report for people not into church reports.

I asked Cavey about some of these comedic videos and he referred to them as "iftobums." He explains, "It's something I came up with a few years ago, and behind the scenes we use it quite a bit. Which is an acronym for 'It's fun to be us moments.' And we'll just every so often say, 'That was a good Iftobum.' That is, it had no purpose except for us to say we're having fun being us. Which is one of the marks of just healthy family, I think. And so I think those – that kind of humour – creates *iftobums*, and that's healthy, that's good."

There was no theological justification offered here – that humour can be found in the Bible, that joy is a virtue, or that humour transcends the mundane as a "rumour of glory" (Berger 1967). Cavey is rarely preachy. He simply invokes the family metaphor, which saturates the rhetoric of the church, and then suggests comedy is a sign of health. The language is more therapeutic and pastoral than theological. However, there is more at work in these antics: it fits too well with a church that proclaims the "irreligion of Jesus" for "a church for people who are not into church." It is reflexively evangelical, shaping an identity distinguished from "sombre" church, especially evangelical churches that take themselves – and their politics – too seriously. "We don't take ourselves seriously; we just take Jesus seriously."

Figure 7.2 Introductory page of TMH 2009 *Spring Report*: glossy final copy spoofs as a draft copy.

THE MEGA-STRICT CHURCH?

Welcome DVDs are free, but they are marketed by TMH for a target audience. Their comedic style cannot be separated from their nature as a commodity. A cursory examination of the literature on megachurches will show that the predominant explanation for understanding their growth and success connects megachurches to the market (Schuurman 2016, 40).[1] Either megachurch leaders are savvy in the marketing of a timely product and mimic the practices of a retail giant or theme park, or the megachurches function as a religious extension of capitalism, its logic, or its neo-liberal ideology. Megachurches are McDonaldized, Disneyized, or Walmart religion.[2]

This literature illuminates the influence of liberal capitalist ideology and suggests that even churches that claim to be against "ritual, rites, and rules" abide by disciplines and habits commensurate with consumer society. The in-house surveys they consistently administer, the extensive labour that goes into branding and marketing, the standardization and predictability of "product" they strive to have across all sites – these are evidence of institutionalized rules and rituals. We have seen in chapter 6 the teamwork that goes into these organizational habits. The disciplinary consumer framework, however, can simultaneously obscure an aspect of religion that is equally present: playfulness. Not just the passive entertainment of consumer theatre, but a grand drama in which a team and audience are actively and enthusiastically participating, energized by the perception of a divine presence. Such a church is not just calculation and manipulation for expansion. It is religious enjoyment, activity that has a significant recreational element, even as they work hard at it.

This is a significant omission in the literature, because by focusing primarily on megachurches' marketing savvy or their similarity with consumer culture, religion is either reduced to economic metaphors or even more radically it is rendered secularized. In fact, I would contend that mixed up with the many consumer practices shaped by marketizing forces are recreational elements *perennially proper to religion*, and evangelicalism in particular. The marketplace situation of religion, especially since the 1960s, shifts religiosity from an obligation to a choice, and that offers fresh opportunities for religious expression, and particularly more experimental, playful, and enchanting expressions. The market gives life to what nationalized religion suppressed. Faith as citizenship and duty becomes faith as choice and leisure, and we end up with the ironic charisma of Cavey's "irreligious" megachurch.

Expectations of loyalty and duty have limits. Although not focused on megachurches, Kelley's (1972) controversial but now landmark book *Why Conservative Churches Are Growing* sparked a debate about why mainline churches were in decline and conservative churches were growing. His conclusion was basically that strict churches who make significant demands upon their members, enforce rules for behaviour, and generally value the group above the individual are those that will grow because they are offering costly religion. While focused on strictness and demands, the tone of these churches was reported to be "serious," a synonym for severity or intensity and contrasted with leniency, promiscuity, or tepidness: serious messages (76), serious adherents (112), serious faith and followers (120), serious purpose (124), serious business (128), serious meaning (164), serious discipleship (177), and seriousness about excluding those who do not measure up to group expectations (178). Those who fail in this regard are "playing" Christianity (121), and once a church is set in a less-than-sombre direction, the inevitable decline in vitality is irreversible.[3]

At first glance, strict church theory seems to have been correct. In fact, almost all megachurches would put themselves on the conservative side of the spectrum in their doctrinal and moral teachings. In the 2008 megachurch survey 65 per cent of respondents self-described as evangelical, 11 per cent as charismatic or Pentecostal, and 18 per cent as fundamentalist, traditional, moderate, or seeker. That leaves only 6 per cent as an uncertain "other" (Thumma and Bird 2008).

We need not conflate seriousness with strictness, however (and Kelley did not intend such, even if some of his language blurred the boundaries). In the same survey, 94 per cent of respondents said "joyful" describes their largest weekend worship service "quite well" or "very well," as opposed to only 42 per cent who reported "reverent" similarly describes it. In fact, most of the popular and theological literature on megachurches describes them as consumer-friendly experiences that allow not only minimal involvement, but even anonymity. These descriptors do not indicate megachurches radiate intense seriousness, strictness, or high costs, even if they are conservative. Free-riders do not seem to feel shunned.[4]

Statistics are never the full story. What is imperative to understand, and what explains the discrepancy between popular perception and these surveys, is that a large church can offer people *a range of choices* concerning their level of commitment, and such churches strategize to move people from the periphery to the core of church participation (Thumma and Travis 2007, 102). Free-riders are welcome because there is room for them, they don't cost anything extra in resources, and they are considered potential future volunteers. Small churches have fewer resources to accommodate that kind of variability in commitment. So there is a freedom to choose that accompanies the strict conservative nature of the church and that reduces the cost of attendance for many.

Mark von de Ruhr (2012) uses an economic model of pricing and signalling, and he tests it against the FACT 2000 survey results to demonstrate this empirically. He finds that megachurches, more so than smaller churches, have multiple easy entry points with low entry costs for seekers or "religious refugees." Multiple service times and styles, as well as a variety of small groups that centre on secular interests like fitness, self-help, or the performing arts are key to drawing seekers' interests. Moreover, von de Ruhr maintains life at a megachurch is a "two-period game." Once attendees have experienced the megachurch as a "high-quality fit product," their participation and commitment increase and the church can raise the price of membership, expecting personal spiritual practices at home, social outreach involvement, and increased volunteer activity. In the long term, megachurches fit the strict church theory as the free-riders become high-participation members.[5]

Overall, statistics show that megachurches have a high level of commitment from their members, even if the congregation also functions as a holding tank for a cluster of free-riders. *All the above evidence of commitment and conservative beliefs, however, does not require Kelley's inadvertent assumption about seriousness, or even his insistence on strictness.* In fact, much of megachurch literature argues that megachurches are conservative and demanding, but they thrive not merely because of their rules and high cost but because they offer a range of participation levels. In short, megachurch Christianity is believed to be consumer religion: faith celebrating free choice, celebrities, and entertainment. This is partly true, but only partly, and it serves as a trenchant critique of some megachurches, especially those immersed in prosperity theology. But theories and surveys are not enough for understanding human groups; one needs to risk a visit in person, venture conversation with staff and patrons, and immerse oneself in the community's everyday life. In sum, megachurches can be conservative and even demanding of their members, but this does not require seriousness. Authenticity, and even joy and irreverence, can be equally compelling to attendees – at the same time, in the same church.

RECREATIONAL CHURCH:
FOOTBALL, LOVE FEASTS, AND DANCE PARTIES

Reflexive evangelicals shape a practice that is playful, but in a way that blends the sacred and secular. In chapter 5 I briefly mentioned the Home Church games nights I attended, as well as gatherings for bowling, soccer, and football. These events are always coupled with food and drink. For example, I played some football at a public school with a group of young men from one Home Church on a Saturday, including such characters as a teacher, a male nurse, a factory worker, and a Sport Chek store manager. We went to the Home Church leader's house afterwards for beer, pizza, and snacks. He had a large wine rack and party fridge in his basement, where we sat and talked about horse racing, the excitement of childbirth, and visiting in-laws for

Christmas. This was quickly and loosely organized and took place beyond the radar of the centralized leadership.

Such recreational events can be more formal and regular. From time to time a regional site will organize a "love feast" on a weekend evening. This alludes back to early Christian "agape feasts" in which believers gathered together with food to strengthen their fellowship. It has also been a Brethren in Christ tradition in North America – originally a weekend-long gathering that included such things as meal-sharing, testimony, communion, foot-washing, baptism or membership ceremonies, and community service.

I attended a "love feast" at the large Oakville site, which began with 400 people and a large potluck in the atrium. We then moved into the main auditorium, where a concert-like worship time erupted in clapping, dancing, whistling, and cheering. The site pastor, Matt Vincent, then took the mic and said, "Sundays are teaching days and we miss hearing each other's stories, celebrating what God has done, where he is moving." He read from Ephesians 3:28, citing that God will do "immensely more than we can ask or imagine." He encouraged people to invite their friends to services and Home Church, and added that he hopes to see dozens more people come to know Jesus. Four people were (re)baptized, three adults from Anglican, Presbyterian, and Catholic backgrounds, and one teen who grew up in TMH. They were dunked three times in a portable hot tub, and as they rose from the water there was loud cheering and clapping. Prayer ended the evening, saturated with notes of gratitude.

I attended two New Year's Eve dance parties at the Oakville site, with Cavey as the DJ. In 2011 the party took place in a smaller auditorium, and Cavey commanded the stage with his equipment: mixers, strobe lights, dry ice machine, and laser lights. He wore a white T-shirt with the slogan "Know God. No Religion" on the front and a giant black polka hat. Christmas decorations still sparkled around the room: large yellow stars hung from the ceiling, poinsettias dotted the stage, and in one corner sat a ten-foot-tall red cone hat.

They began by playing fun songs for the kids, many of whom were dancing with their parents. They did the chicken dance: elbows flapping, clapping, swinging arm-in-arm around the dance floor. Then a "Jump Around, Up and Down" song, followed by "Celebrate Good Times" and "YMCA" with the popular hand-action accompaniment. The children glowed with excitement.

"The Macarena" and "Do the Twist" were followed by "Girls Just Wanna Have Fun." Cavey was always adding commentary, saying now, "This is for the girls, and for the guys who like girls. If you're a guy who doesn't like girls, well, give it time." Balloons appeared as Cavey took requests and then started a "Kiss the DJ Game": he played a re-mix, and if someone could guess the artist and song before the lyrics came, they could "kiss, hug, or shake hands" with the DJ and receive a prize (Smarties). Tim Day was present, serving food and drinks to the partiers just outside the dance hall.

Around midnight Cavey stopped the music and called everyone into a circle for "some family time and prayer." With still over 150 people present, Cavey asked them to share one sentence of praise or thanks with regards to the year. "Who goes first?" he prompted. "If we were Pentecostals they'd be fighting for the microphone." Soon people started to respond, giving thanks for beaches, homes, family, new jobs, engagements, and friends. One young man in a hockey sweater testified, "I'm thankful to God for taking me out of religious ritualism and into a place of true worship." Another ventured thanks that his mother was healed from cancer.

Cavey then interrupted and shared a rare personal moment:

Can I use your mom's healing as an illustration of something? My mom died of cancer in 2011 and I'm still grateful, because whether God chooses to heal or not, whether he chooses to give you a better job or not, no matter what happens, we live in faith that he has a purpose and plan for our lives. What is the worst that could happen to you? You could die and that's better. So once that's the case, what is there to worry about? So when Paul says, "Be grateful in all things," we can actually be grateful in all things, it's not just poetry or pie-in-the-sky. So I love what we are hearing here.

Cavey then introduced his wife and three daughters to the crowd. Then he asked everyone to stand up, "hold hands, hug, whatever," because "we are all family, spiritual family." Tim Day concluded this time with a prayer that they might be bold witnesses, thanking God for TMH, where "we learn to love our enemies, and give to those who need it most, and try to live simply so we can live generously." He also thanked God for the generosity of Meeting Housers who gave during the budget appeal of the last few weeks. Then most people shuffled home.

Many North American churches have special events, fun nights, and potlucks. But the pumpkin-carving evenings, the "Skate and Movie" Saturdays, and the various dance parties at the Meeting House are a distinctive blend of sacred and secular that often plays on the edge of evangelical mores. Football and beer, "love feasts" with dancing, and dance parties with family-friendly Top Forty music – they all seek to make church enjoyable, familiar, and even family-like. This church is not known to be theologically liberal or ethically permissive, but quick investigation will demonstrate neither is it strict or sombre. Evangelical mores still guide the personal lives of most attendees, but church activities like those mentioned above feel liberating for many. It is a sense of freedom that is born out of their joy and confidence in a loving deity who isn't fastidious about rules and regulations; it is also suffused with a deeper sense of cultural legitimacy in a world where what's cool rules, a world where authenticity is more valued than obedience to traditional authority. However, such authenticity comes by shunning evangelical convention and expressing yourself through popular culture's practices and products – an alternative form of convention.

MEGACHURCH AS "FUN"

My fieldwork at TMH suggests there is a basic element of religious life that is implicated in market conditions but is not wholly determined by them. Along with Ellingson (2010, 258), I would hold that the complexities of megachurch life are best captured in a "multi-causal approach" that examines both endogenous and exogenous factors – both internal to the congregation and externally stimulated change – and the relationship between the two. Similarly, we must pay attention to the relationship between the market and the megachurch, the exogenous forces that enable and constrain megachurch practices, as well as the historically evangelical motivations that engage such a consumer context. What I find in that nexus is something hinted at but never expanded upon in any of the literature: *evangelical enjoyment*, which is manifest at TMH in the form of an "irreligious" paradox.

Much of the writing on megachurches has either remarked directly on the playfulness of megachurches or intimated such in an indirect or backhanded way. For example, Nancy Eiesland (1999) describes how Hebron, the local megachurch of her study, organizes the annual Starlight Crusade at the local football stadium. "We rent the stadium ... it's a lot of fun," proclaims the pastor. "Our people want folks to come and be totally relaxed." This is the general atmosphere cultivated at the church, where there is always a friendly welcome, and the pastor begins his sermons with "jocular Christian small talk" and "self-deprecating jokes" (58–9).

Contrasting mainline churches with the new evangelical megachurches is instructive. James Twitchell describes mainline churches as "so similar" with "a hundred white haired members" where "the experience was neither new nor startling ... not a chore but a way to set the clock" (2007, 180–2). While his argument is about the feminization of the church and the new manliness of megachurches, he emphasizes that "the problem is clear enough: it's booooring" (186). By contrast to mainlines, the evangelical megachurches have embraced marketing culture, demonstrating a "religious shift from gatekeeper to carnival barker" (92). "An aspect of modern competitive churching is now, as it always has been, *show business*," he writes, and makes comparisons with P.T. Barnum's circus (226, 269). Twitchell reports, "I've attended many of these churches, and the one thing I'm aware of feeling as I walk back to my car in the spotless parking lot is, 'Hey, that was fun'" (58).[6]

Here is the pivotal question: Is all fun necessarily secular and corrosive of genuine faith? Or is the enjoyment of church life a sacralization of consumer entertainment or pleasure arising from spiritual experience? The answer is not so easily determined. This overview of megachurch research shows that coupling the idea of fun and megachurches is a common observation.[7] It has not been closely theorized yet, and the secular assumption has become the default interpretation for many. The assumption is this: *pleasure in worship must be a failure of faith*. Real religion must be strict, sober, and serious or it has been co-opted.

James Wellman has been researching evangelical congregations for years. In his 2008 study contrasting evangelical and liberal congregations in the Pacific Northwest he reports in passing that the larger and thriving evangelical churches had something the mainline was missing: "New members in particular were attracted to these evangelical churches because they were 'dynamic and fun, full of energy.' One sensed this vitality in the focus groups" (2008, 164). In contrast, he was surprised that "in a region known for its progressive politics," he had "difficulty in discovering vital liberal Protestant churches" (xiii).

Wellman goes further in his subsequent research. Wellman and Corcoran (2014) are doing ethnographic work with twelve megachurches on the West Coast, and their project combines Durkheim's theory of effervescence with Randall Collins's interaction ritual to maintain that megachurches are a place to get excited and enthusiastic, or as they say, "high on God." They argue that the large gatherings in megachurches, combined with their music and charismatic leadership, produce an emotional energy that is related to the brain chemical oxytocin and interpreted by attendees as divine spirit. Wellman explains, "That's what you see when you go into megachurches – you see smiling people; people who are dancing in the aisles, and, in one San Diego megachurch, an interracial mix I've never seen anywhere in my time doing research on American churches. We see this experience of unalloyed joy over and over again in megachurches. That's why we say it's like a drug" (Fowler 2012). In contrast, Wellman and Corcoran focus more on energy and excitement, not just entertainment.[8]

It should be noted here that none of the scholars listed above would say that megachurch Christianity is *only* playful. There are serious aspects to the conservative faith of these adherents, and that seriousness exists in dialectic with the playful parts, and at times the playful parts are in fact seriously playful.[9] Huizinga has noted a similar dynamic of seriousness and play in his classic study of play (1950, 8). At the same time, the modern rationalizing processes of McDonaldization described by George Ritzer (2010) are equally present. But again, they exist in tension with the playful aspects we are highlighting – an "irreligious" paradox of rationalization and religious play. Noting those playful aspects is what is systematically missing from the megachurch research. In the broader social science literature of religion, however, play is not really a new concept, as we shall see.

ONE ROOF DANCE PARTY

Playfulness does not eliminate the need for intense efficiency. The everyday life of TMH includes consistent marketing, management, and introspection. In order to fold up all their church materials, sort it into bins, and vacate the rented movie theatres in time for the Sunday

The Playful Production of Ironic Evangelicalism 175

Figure 7.3 Organizing a portable church in a rented movie theatre.

matinee crowds to freely enter they must be following a protocol that is organized and rationalized. At the main site, to simply get hundreds of cars out of a parking lot and hundreds back in for the second and third service takes intense, directed action. Getting a consistent brand and weekly program out to over seventeen remote sites requires centralized, standardized protocols. Ritzer (2010) summarized modern life as McDonaldized, meaning it was characterized by efficiency, predictability, calculability, and control. When you operate on a gigantic scale, these operational values become necessary virtues.

After the work of those like Michel Foucault, it's conventional in some sociological scholarship to unveil the iron hand beneath the velvet glove, the discipline beneath the apparent humanistic practice (e.g., Shearing and Stenning 1985). But there is more than highly rationalized bureaucratic power operating within this lived religion. There is something deliberately casual, playful, and even cheeky about the everyday life of TMH, and it is this drama and the meanings attached to it that compels people to freely enlist themselves in its service. The iron hand may be iron, but it can form an open palm as well as a fist. Megachurches are routinized institutions, but it's a charismatic spirituality that they seek to routinize. Structural jigs and faithful jest can exist in creative tension. Granted, there were instances I heard of where regional sites chaffed under rigid centralized rules – but it was also the consistency of their brand and identity that attracted and delighted so many people.

Hosting a giant party for thousands of people requires both razor-sharp organizational skill and the creative, celebratory spirit that animates any large urban festival. Discipline and festivity are caught in a delicate dance. On a few occasions the entire Meeting House church population gathers in one place at one time, and these events are symbolically paramount to the life and meaning of TMH's vision – the vision of being an "irreligious" church. June 2011 marked the twenty-fifth anniversary of the church plant, and they rented the PowerAde Centre in Brampton (5,000 seats) to host "One Roof" – an all-sites gathering that included a service of celebration, a tailgate potluck in the parking lot, and a family-friendly dance party with "DJ Bruxy." A similar extravaganza was hosted there in October 2012 to launch the next five-year mission plan called "Transform," which included the goals of growing in faith, opening more sites, inviting 100,000 people to the church, and giving $5 million to compassion agencies in Canada and Africa.

I attended both events, which I consider to be the two most significant "liturgies" of the church. This is where they name their values, celebrate their key stories, symbols, and leaders, and perform rituals that reveal the heart of their identity. Both events could be likened to a giant carnival dance party. The reversals in the biblical banquet parables – where the poor are given the banquet seats intended for the wealthy guests who rejected the invitation – suggest what has been called the "carnivalesque" (Bahktin 2009; Taylor 2007). The carnival, explains Taylor, is the temporary play of anti-structure against the dominant structure that provides relief from the dominant code by asserting a higher code in which the common bond and equality of all human beings is normative. It can be understood, in Victor Turner (1982, 1995) (and Arnold Van Gemp's) language, as a space of "liminality" – which parallels the ludic consciousness discussed by Huizinga in his book on play (1950). It's a transitional state of mind that can be ambiguous, disorienting, but also transformative towards a new identity.

The celebrations were outlined by three main events: a praise music concert, a potluck tailgate party, and a live band dance concert followed by DJ Bruxy Cavey's dance mix party. The fact that they did not choose to use a conference centre, larger church facility, or concert hall indicates the corporate identity they are pursuing. The PowerAde Centre hosts not only popular hockey tournaments, but music concerts and Punjabi female dance festivals. Its adjoining property contains numerous baseball diamonds, cricket fields, and a paintball playing ground. It is a place of play for the average middle-class Ontarian, not a swanky hall for the cultural elite.

The use of sports facilities or park grounds for church events is not a novelty. Revivals since the 1700s were often conducted on recreational grounds, and Billy Graham, Joel Osteen, and Promise Keepers have used sports stadiums to accommodate their vast crowds. Such mass rallies are limited not only to evangelical gatherings, as the second-largest crowd to ever enter the New York Giants Stadium was 82,948 faithful for the Mass celebrated by Pope John Paul II during a rainstorm on 5 October 1995. Stadiums suggest spectacle, crowds, celebration, and cheering.

The One Roof event is different from these Christian spectacles because its recreational nature is not confined to the nature of the building; that is to say, the "liturgy" of what takes place is similarly recreational in style and content. It is not a serious mass with the precious host being passed between celebrants. While there was a formal service of sorts in the middle of the day's events, it felt more like a rally than a traditional worship service. Many congregations host carnivals and fairs as fundraisers or special occasions, although they are usually extracurricular to the worship events of the congregation. The One Roof carnivals celebrated the church and included a worship time and even a short teaching time seamlessly blended into the day's recreation.

On the day of the twenty-fifth anniversary celebration in 2011 it was raining, so the morning's Home Church baseball tournament was cut short, and the pastors' dunk tank along with the parking lot live band "Jimi Jive 5" were cancelled. The wet did not discourage people from coming, though, as a long backup of vehicles required numerous volunteer parking guides to direct the traffic. At the large arena's main entrance, people milled about the multiple bouncy castles, games tables, water bottle tent, cotton candy and sno cone stands, while an ice cream truck and Tiny Tom Donut truck parked nearby.

It was intentionally family friendly, and children buzzed all around with parents in tow. Inside the arena, just past the entrance's canned goods donation table for the Speroway Food Bank (3,300 pounds of food were collected that day) there were clowns, face-painting, balloon animals, and the concession stands all open for business. Glow sticks and colouring booklets with crayons were handed out freely to the kids. "Reptile Bob" wandered the cavernous outer hallway with his ten-foot boa constrictor and a giant tortoise. A merchandise table sold Cavey's book, worship music CDs, baseball caps with the TMH logo, and T-shirts that say "Know God. No Religion. John 17:3."

Some things seemed a little out of place. One of the clowns appeared to have a full-body tattoo and was trembling from what seemed like withdrawal symptoms. Another clown who was attending to a games table was handing out business cards to families that came by, promoting her services for entertaining children's parties. One must keep in mind that while these people were mostly white, middle-class Ontarians, they did not know each other. They shared no denominational identity, and most had only a few years' experience with TMH at best. The church welcomes the crowds, and not everyone is recognized.

Inside the arena proper the noise level was ferocious and the jumbo screen show was impressive, demonstrating hours of careful preparation. It included highlights from the last twenty-five years of teaching, trivia questions, funny in-house videos – including a clip of the moment when Nina Cavey proposed marriage to Cavey during the regular "Q. and Eh?" session one Sunday morning ten years earlier. This is a key moment in the lore of the church: the engagement and remarriage of its central figure. Additionally, a whole rash of pop culture images from 1986 forward flashed across the jumbo screen. A praise band led worship songs as photos from youth events continued to stream. People danced in front of the stage as the strobe lights shifted, dry ice fog floated forward, and people clapped and cheered and the crowd in the stands above did the wave.

Suddenly Cavey bounced out in a T-shirt, jeans, and flip-flops and shouted, "Happy Anniversary! We made it! Hallelujah!" He read off greetings from notable figures, including Bill Hybels, pastor of the Willow Creek megachurch in Chicago, and Gregory Boyd, a megachurch pastor in Minneapolis. Toronto professional football star Pinball Clemens, who is a member of TMH, was called to the stage, but he was in fact absent. Then came a spoof video of greetings from U2 band leader Bono.

Just after a final worship song faded out, the lights went down and a large man in a top hat came onstage. A flash mob suddenly erupted throughout the arena, and dancers in white T-shirts followed a choreographed parade up to the front stage to a parodied version of Usher's song "DJ Got Us Fallin' in Love." The refrain's words had changed to "Jesus got us fallin' in love again," and the dancers included many staff members dressed as ushers. The crowd got more excited and cheered. It was a mix of a concert and a revival meeting.

The founding pastor of TMH, Craig Sider, then came onstage. He said a few words, and then Cavey was re-introduced as "Bruxius Cavius" and received a standing ovation. He prayed and then offered a short meditation on the story of the ten lepers (Luke 17). He explained that ten lepers were healed by Christ and nine went to show themselves to the priest because that was the Jewish law. But one leper, a Samaritan, put relationship with Jesus before the legal rites and turned around to thank Jesus, "praising God in a loud voice." Cavey urged the crowd:

> Let's all shout out our gratitude like Pentecostals and grateful Samaritans ... shout it out like your team has scored a goal, and if you can't think of anything, just shout that word "Hallelujah!" If you can't say that then shout "Yo, Yo!" ... Lord, if you choose to close our doors next month – if that's your will, we thank you for how you've already used us. All of this has been pure privilege. We will turn our backs on our journey towards religion for we see you as everything to us ... we will turn around from what seems good and orderly living if we are putting our faith in good and orderly living for our salvation ... thank you for the gospel that has touched our lives.

The excitement in the crowd was so boisterous it was sometimes hard to hear what Cavey was saying, but it didn't seem to matter – everyone was obviously enjoying the spectacle. Cavey reiterated the church's commitment to precariousness, to vulnerability, and "irreligion." Evangelicals would feel something familiar in the encouragement to celebrate, to shout, and to give thanks for the "gospel that touched our lives."

There was a break in the indoor program for the outdoor parking lot tailgate potluck, and cars were generally clustered around signs with their Meeting House site location. Many opened their back hatch or popped open a table to share their goods with each other. There were rice dishes, pots of chili, all kinds of salads, fried plantains, pizza, honeydew melons, and carrot muffins, and one van had over a hundred tiny cupcakes in the back. People were generous with their offerings, and the atmosphere was giddy, even if the weather was a little wet and cold.

Back inside all the chairs were cleared away and the dance party with the live band Gruv Funktion began. Hundreds of people were dancing as the band sang a series of Top 40 pop cover songs – none of which had any particular Christian content. Everyone had been promised before that this would be a kid-friendly event with a "wedding-dance atmosphere." "Part of the fun is that it's loud," explained Cavey earlier. "You have to cheer and you'll wake up with a great memory and no voice."

The band exited, revealing that the live music was only a warm-up for the climax of the party: DJ Bruxy and his music machines. "OK," he shouted into his mic while turning dials on his electronic deck and mixer, "Let's work up a sweat!" By querying the audience Cavey determined the age range in the arena was six months to eighty. The swirl of electric sound was powerful, and it came in swells and waves, at times shrill to my ears.

"Oh wait," said Cavey, as someone whispered in his ear. "Jack from Kingston turned sixty-five today!" The music stopped and they sang "Happy Birthday" to him and others who had birthdays. Fingers were pointing at Jack in the crowd. The music exploded back on with "We Are Family" by Sister Sledge, and I could feel the bass pumping through my chest. People had balloons on their heads and glow sticks around their necks, teens danced in a circle with each other, kids rolled and flipped on the floor or danced with their parents, holding hands and swinging their arms or bouncing on their parents' shoulders.

Hashtags and Instagrams of attendees dancing on the floor were flashing on the screen and tweets popped up: "This is a taste of heaven," "Best family dance party ever!" "Dancing with my granddaughter!"

Cavey shouted into the mic as the "Conga" by Gloria Estefan came on, and people formed a giant conga line. Cavey was jumping up and down as the dry ice fog billowed around him and he was waving his hands in the air in sync with the beat. Hundreds of people gyrated in the strobe lights, oblivious to the rest of the world. "Everybody just have a good time," says the lyrics to LMFAO's "Party Rock Anthem," "And we gonna make you lose your mind."

The lyrics suggest the liminal space into which the crowd was absorbed. It was ambiguous space, both sacred and secular, a form of play and a form of cultural appropriation. One wonders, Is this church or a dance club? Is Cavey a music DJ or a church pastor? Suddenly Cavey stopped the music and said, "The parents of Meredith are here and can't find their daughter. Meredith, where are you? Does anyone see a little girl by herself?"

The whole arena was silent for a moment. People milled about uncertainly. Suddenly, near the back in the middle of the vast crowd, a four-year-old girl rose up above people's heads and floated on hands right up to the front to her parents beside Cavey. Everyone cheered. Immediately Cavey restarted the music with "Everybody Dance Now" by C + C Music Factory.

Again, all the music was Top 40 tunes, except for one that sticks out called "Range in the Sky" by the Flying W Wranglers – a yodelling techno-country cowboy song. In between the yodelling, the refrain echoes:

I'll sing his praises across the prairie
He's got a range in the sky for me.
Now I can yodel my way home to Jesus
He's got a range in the sky for me.

The quirky song was played tongue-in-cheek, as Cavey openly expresses his dislike for country music. He added the techno beat on top of the country song with his mixer.

Cavey encouraged everyone to sweat it up for the last song, "Sunday Morning," by K-OS, which declared, "Every day is Saturday night but I can't wait for Sunday morning." He then announced that he hosts regular dances in the Hamilton area and if they google "Cavey's Cabin" they can find out when his next dance party would be.

"Who's going to preach tomorrow morning?" Cavey shouted, explaining he would not have a voice in the morning. People filed happily out of the area, and the time was 9:40 p.m. – late, but not absurdly so for a family event. The next morning, a bleary-eyed Cavey preached for three services.

RELIGION AND PLAY

At the heart of much of the discussion above, where on one hand successful religion is deemed necessarily strict and intense and on the other hand religion with an entertaining character is considered commercialized and secularized, is what I am calling the "seriousness fallacy."[10] Religion, in this view, is normatively sombre, and any playful activity in religious contexts is considered inherently less than spiritual. So the consumer critiques of religion are coincidentally the corollary of the strict church theory: both assume that religion is properly serious, sober, and certainly against energetic dancing.[11]

This sort of concern about holy hilarity extends to those who write about congregational religion. Einstein, for example, betrays this bias quite starkly when she critiques megachurches by saying, "Religion isn't supposed to be comfortable," but instead requires that one "step out of the culture" to nurture a faith that "is not easy" and is built on "lots of hard work" (2008, 210). For her the "consumer-friendly, feel-good, easy-listening type of Christianity" does little but conceal dangerous neo-liberal agendas (179). Her politicized lenses obscure the theological aesthetics and the ethnographic reality: evangelicals know how to enjoy their faith in their Jesus.

Ironically, despite the seriousness fallacy that pervades the study of North American religion, some of the most seminal thinkers in the history of the sociology of religion have written about a deep connection between religion and play. Marti (2008) draws our attention to this fact through his ethnographic work on a megachurch in Los Angeles, and more so than any of the studies above, he gives a legitimacy to playful and even entertaining Christian worship. Oasis Christian Center meets in an old movie theatre and provides an unabashedly entertaining spiritual experience. Its attendees often describe their congregation with the word *fun*, and because it is located in the heart of Hollywood, it draws on all the musical, artistic, and acting talent that saturates the district. Rather than suggesting this local incarnation is a loss of religiosity, Marti draws on a theme that lies neglected in Durkheim's *Elementary Forms of Religious Life* (1995) where Durkheim writes, "Since utilitarian purposes are in general alien to them, [religious rituals] make men forget the real world so as to transport them into another where their imagination is more home; they entertain. Sometimes they even go as far as having the outward appearance of recreation. We see those present laughing and openly having fun" (1995, 384; see also Marti, 2008, 117). Durkheim admits to an "outward appearance" that is something less than the substance of what is socially taking place. The recreational nature of religion, which he ties to feasts, festivals, and other celebratory rites, is not alien to religion but rather properly basic to it. Games and art, says Durkheim, are born in religion, because "the cult" by its "inherent logic" is a "form of recreation" that "refreshes a spirit worn down by all that is overburdening in day-to-day labour" (1995, 385). Marti additionally demonstrates how this entertainment constructs a particular Christian identity.

The relationship between play and religion has a history beyond Durkheim, but it remains relatively unattended. Robert Bellah (2011) has claimed a basic connection between play and religion in his extended investigation of the evolution of religion in prehistorical human life. In fact, he argues that "play is central for my argument about religious evolution," for ritual itself "is the primordial form of serious play in human evolutionary history" as it developed from mammalian play (89, 92). Myths, too, "are part of the 'play-habit of the mind,'" writes Bellah, quoting Huizinga's classic work on play. Huizinga maintains, "A half-joking element verging on make-believe is inseparable from true myth" (1950, 148). Bellah takes the discussion through Huizinga back to Plato, who extolled the value of festivals for those who have lost the child-like propensity for play: "So, taking pity on this suffering that is natural to the human race, the gods have ordained the cycle of festivals as times of rest from labour. They have given as fellow celebrants the Muses, with their leader Apollo, and Dionysus – in order that these divinities might set humans right again. Thus men are sustained by their festivals in the company of gods" (Bellah 2011, 109; Plato *Laws* 2.653). In sum, for Bellah, as with Huizinga, ritual, myth, and festival are all a function of play, and play, not so much in opposition to seriousness as in opposition to work, is fundamental to not only religion, but to much of culture itself.

Other significant scholars of religion, like Peter Berger[12] and Andre Droogers,[13] have made similar fundamental connections between religion and play, although they focus on different aspects of the relationship. To summarize, for Durkheim religion is something as opposed to work, and it offers respite and rejuvenation that becomes foundational to other parts of cultural life. Bellah echoes this in his postulating of the key role of play in religious evolutionary history, functioning as a creative source for ritual, myth, and festival. Berger takes a more philosophical, if not theological, approach, arguing that the transcendence of the everyday in play and humour is an intimation of a religious sense. Finally, Droogers insists that it's not just religion, but science and scholarship as well that demand a playful quality in order to be creative and sustaining.

Congregational life in a religious marketplace is a voluntary phenomenon and, as opposed to work, can be considered discretionary or leisure activity. As Durkheim explains, religion should be a relief from labour: "Once we have fulfilled our ritual duties, we return to a profane life with more energy and enthusiasm, not only because we've placed ourselves in contact with a higher source of energy but also because our own capacities have been replenished through living, for a few moments, a life that is less tense, more at ease, and freer" (Durkheim 1995, 386 quoted in Marti 2008, 118). What's so enjoyable about megachurch religiosity is properly contrasted not with "real religion" (meaning strict, sober, serious religion) but rather with the toil of the electronically mediated workplace in an unstable economy. Cultural creatives lead intense lives, fighting the traffic of Toronto, and some of them find relief in their Christianity. The iron cage is challenged by the evangelical preacher's opening joke, and the worshipper's emotional state is enlivened by the swelling music of the praise band.

Says Marti, "To miss out on the entertainment aspect of religion is to miss out on one of the most powerful draws of religion in contemporary life" (2008, 117). If this assessment of religion is correct, then the contextualizing of religious architecture and liturgy to an entertainment culture are not simply diversions from the seriousness sacredness of religion but rather participation in something constitutive of its origins and function. Playfulness is not accidental but basic to evangelical megachurch community life, and religion in general. Contrary to the seriousness fallacy, Huizinga clearly states, "The ritual act, or an important part of it, will always remain within the play category, but in this seeming subordination the recognition of its holiness is not lost" (1950, 27).

Indeed, the secular and the sacred can blend without either overwhelming the other. The sacred has always played with secular forms. Theological critics worry that the medium becomes the message, secularizing the faith. But it is equally possible that by shifting the context and meaning of a cultural practice, secular forms can be sacralized (Ostwalt 2012; deChant 2002). TMH acculturates to a North American concert atmosphere while simultaneously seeking to transform such cultural patterns towards a communitarian expression of the "spirituality of Jesus."

The Playful Production of Ironic Evangelicalism 185

MUSIC AND RELIGIOUS PARODIES

It is said that if something happens twice in a church, it becomes tradition. The second "One Roof" event on 20 October 2012 was intended to launch their new five-year mission. It was like the first One Roof event except that there were more Christianized music parodies, which I will describe here in more detail. *The Oxford Dictionary* defines *parody* as "an imitation of the style of a particular writer, artist, or genre with deliberate exaggeration for comic effect." It is a form of play that in this instance mixes sacred and secular, popular and religious culture, creating a world familiar on two levels – in both music and meaning. The juxtaposition, and even outright incongruity – transports participants to a place where they are caught up in sacred play. Secular songs are sacralized for Christian worship.

To start the stage events, the "Party Rock Anthem" by electronic dance duo LMFAO, retitled "Kingdom Rock Anthem," erupted onstage with flashing coloured lights, dry ice, and about a dozen talented "shufflin'" dancers. Mimicking the original music video, they danced similar moves, including hand-springing and floor-spinning breakdancers, a shiny silver dancing robot, and Cavey himself taking the role of the mysterious beige-robed long-haired bearded "Jesus" figure who enters in the last few seconds of the original music video, except instead of the giant gold bling necklace, he has a sparkling gold cross emblazoned on his robe. Unlike the secular LMFAO version, there is no scene with a sexy blond woman suggestively gyrating before the camera.

The original LMFAO music videos celebrate all-night partying, excessive drinking, licentiousness, and disturbing the peace, and they have used pornographic actors in their videos. The TMH lyrics have necessarily been sanitized and spiritualized: "And we gonna make you lose your mind, everybody just have a good time" was altered at One Roof to say, "And we gonna renew your mind, everybody just have a good time." "In the club party rock, lookin' for your girl, she on my jock (huh) non-stop when we in the spot" was recomposed to express the urgency of Christian mission: "No stop motto cause it's mission go, every culture gonna know, get all these feet out the door." Finally, "I'm running through these hoes like Drano, I got that devilish flow rock and roll no halo" was switched to "We dancin' got get-go like Drano, I got that Spirit – like flow, God in soul, make me whole."

What TMH produces in its music is one indication of its wider approach to broader culture, and especially the nexus of evangelical and popular culture. Seventeenth-century politician Andrew Fletcher wrote, "If a man were permitted to make all the ballads, he need not care who should make the laws of a nation."[14] Music reflects and shapes the values and emotions of a community in powerful and specific ways. It inscribes its feel for the world into ears and onto bodies, solidifying community and mutual identity (Busman 2015).

Unlike non-evangelical listeners, those who listen to CCM actually pay attention to the lyrics and are more likely to internalize them (Reid 1993). It is a way of forging a counter-identity to mainstream secular culture, a way to even "rebel" against secular materialistic and naturalistic world views (Luhr 2009). But the creation, production, and distribution of CCM is a curious and even remarkable blend of secular styles and corporate interests with sacred expressions and intentions.[15] It is this juxtaposition of sacred and secular, faith and popular culture, that leads some insiders to view evangelicalism as irreparably compromised or even "counterfeit culture" (Kyle 2006).[16]

Christian Contemporary Music is a microcosm of evangelical experience.[17] TMH plays with the styles, forms, and content of popular culture – and this approach includes their use of movie theatres as their main meeting space, the pop cultural themes in its marketing and teaching, and its ambivalent recognition of its pastor and DJ Bruxy Cavey as a celebrity figure. This playful engagement with the electronic universe of popular culture contrasts with TMH's purported localized, activist, and organic culture that happens within their weekday Home Churches. My argument is that what is happening in the mashup of popular culture and evangelical Anabaptist sentiments is not necessarily a fraud as some evangelical insiders suggest (Kyle 2006; Peacock 2004) nor is it inherently a form of internal secularization (Sargeant 2000; Bruce 2002) but an act of playful and strategic *parody*. Christianity, perhaps more so than other global religions, has played itself off secular forms, from the Vatican's imitation of imperial Rome to CCM, and the blending of sacred and secular can have both calculated and playful intentions and social trajectories. The Meeting House is taking what is familiar across ethnic and theological boundaries and using it to draw potential attendees into its liminal and ludic space. It is a form of contextualization of Christian teaching that is done in a playful way and requires constant reinvention to keep up with the constant shifts in style and content in popular culture.

Information technologist and self-declared "MennoNerd" Ryan Robinson blogs about the One Roof event at Anabaptist Redux:

"Think being a Christian is no fun? I'd like to think my church proves you wrong." "When my church gets together," he emphasizes, "I get pumped" (11 November 2012). His pastor is not just a preacher; he is a late-night party DJ. Secular forms may strengthen piety as well as corrupt it.

RELIGIOUS LUDISM, EVANGELICAL JOY

My concept of a "dramatic web" suggests a performance that captivates an audience along intersecting storylines and practices. This approach characterizes charismatic authority primarily as an *aesthetic* (Ladkin 2010) – a felt sense, an embodied sensory impression that engages both emotion and imagination, mobilizing followers for a mission and movement that empowers them and increases their sense of self-worth. I imagine the moments when I was caught up in the creativity and excitement of the church as an experience more consistent in many attendees' career at TMH. There is an allusiveness to aesthetics – a nuance and imagination that manifests as beautiful, grotesque, or humorous (Seerveld 1980).

By drawing attention to the ironic nature of this church, my aesthetic focus is the playful and humorous. All play is not the same, however: cheap entertainment that mimics television shows is different from satire that critiques popular culture. Let me be clear: not all play is sacralized recreation. Nevertheless, celebration, feasts, and festivals are inherent in religion, and perhaps we might more playfully call what I am getting at *religious ludism*. In megachurch contexts it manifests as evangelical enjoyment – a way of engaging a perceived invisible Wholly Other, which recreates their collective and personal identities. I am suggesting it could be said that Christian play can be a liminal state that allows personal and corporate transformation to occur, including deconversion.

Huizinga explains that one key characteristic of play is that it is "not serious" and "a stepping out of 'real' life into a temporary sphere of activity with a disposition all its own" (1950, 8). Turner, likewise, explains ritual as a process that involves a liminal phase at the centre that entails a "ludic deconstruction and recombination of familiar cultural configurations" (Deflem 1991, 14). This ludic moment in religious practice allows for an old identity to be broken down and a new one to be constructed. Cheap entertainment that positions the person as passive consumer would not function this way, as it distracts, disempowers, and does not engage the status quo. Charisma that just gives people what they want and keeps them in their place is normatively deficient (Lloyd 2018; see also Wessinger 2012). Such play may transform, but only to shape a person into a passive consumer within a large consumer-capitalist system. Laughing, the audience escapes the political moment while being rendered a partner in the politics of the show.

At the heart of the Meeting House is a drive to recreate evangelical Christianity, to rebrand the movement as well as to re-form individual evangelical believers who live simply, give generously, and act peaceably. Much of the Christian performance at this church is theologically geared towards a liminal state, and the transitory nature of their meetings in rented movie theatres and weeknights at members' homes adds to the "betwixt and between" experience. The theatres are dark, without windows, like what theologians call "the intermediate state." Woven through all the anti-structure, however, is a "play attitude" that contributes to the liminal nature of the church and allows their mission of evangelical transformation to advance – at least to a certain degree. It all happens in the heart of consumer discipline – the mall – but it seeks to deconvert attendees from its allure while appropriating its consumer practices. It is mixed play. What forces get the last word in an ironic scenario like this?

Masters (2007) already applied Victor Turner's ideas of ritual process directly to the Meeting House, and Packard (2012) has subsequently done the same for the broader Emerging Church phenomenon, of which the Meeting House can be said to be a member. But neither of the above connected the liminality of these churches with their playfulness, and neither remarked on playful religious behaviour.[18] Churches like TMH have built their entire existence upon a playful, distanced, critical take on evangelical religion, and it's not only a simple reflection of McDonaldized life. Most members would be highly critical of such an assessment of their religious life, and while some analyses can assume a measure of obliviousness in their subjects, there is simultaneously a deliberate awareness of consumer life in many people I met, an active resistance to "bigger and better," and significant enjoyment not wholly explained by passive consumption. There is more observable ambiguity and paradox in this congregational play.

THE OLD SPICE PARODY

As a final illustration in this chapter, I want to describe one more piece of MH media that demonstrates, in summary fashion, what this book has been saying about TMH, charisma, and Cavey's religion as an interrogation of "religion" and the championing of intimate relationship. In 2012 TMH produced an eighteen-second commercial promoting their church, which would be played in the movie theatres where they had remote sites. This video they titled "Welcome Video," and it is probably their singular most important eighteen seconds of promotional media.

The ad begins with Pastor Cavey, clean-cut in a three-piece suit, standing stiff in front of a drab brown church sanctuary declaring, "When it comes to faith, some people like tradition." A church bell dings, and the camera flashes quickly across three characters: an older woman playing the organ with what looks like evidence of a stroke on her face; a boy groaning while struggling with his tight tie and collar; and then a smartly dressed woman in a pew hovering over a little girl and giving her a strong "Shhhhhhh!" Finally, a woman fans herself distractedly in the sweaty pew, rolling her eyes.

The narrative immediately presents a stark contrast, if not conflict, in the form of a cliché. Conventional church is dull and uncomfortable, if not confining and oppressive. Women are uptight and the men strangled in starched suits. Irony is introduced as Cavey says, "Some people like tradition." Really, who would like *that* caricature of a boring church? The drama has begun as a satire – understood as prophetic criticism made funny (Jemielity 2006, 21). Satire diminishes its subject and makes it look ridiculous, worthy of scorn (Abrams and Harpham 2008, 320).

"Some people like tradition." The stiff, clean-cut Cavey then suddenly announces, "and some people don't!" The organ music immediately winds down and some upbeat rhythm guitar music and percussion take over. Charisma breaks through the routine frame, taking people to a new space, one that is both familiar and strange, offering hope for a closer connection to the core of existence. It is vital to first define a problem or crisis, then offer an attractive solution. Reconstruction must follow deconstruction.

So Cavey then rips off his suit to reveal his casual jeans and plaid white and grey shirt underneath; the toupee he was wearing flies off and his long hair cascades down past his two earrings and onto his shoulders; the church scene vanishes and is instantly replaced with a movie theatre full of happy people with coffees in hand. Cavey invites: "If you're one of the 'don'ts' but still interested in spirituality, well, guess what? You've come to the right place." He dons a fedora, and popcorn and a drink smoothly fall into his hands from skyhooks as he sits himself down into a cushy movie theatre seat. "It's the Meeting House, a church for people who aren't into church," he quips, as the logo and website appear on the screen.

The venue and style are fresh and new. The movie theatre setting acts as sacred space, and the featured fast food becomes sacrament. The cinema is a setting of celebrity, of consumption, of romance and escape. The movie theatres are already a "liminal" place – a dark, betwixt-and-between sort of place that is neither home nor work nor church and functions as the midpoint in personal transformation (Masters 2007). The theatre is one step away from that old spoiled evangelical identity and on the way to a new, more culturally legitimate identity – but not there yet. The Anabaptist element awaits.

What is especially instructive about this video is first of all its cost. I was told they brought in outside video technicians and producers for this commercial and that it cost them thousands of dollars. It was a significant investment and a venture into other institutional contexts. Second, the video is a parody, patterned after a popular series of commercials produced by Old Spice that star African American football celebrities Terry Crews and Isaiah Mustafa (originally titled "The Man Your Man Could Smell Like"). The commercials assure the male viewer that Old Spice will make him as stunningly attractive to females as Mustafa or Crews. This parodic reference draws TMH into broader cultural myths of being innovative, athletic, and cool, of the need to stand out from the crowd, to be an empowered, confident individual who patronizes the right brands, while further blurring sacred and secular binaries. Ironically, the videos exaggerate male sexual power and tap into myths around black male sexuality. For a white church headed by a white pastor who is overweight and openly labels himself as a "beta male," it's doubly ironic. He is a perfect foil for the virile, black, male athlete, and the juxtaposition of the pale rotund Cavey with these dark chiselled figures is certainly comical.[19]

DRAMATIZING AN "IRRELIGIOUS" PARADOX

Megachurches are big, and to be big requires institutionalization – or resignation to chaos and pandemonium. For most, institutionalization follows the paradigm of consumer capitalism – organizational management techniques, in-house research, and clever marketing. For a megachurch like TMH that eschews the rhetoric of institution, rules, and rituals, this becomes a performative contradiction. Unless the contradiction is approached playfully, as a paradox. The fiction that results is what I call the "irreligious" paradox: a large rationalized bureaucracy that envisions itself as an organic, spiritual but not religious movement in touch with the divine Jesus. On a different level, it is an institution of centralized control and intense organizational labour that revels in a culture of play: irony, satire, festival, dancing, and intricately designed parody.

This paradoxical approach creates a liminal space – "a place betwixt and between" – that is normal to play and offers a space in which personal transformation can take place, including deconversion from "religion," consumerism, and, because they are Anabaptist, involvement in the business of the state. This is the goal of TMH: to take the spoiled identity of conservative Christians and train them in the habits and language of becoming more cool – less politically motivated and thus more culturally legitimate. They do this not with angry, bombastic critiques but with irony, parody, and dance parties – a more gentle and enjoyable transformational process that is itself more congenial to a modest Canadian culture. I would venture that much of this analysis could transfer to many churches infected with some form of reflexive evangelicalism.

In the next chapter, I ask the most often-repeated question at TMH and other megachurches across the continent: what happens when the leader leaves, resigns, is deposed, or dies? In dramaturgical terms, how does the megachurch performance *end* – or how do leaders create a new chapter, a next act, or a sequel? A lingering mythology persists, declaring the inevitable end of the religious community immediately following the death of its founder – an assumption that simply has no basis in the history of new religious movements. Team ministry discourse, and the implemented structures that reflect it, are the foundation of the expansion and routinization of charisma within the dynamics of the dramatic web, which has enduring power beyond the life of the leader. The leader's body is a symbol of the charismatic relation, signalling a message, a community, a way of life. The message, community, and way of life, however, can persist without a live body.

8

Dramaturgical Trouble and the End of the Show

Bruxy Cavey: In the BIC every fourteen years a pastor can get a full year off [as a sabbatical]. So see ya! I've been here fifteen, sixteen years. It's not a crisis, it's a pre-emptive strike. I'm going to take three months off to do some reading, writing, with my family. I'll be in community.
    Tim Day: What if things start tanking?
    Cavey: Tanking?
    Day: You'll come in and save it.
    Cavey [*nonplussed*]: Yeah, I'll save it.
Onstage Sunday morning, 6 May 2012

"What if B gets hit by a bus?... Well I'm here next Wednesday night. How about you?" ... Yeah, Bruxy can die, but it has nothing to do with me to a certain extent. This is my group. This is my Bible Study group. This is my Home Church. I'm coming here.
TMH staff member, interview, 11 July 2013

Cavey occasionally conveys to his followers the fleeting nature of their community. At the twenty-fifth anniversary of TMH in 2011, with thousands of people gathered together from all the regional sites of the church, he thanks God in his prayer for all the stories of changed, healed, restored lives. Then he adds, "If you use us for another twenty-five years, that would be our privilege, to pass our torch to the next generation. But if you choose to close our doors next month – if that's your will, we thank you for how you've already used us. All of this has been pure privilege. We will turn our backs on our journey towards religion for we see you as everything to us."

Cavey realizes that to be consistent, he cannot merely preach against the abstraction of "religious rules, roles, and routines" if his own church is becoming a long-standing institution with its own calcifying structures and inertia. So he deliberately nurtures a sense of fragility and impermanence among his followers. If they wanted to be truly "irreligious" and anti-institutional, however, they might arbitrarily set a closing date for their swelling organization.[1] In June 2007 he preached, "Part of the life of any structure is being able to embrace their own demise: that is what it means to follow Jesus ... One of the saddest things on the planet today are the time and energy that people invest in churches and denominations that have long outlived their usefulness.... Shut it down." However, there are no plans for such closure of TMH, suggesting a Weberian paradox of "routinization for people not into routinization."

Cavey does not acknowledge that the contingencies of his own career and life to a large degree create the sense of precariousness in such a large institution. When any organization – and especially a voluntary organization such as a church – centralizes its charisma in one particular personality, the inevitable question arises and becomes more pressing as the leader ages: *What will happen if the leader leaves, retires, is deposed, or suddenly dies?* When power is concentrated narrowly in one charismatic authority, even if Cavey continues to freely delegate so much responsibility, the institutional structures rest on the precarious foundation of the consistent perception of extraordinary performance. The stakes are high; the livelihoods of dozens of staff and the spiritual care and community life of thousands of people are vulnerable to the vicissitudes of charismatic succession. Goffman uses the term *dramaturgical trouble* (1959, 134) in passing to describe moments in the performance in which the performers cannot relax and where control of performance "regions" carries some uncertainties. In fact, Goffman examines performance disruptions and discrepancies at length for the tacit rules and roles they reveal. The dramaturgical trouble I explore in this chapter involves role distance taken to extremes (that is to say, when the leader leaves the role completely by leaving or dying) and may produce alienation much more profound than any instance described in chapter three.

This chapter is less about irony and more about the reflexivity of evangelicals who follow a charismatic leader: how do they reflect on their dependence on this singular figure for their church livelihood? Here I aim to problematize the comprehensive nature of charismatic authority that many assume marks megachurches, and I do so by investigating two types of dramaturgical trouble. The first part of the chapter examines aspects of the performance that discredit the dominant impression they wish to make, including an examination of Cavey's uncomfortable face-to-face encounters with attendees and his limited, if not awkward, involvement in the daily operations of his megachurch. To do this, I observe Cavey's performance inconsistencies in the celebrity pastor role, with significant reliance on the perceptions of his audience gathered from attendee interviews. My strategy in this section is to argue that TMH has been managing weaknesses in Cavey's charismatic authority all along, and the inevitability of his leaving TMH is not as catastrophic a transition as some assume. The dramatic web is fragile, because it hangs by a welter of tenuous threads; but because it hangs by a welter of such threads, it has some stability and a future.

The second part of the chapter introduces the subject of the end of Cavey's performance at the Meeting House. While this dramaturgical crisis remains in the future, anxieties of its eventual reality reach back into the present. Therefore, I move beyond my own data to the broad range of anecdotes on megachurch pastoral succession and suggest possibilities for the future of leadership at the Meeting House, while discrediting the stereotype of an inevitable implosion through scandal.

This is a timely discussion, for many of the megachurch founders from the 1970s and 1980s will be entering retirement age within this decade. Robert Schuller was one of the first to signal transition to new leadership, and if the bitter end of Schuller's Crystal Cathedral signals the paradigm for megachurch *endings* to the same degree it shaped the model for megachurch *beginnings*, many megachurches will be encountering disruptive and even disastrous transitions in the near future. However, while many took advice from Schuller on how to grow a church, many megachurch pastors and their boards may learn the negative lesson from his succession failure, and instead carefully plan ahead for their own leadership transition.

The charismatic diamond suggests charisma is a delicate phenomenon, arising from the confluence of four different factors. Charismatic authority can be destroyed or lost if one of the four elements becomes altered too suddenly or in the wrong direction. Billy Sunday lost the strength of his charismatic authority when the cultural context shifted but Sunday's message did not (Martin 2002). Robert Tilton's charisma was undermined when anti-fans used the democratic possibilities of new media to satirize his show and attack his credibility (Bekkering 2015). Mark Driscoll similarly bore the brunt of negative media scrutiny and resigned in ignominy (Vanderbloemen 2014; Hendersen and Murren 2015). Rob Bell stretched his dramatic web of charisma too far towards the left, and he lost much of his original constituency; with fewer followers, his charismatic authority waned (Wellman 2012). Followers form a deep emotional bond with their charismatic leaders; but when such leaders physically or psychologically abuse followers, reject their love, or spiritually betray them, the bond is threatened and can be severed (Jacobs 1987). The charismatic bond is not a taken-for-granted enduring phenomenon. In terms of the dramatic web of TMH, the nagging thought persists whether the romantic promise that supports the satirical show might not end in a tragic mess. Webs are sticky, and they can hold passing visitors for a time; but they are also delicate and subject to the vicissitudes of the cultural weather.

PERSONALITY CULTS AND THE UNDERSIDE OF CHARISMA

If religion, and evangelicalism in particular, is stigmatized in Canada as discussed in chapter 3, then religious "personality cults" are subject to even greater suspicion. The term *cult* already prejudices the matter, but like the notion of "celebrity worship" (Laderman 2009), any situation where a single leader takes an idealized role that leaves followers passive or dependent provokes severe criticism.[3] This was a constant question when I explained my research to the curious: is he in danger of becoming a narcissistic or authoritarian religious leader?

While scholars use the term *cult of personality* to describe the manufactured media image of political leaders (Corsi 2008; Plamper 2012), it has also been popularly applied to religious leaders who are celebrities in their own communities and who are better known than those communities: new religious movement leaders such as Jimmy Jones or David Koresh and megachurch leaders such as Jerry Falwell, Rick Warren, and Joel Osteen. The term has also been used to describe the enduring role of the charismatic African American church pastor in the midst of the congregation (Royster 2013, 17), leaders of some Buddhist groups in Canada, such as Daisaku Ikeda, the leader of Soka Gakkai International (Shiu 2010, 93), as well as Fo Guang Shan's leader, Master Hsing Yun (Verchery 2010, 233). While the meaning of the term shifts within these different religious contexts, the public suspicion about a cult of personality carries social stigma that can motivate calculated impression management.

Cult can simply mean "worship" but it popularly conjures the impression of blind loyalty and the myth of "brainwashed" followers (Dawson 2006). In fact, charismatic authority is rarely totalizing, and TMH provides a helpful nuanced perspective on the matter. Attendees and staff at TMH are aware of weaknesses in Cavey's charisma and are attuned to the limits of his leadership abilities. For example, some lay leaders demonstrate great reflexivity and ambivalence about Cavey's central role. Their concern is understandable, and Emerging Churches characteristically suspicious of celebrity pastors pursue egalitarian or "flat" leadership structures while ironically depending on charismatic leaders and invisible oligarchies (T. Jones 2011; Marti and Ganiel 2014, 117). There has been a growing cultural disillusionment with charismatic leadership (Khurana 2002; Lloyd 2018). For example, organizational management guru Jim Collins says creating a cult of personality "is the last thing you should do" (Collins and Porras 2002, 135). While charismatic leaders may lead great companies that last, two traits are more important than any charisma, insists Collins: humility and resolve.[4] Charismatic leadership can be a liability, and leaders at TMH are reflexive and savvy enough to know that not everything at the Meeting House depends on Cavey for its life, direction, and future.

The precariousness of a religious group is not confined to the death of its leader. Not everyone is caught up in the charismatic bond, its fellowship and blind obedience. I saw this in numerous ways, as in Home Church discussions where many disagreed openly with Cavey's pacifist views, his emphasis on suffering as normative to the Christian life, or his stance on singlehood as the Christian default status rather than marriage. Despite Cavey's teaching that Christians should not be involved in politics, I met a number who were card-carrying members of the Conservative Party of Canada and were deeply involved in the current election campaigns. I noted that the pastor doing baptisms and the Meeting House *Manifesto* both state that baptism is "an expression of [believers'] decision to follow Christ," but those being baptized interpreted their (re)baptism instead as a rite of passage towards leadership in the church or as a public expression of renewed faith. As a final example, TMH teaches that marriage is not an option for a gay Christian, but in 2014 an "unofficial" Home

Church in Toronto comprised partnered gays and lesbians. I have since heard of a number of "unofficial" Home Churches that meet together and follow the teachings but do not comply with the liability requirements for Home Church as stated by TMH leadership and thus are not formerly recognized, even if they may be informally acknowledged by a site pastor.

As Goffman reports (1961a), there is an "underlife" to large institutions – activities that may not be sanctioned by the institution's officials (Ingram 1982, 1986). For example, the ordinary member of a large institution can "work the system" in a number of ways for personal advantage. I remember how at the large "all sites" gathering for the twenty-fifth anniversary of TMH at the PowerAde Centre in Brampton, clowns made up part of the festivities. As one clown was tying up a balloon for a child, the clown gave the parents her business card, saying, "I do birthday parties for children – check out my website." At one Home Church I attended, a woman was handing out brochures about her jewellery business called "Unmistakably Latasia." I saw other instances where people were taking advantage of the large potential consumer market at TMH, and one interviewee even commented on the practice. She had not attended TMH long, but she said she heard some talk that "it was a good church to make business contacts." She was a public school teacher, so networking opportunities did not attract her; but it was one of her lasting impressions of the church.

I was surprised when a few friendly inquirers did use the term *cult* or *cult-like* when asking about my research. Melton (1991) says that lingering prejudices of "cults" and their charismatic leaders lay behind the assumption that a succession process after the passing of a founder will inevitably involve serious disruption and even the dissolution of the new religious movement (NRMs – the proper term in sociology and religious studies). Many NRMs, he insists, are actually variations on the old religious traditions and have formed transnational networks led by a designated hierarchy within an international headquarters. The establishment of a bureaucratic structure ensures continuity: "Once the founder articulates the group's teachings and practices, they exist independently of him/her and can and do develop a life of their own" (8).

Melton agrees that new religions come and go, but longevity has little to do with the founder's passing. The more salient factors are public response to the founder's ideas and the competence of followers in organizing the group after the founder's retirement or death. Melton concludes quite simply, "What does happen when the founder dies? Generally, the same thing that happens in other types of organizations, that is, very simply, power passes to new leadership with more or less smoothness depending upon the extent and thoroughness of the preparation that has been made ahead of time" (1991, 8).

A founder's passing may be sad, but it generally does not entail the subsequent death of the community. Power struggles may ensue, especially if intellectual property or other assets have not been properly designated. But new legal requirements of corporate structures have given more stability to new religious groups, says Melton, and there have been many "orderly transfers of power," in recent history, including the succession of L. Ron Hubbard (Scientology), Victor Paul Wierwille (the Way), and Herbert W. Armstrong (Worldwide Church of God) (1991, 10).

Although he does not name the process as the routinization of charisma, Melton offers a re-narration of a new religious movement's development that echoes Weber. Contrary to the mythology and rhetoric of "totalizing" NRMs where the leader is in permanent, absolute control, Melton describes a shift from the centrifugal influence of charisma to the centripetal unfolding of bureaucratic structures. The first generation of followers are self-selected because they are drawn to the leader and his or her vision. As the community grows, it needs to experiment and adapt to new situations. Followers give feedback to the leader, and the leader troubleshoots the teachings and followers' needs. Versatility decreases as the movement expands geographically, and branch campuses are set up with intermediaries to oversee community life. "The lines of authority and communication become more impersonal," says Melton, and administration passes to second- and third-echelon leadership (1991, 11). If given enough time, the pattern of self-correcting and fine-tuning will continue through the death of the founder, and on to a second generation of followers.

Charisma has staying power beyond death. With an administrative apparatus in place, oral and written traditions, rites and ceremonies to transfer charisma to others, and a successor committed to the founder's mission and continued identification with that mission, charisma can be effectively routinized (Trice and Beyer 1986). Historically speaking, the careers of megachurch pastors such as Aimee Semple McPherson, Daddy Grace, and Frank Norris mushroomed into new denominations rather than fizzled out, and other megachurch pastors such as William B. Riley, Dan Malone, Charles Spurgeon, and Jerry Falwell began their own university to ensure a long and culturally expansive legacy. Charisma, as Weber said, becomes routinized by followers, and this ensures the continuity of the group far beyond the life of the leader. The dramatic web of charisma may stretch and grow exponentially rather than shrink and wilt upon the passing of the leader as new lines of vision, administration, and marketing are spun.

In what follows I will describe three aspects of Meeting House culture that qualify the charismatic authority of Cavey. The first examines the passive nature of Cavey's personality, the second his relatively minor role in many executive decisions, and finally, some followers' ambivalence about his central role. As I argued in chapter 6 on teamwork, Cavey's charisma and executive powers are already qualified in many ways, and the routinization of his charisma has already begun, long before he has left the premises.

ENTREPRENEURIAL AND DISINTERESTED

The emerging concept of institutional entrepreneur offers another frame in which to analyze Cavey – a leadership concept confined mostly to the sociology of institutions and management. Marti and Ganiel (2014) find the concept helpful in understanding the leaders of the Emerging Church Movement, even though the literature on institutional entrepreneurs has yet to be systematically applied to religious settings. Marti himself has coined the term *entrepreneurial evangelicalism* (2005, xi), which he describes as a religious orientation that "creatively and intentionally engages 'culture'" (xii).

The role of entrepreneurial wizard fits Cavey only loosely. He is the star of the show, but he does not run the show. He has an intuitive knack for connecting with the "spiritual but not religious" sentiment, and I am told he has provided some novel ideas in shaping the structure of the Meeting House, especially in its marketing in the earlier days. But overseers (trustees) have told me he is reserved at their board meetings and can look distracted or disinterested at times, even though whenever he's asked to speak he is perceived as prescient. He does not present as the passionate visionary driven to inspire and control his board, which is the impression given by such megachurch leaders as Robert Schuller, Bill Hybels, and Mark Driscoll. In fact, numerous

MH leaders have told me that he was quite reluctant to set up closed circuit television in the school where they used to have their Sunday services and then unenthusiastic about expanding the church through projected teachings at multiple sites. This may be false modesty, but it tells the story that Cavey is not a self-made man.

Even after Tim Day left, many of the administrative matters handled by Day were transferred to other staff, and they slowly transitioned to a leadership triad: Bruxy Cavey, teaching pastor; Rod Tombs, senior pastor of operations; and Darryl Winger, senior pastor of congregational life and compassion ministries. Cavey consistently articulates and practises a shared leadership model.

Furthermore, his disorganized behaviour is legendary; he has missed various appointments, including a church Christmas party. "He's lost his wallet, like, four times," mused a family friend. One newly hired site pastor told me that he met Cavey at the main site for an introductory interview. Cavey arrived late and asked, "What are we supposed to be doing here?" "You are supposed to interview me," replied the young recruit. In some ways, Cavey resembles the absent-minded professor more than the driven megachurch entrepreneur-pastor. He needs administrative support to make it through the week's work.

This mild-mannered performance is consistently reported. "He's no alpha male," said Cavey's wife to me in passing during one of my interviews in their home. Cavey has spoken on occasion of TMH as a culture of beta males and often calls himself a geek. He tells his followers, "My idea of a good time is a bigger book." He lives far away from the main campus of the church, he has no permanent office he consistently uses within the main building,[5] and the majority of his time he spends preparing for his teaching moments and answering questions from those who pursue his attention – or on the road speaking at a variety of venues, where his "handler" guides him to his rooms and ensures he takes time to eat meals. In some ways, he fits the role of a guru or lama[6] more than a visionary megachurch pastor or MacNair's (2009) all-powerful megachurch "regal pastor"; he lives on the mountain (actually, at the foot of Hamilton Mountain in Dundas), and people must seek him out to have an audience. His primary mode of conversation with pastors, his board, and attendees is passive; he patiently waits to be asked a question. In sum, like Korean megachurch pastor David Yonggi Cho (Hong 2000b), Cavey appears disinterested in controlling mundane church operations; he delegates to others quickly and thus frees himself for the tasks he enjoys. His charismatic authority is already routinized through tasks he has handed on to other Meeting House leaders on his team.

People intuitively believe, and research suggests, that overdependence on a single charismatic leader presents numerous dangers (Hey 2013, 192). So limits on Cavey's involvement, control, and governance can be healthy and likewise demonstrate that the dramatic web depends on a team, not solely on Cavey's personality. In fact, his personality may be a liability in some unexpected ways. Webs, after all, are riddled with holes. These gaps are already being tended to, while Cavey still resides in the central role.

CAVEY'S AWKWARDNESS AND CHARISMA'S BOUNDARIES

In this section, I want to demonstrate the limits of Cavey's charismatic bond and show some of the ambivalences of attendees towards his central role. In most conversations about Cavey, the sense of wonder at his talent and character spares few superlatives.

Cavey's charisma, however, is not a universally experienced phenomenon. To state the obvious, not everyone who encounters Cavey becomes enamoured with him. The most virulent response I received was from a clergyman who said he had detailed knowledge about Cavey, and he became agitated when I mentioned my case study, exclaiming, "Cavey's a manipulator!" Because he refused to explain what he meant and walked away, I can only guess at his meaning and possible motives. The significant and simultaneously ironic reality remains that all charisma has its limits, and any accusations of brainwashing or even manipulation are rhetorical exaggerations that tap into the lingering mythology of "cults" (Melton 1991). Cavey may captivate some audiences, but his teaching, appearance, and personality certainly do not appeal to everyone. Only 5,000 people attend his church in a densely populated metropolitan area of millions.

Additionally, while extolled as a charismatic speaker, Cavey lacks the spiritual charismata expected of Pentecostal leaders in his childhood tradition. Some megachurch pastors speak in tongues, initiate miraculous healings, and claim special revelation (Miller 1997; Hey 2013, 97). As chronicled in chapter 3, Cavey repeatedly tried to receive the gift of tongues as a young leader in his Pentecostal church, but he never manifested any such supernatural experiences or gifts. This limitation is appropriate for a post-evangelical dramatic web of charisma; while many Christians seeking the miraculous as evidence of divine presence will flock to such venues as Catch the Fire Toronto (formerly known as the Toronto Airport Christian Fellowship), few skeptics would feel comfortable among a crowd being "slain in the Spirit." Cavey offers a biography that knows the charismatic subculture well, and he distinguishes himself from it in a winsome way.

More significantly, his awe-inspiring and renegade performance lands in dramaturgical trouble when people encounter Cavey face-to-face. When Cavey is offstage and off-camera, he often appears sharply out of character, and the experience can be jarring for attendees.[7] Cavey's presence in the halls of the Oakville site, for example, where he stands between Sunday performances to answer questions and get audience feedback on his teaching, demonstrates this disruption. If the auditorium stage is a Goffmanian performance "front region," Cavey's casual availability after the service is not precisely a back region or "outside" region, as he is still addressing his audience and not relaxing with colleagues or members of his team. It's not quite a front region, as no exchanges in the hall are recorded and podcast for transnational consumption. In effect, it is a new pose, a second "out of character" performance habituated over time (Goffman 1959, 134).

The hallway does give the *appearance* of a back region, however. Vulnerable to hundreds of potential questions, Cavey fosters the impression of accessibility and familiarity. He even invites Meeting Housers to his private residence and regularly hosts dance parties for those eager to connect with him in such a way. Yet he presents in a radically different character, not unlike Goffman's reference to Kenneth Burkes's musician, "who is assertive in his art and self-effacing in his personal relationships" (1959, 136). Audience members become confused, even disillusioned (what I have called an alienation effect) as "what they had taken as the performer's essential self [now appears] not so essential" (139).

In short, as Cavey transitions through the literal backstage and takes up his usual post standing by the Meeting House bookstore, he is no longer "on." Goffman uses the language of "regression" for back region behaviour, but Cavey does not show the casual familiarity of back region behaviour. Cavey simply turns his stage persona "off": gregarious, outgoing, and dynamic on stage, he is quiet, uncomfortable, and almost expressionless offstage. While on one hand such radical contradictions may enlarge the enigmatic nature of Cavey's persona, on the other hand, accidental backstage interactions with charismatic leaders can be damaging to their charismatic authority when they reveal the leader's mundane existence (Joosse 2012). Wellman and Corcoran (2016) point out, however, that this disillusionment occurs only if the leader is considered divine; confessions and demonstrations of humanness convey authenticity, increasing trust and relatability, intensifying the charismatic bond.

Meeting House attendees' personal encounters with their celebrated teacher are less than ecstatic experiences, but they do leave followers with a deeper sense of wonder and mystery associated with their leader. "He's one of the most introverted people that I have ever met," said one older attendee. When in small gatherings with Meeting Housers, he is often distracted and "seems really small." His body language communicates "Don't bother me" or "Don't come near me please." *Awkward* and *shy* were among the most frequently used words to describe his social skills, but as one Cavey friend pointed out, he is not entirely shy. He will engage his conversation partners directly and deeply. "He's just introverted and would often rather go off in a corner and read a book."

One friend of Cavey told me the shy and awkward Cavey is the "real" Cavey and that his onstage persona "is an act." Cavey and other Meeting House leaders have, in fact, offered this explanation onstage and in "First Steps" orientation classes, warning attendees that they ought not to be offended if Cavey seems out of character when they meet him. "He is not being rude," they are told, "just reserved." This "plea of forgiveness" for out-of-character communication, says Goffman, strategically softens the disjuncture that audience members may feel (1959, 169) and becomes an "inside secret" of the whole performance, unavailable to outsiders (142), which now include podcast viewers.

Another Home Church leader said something similar. "He somewhat psyches himself up for Sunday mornings, because that's not his typical way of doing things ... He's a bit of an enigma ... I find it intriguing that he could be one way in some circumstances ... I feel like his real self is that introverted, quiet spirit that is really seeking after God, and who is passionate about what he does. So I really admire him." In other words, not only does he teach in an admirable fashion, but knowing that public teaching is stressful for him adds to the mystery, and thus may even spin another line in the dramatic web of charisma.

Rojek (2001, 11) explains that celebrity status "always implies a split between a private self and a public self" and that the human actor "presents a 'front' or 'face' to others while keeping a significant portion of the self in reserve." In George Herbert Mead (1934) terminology, Rojek explains, the split between the I (the veridical self) and the Me (the self as seen by others) is basic to human life but exacerbated by the overwhelming power of the celebrity *Me*. Rojek suggests this tension may be disturbing if not pathological for the celebrity performer if the *Me* colonizes the *I*.

Another insight into the contradiction suggests that Cavey pre-empts the definition of the situation with the face he puts on. Said one attendee, "He doesn't want to be your friend." Typically, charismatic leaders "are known for their seeming sensitivity to the needs of others – they make a personal connection with those they meet, showing interest in their lives, no matter how brief the encounter may be" (Dawson 2011, 116). Self-help manuals for developing charisma give advice that says something similar: charismatic individuals listen intently to others and make them feel comfortable and valuable (Alessandra 2000; Morgan 2008). A consistent report from Meeting House staff – including site pastors – was that Cavey did not recognize them at meetings, and even a day after interviewing them for a new position, could not remember their names. Cavey publicly admits this; he makes jokes about missing appointments and not remembering people's names or the events in their lives.

Could his indifference be associated with his ironic shtick? David Foster Wallace writes before the dawn of the ubiquitous internet about pop culture's ironic character, saying, "Exhaustive TV-training in how to worry about how he [Joe Briefcase] may come across, seem to other eyes, makes riskily genuine human encounters seem even scarier." A steady diet of Hollywood movies offers "lessons in the blank, bored, too-wise expression that Joe must learn how to wear" for the crowds that he passes. In fact, "the numb blank bored demeanour" he contends, "has become my generation's version of cool" and treats everything like it's on a screen, far away (1993, 181). Cavey may have this face, but in personal conversation he does not convey indifference. A similar exhaustion, however, born from matters of scale may be at work.

A former overseer contrasted Cavey with another leader of a large local Christian institution who remembered "names, children's names, and what you did last month," and with another business CEO he knew who made a point of coming to the employee lounge and chatting about hockey news. Cavey, he said, "doesn't have the energy to invest in anything but teaching." A former attendee who had spent considerable time as part of Cavey's Home Church said he bumped into Cavey and his wife at a CD store and greeted him. "Cavey barely responded," he said. "He looked at me, unrecognizing, as if he was a group home client being led around on a day out."

I noticed some attendees develop a faux sense of intimacy with Cavey, who, though a very familiar presence to the attendee, has no cognizance of his or her personal existence. As one attendee said, "I never know what to talk about with him. It's kind of like this deity complex, right? I didn't treat him like God, but it was weird. It was awkward." Connections with Cavey remain a mediated, one-sided relationship, something critics variously describe as a pseudo-relation (Boorstin 1961), parasocial relationship (Rubin and McHugh 1987), or intimate stranger (Schickel 2000). It is the *image* of Cavey and his vision that develop a sense of solidarity between attendees and offer them a "sacred matrix" in which to locate their busy "irreligious" lives (Shoemaker and Simpson 2014). It is not the actual person, Bruxy Cavey.

Another example of his introverted and detached nature when offstage was when he was asked to take his father's place as Santa for the Oakville Meeting House Christmas party. Cavey relented, but not without reluctance. "I hated it," he told me in one interview, laughing at himself. "I'm no Santa. I'm not a fan of kids. I love my own." Those who have attended his parties, too, say that he is awkward, sometimes quiet, content to do his own thing in a corner, expecting people to mix, enjoy themselves, and when it's time, leave his house.

Goffman describes the back region as a physical "buffer" from the deterministic demands of their front region performance (1959, 114). People of higher social status, says Goffman, including "sacred" performers such as clergy (133, 137), have a very small back region. Megachurch pastors, with their thousands of congregants and multiple thousands of viewers and outsiders, certainly have a limited back region in which to relax. I would suggest that Cavey has created a *psychological* buffer for himself by cultivating an additional persona that enables him to give the impression of accessibility while maintaining a level of guardedness. Compared to his animated teaching persona, he is very gentle yet stiff when addressing particular audience members from the stage, who can come with high expectations and, at worst, with aggressive questions, the desire to stump him, embarrass him, or even provoke him. His commitment to pacifism and convictions about anger further requires consistency in these moments, and the formality with which he answers questions maintains both the politeness and decorum necessary for front region behaviour while reserving energy for his next big performance (1959, 108). Significantly, Cavey is certainly not the only charismatic leader to be introverted in intimate settings (Martin 2002, 9; Goodbrand 2010, 151; Wellman 2012, 49).

This is not to say he does not break out of this docile character at times. He is not eager to please and can become impatient with impertinent questions. "He can't stand people who challenge him just for the sake of challenging him and don't care about the answers," I was told by a Cavey friend. People who are looking for loopholes, who want to quibble about minutia or the proper definition of "religion" can raise his ire. Rarely does his impatience lead to a visible display of anger.[8]

To summarize thus far, I am arguing that the charismatic authority of Cavey has its limits. I am not discussing the proverbial clay feet, Achilles heel, or even the classical hubris that may diminish a megachurch pastor's charisma but merely the non-totalizing character of such charisma, what Goffman called the discrediting of the fostered impression. If Cavey is dynamic and brilliantly charismatic onstage, he is flat, guarded, and meek in person. This challenges the lingering caricatures of personality cults and their totalitarian charismatic leaders; my detailed empirical descriptions of one particular charismatic individual demonstrates the nuances and limits of charismatic power.

FOLLOWER AMBIVALENCE ABOUT CAVEY'S APPARENT INDISPENSABILITY

MH attendees are not only puzzled by Cavey's lack of charisma in person, however, they are ambivalent about his excess of charismatic authority within their church. Gamson (1994, 146) constructs a typology of audiences from his empirical research, which has five categories that range from naive believers in the deserving fame of a celebrity to those who see the manufacturing of celebrityhood and then either strive to unmask the mechanics of desire or just enjoy the play of representations and gossip about them.

The Meeting Housers typically fit in Gamson's first category, what he calls the "traditional audience." They trust in their own ability to discern authenticity and see Cavey as a deserving celebrity. They identify with him, not fantasizing about him as Gamson says some traditional audiences might do, but rather seeing him as a model for their lives. Attendees typically do not see Cavey's celebrity status as a function of media processes but rather simply a result of his teaching skill and spiritual gifts. Attendees, however, generally understand charisma as Cavey's unique possession, as a form of biblical *charism*, not as a Weberian charismatic bond or a dramatic web.

That said, a few interviewees expressed recognition that the "Bruxy" they knew was packaged, polished, and controlled by intermediaries and that "Bruxy" was in fact an image, a persona that they interacted with through a screen or podcast from a distance. One site pastor, with the knowledge of his superiors, began a blog that critiqued "pixilated pastors" but did not mention TMH or his role within it (he resigned soon after). The average education of attendees is higher than the average in Canada, and, when pressed, many would acknowledge their mediated relationship with their pastor. Still, simply the fact that he is called "Bruxy" betrays the illusion of intimacy with him.

Some attendees are wary of being part of a church too dependent on one personality. One university student thought having Sunday teachings led by different teachers was a good idea. "There's a lot of people at the Meeting House that follow Bruxy and they don't follow Jesus," she laughed. When other teachers come, "there is either less people at church or there's people who are visibly like 'Oh, it's just [some other staff member]. Whatever.'"

A nurse said that the uncomfortable thought crossed his mind that "this could be a church full of people just wanting to hear Bruxy speak," but he shrugged it off, suppressing the thought. I asked a middle-aged woman who only attends a Home Church (she gets the teachings on podcasts) if the Meeting House had any weaknesses. She explained,

> Bruxy is the key. He explains big concepts by putting them in laymen terms and shows practical ways of living it out. I wouldn't be at the Meeting House if it weren't for him. I like to see and hear him. I do listen to the others, and I try to get something out of them, but Bruxy touches me most. "When is he coming back to teach?" I always ask. The church in my eyes is Bruxy. I know that's not right, but that's where my attachment is. If he

would move on ... well, I would still go but I wouldn't get as much out of it.

Attendees feel some ambivalence about the indispensable role of Cavey ("I know that's not right") while at the same time coveting his consistent presence and teaching. He is the megachurch pastor for those not into megachurch pastors. It is a weak form of resistance to his celebrity status, but it demonstrates an awareness that is a few steps beyond denial and naive celebrity worship.

Those who were deeply involved in a Home Church often insisted that their loyalties had switched to this local ministry group. I opened this chapter with such a quote, and here is the extended quote, spoken by one church employee who had been converted to the Christian faith through TMH,

> There's a lot more to us than just the Sunday morning teaching. It's significant for sure, but all those other things we've talked about that makes us unique, and our focus on our small groups, one of the guys in my particular Home Church, the topic came up "What if Bruxy gets hit by a bus" Right? And he said – and it's stuck with me for a long time – he said, "Well I'm here next Wednesday night. How about you?" Right? So that's all he was saying. Yeah, Bruxy can die, but it had nothing to do with me to a certain extent. This is my group. This is my Bible Study group. This is my Home Church. I'm coming here. Right? Are you coming, or are you stopping coming just because Bruxy died? Right? And I think that's a reality for a lot of people.

This is an important testimony, which should not be read as a dismissal of Cavey as much as a depth of commitment to his vision. Even if Cavey dies, this man will continue Cavey's legacy by being faithful to the church.

A few interviewees repeated impressive stories of committed people who come faithfully to Home Church but do not attend Sunday – as evidence that Home Church is the primary locus of their commitment, not Cavey. These circulating stories, in my estimation, allow attendees to believe Cavey's teaching and personality are incidental to the church, and that the pure relationships of Home Church will endure, regardless of Cavey's presence. This ignores the actual fluidity of Home Churches and the fact that their weekly gatherings are structured around Cavey's

Sunday teachings. The stories, however, soften the precariousness of their church situation and quell the anxiety that may surface when they think of Cavey's departure from their community.

In sum, this section has sought to demonstrate numerous ways in which Cavey's charismatic authority is disrupted. The looming prospect of his eventual retirement and death are thus not so much a novel and insurmountable catastrophe for TMH leadership to navigate as another challenge for them to address and engage as they seek to routinize the charisma of his presence, teaching, and vision. Not only is charismatic authority always dependent on follower recognition and cultural support, but it is never so overwhelming that it does not need the organization and planning of a committed staff and leadership team.

OUTSIDE CRITICS

As mentioned earlier, not everyone is captivated by the dramatic web of Cavey's charisma. Only 5,000 people currently attend his church, and only about 30,000 have attended over the last twenty years from a population of millions. But there are some people who actively oppose Cavey, and paradoxically, while they acknowledge his charismatic power, they oppose his teaching and seek to undermine his reputation within the conservative Christian subculture in North America. Ironically, some of their attacks on his ministry work to strengthen Cavey's charismatic bond with his followers.

Calvinism no doubt raises Cavey's ire.[9] Still, Cavey has interviewed a Harvest Bible Chapel pastor on a Sunday morning and then given him the microphone to preach in their church (Pastor Robbie Symons of Oakville HBC). The HBC's global leader James MacDonald had affinities with Mark Driscoll and wider "neo-Reformed" American groups, but "Pastor Robbie" and Cavey have been able to talk casually with each other, as their church members do switch back and forth between the two megachurches (although more often towards HBC, I suspect).

Jacob Reaume has been the pastor at Harvest Bible Chapel in Waterloo, Ontario, since 2009 (in 2018 it changed its name to Trinity Bible Chapel). This is about an hour from Cavey's main site, but just down the road from two MH regional sites – the Waterloo and Kitchener sites. To put it mildly, Reaume's been less cordial with Cavey. One clue may be that Symons has an undergraduate degree from

Wilfrid Laurier University in Waterloo and went to McMaster Divinity School in Hamilton, Ontario, but Reaume (born and raised in Guelph, Ontario) obtained a master of divinity degree in the more embattled American South – the Southern Baptist Theological Seminary in Louisville, Kentucky. Using his platform as a pastor, Reaume had made scathing public critiques of Bruxy Cavey (on his church's website) but in early 2017 he attacked Cavey's Christian identity in a more sustained way through his regular blog post, which circulated through evangelical circles and was brought to my attention by someone outside both churches. Reaume wrote online, 17 July 2018, "Bruxy Cavey is, in my opinion, the most significant theological controversy Canadian Evangelicals have faced in 70 years."

What is noteworthy is that Reaume's critique starts with an acknowledgement of Cavey's charismatic powers. He mentions numerous times that Cavey "is the pastor of one of Canada's largest churches" and "is perhaps Canada's most recognizable church leader." While he doesn't use the word *charisma*, in some 2018 posts Reaume describes Cavey as having "charm," being "diplomatic" and a "master magician ... who plays with words and phrases like magicians play with cards." At one point he admits, "[Cavey] is warm, friendly, and good at listening" but this, he warns, is a false humility, because Cavey "mocks God's Word" rather than "trembling" at it. Cavey can "disarm people with some tomfoolery" but "frankly, it reeks of an attempt to manipulate his people." He is, in disguise, a "predatory wolf," and not "the Disneyland type" of wolf.[10]

All his charges against Cavey relate to Cavey's "irreligious" quest. First, with regards to gay marriage, Cavey appears on a video in January 2017 in which he apologizes to the gay community for the way the Church has treated the LGBTQ community and for the "absolutely asinine" way in which particularly conservative Christians "have approached disagreements over this topic." Reaume charges Cavey with "bearing false witness" (the ninth of the Ten Commandments) and one who calls "evil good and good evil." "While he might be a Christian," Reaume blogs, "he's not conservative and he's not speaking on our behalf."[11]

Second, Cavey's views of inerrancy and the substitutionary atonement raise Reaume's evangelical hackles even higher. Cavey has said publicly that he does not hold to the inerrancy of everything in the biblical text because the Word of God is first and foremost Jesus himself. Jesus appears to be accessed apart from the Bible, a view that Reaume finds just "bananas." Cavey also finds the substitutionary atonement doctrine abhorrent, and as a *theory* of the meaning of Jesus's work on the cross, he wants to "convert everyone away from it." This incites Reaume to suggest Cavey is a "false-teacher" just "like the old liberals" who "misrepresent Scripture ... and church history" and "pull people straight to hell." Cavey's denial of substitutionary atonement indicates a false gospel, and "a man who denies the Gospel is eternally condemned." Reaume concludes, "Is Cavey teaching Christianity or Bruxyianity?"[12]

Reaume writes in a footnote that he received most of the research into Cavey's teaching from Eric Schneider, a carpenter, blogger, and member of Trinity Bible Chapel whose posts are all critically directed at Cavey's teaching. Schneider has also posted a letter he wrote to Tyndale Theological Seminary president and board in which he contrasts Cavey's public statements on inerrancy and atonement with Tyndale's Statement of Faith.[13] This casts aspersion on Cavey, who has signed the Statement of Faith as an occasional instructor at Tyndale. Curt response letters from the Tyndale President are also posted on Schneider's blog. Another blogger, Randall Rauser, jumped into the fray, defending Cavey and calling Schneider pharisaic and a bully who risks a defamation suit.[14] Cavey himself responded at the time, but not directly. He posted some blogs explaining his view of the atonement[15] and another blog on dealing with divisive Christians, including a vlog entitled "Who Are Our Enemies?"[16] But he nowhere names Reaume or Schneider or their charges against him. He refuses to address his accusers directly in public or mention their names on these uploads.

This is a rough summary of numerous contentious web exchanges that continued even more intensely into 2018. There is more beyond them from other bloggers and preachers,[17] including Pastor Paul Carter, a Baptist pastor in Orillia who personally interviewed Cavey about his controversial views about the Bible and atonement and concluded his analysis by writing:

> Having summarized my observations, I am ready to render my conclusion.
> Bruxy Cavey is not a heretic.
> He's an Anabaptist.[18]

My point in mentioning this theological scrutiny is to show that Cavey has had detractors for years, and his charisma is not universally received. Paradoxically, having enemies can help intensify one's charismatic authority and can garner deeper loyalty from followers. That Randall Rauser took the time to defend Cavey by writing a short essay addressed to Cavey's detractors – whom he calls "bullies" – shows how emotions can be ignited through online debates. Followers rally in the face of perceived aggression against their tribe. Cavey's final comment when addressing this debate once again cautioned against retaliation. "If any of you feel persecuted and feel that this is really harsh, just think back a few hundred years to the early Anabaptists and realize you have it good [*restrained laughter*]. This is not persecution, even if we are being called non-Christians or heretics by this small stream of the Christian family tree. We want to love them back and embrace them as family, even if they don't return the favour."[19]

In the wide scheme of things, I suspect these exchanges have inflated Cavey's reputation in North American evangelical circles. They certainly confirm to HBC attendees the orthodoxy of their own church and simultaneously confirm to TMH attendees, as evidenced in Cavey's measured response, the orthopraxy of their gentle-hearted, persecuted leader. It also proves once again to Cavey's followers that the right-wing evangelical community remains contentious and judgmental – something they resist. In sum, the internet more often works as a "big sort" – reinforcing confirmation bias and retrenching people in their own subcultures (Bishop 2009). "Canadian Evangelicals are now being forced to define who we are," blogs Reaume.[20] His definition, however, does not come in the reflexive evangelical style, and he perpetuates a contentious stereotype that Cavey persists in challenging. Cavey has become increasingly the subversive evangelical.

THE END OF THE SHOW: A DRAMATURGICAL TYPOLOGY

When Cavey was set to go on sabbatical for three months in 2012, there was some concern expressed at the Annual General Meeting that spring. First of all, people wondered if attendance would plunge. "We'll be fine as long as everyone is on automatic withdrawal," quipped Day. There was also some concern as to whether Cavey could be transitioning out. "I have pledged to retire at the Meeting House," said Cavey, adding with a joke, "That's in two years." They were all assured the best days were ahead, and everyone cheered.

Still, what will happen to TMH and its attendees if Bruxy Cavey suddenly leaves, dies, or is deposed? Someday he will retire, and TMH will have to move forward without him or close its doors. I made the question of Cavey's passing a standard part of my interviews (and I didn't always need to ask the question – it was sometimes brought up by the interviewee). In many of my discussions and in the wider literature, the question takes the form of "What would happen if the leader was hit by a bus?" (Vanderbloemen and Bird 2014, 33, 37, 132). Besides suggesting an unexpected death happening in the daily routine of pedestrian life, the scenario is a popular culture trope – a device used in TV and other media for killing off a character (sometimes referred to as the "Look Both Ways" trope) (TV Tropes n.d.). The scene usually consists of two main characters having a conversation on the side of the road, and the camera centres on just one of them. A bus suddenly enters the frame of the picture from one side and sweeps the victim right off the screen. The scene deliberately provokes shock, a reaction appropriate to a church that will lose the one character so centrally important to its life, history, and identity. The trope itself is also symbolically apt for a church thoroughly permeated with popular culture.

According to Vanderbloemen and Bird, most churches and many megachurches do *not* plan for the succession of their current pastor.[21] Many leadership transitions are disruptive and potentially destructive to the church. Some megachurch leaders, such as Frank Harrington (Peach Tree Presbyterian Church), who suddenly died of pneumonia in 2000, leave their church without a succession plan and risk a power struggle for leadership control and assets. Others, such as the prominent case of Wallie Amos Criswell (First Baptist Church, Dallas, Texas) call a successor (Joel Gregory), but once he comes on board, the old pastor, his family, and/or even the board refuse to transfer authority to the new leader. In this instance, Gregory left in frustration after two years on staff and wrote a book about his experience (Gregory 1994). Leadership scholar Ronald Heifetz (1994) called such cases where a constituency refuses to accept the adaptive changes urged by a leader an "assassination." Their ability to influence the organization has been nullified.

This need not be the case in every one of the 1,800 megachurches in North America; succession can happen in several ways. I surveyed over 100 different scenarios of megachurch leadership succession through megachurch literature, and by searching the web and I developed a rough typology of succession scenarios consonant with some succession themes noted by Weber.[22] First of all, I found twenty-four instances where leadership is passed down to another family member, and I would estimate this covers up to 40 per cent of megachurch successions. This almost surely will not happen with Cavey, as his children have not shown an inclination to even cursory involvement in the life of TMH. Second, I found thirty-five cases in which the megachurch board set up some sort of bureaucratic process for succession, often involving a consultant, and it seems this represents the larger proportion of succession scenarios – I estimate up to 60 per cent. This is thus the most likely scenario for TMH, too, especially since Cavey has habitually deferred to his board. Some succession anecdotes seemed to be a combination of the two types, but as a third scenario, I surveyed twenty-nine instances where succession came through some sort of scandal, but as you will see below, the percentage of megachurches that transition this way is actually quite small.

I want to unpack this third scenario in more detail, because it is the dominant assumption created by media attention to leadership failure and creates a stereotype that stretches into the academic literature. Starks (2013) creates the false impression that sexual misconduct is a particularly significant issue for megachurch pastors. But he does not offer any evidence for his claims – for example, by comparing the amount of sexual misconduct discovered in the lives of megachurch pastors with smaller church pastors, CEOs of large corporations, politicians, military leaders, or those in show business. Starks cites mostly psychological literature, which either addresses all pastors generally or even wider populations. The myth of Elmer Gantry lingers, and mass media coverage of celebrity scandals – and the ensuing gossip – only feeds these misperceptions.

A brief comparison with corporate experience of disruptive leadership transition suggests churches – including megachurches – may fare considerably better. An oft-cited article published by the Center for Creative Leadership actually estimates 38–50 per cent of new CEOs fail within the first eighteen months (Riddle 2009). Professor and leadership consultant Clutterbuck (2012, 8) talks about a "crisis in succession planning" and cites the Human Capital Institute claim that 70 per cent of new CEOs fail within two years. Hogan, Hogan, and Kaiser (2011) summarize twelve studies of management failure from 1985 to 2005, which maintain failure rates of 30–67 per cent, with an average of about 50 per cent. Reasons for failure fell into categories of team mismanagement, lack of business acumen, poor working relationships, and inappropriate or immature behaviour.[23] "Based on the data," they conclude, "two-thirds of existing managers are insufferable and at least half will eventually be fired" (3). Aasland et al. (2010) estimate the prevalence of destructive leadership behaviour (which includes passive, disloyal, and tyrannical behaviours) to range from 33 to 61 per cent, as determined by surveys gleaned from 2,539 employees. Those are startlingly high statistics – higher than most would expect in the world of business leadership.

We must grant, however, that it is difficult to give precise definitional boundaries for failure, and what it exactly entails can be widely diverse. However, if we assume it results in termination, we can make a rough comparison. The FACT 2010 survey covers 12,000 religious groups of all sizes and traditions and reports that in the last five years of these groups' history, because of the leader's personal behaviour, 7 per cent of the groups surveyed had congregation members leave, 3 per cent of them had members withhold donations, and 5 per cent of them resulted in a leader or staff member leaving (Hadaway 2011).[24] Other statistics show that 28 per cent of current pastors in the United States have been fired or forced to resign at some point in their career, and 42 per cent of these seriously considered leaving the ministry (Tanner, Zvonkovic, and Adams 2012).

There are no statistics available on the number of megachurches that experience scandals, a category that is admittedly difficult to operationalize for a survey. My correspondence with Scott Thumma, Warren Bird, and Dave Travis – all experts on megachurch research – shows them agreeing that under 5 per cent of all current megachurch pastors will end their careers in some "significant conflict," including financial, sexual, or criminal scandal. With 1,800 megachurches across North America, that means ninety megachurch pastors' conflicts will most likely be covered in the media as their tenure ends. That could be a lot of bad press.

This suggests, first of all, that the vast majority of megachurch pastors do *not* end their career in scandal. Most of their succession narratives will follow the two succession scenarios I described above. Second, the vast discrepancy between perception and reality goes to show only the powerful and yet distorting character of the mass media, because the most readily available cultural narrative of megachurch pastor careers remains the ignominious ending, reinforcing the cynical Elmer Gantry stereotype. Granted, megachurch leaders deserve more scrutiny because they have more power, and more power generally entails greater ethical dilemmas affecting more people (Paschen and Dihsmaier 2013, 7).[25] So as a warning or morality tale, these stories are apt, but they do not reflect the reality of the prevalence of disgraceful endings.

Megachurch scandals are well publicized and easily accessible on the internet, fulfilling the promise of "If it bleeds, it leads." Bill Hybels ended his illustrious career in ignominy over sexual misconduct allegations (Sanders 2018). Other recent disgraces include Ted Haggard (New Life Church, Colorado Springs, Colorado), who resigned in 2007 from his church after it was revealed he had sexual liaisons with a male prostitute and used crystal methamphetamine; Jack Schaap (First Church Hammond, Illinois), who left his megachurch in 2012 and now is serving a twelve-year prison term for having sex with a minor; Isaac Hunter (Summit Church, Orlando, Florida), who committed suicide in 2013 when it was discovered he was having an affair with a member of his church staff; Mark Driscoll (Mars Hill, Seattle), who resigned from his leadership position under accusations of bullying, plagiarism, and financial impropriety (Johnson 2018); and David Yonggi Cho (Yoido Full Gospel Church, Seoul, Korea – the world's largest megachurch), who in early 2015 was sentenced to three years in prison for embezzling the equivalent of $12 million from his church (Morgan 2014). Buddenbaum (2013) summarizes the history of evangelical scandals, arguing that while older scenarios involved evangelicals acting scandalously "in spite of their faith" (such as megachurch leaders Aimee Semple McPherson and J. Frank Norris), more recent examples generate scandals by evangelicals "acting because of their faith" (referring primarily to the political manoeuvrings of the Religious Right, such as Chief Justice Roy Moore and Republican Tom DeLay). She concludes, "The acts of a few have, in recent years, tarnished the image of the many" (123).

Goodman (2010) reifies the celebrity scandal trope when he says, "The old law of tragedy says stars must fall. If the persona is the product, the person is the victim, swallowed up in the persona." When it comes to celebrity megachurch pastors, at least, scandal is not inevitable. As Hey (2013) suggests, there are ways to structure support and accountability that help prevent abuse and scandal. He mentions such practices as establishing strong ties with other congregations, denominations, and government agencies, increasing lay empowerment, and pursuing a transformational leadership model

(215, 276). Clergyman Brian Bork (2018) warns, however, "An evil that depends on a delusion will always resist being fully understood. It will also, if it so desires, find a way to evade the structural safeguards we put in its way." .

Some megachurch pastors can continue after a scandal, as the financial scandals of Charles Blair in the 1970s (Calvary Temple, Denver, Colorado) were forgiven by many followers (Ingold 2009), and more surprisingly Bishop Eddie Long (New Birth Missionary Baptist Church, Atlanta, Georgia), who, despite being divorced twice, charged with tax evasion and sexual misconduct with minors, remains the pastor of his megachurch, although with diminished attendance. An *Atlantic* journalist attended Long's church after some of the scandal erupted and concluded from the boisterous support of the audience that "there would be no disillusionment, no void in the spirit as Long was guilt proof" (Coates 2010).[26] While a core of followers may never turn from their charismatic leader, the tarnish of scandal usually does some lasting damage.[27] Vanderbloemen and Bird suggest the aphorism: "People will remember how you leave long after they forget what you did while you were there" (2014, 141).

Scott Thumma (1996) offers a careful analysis of the scandals that plagued Earl Paulk Jr at his Chapel Hill Harvester Church in Atlanta. He specifically emphasizes how Paulk's charismatic presence and rhetoric could no longer carry charismatic authority, as the latter is determined by recognition from followers, who were largely beginning to leave his church after receiving scandalous news about their pastor. "I came because of one man," said one staff member and singer in the worship band, "and now I'm leaving because of one man." Thumma concludes, "Paulk's charismatic vision could not have arisen without a supportive community; and neither could it be maintained in social isolation" (454). As I have maintained throughout this book, if supporting actors and audience turn away, the dramatic web of charisma falls apart.

People are intrigued by speculation about the psychology of megachurch scandals, and there is some literature on this (Willimon 2012; Starks 2013; Hey 2013). Is it simply that excessive power corrupts those who wield it? But only a minority of megachurch pastors are known to have abused their powers. Do all of them have a level of responsibility at which their competence exceeds their character, and their character collapses under the weight? This would be something to explore case by case and would be hard to ever measure accurately.

Could it be that leaders who start to burn out may opt to unconsciously self-sabotage as a way to quickly escape the role and its responsibilities? But that presents the question why many plead innocence or beg forgiveness in an attempt to be honourably reinstated in their role. I do not have a psychological theory that adequately explains why scandals happen. They occur in every sector of society, in all kinds of institutions, and suffice it to say power comes with many temptations. It could be that once you've seen one leadership scandal, you've seen one leadership scandal. My main point here is that megachurch scandal does not occur as often as it is publicly perceived to happen.

Some megachurch pastors actually leave the ministry by choice – not under the pressure of moral, financial, or criminal wrongdoing. While their charismatic authority is not dissolved by scandal, it is dissipated by their exit from both their congregation and the Christian ministry. While this remains a rare occurrence, examples include Allen Hunt (Mount Pigsah United Methodist Church, Atlanta, Georgia), who left his megachurch of 8,000 to focus on his radio show in 2007 and then converted to Catholicism in 2008 (Hunt 2010). In 2010 the wildly popular author Francis Chan left as senior pastor of Cornerstone Community Church, Ventura County, California, because he said he felt God calling him to work on developing a church planting movement. Another case would be Rob Bell (Mars Hill, Grandville, Michigan), who left his church after some controversy surrounding his latest book (*Love Wins* 2012) to produce a TV show in Hollywood (which failed to materialize). In his biography of Rob Bell, James Wellman reports that some say Bell's "charisma has passed" and his fifteen minutes of fame read at "14:45 and ticking" (2012, 59, 63). As we have established in earlier chapters, charisma develops from the nexus of several factors including audience recognition in the context of cultural crisis or uncertainty. Charismatic succession, like charisma itself, remains precarious, unpredictable, and potentially fleeting. Glassman (1975) examines briefly the notion of "de-charismatization" – when rationalistic and even cynical perspectives infect the enchantment that surrounds a particular leader, and the charismatic bond corrupts and fades. Charismatic authority comes with no guarantees, but with a team effort, a charismatic legacy may endure.

THE IRON BRAND

I want to entertain the opposite idea for a moment – that megachurch charisma is incredibly strong and may become its own trap. How strong are the bonds of this web – does an iron brand lie beneath the silk threads?

By "iron brand" I mean the solid and static nature of a corporate identity and its brand logo. "I am the brand," said pastor Mark Driscoll, and when he was dismissed, his church imploded and closed (Graham 2014). Celebrity mixes with Weberian charisma to make a potent blend. As I thought about TMH, its success in numbers, and Cavey's central role in its life and growth, I began to speculate about how difficult it would be for Cavey to either change or leave. In an interview I said to him that he has worked so hard to create this "irreligious" identity, it would be hard to move on from it. "For example," I went on, "it would be difficult if you cut your hair."

His long hair is emblematic of his "irreligious" brand and would seem difficult to change. Like his tattoo. It would disappoint many people. Thousands, perhaps. Likewise, if he were to resign and move to a new church. Small church pastors generally move from church to church through their career – many as often as every five to ten years. In fact, Thumma and Bird write, "The increasing tenure of the senior pastor is negatively related to spiritual vitality and a clear mission and purpose of the church" (2015, 12). After twenty years with an incumbent pastor, the stats show fewer megachurch attendees "strongly agree" their church is alive with purpose. Cavey's developed persona, however, seems too large and heavy for much mobility. He's become an institution, TMH brand, and even to some degree he has indelibly marked the small BIC denomination in Canada with his popular appeal and vision. It depends on him. If bureaucracy can become an iron cage, as Weber said, to mix metaphors, the dramatic web can become a gilded cage, a sparkling, frozen web. As Clifford Geertz said, "Man [sic] is an animal suspended in webs of significance he himself has spun" (Geertz 1977). Followers believe they have an intimate relationship with your persona, and it's meaningful and even vital to them. This calcifying of a brand is both different and the same as institutional hardening – it is difficult for a leader to alter or leave. The persona sticks in its own web of meanings. Attendee and public expectations are reluctant and slow to change.

"Everyone wants to be Cary Grant. Even I want to be Cary Grant," said Cary Grant (Preston 2005). But he could equally have lamented that he would rather not be cocooned into Cary Grant. The persona hardens and reifies after time, and it's hard to change the popular, recognized image. On another occasion Grant said, "I pretended to be somebody I wanted to be until finally I became that person. Or he became me."[28] A persona can colonize one's identity. The moral might be: Be careful what webs you spin. Spiders can get caught in their own web.

If I could speculate further, having spent some time thinking about evangelical celebrity, I wonder if media scandals might not be a way out of a reified image. It's hard to gently leave a well-developed and well-loved persona, especially one that presupposes a saintliness that the bearer knows disguises his or her true deficiency and defects. One might feel like a fraud, or at least confined and burdened by the sycophantic gaze. A courteous parting would not suffice for followers caught in a charismatic bond – the courtesy might even strengthen the bond. To simply alter a successful persona would be an equally delicate endeavour – followers have adored a familiar image they may not like to see change. In such as case, self-sabotage through crimes and misdemeanours could be a means of escape, an abrupt severing of a charismatic bond grown too burdensome. I further imagine that as much as these charismatic leaders long for escape, they are equally terrified of the uncertainty that lies beyond the bond with their followers, and so they fight to restore the image as soon as they risk losing it. They are loath to lose its popular cachet, its currency in the mediascape, its status. Like the hungry spider in its web, the charismatic bond provides food for them, and they know little other nourishment.

That said, I have demonstrated that scandals are relatively infrequent compared with other similar leadership professions. There are over 1,800 megachurches in North America, and 20 per cent of them had pastors over the age of sixty in 2015 (Thumma and Bird 2015). The dramatic web of charisma can be a comfortable place to rest – the silk threads I hope suggest something softer and perhaps more pliable than an iron brand, or the gilded cage, if these pastors are to transition well to their successors. Succession will be a significant issue in the coming years as more charismatic leaders move towards retirement.

THE END OF THE MEETING HOUSE

When Cavey retires, dies, or is deposed, it is mostly likely that TMH will follow some form of the second scenario I have suggested – a board process, guided by professional consultants, as there does not seem to be an heir apparent in the Cavey family. The overseers of TMH would take charge and begin a search or potentially give a mandate to a search committee for the task with the aid of a management consultant group. TMH would inevitably suffer a loss of membership, but this need not be equated with the dissolution of the church or all its regional sites.

In fact, a town hall meeting in June 2018 showed that now that Tim Day had left and Bruxy has rounded the age of fifty, one of four areas of strategic focus was "developing leaders." TMH leadership admit this was not a core strength of TMH, but they will begin to give more attention to the matter. Cavey himself said that night that he imagines retirement around the year 2030, and they need to think backwards from that point. His new slogan, "From one church in many locations to one family, many expressions" suggests an option for TMH would be to turn all the sites into separate church plants under TMH brand. Time will tell.

Close observers of megachurches seem to agree that there is no formula for megachurch pastor succession, but it can be a relatively smooth and healthy transition if planned carefully well ahead of time. Thumma and Travis say the key factor is "the former senior pastor's willingness to give up power, status, and a prominent public role within the worship life of the church" (2007, 75). Wheeler (2008) explains how a "relay succession" (called "intentional overlap" by Bird 2014a) was the plan with all three of his case studies of megachurch leadership transition, and they provided important mentoring for a "home-grown" successor and significant continuity and stability for the congregation. Vanderbloemen and Bird (2014) make numerous suggestions, including helping the former pastor find a new identity, giving the congregation time to grieve the loss of their beloved leader, cultivating internal candidates who have had some training elsewhere, and encouraging the new leader to honour the former pastor and his family.

Vanderbloemen and Bird (2014, 36) offer Larry Osborne (North Coast Church, Vista, California) as their role model for successful succession planning. Osborne inherited a small church plant from a friend in 1980 and grew it to megachurch size, with 11,000 people in attendance at four different sites in 2013. Nurturing a culture of leadership development, Osborne set a standard for his subordinate leaders by creating a preaching team and an executive team of senior pastor peers. One particular teaching pastor, Chris Brown, is seventeen years younger than Osborne and has been teaching as often as Osborne has. North Coast Church is the model church, not because it has a succession plan on paper, but because replication of leadership and its distributed character has been built into the culture of the church at every level, preparing it for almost any kind of leadership transition.

The anti-cult scares of the 1960s and 1970s linger in the media and transfer onto discussions of the charismatic leaders of megachurches in North America. I have demonstrated that rather than the myth of totalizing power over their followers, the charismatic leaders of megachurches suffer different kinds of dramaturgical trouble, and this stems from weaknesses in the charismatic leader, anxieties about the group's over-dependence on a single leader, media criticism, and nervousness about approaching leadership succession. Yet the impending death of the prophet does not likely entail the disbanding of the group – for there are many likely scenarios that result in the continuation and eventual expansion of the church. As a case study, the Meeting House demonstrates that the routinization of charisma expands in parallel to charismatic authority – through teamwork and dedicated staff, and the church most likely will continue long after Bruxy Cavey has retired, died, or been removed from his position of leadership. The dramatic web of charisma is fragile, but it's also flexible and sticky, and easily re-spun.

9

Epilogue

Reflecting on Reflexive Evangelicals

I want to convince you that irony, poker-faced silence, and fear of ridicule are distinctive of those features of contemporary U.S. culture ... that enjoy any significant relation to the television whose weird pretty hand has my generation by the throat. I'm going to argue that irony and ridicule are entertaining and effective, and that at the same time they are agents of a great despair and stasis in U.S. culture.

David Foster Wallace

Our devotion, after all, *takes form*. We're standing in it, walking through it, breathing it, holding it. What shall we do with it? Is it worthy?

David Dark

"I'm considering getting Hebrews 8:13 on my other arm," writes Cavey in jest in his second book (2017, 5). This would help explain the Leviticus 19:28 tattoo on his left arm. The Hebrews text says, "By calling this covenant 'new,' he has made the first one obsolete; and what is obsolete and outdated will soon disappear." In other words, ancient Old Testament rules from Leviticus like "Don't wear tattoos" are null and void after Jesus Christ. Cavey emphasizes the discontinuities between testaments, at times characterizing the Old Testament as "religious."[1] The new covenant offers freedom from the old rules, and with such freedom preachers can have as many tattoos as they like. In Cavey's case, the tattoos may even be Bible texts that create an inter-testamental dialogue across his body. Such tension is his brand.

At the heart of TMH is Cavey's body, an icon of the retro-hippie culture, and branded with his ironic tattoo. He is the unclerical pastor leading a movie theatre–based church in a subversive mission to eradicate "religion." It all plays in paradox, even a performative contradiction, and it cultivates ambivalence not just in its attendees, but also in myself, the researcher. In what follows I want to investigate some of those ambivalences and engage a few lingering questions. What is the future of reflexive evangelicalism, and those within it who tend to satire and irony? Am I assuming this "irreligious" drama is just a "show"? Do people at TMH really grow and change for the common good? Can there be religion without rules? And finally, if evangelical faith dances with consumerist practices and spaces, who takes the lead?

REFLEXIVE EVANGELICAL FUTURES

My research is centred on a case study of one church, but this church is an indicator of a broader movement. James K.A. Smith in his book *How (Not) to Be Secular* (2014) captures the cultural movement: "Faith is fraught; confession is haunted by an inescapable sense of its contestability. We don't believe instead of doubting; we believe while doubting. We're all Thomas now." Smith claims the secular mind is haunted by faith, and the heart of the faithful is haunted by doubt. I began this book talking about the self-consciousness of religious belief and the desire of many North Americans to avoid the fundamentalisms that claim certainty without a doubt – whether atheist or religious. This entails shunning the hard-line liberal or conservative camps. Is there a third way?

Donald Trump has exacerbated the ambivalence of evangelicals for their own species of faith. Some are angry, some are defensive, and many are embarrassed. What I call reflexive evangelicals eschew this spoiled identity and are searching for a way out, a redemption of their reputation and status. The Meeting House pursues the route of iconoclastic repudiation, promising conservative Christians a way out towards a more culturally hip identity as "irreligious" followers of a subversive Jesus. They do this mostly through satire, and the playfulness of paradox and irony, epitomized by the vision of a charismatic leader, Bruxy Cavey.

Where do they go next? Some suggest divesting themselves of the name "evangelical" and using a new label, like "Red Letter Christian" will solve the identity crisis. Campolo and Claiborne (2016) suggest highlighting the words of Jesus, as a "red letter" Bible does, will keep the faith focused on the Beatitudes and parables and less on political machinations. Others claim it's a canon within the canon – a selective approach to the scriptures and too narrow a focus for the faithful.

The idea of a "third way" seems broader and more inclusive, but the decision of what lies beyond the current evangelical identity crisis may lie in other hands. Campolo and Claiborne further declare the future of evangelicalism lies no longer with "old white men" but with other ethnic leaders and their faith communities. This is certainly true, as the majority world continues to swell with Pentecostal fervour and the West continues to cultivate a growing demographic of religious "nones." Reflexivity may give way to something more ecstatic, more enchanted, and possibly more attentive to such things as healing, spiritual warfare, and miracles. This is, incidentally, the kind of faith that Cavey deconverted from in his twenties.

A SEASON OF IRONY

I have made numerous plays in this book on the motto "church for people not into church" substituting religion, megachurch, evangelicalism, institutions, and Anabaptism for "church." TMH is also pacifism for those into horror movies, and satire for those not into anger. The list of creative tensions and performative contradictions is long and often embraced.

Satire and its complement of irony are as old as humour, but some consider the culture of the 1990s to have been more substantially ironic.[2] David Foster Wallace associates "postmodernism's rebellious irony" with white male fiction writers nurtured by television and the "rebellious youth culture" of the sixties and seventies. "For irony – exploding the gaps between what's said and what's meant, between how things try to appear and how they really are – is the time-honoured way artists seek to illuminate and explode hypocrisy" (1993, 182). This describes well Cavey's drive to expose the anger, violence, and political ambitions of groups claiming to follow a Jesus he claims was all about love and peace.

Wallace, however, is critical of the self-referential irony that saturates popular culture. "What do you do when postmodern rebellion become a pop-cultural institution?" he asks. He mentions Burger King and Chrysler ads that urge the consumer to "break the rules" and then adds, "If rulelessness becomes the rule, then protest and change become not just impossible but incoherent." Irony can be tiresome, he claims. "It's not a mode that wears especially well" and in fact, "make no mistake, irony tyrannizes us" (183).

Irony assumes a lost ideal, and it serves a prophetic function. But it has a season, after which it becomes weary, cynical, and even nihilistic. Wallace yearns for "anti-rebels" who move beyond cleverness to risk some sort of reverence, eschewing self-consciousness and fatigue. This may be a second naivety, a new earnestness on the other side of ironic critique and disillusionment. Something beyond the self-referential universe of television and the hyperlinks of the internet that nurtures hope and an ambition for public responsibility to care for "common things" (Purdy 1999).

I do not expect Anabaptists to run for political office,[3] but there is something they certainly offer to cultivate and enrich civil society. Canadians, more so than Americans, do look first to their government to solve social issues, but the mediating institutions of churches, neighbourhood societies, charitable organizations, and other associations can promise a better life than private cynicism nurtured by permanent residency in an endless electronic labyrinth. Common things, like friendly, interactive neighbourhoods, a healthy natural environment, and public accessibility to the arts require a sense of civic responsibility that lies beyond an ironic attitude.

I believe Cavey has some awareness of the limits of irony, as his second book (2017b) takes more risks to dwell more positively on his faith and theology. Deconstructive play, if it is to be true to its ideals, should move toward a season of reconstruction. Charisma cannot merely destroy the old regime and identity; it must be more than rhetorical, and it must provide followers with a way out to a promised land, a new identity and purpose. Cavey's denominational connections offer him some tools here, and while denominations add bureaucratic rules, they also provide a stabilizing tradition, the two other authorities that Weber contrasted with charismatic authority. These other sources of authority help routinize the charisma and decentre Cavey for the future another generation anticipates but that he will not see.

IS IT ALL JUST A SHOW?

Why did I use drama as a frame for my analysis? I could have just described TMH without putting it into theatrical terms. But this was a strategy on my part, first of all to communicate something about religion and charisma, two closely related subjects. The persons committed to this church are not dedicated to its mission out of intellectual conviction alone. People devote themselves to what they love, and what they love has intrigued them in such a way that, for much of the relationship, they operate under a suspension of disbelief. Their imagination has been enchanted by a performance that wants to make a certain impression about the world and to the world. They are caught up in this drama, and take a role, play their part in its evolving conflict and resolution, following and improvising on the script they are given. This is not just a world view, it's a way of acting in the world, participating in its tragic ("religion") and comic (Jesus's spirituality) twists.

Theatre is also an exchange, and while an audience can passively consume the show, in interactive theatre, the audience actually contributes to the drama, adding to its meaning and innovating its themes. Charisma is not simply the downloading of ideas, but the recruitment of actors for the magnification and dissemination of the drama. A dramatic web requires a trusted team of dedicated followers who model the new identity and build confidence in their leader. It is not a one-man show.

I am wary that the reader may erroneously assume I am suggesting megachurches are "just a show" and that their leaders' convictions are "just an act." Goffman's writings have been accused of promoting a view of humans as cynical manipulators, and I have argued elsewhere that this was not the case for Goffman, and neither is it the case at the Meeting House (Schuurman 2016, 67). I do not suggest the opposite – a naive view that all religion at megachurches is sincere, unpretentious, and done in good faith, but I try to keep the scope of action open to the full range of human aspiration and failure; religious drama can be manipulative, but it can also cultivate the better parts of our humanity, and sometimes it can be quite ironic and playful. A performance, if nothing else, is play. Drama is a metaphor for human action, although human action can be more or less intentionally dramatic.

Cavey sometimes displays a knowingness about this paradox of "irreligious" religion, which some may interpret as duplicity. He insists that his idiosyncratic, pejorative definition of religion as a systemic effort to "earn salvation" makes the paradox sincere and the paradoxical slogan of the church prophetic. Yet his tongue is often in his cheek, too, so it's hard to believe his mischievousness has any hard boundaries. There is something of the trickster in his approach. This is not a church for literalists.

DOES TMH CHANGE PEOPLE?

A Willow Creek Church study concluded that their church activities did not significantly influence spiritual growth and that 25 per cent of their constituents were "stalled" or "dissatisfied" with their spiritual growth (Hawkins, Parkinson, and Arnson 2007). Leaders said in response that "one-size-fits-all" does not work for everyone and they needed to encourage more individually customized spiritual disciplines. Still, if 75 per cent of attendees are reporting some personal growth, that suggests at least one megachurch is creating an adequate environment for some degree of spiritual transformation.

One of my contentions throughout the book is that reflexive churches like TMH offer a third space, a playful, liminal space, "betwixt-and-between" that offers opportunity for personal transformation, and that at TMH this transformation is towards the image of the subversive, peace-loving Jesus that Cavey preaches. The reader might well ask, "Well, does it work?" I already give an assessment of the life of Home Churches in chapter 5. The question here is, Do individual attendees come to embrace the radically simple, generous, "irreligious" life?

Ultimately, TMH is a place that welcomes all people curious about their mission, and they can be in any stage of growth and change. People are always changing towards some end, and the variables involved in change are part of an open system. It's hard to measure personal change and its roots, although people can offer a subjective self-assessment. One standard question I asked in the interviews was "How has TMH changed you?"

The responses were predictably varied. "It got me excited about opening up the Bible again," said a graduate philosophy student with a background in theology. A service worker in a hotel told me TMH showed him he can be accepted for his faith in Christ and not on the basis of doctrinal alignment. A young woman whose husband never comes with her to church said Cavey helped her face her doubts. She came from a background with lots of judgment, and he's eased her worries, allowed her to be honest with herself. An undergraduate student whose parents she described as "non-Christians" said that Cavey helped her see the intellectual side of faith as well as its applicability in everyday life. It also taught her to "completely debunk religion." This last testimony was frequent, suggesting that the message was getting through.

Growth and regression both happen in any church. One series Cavey taught suggested his "irreligious" message was being conveniently misinterpreted. "Licence to Sin" (February/March 2011) focused on the first letter to the Corinthians and how the recipients of the letter pushed the boundaries of God's grace, using it as a licence to sin. "Getting drunk? Sleeping around? Free and easy divorce?" asks Cavey in his introduction to the series. This was the state of the church in Corinth, and in part, an attitude Cavey wanted to address in his own church. Cavey suggested at one point that his anti-religious gospel, calling people beyond the rules and rituals of a system, was being abused by a few Corinthian-like people who did "whatever made them happy," overlooking the "devastating impact of sin."

When I asked attendees if they were coming to identify as Anabaptist or pacifist, the most common answer was in the negative. One member of the executive leadership team acknowledged this, explaining that the BIC connection was "family business ... and the allegiance [from attendees] is just not there." She went on to argue, however, that most attendees still unconsciously carry some of the heritage with them: "The values of simplicity, the values of peace, the values of community that Jesus permeated – that, I think, is what deeply resonates with people. Which is all the right stuff to deeply resonate with."

My interviews broadly confirm she makes a pertinent point. The attendees I talked to would mention that Cavey had provoked them to think more deliberately about their views on pacifism, as well as other BIC core values such as voluntarism, simplicity, community, and generosity. For example, one middle-aged woman I interviewed had her children leaving the house for college, and they decided to downsize to a smaller house. She narrated this as an application of the simplicity teachings she and her husband had recently absorbed at TMH. She did not self-identify as Anabaptist, but some of the Anabaptist themes had influenced her behaviour.

My study did not focus on the "compassion" work of this church, and I did not extensively observe and catalogue all the different ways in which people serve, sacrifice, and contribute to (or ignore) their communities and the needs of the world beyond. Wilford (2012) concludes that Rick Warren's megachurch reinforces the individualistic structures of post-suburban life. Elisha (2011), however, follows what he calls "socially engaged evangelicals" in two Kentucky megachurches to argue "American evangelicalism cannot and should not be reduced categorically to notions of individualism" (21). Inside these megachurches he discerned an ambition rooted in "the kingdom of God" that presses members to "expand their cultural influence and authority" (212) and "complicate (but not completely erase) the conventional boundaries of religion and secularity" (220). This suggests social action beyond charity, a participation in wider culture that goes beyond paralyzed ambivalence or an inward-focused ecclesial feudal order that cares only for its own.

LEADERLESS MYTHS

This book is not a manual on "how to build a megachurch like TMH." It should appear in the library catalogue under reflexive evangelicalism and charismatic leadership, not under church growth literature. But even charismatic leadership as a rubric can be misleading, as I argue that it is more an unfolding cooperative dramatic event than the story of a singular figure's power, personality, and vision. There is no simple recipe to follow in this understanding of a church that grows numerically, for it involves the serendipitous confluence of a variety of factors, including the audience, the staff, and a cultural crisis of some sort. You can't plan for a successful megachurch.

As I said earlier, reflexive evangelicals are shy about their megachurches, if they have one at all. We saw in chapter 6 how wary Meeting House staff are about being perceived as a "cult" and so they downplay the significance of Cavey. Some church growth literature, called the "missional church" movement,[4] eschews the romance of a charismatic leader. They distinguish their ecclesiology from the church growth megachurch models. It critiques the "CEO leader who takes charge, sets growth goals, and targets 'turnaround congregations' ... rooted in the North American myth of the heroic, charismatic personality" (Roxburgh, Romanuk, and Gibbs, 2006, 27). Instead, missional leadership cultivates an environment in which people can imagine and follow what they perceive God is already doing in their local community (29; Sparks, Soerens, and Friesen 2010). Such leadership orients itself not at growth, strategy, or charisma as much as the needs and opportunities for holistic ministry in the local neighbourhood (Roxburgh 2013).

Wouldn't a truly reflexive evangelical, weary of the media-hyped scandals and Elmer Gantry stereotype, pursue a *leaderless* evangelicalism, a faith without celebrity? Emerging Church Movement discussions share a "missional" foundation for leadership but orient themselves to postmodern culture as much as local community, emphasizing a broader socially active "kingdom theology" rather than numerical church growth (Bielo 2011, 138–56). They begin with an aversion not only to CEO models of leadership but modern hierarchy, control, and patriarchy in general (Morgenthaler 2007), symbolically taking collaborative Dorothy as an icon in opposition to the expert authority of the Wizard of Oz (McLaren and Campolo 2003, 141–51). Pushing off from bad experiences with controlling charismatic leadership in their past and inspired by the 1960s counterculture, these Generation-X pastors experimented with democratic, collaborative, rotating, and even "leaderless" forms of group leadership that focus on a person's particular passion, gifting, or the nature of a task rather than a specific person and position (Gibbs and Bolger 2005, 191–215). This brand of pastor pursues more of a facilitative role than a directive one, which may mirror the academic socialization that many emerging attendees have experienced, as they tend to have higher education levels than the average evangelical church (Marti and Ganiel 2014, 23). Leaders are not some hired know-it-alls, but fellow travellers who arise from the group and vulnerably share their brokenness with others in compelling ways (Burke 2003, 35–45). If church growth specialists value the decisive visionary leader, the Emerging Church communities groom leaders for humility, thoughtfulness, genuineness, and warmth (Marti and Ganiel 2014, 118). Cavey embraces much of this kind of discourse.

Still, many have learned that the leaderless ideal can cause frustration, and unspoken forms of leadership inevitably develop (Gibbs and Bolger 2005, 198). Packard explains that while they have a democratic, egalitarian vision, Emerging Church pastors' charismatic authority casts a "long shadow" on their congregations, and often in the push-and-pull of congregational life "power is still very much connected to status in the organization" (2012, 117–18). Some leaders exude a "guru-like quality" that attracts the crowd in the first place, such that members declare they would be lost without their leader (Marti and Ganiel 2014, 118–19). Some Emerging Church leaders, such as Peter Rollins, take on the role of intellectual celebrity, as he draws deeply on philosophers such as Jacques Derrida, John Caputo, and Slavoj Žižek (Marti and Ganiel 2014, 169). In other words, the anti-modern, often negative identity of the Emerging Church does not always provide clear alternatives to what it seeks to transcend.

D.G. Hart says evangelicalism can never become a tradition, because celebrity cannot be handed down (2004, 185), but he overlooks not only the tendency to routinize charisma (and successes such as Aimee Semple McPherson's Foursquare Church), but also how large personalities played vital roles in many religious traditions, including Calvinism, Lutheranism, Mormonism, and Buddhism. American evangelicalism is not distinguished only by celebrity personalities, but as much by the particularly American quality of those personalities – championing revolution, innovation, expansion, and marketing while bureaucratizing the movement. In Canada this legacy is a more tempered evangelical performance, due to a smaller religious marketplace and stronger ties to historical denominations. But it is not a passing phenomenon.

If anything, I would venture that the proliferation of the megachurch offers a new structure to Protestantism, a new ecclesial feudalism. Megachurches can dominate the religious landscape of a region and draw a wide diversity of people into their institutional shelter with its dramatic web and accompanying offerings of teaching and ministry. They may also offer services and inspiration to smaller local churches rather than simply be the big box competition. In fact, megachurches in the same region, like TMH and Oakville HBC, can become feudal competitors. Megachurches are the home for religious refugees and free agents, and they often offer a strong, culturally savvy Christian identity for a post-denominational, electronically networked age. Reflexive evangelicals may join them, but mostly with an ironic sensibility about their membership.

BAD RELIGION, BAD RELATIONSHIP

My reflections so far have reviewed the themes of reflexivity, irony, drama, and charismatic leadership, and now I turn to religion. What is the "religion" to which we have become so allergic? "Religion" has become a bad word, a curse upon the land. "Relationship," on the other hand, conjures coffee with friends. However, religion, anthropologically speaking, is a way of life consisting of creeds, codes, cultus, and community (Albanese 2008). Popularly, it refers to belief in aligning oneself with God or the gods. In this sense, reflexive evangelical churches are as "religious" as any other Christian congregation, Hindu temple, or, arguably, fan club for a sports team.

Religion (from the Latin *religare*) literally means "to bind again, to re-tie." This could mean bondage or bonding, and the ambiguity is accurate. Religion can be a trap, but it can also be connection. In other words, religion *is* relationship. Good religion in Christian terms is a liturgy that heightens a sense of our interdependence and nurtures peace with our divine, human, and creaturely connections. Bad religion is what Cavey identifies: judgmental, legalistic, and bent on procuring its own justification.

This etymological exploration also assumes then, that "relationship" – even "pure relationship" – can be both bondage and bonding, hurt or healing, distance or intimacy. Communities like Home Church and Huddles can also carry toxic, suffocating, or exhausting intimate relationships. People thrive when they cultivate the right boundaries, bridges, and bonds for their personal growth and service in church and society.

So the religion/relationship dichotomy is a false one, but it has its rhetorical purposes and in an age of institutional skepticism, where residential school memories are fresh, sexual abuse by priests frequents the headlines, and moralistic preachers have their own television stations. In the face of this, evangelical leaders like Cavey want to self-define, shaking up the categories, and that means using words idiosyncratically, like *religion* and *irreligion*. He is not alone. Religion as oppressive, evil, violent, hypocritical has become cliché.

At the core of this discussion, *much depends upon one's definition of religion*. In his second appendix Cavey (2007) warns people through the words of 2 Timothy 2:14 to "stop fighting over words" and focus on his message, not his definition of religion. People who are emotionally bonded to certain words are caught in a "linguistic idolatry" of pseudo-academic debates rather than love. Focus on meaning, not terminology; listen to the heart, not the semantics of the conversation.

I understand the prophetic colour of Cavey's vision and I did not quarrel with Cavey or any attendees about this "irreligious" approach during my study of the church. It has been a place of healing for many who are disaffected with Christianity and church. In rejecting "religion" they are really shunning the judgmentalism, legalism, works righteousness, and angry tones of blustery evangelicalism and instead focus on God's grace to those seeking, hurting, and questioning. Their rhetoric is evangelistically strategic and comes in the context of a specific culture of disdain towards especially conservative forms of Christian faith.

Yet words like *religion* matter, as they open, steer, trap, and reshape the imagination. Taking the pejorative definition of religion too religiously can be confusing, and misconstrue the life of others. I note that Roman Catholics tend to be much more defensive about "religion" – as they understand it as referring more directly to the Church herself. Some atheists and social scientists understand "irreligion" to be a form of naturalistic philosophy, and dictionaries define it as an indifference, rejection of or hostility towards religion – meaning belief in a God or gods.

The "irreligious" approach becomes additionally problematic insofar as it downplays both the formative and sacramental role of religion, rituals, and rules. James K.A. Smith (2016b) maintains that religion, as rituals, rites, and regulations, is not only an *expressive* practice, but a *formative* practice as well. That is to say, all of life is liturgy (or drama, if you will), and our liturgical practices shape our desires towards certain telos or ends. Rituals train people to love particular objects. They become the habits of the heart and participate in human spiritual growth or corruption.[5] Again, relationship and ritual are in an intricate, reciprocal, inseparable dialectic.

This transparent acknowledgment of the liturgies of life can be a refreshing embrace of one's deepest allegiances. One young man mentioned earlier had been a worship leader and musician in the Meeting House for almost ten years, but he became disillusioned with "irreligion" and joined the Anglicans (and was even leaning towards the Roman Catholic tradition). What he said bears repeating: "I want something with roots, and you know, sense of history, and tradition. And actually I want ritual, and I want religion, and maybe we might interpret it different ways, but you know I actually want that stuff. I want my imagination formed, and I want to spend some connection with the past. And yes, I want religion, maybe not as you might find it, but that's what I want."

There was something missing at TMH that he felt he needed and in fact longed for. Theologically speaking, as prophetically necessary as it is to denounce religion, religion is still an inescapable priestly vehicle for spiritual formation and transformation. Religion is not only opposed to relationship, it also depends on relationship: to the divine and to others, both in the present and past.

Cavey knows all this, and he has chosen his idiosyncratic definition as a rhetorical strategy and, because he believes the weight of biblical material on the subject favours his view, he leans towards his pejorative definition. He says his vocation lies with seekers, and that means starting with their spiritual location. But as David Dark persuasively argues in his small book *Life's Too Short to Pretend You're Not Religious* (2016) that, being the self-deceptive creatures we are, we tend in our minds to save the undesirable forms of religion to refer to *someone else's* religion and we can avoid awareness of our own messy allegiances, our "unexamined liturgies" (180). "I'm never not being religious," he writes, "We're all in it ... We are never not worshipping in one way or another" (178–9). He insists, "Your religion is your witness is the shape your love takes. In all things" (23).

Over-using the "evil religion" cliché can prevent us from being fully alive to our own liturgies. Now it's clear that TMH has many distinctive Christian practices including communion, love feasts, simple living, tithes, baptism, and musical worship. But because of their "irreligious" theme and infrastructure, they also practise going to the mall each Sunday, buying their Starbucks coffee, sitting in movie theatres, watching movie clips from celebrity-studded films during the teaching time, and often eating out afterwards at the food court or East Side Mario's. Similarly, TMH has a rigorously timed service schedule, complete with a countdown to the starting time displayed on the big screen; these services are as predictable, efficient, and calculated as any movie theatre experience. Such routines train attendees in a way that reinforces their training in other consumer experiences, even if the teaching instructs otherwise. Much of this can operate at odds with the other Christian spiritual practices mentioned above, especially when there is no attempt made to reshape and transform the wider cultural institutions they inhabit. The malls are used instrumentally, more as familiar space for evangelistic outreach than as space to be reshaped for the common good. So the practices of passive consumption become rival liturgies mixed with church liturgies. Granted, such tensions affect every North American religious person and organization today (Slagle 2011). We are all in it, but the question is one of awareness, confession, and strategic retraining.

Attending church at the mall may not feel "religious," because it lacks such significant symbols as a cross, a communion table, or an open Bible, but it also misses the best imaginative work that these symbols – and other Christian symbolic alternatives – can muster.

Malls have their own "religious" symbols – the brand names and logos revered by their consumer attendants. But if religion is ritual and ritual shapes the heart by the spirit that animates that ritual, architecture matters. Some say architecture always has the last word. Symbols, structures, and routines shape our desires in mostly tacit, unconscious ways (Smith 2016b). We may end up wanting things we would not think we want. Or thinking we want things that we do not really want anymore, deep down. Meeting in a movie theatre carries and nurtures unintended meanings and practices.

I am not suggesting Cavey rearrange his vocabulary, but I do think championing both trajectories of "religion" more transparently will intensify the paradox and the creative tension in which he takes such delight. This is the paradox articulated in a deeper and more intense way: religion – as an everyday liturgy, including my own – can be a burdensome legalism and xenophobic chauvinism, and the same religion offers an opportunity for training in virtue and cosmopolitanism. Religion can be constraint, but also a beautiful, playful constraint (Morgan and Barden 2015) that could also be seen as a jig – a device that guides action to help it move smoothly (Smith 2016a). To the degree that reflexive evangelicals deny their religious and institutional character, they lean to a negative identity, a countercultural stereotype and short-sighted neglect for structures that can be a scaffold for human flourishing.

Cavey claims to stand outside "religion" and the constraints and artifice of institutions – he is the characteristic cool "outsider" who satirizes and critiques with prophetic authenticity (Hale 2011). The irony of his ironic attitude, however, is that irony has become mainstream – the counterculture has become the dominant culture, and postured authenticity has become a market commodity (Purdy 2000; Heath and Potter 2005; Gilmore and Pine II 2007; Potter 2011). To build and preserve institutions within a long-term commitment to their sustainability – this would be a true challenge to mainstream consumer culture.

In sum, I am arguing that reflexive evangelicals who embrace this polemical approach to religion are at their best when they fully recognize their paradoxical, if not contradictory, stance. This is especially true for a megachurch – embracing their anti-institutional bureaucratic nature, their tradition-spurning traditions, and the rules of their anti-ritualistic ethos. Being radical has its own rules and rituals, and embracing the ordinariness of institutional stewardship at the same time one denounces oppressive routine can increase social capital and human flourishing (Horton 2014). In theological terms, this means intentionally embracing not only prophetic roles against religion, but the priestly religious roles they already exemplify in sacrament and service.

This prompts a re-examination of what might be meant by "the end of religion" in the Canadian context. If there is an end to religion in this millennium, it's not the end of religiosity or religious institutions, but the end of Christendom in Canada, the end of Christian privilege, authority, and even legitimacy; this includes the end of faith as an appendage to citizenship, the end of church as denominational silos, the end of giant bureaucratic centralized religious institutions as the dominant religious presence in the country, and the end of faith as merely intellectual consent. Diane Butler Bass has said the goal is to see the world as it is, not as it was, for the old jig is up; Christianity as we knew it does not work anymore. It has failed (2012, 36). At least it has failed in its nationalistic forms. The Christian Church, in order to thrive, constantly needs a fresh drama to play into its shifting context, and currently a drama that intensifies the paradox of "irreligious" religion may have more truly countercultural use, if liquid consumer modernity is to be resisted. Religion destroys life; religion offers new life. It is our fractured response to a muffled presence; it is a broken hallelujah.

THE FUTURE OF THE MEETING HOUSE

Success brings many challenges. At TMH, attendee mobility remains high, as many come and go without making deep investments in the fabric of the church, while a smaller number give immensely of their time and energy to keep the quality of community high. I am told that in the last twenty years up to 2016 there are over 33,000 email addresses gathered on their email list. The core group of faithful followers and staff could burn out, especially as change seems to be constant and at times very intense. Another issue is the whiteness of the church, even at regional sites located in deeply diverse ethnic communities such as Brampton and Toronto. The disjuncture between the church and its surrounding demographics has been a matter of internal discussion, but until 2017 I noted there was only sporadic talk of addressing these anomalies.[6] Additionally, some members were agitating for more specialized programming, as Young Adult Home

Churches had begun to spring up, as well as a number of "unofficial" Home Churches, including one composed of LGBT persons not fully in agreement with TMH's stance on same-sex marriage.

The site pastors were generally male, with a few exceptions. Christa Hesselink was site pastor at Brampton and Waterloo for a time, and another female became site pastor at East Hamilton in 2012. This second female pastor came out publicly as a lesbian in 2014 through a video broadcast during a summer teaching, declaring her long-time celibacy and the supportive embrace she felt by TMH. Leadership explained to me that TMH was open to hiring more female pastors, as Cavey champions the "egalitarian" gender ethic of the church; Tim Day, however, explained to me that qualified female candidates formed only a tiny pool of applicants. That soon changed after the bulk of my research was complete.[7]

As with any church, there were staff tensions, personnel changes, and other growing pains. Numerous leaders and pastors have come and gone in Cavey's two-decade tenure and the executive level structure, like that of the rest of its labour force, has constantly changed. Currently in 2018, a trio of senior pastors shifted into place – Cavey, Darryl Winger, and Rod Tombs – all who had functioned at the executive level in some way for many years. Looking at the big picture, the organization has had its share of growing pains and internal conflicts but has yet to experience any significant division or scandal.

Research suggests that a charismatic leader's propensity to be disconnected from the day-to-day operations of the organization could create a bifurcation at some point that may be hard to bridge. Johnson (1992, 5) calls this the emergence of "two worlds" – one of the followers and one of the leader and his inner circle. Charismatic leaders like Cavey best keep in lock-step with their executive team and resist the inclination to be a guru by the mountain only who speaks on Sundays, reads books, engages social media, and travels on speaking tours. Most importantly, if Cavey's charismatic authority is to be passed on beyond his own persona, he will need to strategize about internal leadership development. Cavey has a poor reputation in this regard, and if his legacy is to reach beyond his own celebrity, the active mentoring of a new generation of leaders would be an essential task. Some recent shifts in 2017–18 seem to move in this direction – towards Cavey's closer involvement with administration and internal leadership development.

The routinization of charisma requires a delicate balance between centralization/consolidation and flexibility/creativity. Hey (2013) calls this the balance between innovation and institutionalization the most significant challenge for the sustainability of megachurches. Cavey would call it the challenge of confining religion over against the movement of the Spirit. The point is, the Meeting House can become its own worst monster, and switching metaphors, as mentioned above, Cavey himself can become confined to a web he himself has spun. Would he shut down TMH if it became too institutionalized? How would he measure that, and what process would guide such a decision? Institutions have an inertia that cannot be suddenly collapsed on a whim.

What does the future hold for TMH? The relationship between TMH and the BIC seems strong, as the BIC in Canada, which doubled in size by 2007 because of the swelling of TMH, has become independent in polity and name from its larger American sibling. There is some momentum and a synergy between the two organizations that is changing the BIC culture across Canada (Schuurman 2014). The relationship between TMH and other megachurches and para-church organizations continues to evolve. New regional sites continue to be added every year. The overall attendance numbers have plateaued, with only slight increases as new regional sites are added. What organizational culture and enduring legacy of Christian identity will settle into this network of communities remains unclear, but it promises to be a distinctive and significant contribution to religious landscape of southern Ontario.

Scholars such as Martin Marty have predicted for over two decades that megachurches, as a fad in evangelical congregational culture, would soon fade from the North American landscape (Marty 1995, 2010). The dramatic web of charisma that animates most megachurches may be as fragile as it is sticky, but there are many ways in which a pastor's vision can be routinized by followers. In short, if megachurches are indeed a compelling drama co-produced by leader and follower that brings meaning, purpose, and "festive flair" to followers' lives in the midst of cultural tension, megachurches as religious organizations are not just a passing fad or vulnerable personality cult, but a viable and likely enduring North American religious institution.

PROPHETIC PLAY AT THE MOVIES

Evangelical charismatic leaders have a dubious reputation – some of it well deserved, some of it bad press, and some of it due to the perpetuation of the Elmer Gantry stereotype in both popular and academic writing on the megachurch. Shysters, frauds, and other preying pastors and "profit" figures seem like a trope (Chidester 2005), as in the movies *Leap of Faith* (1992) and *Megachurch Murder* (2015). Furthermore, the megachurch institution has been narrowly characterized as "the cruise ship" of congregational life (Jethani 2014), McDonaldized church (Drane 2009), "capitalism's cathedral" (Maddox 2012), and "the 800-pound gorilla in the voting booth" (Einstein 2007). One of my goals was to problematize these caricatures by showing how at least one evangelical leader can be reflexive in addressing this inherited legacy and protest rigid, negative expectations for evangelical life.

Cowan (2008) has argued that against the fallacy that religion is "good, decent, and moral" in order to disabuse readers of the assumption that religion by nature occupies some ethical high ground. In light of Hitchens (2009) and other new atheists, it may be necessary to also posit a "bad, poisonous, and violent" fallacy with regards to the nature of religion. After my fieldwork at TMH, however, I am struck by common assumptions about the necessary "seriousness" of religion – what might be called the "serious, strict, and sacred" fallacy, and how that denies the celebratory, silly, romantic, or satirical religiosity I witnessed. This assessment echoes older claims in the sociology of religion that explore a close connection between religion and play, claiming that religion, at heart, must refresh people for the ordinary work of their lives, and that within the origins of ritual is a form of play that harbours a signal transcendence, the echo a forgotten voice, the rumours of angels (Berger 1970).

What does this assertion of playful religion mean for the image of the prophet, protesting with righteous anger? The prophet figure is well recognized in the study of religion, as he is basic to many traditions (Heschel 1972; Brueggemann 2001). To use Judeo-Christian examples, the ancient Hebrew prophets railed against idolatry and injustice and called people to return to faithfulness and service to God. Mohammad follows a mission with some overlapping concerns. More recently the iconic Martin Luther King Jr denounced institutionalized racism and oppression against blacks in America and championed the civil and human rights of all people. The prophetic figure garners popular admiration and scholarly approbation even while attracting disdain and dismissal from those invested in business-as-usual. The prophet, however, is usually a serious, if not grave figure.

The serious prophet's foil is the shyster, the fraud, the Elmer Gantry-type who preys upon the hopes and fears of vulnerable believers for personal gain. Spotting such a con artist requires a posture of skepticism or suspicion rather than the credulity often assumed to characterize the faith of the laity. As mentioned, both popular culture and news media ensure this stereotyped "profit" figure remains firm in popular imagination. Truly, some mega-pastors have been exposed to be motivated by greed or the need for power, sex, and control. They can be criticized as clowns for the credulous, but they are manipulators and criminals (Chidester 2005; Starks 2013).

One archetypal figure that gets less attention but deserves more consideration is the holy fool. Coming in different forms, from the mythical trickster figure to the Christian clown or comic, the fool can catalyze liminal states and disrupt rigid perspectives (Lemert 2003; Campbell and Cilliers 2012). Understood as a Shakespearean character, one of "the most revered" types of Orthodox saints (Ivanov 2006), or as Christ himself (Stewart 1999), the fool carries a significant connection to both religious history and theology, and the lack of attention to this archetype is comparable to a certain neglect in the study of congregations. Scholars seem shy to investigate foolishness; it may a liability to credibility.

What I have done in this book is claim that irony is a form of reflexivity, and such reflexivity has a playful component not alien to prophetic critique. Every time Cavey rolls up his sleeves or wears a T-shirt, which is his typical uniform, his Leviticus 19:28 tattoo is revealed, challenging evangelical mores about tattoos and declaring his ironic posture toward his biblical heritage. Cavey is not brash, insolent, or deliberately controversial; he a gentle man, gregarious on stage, and often witty. His subversive streak is directed at the stereotype of the angry, judgmental evangelical. So his tattoo shouts his ironic creed, denouncing those who would defend the religious rules as the way to life and salvation. With his long hair and thumb rings, he dresses the clown, rejecting the conventions of his evangelical tradition in order to champion the therapy of trusted relationships in which everyday personal struggles are shared. For him this is the way of Jesus in a culture of impersonal systems – religious, technological, and consumerist – that promise more than they deliver. In a 2009 teaching series on the narcissistic "culture of ME" he exclaimed that "the solution" was to become "integrated into a counter-cultural community that promotes other-centredness and self-sacrifice ... [T]his is the shape rebellion takes."

Cavey is a fool for Jesus and his perceived "rebellious" way. The fool is less valorized than the prophet, especially in a consumerist age. Moore (1995) says the paradigm-busters are rare, and he longs for apocalyptic prophets to warn the masses who have their prayer breakfasts beneath the Golden Arches that the world is on the edge of environmental collapse. "Where are the real prophets?" asks Moore, sounding nostalgic, and turning away from his otherwise dispassionate historical narrative. "Can there be any in a country whose self-image rests on fast, friendly, and guiltless consumption?" (276). We might additionally ask, "Can a prophetic voice arise from a church that meets in movie theatres and malls?"

The analogy between megachurches and McDonald's or Disney comes with several ambiguities the prophetic approach may not acknowledge, ambiguities that Moore himself elucidates quite clearly in his history of commercialization and religion in America. Sometimes the comparisons of megachurches with the corporate giants of popular culture are simply put-downs or snobbish condescension. But a critical posture is vitally important. "In so far as it trivializes truth, simplifies suffering, and sucks us into its simulated realities as extras in the spectacle, it can hardly expect to go unchallenged," says sociologist David Lyon (2000) about consumer religion in general. Religion that merely entertains will distract and disempower its adherents.

The Disney dismissals, however, unintentionally reveal that there is something pleasurable and alluring about these popular, institutionalized festivals. Lyon waxes ambivalently about this situation, saying Disneyized domains may "recall the significance of story-telling, or remind us about the place of emotion and even spirituality in fractured and coldly rationalized societies. They simply join the protest against a narcissistic modernity, in love with its own image" (148). In effect, argues Lyon, there is something compellingly enchanting and dramatic about Disney-like religion. The animated mouse may be rattling the iron cage of technocratic efficiency, even as it depends on such infrastructure for its life. Similarly, and quite ironically, in his critique of the McDonaldization of the church, Drane (2009) sees celebration, humour, mime, story, drama, and dance as *antidotes* to McDonald's iron cage. There are more nuances and subtle distinctions to be made in what has been too easily rejected as simply consumer religion. This book has elaborated on the contrasting impulses of modern rationality and evangelical enjoyment as they "play out" in a contemporary megachurch. Ronald McDonald serves billions of factory-made burgers, but he does so dressed as a clown. Corporate powers appropriate an archetype that has the capacity to subvert their greedy, calculating disciplines.

Lloyd (2018) writes quite persuasively about the need for a normative understanding of charisma. Charisma, he explains, can be authoritarian and reinforce the power of a few over the many, keeping them subservient, oblivious to the contingency of the current cultural moment and its liabilities. Charisma can mystify and enslave. But charisma, reflexively approached, can also be democratic, disclosing its own mediated mechanisms and empowering the crowds to imagine better, alternative worlds. Cavey's rhetoric is certainly most often democratic in tone; I would venture, too, that while irony can also slip into cynicism and paralysis, Cavey's followers have moments that lead to the kind of personal transformation he speaks of, and this, in turn, engages the business-as-usual of the status quo – insofar as an Anabaptist's quietist ethic may allow.

This is what I learned in my years of megachurch research: megachurches, like evangelicalism, come in diverse shapes and colours, and generalizations are difficult to make. Nevertheless, one generalization that seems to hold true in the literature is that their members do not perceive their churches as strict, serious, or costly. Neither would they agree their worship is merely consumerized McDonaldization. Instead, the overall self-perception is that they are enjoyable communities of passionate faith that offer considerable choice for those wishing to participate. In the case of TMH, they self-identify as a form of modern urban Mennonite, *inside* the capitalist system but not *of* it. Such insider perceptions count for something in sociological and anthropological research, even if they are not sacrosanct.

While most scholars of the megachurch have made passing mention of the celebratory atmosphere in megachurches, no one has yet elaborated at length on this characteristic, in part because it is viewed as incidental to more serious political and economic matrices, and, related to that, enjoyment is not considered a truly *religious* activity. Insofar as they are enjoyable, megachurches are perceived to be secularized. But what I have done in this project is argue that the reverse may in fact be equally true, if religion is – as Durkheim maintains – a recreational activity. Play, joy, and even irony are not contrary to religion, but in fact betray its heart of celebration, festival, and in many traditions at least, grace. Some evangelicals display this characteristic of religion quite clearly in their in-house activities, and it's magnified in a megachurch. They are "breaking up the lines of expectation" for their visitors and critics.

Recall the story at the beginning of chapter 7 – where there was joking and laughter in prayer. Harvey Cox said, "Our ability to laugh while praying is an invaluable gift" (1969, 144). A subtle wisdom lies in such foolishness. It reveals the intuition that our religious practices are human responses – contingent, imperfect, changeable. Similarly, the holy fool may be a prophet for a culture bound within the iron cage of McDonaldized and digitized rationality, disturbing business-as-usual, revealing that these systems, too, are not sacrosanct but alterable. They, too, can be bad religion. Cox calls Christ the harlequin, "the spirit of play in a world of calculated utilitarian seriousness" (145). The holy fool surprises us into a reflexivity, awaking us to our captivity, as well as to the possibilities of a beautiful, playful constraint. Beyond the supposedly magic kingdom lies a more peaceable kingdom, which recognizes our wounds and instigates a care for common things. This suggests a third way, neither status quo nor violent revolution, dancing between disbelief and credulity – not just in the divine, but in our own evolving electronic matrix.

APPENDIX

Method

Fieldwork and Posture

Ellingson's (2010) seminal review of megachurch research declares that "the emergence and rapid growth of megachurches in North America and Asia represent one of the most significant changes to Christianity in the past twenty to thirty years" and in research on megachurches there "is no shortage of work to be done" (247, 263). Significantly, megachurch research offers "an opportunity to extend accounts of how religion is being reshaped or restructured in the 21st century and develop new explanations of religious innovation, change, and power" (264). Ellingson contends that studies need to focus "beyond descriptive research and develop more systematic and robust explanations" that engage debates in the sociology of religion, as well as organizational and cultural sociology.

This study offers a recent ethnographic snapshot of a Canadian megachurch in order to elaborate on the new reflexive evangelicalism and its ironic charisma. One of my goals was to learn the craft of ethnography, in which one immerses oneself in a subculture in order to understand it from the inside out. I wanted to investigate how people lived their faith, not just what was said or written about it on the website. It's easy to offer an opinion on the new culture of megachurches from an armchair, but it's more valuable and interesting to observe it first-hand and hear how the people themselves interpret their own experience, even if everything that shapes their life is not transparent to them.

Some have said that ethnographic case studies like this can be "critical" – a means of social activism or advocacy, of giving a voice to the marginalized and advocating for their cause. Attendees at the Meeting House are not marginal in class, race, or education, although

I do argue that they are a stigmatized group in Canada – as conservative evangelicals. I did not choose this research project to advocate for them, or conversely to critique them as a bourgeois group mainly perpetuating larger systems of social inequality. I wanted to understand (Weber's *verstehen*) what drew so many people to the church and so observe the performance of their religion – sympathetically but not simply in their own terms. I sought to create a cultural portrait of the Meeting House through a "literary, almost storytelling approach" that characterizes some of the best qualitative research (Creswell 2006, 72). This does not negate explanatory approaches or other critical perspectives; however, it does scrutinize dismissive labels that would hardly be recognizable to the persons being studied.

My ethnographic work focuses on the leader, which some may argue defies the nature of ethnography. But the focus of my project is that the leader cannot be understood apart from the relationship and work of the people, and conversely, the people cannot be understood apart from their primary symbol, their charismatic icon. This ethnography suggests a vital dialectic between leader and led that arises out of my fieldwork.

My method consists of six basic fields. *First*, I was a participant observer at many larger events for about two years (fall 2011 to spring 2014), with one full year as a regular attender. I attended at least thirty-eight Sunday services, often at Oakville headquarters but also visiting most of the regional sites for at least one Sunday morning. Other events I attended included two all-site rallies at a large sports arena, New Year's Eve dance parties, baptism events, recreational events, various external speaking events for Cavey, and general membership meetings.

A *second*, more intimate field of research was their small groups, internally known as Home Churches. I visited five different groups associated with three different MH sites for eleven weeks each – for sixty-eight group meetings. The general venue was a review of Cavey's Sunday teaching, followed by snacks and then a time of prayer. My Home Church visits also included various other events: I worked alongside church members at their volunteer activities, exchanged presents at Christmas, joined in football, soccer, and bowling, and attended games nights, a pool party, and a progressive dinner.

My *third* field of research consisted of formal interviews with eighty-two people (fifty-five male and twenty-seven female),[1] using an open-ended interview style guided by some standard questions. Most interviewees were attendees or staff whom I encountered through snowball sampling. To get a wider perspective I interviewed two pastors from neighbouring churches and six ex-MH attendees. I had three interviews with each of the top executive leaders, Pastors Bruxy Cavey and Tim Day, as well as multiple interviews with other executive leaders, and two former Overseer (church board) chairs. This is quite an opportunity, as others who study megachurch pastors cannot get access to the senior pastor (Sinitiere 2015; Johnson 2018). I conducted dozens of casual interviews, too, as I made my way through the different venues and entry points of the church community. I have used aliases for attendees but not for executive staff such as Tim Day and Bruxy Cavey.

Meeting House staff supplied me with a *fourth* source of data. They conduct in-house surveys of their attendees every fall and spring, and they made the results of these surveys available to me without conditions attached. The surveys cover basic demographic data such as gender and age, but also frequency of attendance at Sunday services and Home Church, length of time they have been with the Meeting House, and their general religious identity before and since coming to the church (Christian, non-Christian, other religion). These surveys generally had a very high response rate and gave me a good indication of the bigger picture of the constituency.

A *fifth* field of study included textual analysis of primary data in the form of diverse media, including 112 sermons, numerous websites and social media texts, Cavey's books *The End of Religion* (2007) and *(Re)Union* (2017), as well as Tim Day's *Plot Twist* (2014).[2] TMH reveals an oral culture, as Cavey and Day do not spend much time writing, and Cavey relies on significant editorial help from staff, who also ghost-write some of Cavey's blogs. The church operates around their video podcasts more than any particular texts, creeds, or polity documents. In this sense, it is more a church of the new media than a church of the book; it is a fluid community lived in rental spaces and online, connected by regional site Facebook pages and a podcast archive of almost fifteen years of sermons. The "teaching archive" or what I call their *electronic oral tradition* was a primary source for understanding their theology, and especially helpful was the search engine they added to a new website in 2012, which allowed me to search for teaching topics and key words through about fifteen years of teaching by Cavey (on audio and video).

Finally, I collected some secondary material on the Meeting House as a *sixth* field of study – from newspapers, blogs, and one master's thesis (Masters 2007). This is not a large volume of commentary, as

TMH operates under the radar of many mainstream journalists' vision in Ontario. There are copious amounts of journalistic material on megachurches and their leaders in North America and beyond, and this secondary material forms much of my contextual understanding of TMH and the general discourse that surrounds it – especially my discussion on succession and the future of TMH in chapter 8.

I began listening to Bruxy Cavey's teaching podcasts in February 2010, and my first interviews took place in October of that year, when I began attending a Home Church at the same time. I first personally asked Senior Pastor Tim Day for permission to study the church and interview attendees, then I sought the consent of site pastors who were responsible for the Home Churches in which I was a participant observer. Then I connected with the Home Church leaders and introduced myself, explaining the channels I had already gone through. My participant observation intensified in June 2011 as I began regularly attending the Sunday services and other special events, including new member classes and new regional site promotion evenings. This tapered off in June 2012 as I began to analyze my data and write my thesis but continued with sporadic attendance into the summer of 2014.

I enjoyed relatively free reign in the social network of the Meeting House. Senior Pastor Tim Day was always gracious and helpful, as was Cavey when I could get an audience. The staff varied in their enthusiasm for my project, some becoming key informants and a few others reticent, perhaps protective of their church and workplace, making email connections and interviews difficult. As for attendees, except for a media personality, two gay members, and the odd logistical impasse, my requests for interviews were always accommodated.

Many social scientists today identify themselves on an insider-outsider spectrum. Raymond L. Gold wrote of four potential roles for the qualitative researcher: the complete participant, the participant-as-observer, the observer-as-participant, and the complete observer (Gold 1958, 217–23). While I would suggest that the two poles of the spectrum would be difficult to inhabit in any pure way, my research falls quite directly in the camp of observer-as-participant. Unlike others who studied a church in which they were members or even associate leaders (Thumma 1996; Wellman 1999; Poloma 2003; Marti 2005; Stewart 2015), I began my research with a church I had never attended before choosing it as an object of study.

I had a brief encounter with Cavey many years ago. While I never attended any Sunday services in which he was preaching, I interviewed him in 1992 for an undergraduate sociology paper on the vocation of pastors (a cassette-taped recording I unfortunately lost). He was pastor at Heritage Fellowship Baptist church at the time, a few years before his divorce and his ministerial migration to the Brethren in Christ. I remember him saying something about being a pastor and retaining his humanity, so that if he exited the church and stepped in something left behind by a dog, he would call it as it is.

I was raised in an immigrant-based branch of the Reformed-Presbyterian tradition and continue to participate in a local Reformed congregation with my family – a tradition historically at odds with Anabaptism. Cavey's feelings for my particular tradition range from gracious to pugnacious, and as mentioned, during my fieldwork he presented an entire teaching series (seven Sundays) that rigorously critiqued Calvinist soteriology (specifically, the five points of Calvinism). So while I am an insider on the basis of my general Christian identity, I am an outsider on the basis of my affiliation with what could be called a rival Christian tradition and (at the time) as a student of religious studies at a public Canadian university. As I noted in chapter 3, some Canadian evangelicals and many public university leaders view each other with a suspicious eye.

Fieldwork is prone to challenge the conventional wisdom, bring nuance to neat theory, and allow for contradictions and partial accounts, because it examines religion in its messy and diverse particularity (Becker and Eiesland 1997, 19). One goal of this project was to introduce an evangelical megachurch without resorting to the McDonaldization epithets, and more specifically, investigate a megachurch congregation that deliberately differentiates itself from the rigid caricature of the militant, patriarchal, anti-intellectual, right-wing Moral Majority evangelical megachurch (Einstein 2007, 190; Teel 2008).

Scholars press for a conscientious approach to research on evangelicals, as they have been subject to academic bias that characterizes them as aberrant or duped subjects (Harding 1991; Bramadat 2000; Bielo 2009). As mentioned earlier, megachurch pastors similarly battle the cynical stereotype of Elmer Gantry, and popular discourse often portrays them as powerful demagogues doomed to scandal and career collapse. I would not feign objectivity, but I did guard myself against the dismissive attitude towards megachurches and their pastors, as well as the air of moral superiority that surrounds the epithets of "McChurch." I also noticed a mixture of resentment and envy lacing some conversations I had with pastors about my research subject. Others sought a more instrumental approach, querying me for tips that would offer some secret formula for their own numerical success.

Unlike McCarthy-Brown (1991), Salomonsen (2002), and Moon (2004), whose participation in their host communities involved initiation, submersion, and for Moon, constant confrontation, I kept to a "minimal participation" research ethic that aspired to inconspicuousness. When at Home Church, if I was in line to pray, I prayed. If it was my turn to bring snacks, I brought the food. Understandably, Home Church leaders did not permit recording devices in their gatherings, so I would scribble the odd note and work backwards from memory immediately afterwards, to be accurate as possible.

Sometimes I was caught up in the excitement around me, as Cavey's charisma can be contagious. Other times I felt duplicitous, voyeuristic, or even ashamed that I was observing, gathering data, and not immersed in the prayers, testimonies, and intimate sharing of personal struggles. There were also moments I felt critical of this church: the highly centralized ecclesiology, its obliviousness to current events and the arts, and Cavey's contentious caricature of Calvinism – all grated against my own predilections.[3] Working within a scholarly discipline, I consciously tried to monitor these emotional responses to keep them from unduly distorting my observations.

Finally, evangelical research subjects have been known to constantly ask their scholarly investigators about their religious identity (Bramadat 2000; Bielo 2009; Elisha 2011). Meeting Housers (as they call themselves) were only mildly interested in my background and purpose, and usually a brief summary of my affiliations would satisfy the casually curious. Once they discovered I was Christian and taught part-time at a recognized Christian liberal arts university, the conversation often freely moved to other topics. I do not recall anyone trying to convince me to transfer my allegiances to TMH, although a few were interested to hear if I had a critical perspective on Cavey's teaching. Overall, I do believe my own Christian identity helped Meeting Housers trust me, and confide in me with their thoughts, hopes, and fears concerning their life and growth in this megachurch. I hope I have stewarded such trust well, while keeping to the rigours of my academic profession.

Notes

PREFACE

1 The word *irreligious* is always in quotation marks throughout this book because the term is indigenous to TMH and it needs to be understood ironically. To be clear: Cavey and his church are just as religious as any other Christian church – being a community of prayer, scriptures, rituals, and doctrine. But being "irreligious" is how they understand themselves, in their own idiosyncratic way, and I've chosen to allow that rhetorical twist to remain in this volume, just in quotes to indicate its special, iconoclastic usage. It suggests a style defiant of convention, consistently casual and irreverent, and wed to popular anti-institutional cultural tropes. I did the same for "religion" – when it is meant in purely the pejorative sense, as Cavey prefers (although I am not consistent, as there are many nuances in the context of some sentences).
2 Winifred Gallagher, author of *Working on God* (2000) is a science writer who cannot shake the faith of her childhood. Cited in Georgescu (2013). See also James K.A. Smith *How (Not) to Be Secular* (2014).
3 Within days of the election, Campolo and Claiborne (2016) declared "the evangelicalism of old white men" is dead and suggested a new label: Red Letter Christians. Kelly Brown Douglas (2018) sees Trump's election as the resolve of a white supremacist nation, adding that 58 per cent of non-evangelical white Protestants and 60 per cent of white Catholics also voted for Trump. Ed Stetzer (2018) polled 3,000 Americans through LifeWay Research to "debunk" the 81 per

cent statistic. He apologetically concludes that the figure doesn't reveal motivations, that it wasn't about abortion or the Supreme Court, that evangelicals would cross party lines if given a pro-life alternative, and that they will overlook personal character if they can see a strategy for the long run. The research also showed that "only" one in four Americans report that their perception of evangelicals has worsened since the election. He admits the uncomfortable question evangelicals "will probably wrestle with for years to come" is this: Was it worth it?

4 I develop this further in chapter 3. It may have an edge of status anxiety (de Botton 2004) in an increasingly fragmented post-Christian context, as de Botton says such anxiety includes a worry that we are "in danger of failing to conform to the ideals of success laid down by our society and that we may as a result be stripped of dignity and respect" (4). But I think the deeper issue is one of redeeming a spoiled identity, as Goffman describes it.

5 A telling indicator of this perception is journalist Marci MacDonald's *The Armageddon Factor: The Rise of Christian Nationalism in Canada* (2010), which was widely received through the Canadian media circuit, and capitalizes on fears that right-wing American "dominionism" poses an imminent threat to Canadian democracy through Canadian evangelical political mobilization. This "retrograde and exclusionary" "militant charismatic fringe" with connections to Prime Minister Stephen Harper was supposedly on the brink of "remaking Canada as a distinctly Christian nation" (10). See McKeen (2015) for a critical perspective on this book, as well as Stackhouse (2010).

6 If evangelicalism is conceived as an impulse and network as much as specific theological commitments (Bebbington 1989), Cavey and TMH find affinity with central players in the evangelical world. His favourite theologians when I interviewed him were N.T. Wright, Dallas Willard, and Greg Boyd. TMH partners with World Vision, gleans from Willow Creek Church resources, invites Tony Campolo and Philip Yancey as guest teachers, and hosts Teen Compass and Outreach Canada events (the latter being a church planting network that can trace its lineage back to Donald McGavran and Fuller Theological Seminary's church growth program). Cavey teaches at Toronto's Tyndale Seminary (a flagship evangelical seminary in central Canada from which Cavey graduated). He has occasional guest appearances on Crossroads Television (CTS), and he periodically features in *Faith Today*, the Canadian equivalent of the American *Christianity Today*.

7 Johnson (2018) examines the polar opposite evangelical community to TMH: Mark Driscoll's Mars Hill Church, a venture into "biblical

porn" and muscular Christianity that she calls an "Arousing Empire" of "sexualized and militarized dynamics of power" that are "structurally embedded and bodily networked through visual and digital media" (37). Her theoretical commitments lie with Foucault and his notion of "biopower" and connect with what Jethani (2012) has called "The Evangelical Industrial Complex." While I follow the importance of the body and power dynamics, I have less affinity with Foucault's negative appraisal of discipline (Schuurman 1995; Lyon 2007, 2018).

8 This series from October 2014 highlights one of Cavey's theological themes: a sharp discontinuity between Old and New Testaments. He looks at texts that use the word *but* to show "before-and-after images" that "convey the radical change that Jesus brings. From law to grace, from animal sacrifice to living sacrifice, from enemies to friends."

CHAPTER ONE

1 Cavey's presentations on other religions, including some discussions in his first book (2007), demonstrate his versatility as well as an openness to acknowledge the religious other. He is not shy about pointing out differences between Christianity and other religions, often examining them through his prism of "religion" as rules, roles, and rituals, and Christianity as normatively centred on loving relationship with Jesus.
2 About five thousand attend on Sundays, but many do not attend weekly. Some attend only Home Churches. They do not keep membership lists.
3 The language of "new evangelicals" is found in Pally (2011), Steenland and Goff (2013), and Markofski (2015) and refers to more activist, left-leaning young evangelicals; the "Emerging Church" or "emergent evangelicals" is a similar but broader term with a vast literature discussed later here. *Post-evangelical* does not necessarily mean "beyond" evangelicalism, for the prefix *post* can assume continuity with its root word. Often taken as a synonym for the Emerging Church Movement, it more properly designates evangelicals who wish to distance themselves from mainstream evangelicalism – more specifically conservative megachurch evangelicalism. So if evangelicalism is a centred set, a post-evangelical would be more marginal to the core while not being out of its orbit (Tomlinson 2003). Willey (2016) uses the term *post-conservative* in her Canadian study.
4 Paul Bramadat suggests a Canadian secular elite have a taken-for-granted view based on secularization theory and are "lagging behind popular convictions and the mounting evidence" that religion persists in spite of secular assumptions and institutions. He argues that in

Canada there is a "common elite reticence about engaging religious (non-Christian as well as Christian) issues and groups openly.... [M]any policy-makers, academics, and journalists continue to assume and even hope that religion will eventually recede in the face of modernization or industrialization" (Bramadat and Seljak 2008, 7). See also Bowen (2004). *Post-secular* does not mean a return to Christendom or some form of theocracy but rather a public life where secular forms welcome religious identities and expressions (Habermas 2005, 2010; Knauss and Ornella 2007; B.S. Turner 2010; Nynas, Lassander, and Utriainen 2012; Gorski et al. 2012; Casanova 2012; Beaumont and Baker 2011).

5 Reflexive performances are typical of the Emerging Church movement (Marti and Ganiel 2014). Giddens (1991) sees reflexivity as endemic to late modernity and its disembedding character. Archer (2009) agrees that globalization facilitates the dynamics of reflexivity, which creates "more 'problematic situations' confronting more people everywhere and fewer and fewer suitable, habitual responses." *Reflexivity* she defines as more than reflection on an object – its distinguishing feature is "the self-referential characteristic of 'bending-back' some thought upon the self, such that it takes the form of subject-object-subject." It involves an internal conversation, an inner drama or "musement" that can lead to some creative or novel course of action. Scholars who champion reflexivity write in tension with those who see only habitus at work (Pierre Bourdieu) and rational choice scholars who limit subjectivity to instrumental rationality. The reflexive agent is active, evaluating, and emotionally involved in a dynamic interplay with surrounding and partly internalized structures (Archer 2009, 2, 7, 12). In chapter 4 I connect this concept with Goffman's idea of "role distance" – detachment from the role one is performing.

6 When I say "liturgy," I mean it as a theologically informed practice for life, not just worship, as used by James K.A. Smith (2009, 2016b). Incidentally, *fresh expressions* is a term used by the Anglican Church and has been defined as "new forms of church that emerge within contemporary culture and engage primarily with those who don't 'go to church.'" There would be some overlap here with the demographic I'm talking about, although this is a denominational program rather than a broad social movement.

7 A megachurch is any congregation with 2,000 weekly attenders. Bird (2012) reports 1,750 in the United States and Bird (2015) reports 50 in Canada (150 congregations over 1,000).

8 The discipline of performance studies is a growing and contested interdisciplinary field (Schechner 1988, 2013; Butler 1988; Strine, Long, and Hopkins 1990; Alexander 2004; Alexander 2006; Madison and Hamera 2006; Fenske 2007; Fuist 2014). The writings of Canadian-born sociologist Erving Goffman (1959, 1961a, 1961b, 1963, 1967, 1981, 1986), and specifically his notion of dramaturgical analysis, form a foundation for performance studies (Jacobsen and Kristiansen 2015). Along with Clifford Geertz and Kenneth Burke, Goffman wanted to highlight the cultural element in human action, the manner in which human activities are "expressive rather than instrumental, irrational rather than rational, more like theatrical performance than economic exchange" (Alexander 2006, 2). Alexander has championed this perspective and advanced its theoretical rigour to form a "cultural pragmatics" that shows "how social actors, embedded in collective representations and working through symbolic and material means, implicitly orient towards others as if they were actors on a stage seeking identification with their experiences and understandings from their audiences" (2).

9 Only recently, U.S. scholar Nancy Ammerman's landmark work firmly established the field of congregational studies and laid out its basic parameters (Ammerman 1987, 1994, 1996, 2005; Ammerman et al. 1998; Ammerman and Dudley 2002). Others have contributed significantly to the field, either through congregational case study or more quantitative and theoretical work (Neitz 1987; Warner 1988, 2005; Becker 1999; Wellman 1999; Harding 2001; Tamney 2002; Ault 2004; Chaves 2004, 2011; Marti 2005, 2008, 2012; Marti and Ganiel 2014; Fulkerson 2007; Bielo 2009, 2011). Still, scholarly books on Canada's 30,000 congregations remain much more sparse and disparate (Lyon 1995; Poloma 2003; Duncan 2008; Bean 2009; W.C. James 2011; Stewart 2015; Wilkinson and Althouse 2012; Reimer and Wilkinson 2015). A number of postgraduate theses examine Canadian congregations (Skinner 2009; Penney 1980; Sam 1982; Bacon 1982; Day 1982; Wildeboer 1983; Millin 1988; May 1989; Vautour 1995; Spate 1996; Cummergen 1997; Carroll and Jarvis 1997; Harding 1998; Gowing 2003; Aicken 2004; Van Holten 2005; Ko 2008; Kao 2009; J.G. Smith 2009; McMenamie 2009; Hinds 2013).

10 As Sam Reimer has demonstrated, "evangelicals, particularly active evangelicals, in both countries resemble each other far more than they resemble their fellow countrymen" (2003, 6). The Meeting House has a close history or sibling relationship with US megachurches like

Willow Creek (Chicago), Woodland Hills Church (St Paul), and EastLake Community Church (Seattle).

11 American megachurches have received some academic attention (Vaughan 1993; Eiesland 1999; D. Miller 1997; Sargeant 2000; Twitchell 2004, 2007; Thumma and Travis 2007; Thumma and Bird 2011, 2015; Marti 2005, 2008; Elisha 2011; Wilford 2012), including black megachurches with their distinctive cultural history (Johnson 2008; Drewery 2008; Barnes 2010, 2012; Tucker-Worgs 2001, 2011; Benson 2011; McGee 2012; Barber 2011, 2012). On the Canadian megachurch scene, consider Poloma (2003), although it focuses more on the Toronto Blessing and global charismatic Christianity.

12 At the broadest level, the language of "spiritual marketplace" is foundational to studying religion in the West (Berger 1967; Wuthnow 1998; Roof 2001; S. Lee and Sinitiere 2009; Slagle 2011) and is supported explicitly by religious economy theory (Iannaccone 1994; Warner 1997; Stark and Finke 2000; Twitchell 2007; Einstein 2007; Stark 2008; S. Lee and Sinitiere 2009). With regards to megachurches specifically, comparing them to big-box stores, restaurants, and amusement parks is common, including Home Depot (Cimino 1999), Walmart (Wollschleger and Porter 2011; McGee 2012), Disneyland (Aycock 2003; Twitchell 2004, 2007; Crowe, McWilliams, and Beienburg 2010), and McDonalds (Ritzer 2010; Drane 2009). Ellingson (2007) and Maddox (2012, 2013) use the language of consumerism to analyze megachurches from a perspective sympathetic to critical theory. Theologians and other Christian writers have similarly railed against the consumerist practices of megachurches (Guinness 1993; Packer et al. 1997; Wells 2005; Tucker 2006; Horton 2008; White and Yeats 2009; MacArthur 2010) and church marketing more generally (Webster 1992; Shelley and Shelley 1992; Dawn 1995; Kenneson and Street 1997; Cimino and Lattin 1998; Gilley 2002; Middelmann 2004; Wells 2008; MacDonald 2010). Not to be dissuaded, some Christian writers see consumerism as an opportunity for incarnational ministry and promote the evangelistic power of marketing, metrics, and management (Barna 1988, 1992; Reising 2006; Cooke 2008; Meyer 2009; Hutchins and Stielstra 2009; Dixit 2010).

13 A plethora of novels portray the ambitious clerical egomaniac, building upon Sinclair Lewis's 1927 novel and subsequent film *Elmer Gantry* (Raabe 1991; Pollard 2007; Stennett 2008; Strobel 2011; K.C. Boyd 2012; Willimon 2012; Cable 2012; Cullen 2013; Cron 2013). Sorensen (2014) examines numerous themes in clergy films, shows,

and novels, including the holy fool, the failure, the detective, the suffering hero, the counsellor, and the lover. Her last chapter specifically examines clergy portrayals in Canadian fiction, which she summarizes as – appropriate to this book – "mildly iconoclastic" (241). The term *personality cult* is used by a number of sociologists of evangelicalism (Quebedeaux 1982; Balmer 2014; Kyle 2006) and in a more explicitly consumerist vein, CEO *pastor* or *pastorpreneur* (Guinness 1993, 53; Kyle 2006, 221; Thumma and Travis 2007, 67; Twitchell 2007, 3; White and Yeats 2009, 77; James 2015, 10). Significantly, (auto)biographies authorized by megachurch leaders read as hagiographies and reinforce the assumption of personality-centred megachurches (Billington 1972; Penner 1993; Hurston 1994; Hybels and Hybels 1995; Schaap 1998; Myung and Hong 2003; Vick 2003; Patterson and Rogers 2005; R. Young 2007; Falwell 2008; Sheler 2009; Keith 2011; Rawlings 2013).

14 There is a plethora of books by evangelicals who echo the "spiritual but not religious" rhetoric (Arterburn and Felton 2000; D. Miller 2003; G. Boyd 2004; Palmer 2006; Schmelzer 2008; Young 2008; Farley 2011; Wolsey 2011; Dollar 2015; Bussie 2016). As Hatch (1989) demonstrates, evangelicals have a long history of rebellion against ritual and formal religion. Fuller (2001), however, argues that of late they have been influenced by popular metaphysical spiritualities. The genealogical lines are blurry, as evangelicals will claim origins in Jesus's anti-Pharisaical approach; but their practice of contextualizing with culture – and just being habituated in a culture where metaphysical religion has a long and at times significant presence – certainly suggests Fuller has a point. "Spiritual but not religious" or "SBNR" – variously called "monism," "the new spirituality," and the "metaphysical tradition," – is a historical stream of North American religion that has achieved increased prominence and legitimation since the 1960s (Porterfield 2001; Fuller 2001; Tacey 2003; Heelas and Woodhead 2005; Schmidt 2006; Herrick 2006; Chandler 2008; Heelas 2008; Albanese 2008; Mercadante 2014). Cavey certainly plays with SBNR language and sensibilities, and directly engages it in his teaching series "The Secret Revealed" (May/June 2007).

15 Ronald Glassman, in an analysis of manufactured charisma and movie stars, writes that "the darkness of the theater puts the individual into a dream-state in which fantasy projections and identifications become easy to attain" (1975, 631).

16 In *(Re)union*, Cavey writes of being a Doubting Thomas, having "an inner skeptic who never sleeps." Seeing the brutality of nature, he

questions the reality of a loving God. He confesses, "I'm the guy who is always questioning, always wondering, always double-checking, always asking for evidence" (2017, 83).

17 I maintain that Cavey falls within the broad sweep of the evangelical network because of his affiliations with mainstream Canadian evangelical agencies and because his faith and practice fall generally within Bebbington's (1989) quadrilateral of historical evangelicalism: biblicism, crucicentrism, conversionism, and activism. Cavey reflexively self-identifies as an evangelical – in his own way: "I wear that label with them because they know what it means. I don't wear it with non-Christians because they don't know what the word means, but they do know what the subculture means to them ... right wing with a certain subculture of Christian cheese ... Go and ask non-Christian friends what words come to mind when you say the word 'evangelical.' See how many words get listed before they say Jesus or gospel" (Stiller 2007).

18 "Cognitive dissonance" is the language of Berger (1976), but I don't believe the faith is thus simply precarious. As Neitz (1987) demonstrates, a faith tested and chosen may be even more firm and secure than one that is taken for granted.

19 There are many different ways to label the seeker-sensitive congregational form: "the new Reformation" category (Schaller 1996), "new paradigm churches" (D. Miller 1997), "faith brands" (Einstein 2007), and the post-denominational designation (Wilford 2012). Each category label emphasizes different characteristics of what is essentially a post-1960s baby boomer–shaped Protestant ecclesiology.

20 *Time* magazine did a feature on the shift in evangelical culture, focusing on views of gay marriage, and featured EastLake and what they called "third way" churches (Dias 2015). In January 2015 Meeks announced full inclusion of LGBT persons in his church, which followed with a 50 per cent loss in attendance and a 42 per cent loss in giving, which translates to $2.8 million of their budget. This seems to have cooled the relationship with TMH. EastLake has firm connections to the Emerging Church networks, as Meeks has spoken about his "friend, Rob Bell," and they hosted Peter Rollins on a Sunday morning.

In conversation with me, James Wellman (see Wellman 2012) saw many similarities between Cavey and Rob Bell, as well as between Cavey and the "pyrotheology" of Peter Rollins. "Pyrotheology" was inspired by the Spanish anarchist Buenaventura Durruti's statement that "the only church that illuminates is a burning church" (Moody 2015). Certainly they all swim in similar Emerging Church waters.

Bell, however, is hardly tethered to any Christian tradition as Cavey is, and Rollins is much more postmodern and philosophical than Cavey. The anti-religious attitude, however, is a shared trait and to some degree a shared theology.

21 Essentially, the emergent project translates "the way of Jesus" into postmodern forms (Gibbs and Bolger 2005, 44), which means epistemologically "deconstructive" (Marti and Ganiel 2014) and post-foundationalist (Middleton and Walsh 1995), embracing a post-Christendom model politically, and ultimately a "post-evangelical" posture (Tomlinson 2003). In other words, it embraces a more narrative than rationalistic apologetic, sees the church as a subculture rather than as part of the political establishment, and operates as a protest movement to the world of pragmatic Boomer megachurches (Bielo 2011, 13). Books by social scientists (Gibbs and Bolger 2005; Bielo 2011; Packard 2012; Labanow 2009; Marti and Ganiel 2014) and dissertations that have studied the movement (Teusner 2010; Chia 2010; Duncan 2011; Steele 2012) follow on the wave of "emerging" networking that began in the late 1990s, with key writers following in the millennium, such as McLaren (2001, 2003, 2006), T. Jones (2008), Kimball (2003, 2007), S. Burke (2003, 2007), Pagitt (2004, 2008) and Rollins (2006). McLaren has spoken at TMH and endorsed Cavey's 2007 book, but like other Anabaptists, Cavey does not seek to identify publicly with The Emerging Church (Claiborne 2011).

22 "Emergents would much rather be part of a megasubversion than a megachurch, for they are more interested in critiquing the *status quo* than reflecting it" (Snider and Bowen 2010, 109). Bielo's (2011) second chapter, "The Ironies of Faith," highlights what I am calling ironic charisma.

23 Bruxy Cavey, 30 October 2013, Toronto Mennonite Theological Centre.

24 This alludes to Berger's work on the comic and religion (Berger 1970, 1997). I elaborate on the relationship between play and religion in the seventh chapter.

25 Like many North American megachurches, TMH moved through many different venues in the early years. They began renting Munn's Public School, Oakville, with an oak tree as their logo. The "Upper Oaks" name was a combination of the geographical references points of Upper Middle Road and Oakville. "Community Church" was becoming a popular way for churches to identify themselves without denominational markings. They also opened an office space in a plaza nearby. In the fall of 1988 they moved to General Wolfe High School down

the street (now known as White Oaks North Campus), since Munn's school was starting renovations to accommodate the ever-growing north Oakville population. Through worship services, baptisms, picnics, summer children's camps, and backyard clubs, the small church plant began to grow. By 1990 attendance was up to about one hundred people.

In September 1994 a new high school opened in town – Iroquois Ridge High School – and services were moved to this larger facility with about 150 seats and a stage. Through prayer, the leadership perceived God was giving them a ten-year vision to attract a thousand people by the year 2000. Before that vision was fully pursued, the Siders moved south of the border, as Craig Sider accepted a position as bishop with the Brethren in Christ in Pennsylvania. It was 1996, the tenth anniversary of the church, and they had no pastor.

26 Taylor (2007) investigates the "buffered self" of the naturalistic paradigm, restricted to the "closed world structures" of an "immanent frame." Yet in the "cross-pressures" of this secular age, he contends many remain haunted by belief in something transcendent.

27 For details on my method and fieldwork, see the appendix.

CHAPTER TWO

1 Warren Bird was the research director at Leadership Network at the time of this writing and kept a database on global megachurches, based on reports he receives from people around the world. In December 2013 his list includes 55 in Africa (with 20 in Nigeria, 10 in Kenya and 9 in South Africa), 107 in Asia (39 in Korea), 16 in Australia and New Zealand, 35 in Europe (13 in U.K.), 39 in Latin America and Caribbean (14 in Brazil). The research on global megachurches, which often emphasizes their Pentecostal spirituality and prosperity gospel theology, is growing (Hong 2000a, 2000b, 2003; Kim 2001; Fath 2005, 2008; Gustafsson 2005; Coleman 2000; Kim 2007; Kitiarsa 2008; Tong 2008, 2011; O'Neill 2009; Asamoah-Gyadu 2010; Agadjanian 2012; Algranti 2012; Barnes 2012; Kim 2011; Hey 2013; Kay 2013; James 2015; Chong 2018; Gitau 2018). Hillsong Church, Australia, is a well-developed case study in globalized megachurches (Connel 2005; Goh 2008; Riches and Wagner 2012; Maddox 2012, 2013; Hynes and Wade 2013; Marti 2018; Schuurman 2018b).

2 It has been called the "new paradigm" in the sociology of religion (Warner 1997) and has close ties to religious economy and rational choice theories (Stark and Finke 2000). Their distinctive language of churches as "firms" or "faith brands" that sell religion as a "product" to impressionable "consumers" has become its own tradition with its own terminology (Iannaccone 1994; Stark and Finke 2000; Twitchell 2007; Einstein 2007; Stark 2008; S. Lee and Sinitiere 2009). They assume that growing churches such as megachurches are "winners" on the religious market because they are savvy cultural leaders that know how to address the religious needs of modern North Americans. While at times bordering on tautology (successful churches are those that appeal to the largest share of the market), this approach offers explanations on a macro-scale that have ignited fierce debates and expanded significant research programs (Young 1997; Bruce 2000, 2002; Jelen 2003; Imber 2007; Foltz 2007; L. Clark 2007; Ekelund, Hébert, and Tollison 2008; Kitiarsa 2008; Janes 2008; Witham 2010; Gauthier and Martikainen 2013; Usunier and Stolz 2014).

3 The history of the American church growth movement can be discerned from some dissertations (Works 1974; Tucker 1998; Bates 2005; Middleton 2011; Walters 2011), the historical accounts of its leaders such as Donald McGavran and the role of Fuller Theological Seminary (Wagner 1980; Glasser 1986; McIntosh 2005; Stetzer 2008) and from the commentary coming from its critics, which include Lutheran (Scudieri 1996), Baptist (Wise 1995), Reformed (Conn 1977; Newbigin 1995), Pentecostal (McClung 1985), liberationist (Terry 1997), and other quarters (Shenk 1983; Inskeep 1993; Roozen and Hadaway 1993; McIntosh 2004). The church growth movement literature itself is extensive, flowing out of a large industry of publishers, consultants, agencies, and church planting networks, and includes all manner of manuals on everything from marketing to management to measurement. Many denominations, including mainline denominations (Kelley 1972; Hoge 1979) have made some foray into this church growth field.

4 "Rage against the Machine" was a teaching series in May/June 2011, five Sundays dedicated to "putting technology in its place." Another teaching series, "What Really Makes Us Happy" (December 2010) challenged some of the materialistic myths of Christmas. The core Anabaptist value of simplicity appears regularly, as in "The Simple Life" (26 March 2006) and "The Maggots of Materialism"

(14 January 2017, part of a series entitled "Travel Light: Going Further with Less"). See also pastor Paul Morris "Confessions of an Urban Mennonite" (2 July 2006).

5 Thumma and Bird (2009) surveyed 24,900 megachurch members from twelve megachurches, and their top three reasons for initially attending their respective megachurch were the worship style, the senior pastor, and the reputation of the church, in that order, although each of these three reasons was just one decimal point different (on a scale of 1–5). It is also in the top three reasons pastors of large churches report growth in their own churches (Thumma and Warren 2015, 7). See also Malick (1996, 26–7).

6 This literature is examined in more detail in Schuurman (2016). Some megachurch studies barely touch the concept of charisma (D. Miller 1997; Sargeant 2000; Marti 2005, 2008; Elisha 2011; Wilford 2012; Bratton 2016; Johnson 2018; Gitau 2018). Balmer (2014) provides a number of case studies of megachurch leaders, but his analysis follows formulaic lines. More detailed analysis of leadership can be found in Thumma (1996), Myung and Hong (2003), and Lee (2005). Psychological views of megachurch leader charisma are found in Hey (2013), and Wellman (2012) brings the cultural context and crisis into play in his biography of Rob Bell. Gitau offers the kind of statement that is common in the literature, without the depth of analysis into charisma's power: "[Kenyan megachurch Pastor Muriithi Wanjau's] pastoral success is not in spite of the intellect demonstrated by his personal educational biography and charisma. It is because of it" (2018, 93). She does, however, highlight how such charisma offers a stabilizing force in a highly destabilized cultural context.

7 This term comes from Charles Taylor, which is not disengaged intellectual ideas but "ways *people imagine their social existence*, how they fit together with others, how things go on between them and their fellows, the expectations that are normally met, and the deeper normative notions and images that underlie these expectations" (2007, 171; emphasis in original).

8 This term is used in Johnson (2018, 5) and is developed in Stromberg (2009). Stromberg builds on Huizinga (1955), arguing that play is something into which we are "caught up," and deep absorption shapes us in subtle ways: "Most of us have at some point become immersed in a book or game or movie such that – on the cognitive and emotional levels – the activity temporarily assumes a profound significance and the importance of the outside world begins to fade" (2–3). Our culture

of entertainment, he continues, "is arguably the most influential ideological system on the planet." He worries that much entertainment culture today suggests an escape into romantic fiction, which dulls and disempowers people. I avoid the use of the word *entertainment* in this book for that reason, suggesting that play, unlike entertainment, can transform and empower people for good.

9 Charisma as a concept has been assessed as passé, dissolved in the manipulations of electronic media (Bensman and Givant 1975; S. Turner 2003) or considered unempirical and too mystical to measure (Burke and Brinkerhoff 1981; Bourdieu 1987; Oakes 1997; Kotter 1999; P. Smith 2000; Joosse 2014). Theories about charisma receive further treatment in Schuurman (2016) because the literature on charisma still grows, and spans a diversity of disciplines, including anthropology (Lindholm 1990, 2013; Csordas 1997; P. Smith 2000; Falco 2011; Dyer and McDonald 2002), celebrity studies (Dyer and McDonald 2002), cultural studies (Horn 2011), history (W. Clark 2007; Potts 2009; Berenson and Giloi 2012), management studies (Conger and Kanungo 1988; Conger 1989; Khurana 2002), philosophy (Bro 1955), political science (Madsen and Snow 1991; Aberbach 1996; Horvath 2013), psychology (Oakes 1997; Schiffer 1973), religion (C.R. Smith 2000; Lloyd 2018), and sociology (O'Dea and Yinger 1961; Berger 1963; Shils 1965; Eisenstadt 1968; Friedland 1964; Tucker 1968; Downton 1973; Wilson 1975; Barnes 1978; Zablocki 1980; Wallis 1982, 1993; Glassman and Swatos 1986; Bryman 1992; D.N. Smith 1998; S. Turner 2003; Rieff 2008; Feuchtwang 2008; Carter 2010; Dawson 2011; Hava and Kwokbun 2012; Hofmann and Dawson 2014).

10 Miller (1997) uses the word *charisma* in a variety of ways. He explicitly states the relevance of the concept of the routinization of charisma for the Calvary, Vineyard, and Hope church movements out of California. In some parts of the book he emphasizes charisma as a prophetic revelation that is routinized by disciples over time (1997, 25–6, 123, 148). In other parts of the text, he refers to "personal charisma" as a personality trait of a leader (14, 149, 163). Yet in other places he refers to charismatic gifts and charismatic worship in a clearly Pauline sense, in one instance stating that their religious expression was "too charismatic" (36, 43, 48). In sum, Miller uses three different meanings of charisma – as a personality trait, as a movement led by a spiritual leader, and as a tradition of expressive worship. In terms of usage, this is certainly legitimate; my goal here, however, is to bring some clarity to such variations in usage.

11 The Romans 12 text includes more ordinary gifts such as teaching, mercy, aid, service, and encouraging. Because the lists are different, I would argue they are not intended to be considered as rigid lists or exhaustive in their scope.

12 Even within the Weberian concept of charisma$_2$ are numerous distinctions and debates. For example, Riesebrodt (1999) claims Weber is inconsistent, and subsequent interpretations have defined Weberian charisma as heroic leadership (Joas 1996) or as an impersonal sacred force (Eisenstadt 1968; Shils 1965). While I can imagine an argument for some overlap between the two, my definition rests more in the former notion.

13 Many uses of the word *charisma* do in fact understand it as a form of personal magnetism. While some find traces of this in Weber (Friedland 1964; Horn 2011, 7) and others level the charge at social psychology (P. Smith 2000), it is best compared to the "Great Man" theory of history, which dates back to the 1840s and the Scottish writer Thomas Carlyle, who declared, "The history of the world is but the biography of great men" (and he meant "males"). His book entitled *On Heroes, Hero-Worship and the Heroic in History* (1840/1993) assumes that by learning about Great Men, one might come to find one's own inner hero.

14 Weber did not make clear that charisma$_2$ can have oppressive, if not horrific, manifestations, such as in the cases of Adolf Hitler, Charles Manson, and Jim Jones (Lindholm 1990; Feuchtwang 2008). Significantly, Weber's notion of charisma as a legitimate form of authority was used by political theorist Theodore Abel to make a "persuasive case" in 1938 for Hitler's rule, even if Weber himself may have objected to such use if he had lived to see the rise of the Nazi regime in his country (Potts 2009, 129).

15 I have been asked when defending my research to apply the model to non-religious figures, like Barack Obama or Donald Trump. Obama offered marginalized and left-leaning Americans disillusioned by the Bush era a positive "Yes, we can" vision of a new, collaborative, multiracial America, and his social media-savvy followers helped create his messianic-like campaign a success. Trump similarly offered working-class and right-wing Americans who were worried about economic shifts and afraid of foreign threats a dream of "making America great again." It's a compelling personality presenting a hopeful vision from within a (perceived or real) social crisis that captures the hearts and participation of a significant group of people. Charisma is the

relationship, the cooperative dramatic production between a leader and staff and a mission-hungry population, which energizes their restless or imperilled subculture.

16 Seminal studies in celebrity culture analysis include Dyer (1987), Gledhill (1991), Lewis (1992), Gamson (1994), Marshall (1997), Braudy (1997), Rojek (2001), Dyer and McDonald (2002), G. Turner (2004, 2010), and Ferris (2007).

17 Forms of celebrity as public renown have existed to some degree as long as there have been media, from Caesar's face on a coin to the portraits of Louis XIV, but the advent of electronic media allows celebrities to be more immediately known, more pervasively displayed, and more frequently described and discussed (Inglis 2010). Early modern celebrity first emerged in print culture as a moral touchstone for readers, as writers highlighted people of renown as examples of virtue (First 2009, 9).

18 Boorstin says, "Two centuries ago when a great man appeared, people looked for God's purpose in him; today we look for his press agent" (1961, 45). In contemporary terms, there is a large industry of agents, coaches, public relations experts, marketers, bloggers, and journalists who did not exist in previous eras in such numbers or with such readily accessible and transnationally mobile powers of communication. Already mid-century Boorstin was saying the "premium on quickly impressive, attractive images" has created a "new Iconography of Speed" (199). See also Kurzman et al. (2007, 363): "Celebrity is status on speed."

19 The *pseudo* prefix is not used by Boorstin but fits his consistent use of the prefix in the book. Bensman and Givant (1975) used the term in the context of a discussion of modern charisma and media, with reference to Boorstin's book. See also Hofmann and Dawson (2014, 353).

20 Boorstin's dualistic approach continues. He urges suspicion of those who appear to have "superhuman" qualities and endorses instead the "authentic leader," who is trustworthy, "what he seems to be," and who is "not trying to be something he is not" (1988).

21 Consider Carnegie (2010), Alessandra (2000), Benton (2005), Morgan (2008), Mortensen (2010), and Cabane (2012).

22 Alessandra's book says it most starkly: charisma is not an "effortless gift of the gods or something you are born with" but a tool that lies within you, waiting to be honed (2000, 7).

23 Dawson (2011, 115) writes, "An element of mystery clings to the idea of charismatic authority, which is more than the by-product of our

ignorance. In its very conception charisma is designed to capture and express our profound and repeated sense that certain leaders have an uncanny ability to win and hold our attention, to persuade and motivate us, to earn our approval. Like it or not, mystery is a defining feature of the phenomenon, and when social scientific explanations become too complete or reductive in nature, there is a sense that we are no longer dealing with charisma per se." Lloyd (2018) compares charisma to religion, which can both positively enchant and more menacingly mystify. At heart, he says charisma communicates our humanity, a certain inwardness and excess, "a point in the world that is essentially opaque" (48).

24 Crandall University professor of religious studies John Stackhouse (2010) – a specialist in evangelical history in Canada – offers a scathing three-part review of the book, arguing that on two key components of journalism and history (information and interpretation) MacDonald frequently fails to pass even minimal journalistic standards. That is to say, even her facts are wrong. In her ethnographic study of the Christian Heritage Party of Canada, McKeen critically summarizes the bestseller as "journalist hyperbole about a surreptitious takeover of Canadian politics by a frightening, apocalyptic Christian Right" (2015, 2). Incidentally, Bird (2009, 9) reports that in the United States actually only 22 per cent of megachurch pastors ever pray for political leaders, although 58 per cent identify as Republican.

25 Cavey spoke at the Exodus Global Alliance, 5th International Conference, 8–10 May 2008, in Toronto, entitled "Sexuality, Truth and Grace." A promotional brochure states one of the themes of the conference was "Change is possible! Freedom from homosexuality not through a method, but through a person, the Lord Jesus Christ!" As of 2013, this Exodus agency ceased to exist. To be clear, in a 2013 document entitled "Same-Sex Marriage: A Third-Way Approach" available on the TMH website, Cavey writes, "Biological determinism is never the answer. Biology is not destiny. Life is about choice. I am not suggesting we can choose our sexual orientation, but I am saying we can all choose how we live" (5).

26 For example, "BIC pastor promotes new approach to homosexuality" on the BIC news website (Carter 2014).

27 http://www.themeetinghouse.com/teaching/resources/.

28 Cavey had two previous Sunday teachings on singleness, in which he argued that singleness should be the default for Christians and that singleness and marriage were "two versions of awesome."

29 I did hear the story from one gay Meeting Houser that he came out of the closet while employed as a camp counsellor at a Christian camp where Cavey was the camp chaplain for a week. The camp director called him to the office, with Cavey as pastoral support. The director told him, reluctantly, he'd have to be sent home because his new identity "looked bad" for the camp. Cavey then piped up: "If he goes, I go, too." In brief, Cavey said all the camp counsellors were holding their sexual appetites in check for the sake of Jesus, not just this young man. "We're both not getting any because we love Jesus. So if he goes, I go, too." In the end, they both stayed.

CHAPTER THREE

1 This line intentionally mimics Brian McLaren's celebrated Emergent Church fiction series: *A New Kind of Christian: A Tale of Two Friends on a Spiritual Journey* (Jossey-Bass, 2001).
2 Willner (1984) qualifies the crisis criteria for charismatic authority, saying it may be constructed by the leader as much as it can be evident in sociological or political upheaval. Conger (1989), speaking from within management studies, suggests an opportunity could be just as efficacious for charisma as a crisis. For Ingram (2014) a crisis is vital and includes a breakdown of tradition, conditions of uncertainty, and a threatening "other." Tucker (1968, 743) insists that the leader's promise of deliverance in the face of distress "may be the quality that most of all underlies their charisma and explains the extreme devotion and loyalty that they inspire in their followers." Dyer (1987, 58) comes closest to what I interpret to be the case at TMH: it's not that the whole culture need be in crisis but "specific instabilities, ambiguities and contradictions in the culture" – specific ideological configurations irritating specific audiences, especially those who experience role/identity conflict and pressure. A celebrity or star can embody or "be" some social tension of the day.
3 Putnam and Campbell (2010) document a similar polarization in the United States. Bishop (2009) calls it "the big sort" that clusters like-minded people into particular US regions.
4 Emerging Church participants respond with "an anxiety to avoid the stigma associated with conservative Christians" (Marti and Ganiel 2014, 59). TV Ontario aired a show entitled "An Evangelical Pitch to Millennials" on *The Agenda* with Steve Paikin on 12 February 2018. A number of young evangelical leaders were interviewed by Nam

Kiwanuka, and all her guests expressed a sense of being stigmatized. For example, Silka "Eternia" Kaya, host of Global's *Love Is Moving*, said it most directly:

> There is a stigma, and I hear it in my social circles, because a lot of my friends don't go to church. So it's like "They are hypocrites, they say this and then they live this other lifestyle, doing something else. I'd rather live with people who are just open about all the stuff they are doing." There is the traditional, especially the American media, you know, the right-wing, conservative, anti-abortion, anti-gay. These are the stigmas, the stereotypes, and it's not part of the community I'm a part of, it's not part of the church I'm a part of. But this is what people who generally don't attend church assume of church goers.

5 Incidentally, Reimer and Wilkinson's (2015) study of evangelical congregations shows that political mobilization is a low priority for them.
6 In an article different from the one listed above, Todd puts the number at 8–10 per cent of Canadians (2011). Bibby tallies evangelicals by denominational identification and labels them as "conservative Christians" (1987, 2004).
7 Zawadzki says hostility to Christianity, in particular on campus, causes students to hide their faith: "Censoring themselves in front of recent acquaintances is a way to ensure that their Christianity does not become entangled in the popular stereotypes" (2008, 73).
8 This is not to say that this cultural context has created Cavey and his vision, but his religious innovation is not independent of that context. In Weberian terms, this strategic counter-performance has an "elective affinity" with social structures (Berger 1963, 950).
9 Queen's University professor David Lyon, who has identified as an evangelical in the past, writes, "Forty years ago, I would have been fairly content with the Evangelical label but today I simply do not identify as such for fear that I might for example be seen as supporting Israeli policies in Palestine, denying climate change, or agreeing that gay people should be excluded from the church" (Lyon 2018).
10 Jeffrey Alexander chronicles how the 2008 US election campaign was determined by a symbolic struggle over which presidential candidate would retain the image of "hero." Republicans narrated John McCain as a national war hero while airing an ad that characterized Obama as a pampered, superficial "celebrity." "It is poetics not economic power," says Alexander, "that makes [the ad's] performative success great" (2010a, 415). The ad did do symbolic damage to Obama, but Obama

and his advisors corrected his presentation style in time to retake the image of cultural hero and win the election.

11 People's Church has 3,000 attendees and Agincourt Pentecostal has 2,370 attendees, according to Warren Bird's Leadership Network database of large churches in Canada, shared with me in April 2015.

12 The West Hamilton (Ancaster) site launched in 2001 at a Silver City theatre a few hundred metres from Cavey's previous church, Heritage Baptist. By February 2003, Cavey had three Sunday morning services running in Oakville. North or Uptown Toronto launched in the fall of 2003 (Yorkdale Station on the subway line), Brampton launched in fall 2004 (just north of Oakville), and a downtown Toronto site was launched a year later in the fall of 2005 for the younger professional demographic of the area. The diversity of locations separated Meeting Housers (as they soon called themselves) from each other and from the physical presence of their central personality, but a common board, budget, brand, structure, and weekly Sunday teaching continued to keep them connected in identity and operations. The "Tri-Cities" regional site (Kitchener, Waterloo, and Cambridge) opened in 2006 – a part of Ontario some call "the Bible Belt" for its many churches drawn significantly from a dense German Lutheran and Anabaptist population. They now had five remote sites, adding two more in October 2008 – East Hamilton (Mountain) and Ottawa, the nation's capital brimming with educated professionals and civil servants. In 2008 TMH went on satellite, broadcasting to the now seven sites across Ontario. The set-up was convenient, as the new building was directly across from the Weather Network, where the technology was readily available. But after about a year of live satellite feed, the six-digit figure costs convinced leadership to revert to a week's delay via a DVD couriered to regional sites. In July 2009 the first non-movie theatre site was launched – at a public school in Parry Sound. Waterloo was launched in 2010 as a way to deal with the large size of the "Tri-Cities" site, and Burlington launched in 2011 to relieve some of the crowds in Oakville who lived in that area. Richmond Hill and Newmarket launched in March 2012, with Brantford following in the fall of 2013. London, Hamilton Downtown, High Park Toronto, and East Toronto would follow after 2015. Owen Sound opened as a teaching site (no full launch yet) in 2016.

13 The Hartford Institute for Religion Research reports similar statistics for megachurches in North America: over two-thirds (68 per cent) of those attending a megachurch any given week have been there five

years or less, compared to 40 per cent in churches of all sizes. Twelve per cent claimed the megachurch as "home" but said they also attended other churches as well (Thumma and Bird 2009), a practice Wuthnow (2010, 124) has called "congregational bigamy." There is a greater fluidity, turnover, and instability to the population of a megachurch compared with smaller churches. Megachurches take advantage of this congregational diversity. Rick Warren at Saddleback Church, for example, recognizes five concentric circles that form their constituency: community, crowd, congregation, committed, and finally the core. He has a scheme that promises to take attendees "around the bases" from membership to maturity, ministry, and then home plate: missions (Sargeant 2000, 113).

14 This assessment is based on information from Statistics Canada and other sources.

15 For Cavey, even working in private security is a direct challenge to his pacifist convictions, as it includes the option of using coercive or violent means to protect people and property.

CHAPTER FOUR

1 For a more intensive exploration of humour, religion, and popular culture, see David Feltmate (2017).

2 Marti and Ganiel quote one Emerging Church member who said the church offers "Christianity for people who don't like Christianity" (2014, 76). Emerging Church participants are notoriously ambivalent about their Christian faith.

3 I originally stumbled on this term in a creative but grammatically appalling electronic book on the charisma of Barack Obama (Bac 2013). Bac suggests Obama uses a form of alienation effect when he transitions from his visionary performance of the American Dream (made real in his own life) to attend to the mundane political issues of the day. She concludes that this strategy worked only partially for Obama; rather than mobilizing people for political action, the alienated audience often still retained strong emotional connections to the aspiring president's charisma.

4 On Brecht, see also Furman (1988); Brooker (1994); Biehl-Missal (2010). The original German word – *Verfremdungseffekt* – has been variously translated as "alienation effect," "de-familiarization effect," "distancing effect," or "estrangement effect" (Sargisson 2007).

5 Note all the anti-religious quotes that form the background of this flyer. It came in a number of different versions, as promotion for

different series or the opening of a new regional site. Another version, for the opening of the Parry Sound site, quotes Jonathan Swift on the front: "We have just enough religion to make us hate, but not enough to make us love one another." On the back is an invitation to attend a Sunday service, adding that TMH is "trying to push back through 2,000 years of religious tradition to learn from the biblical Jesus." Church history is interpreted as the history of a long corruption.

6 NBC, for example, has been critical of megachurch pastor Steve Furtick's ceremonies, where he purportedly manufactures baptisms by the thousands for his Elevation Church in Atlanta (Watson 2014). They are also critical of another matter of scale: his $1.7 million, 16,000 square foot mansion. By contrast, the various baptism events I witnessed at TMH usually included three to five baptisms, with short testimonies.

7 For example, "Say What? Getting, Living and Giving the Good News" covered eight Sundays in June/July 2010.

8 Other places the ritual has been discussed include blogs at unseminary .com (7 November 2013), fulfilledprophesy.com (10 July 2005), churchmarketingsucks.com (14 April 2005), and transformingsermons .blogspot.ca (18 March 2005). All enthusiastically approve of the practice.

9 James Davison Hunter states that a consumer logic characterizes the trendy anti-institutional, "new 'revolutionary' expression of Christianity" that caters to specific demographic groups. "In the end, church is one more consumer choice for Christian believers; not much different in character from any other consumer choice," and reinforces modern individualism and consumerism rather than the structures that would resist them (2010, 283). Hunter's macro view, however, neglects the ethnographic view, which can demonstrate how choice can allow people a chance to test options and then make a personal commitment that is more than mere preference (Neitz 1987; see also Smith 1998; and Taylor 2007).

10 Cavey's sermon titles, while focusing on Christians being "dead" to sin, will play off zombie films: "Night of the Living Dead" (2000), "Return of the Living Dead" (2003), "The Living Dead" (2005).

11 The obvious contradiction does not seem to faze Cavey. A friend of Cavey who said Cavey enjoys *The Saw*, *Halloween*, *Exorcist*, and *Nightmare on Elm Street* films, described his shock when Cavey first mentioned zombies publicly. "I turned to my wife and said, 'Did he just say what I thought he said?'" He added that one older woman left the service when Cavey played an (evangelically speaking) risqué clip from

Lord of the Rings during his teaching time. On 10 August 2018 he wrote on his blog (a meditation on the thriller *A Quiet Place*), "Why do I like scary movies? Maybe for the same reason people enjoy challenging themselves to ride roller coasters: it's a safe way to engage our own fears, to practice bravery, to develop courage, and to enjoy the thrill." http://www.bruxy.com/category/movies/.

12 Cavey began the service on 10 October 2017 with the trailer of child zombie movie *The Girl with All the Gifts* (2016). His first words after the clip were: "Oh, just another typical Sunday morning in kidmax" (TMH Sunday school).

13 Compare this with the American evangelical organization Focus on the Family's review of the show, which quotes film reviewer Jeff Otto: "This may well be the bloodiest show ever seen on television." While the review admits there is some depth to the show with regards to family, friendship, and faith, it concludes by warning, "This is munching-on-entrails, stab-that-shambler-in-the-eye-socket violence. And it's turned into something of an illustration of just what you can and can't do on cable these days" (Asay and Whitmore 2014). The profanity used in each episode is listed, with the key consonants and the proper number of dashes inserted for each term.

14 Cavey did a teaching series entitled "Modern Family" in October 2013 that used numerous clips from the situational comedy show of the same name. While the show celebrates the de-centring of the nuclear family, Cavey used it to emphasize a theology that emphasizes the church as a family-like community, one in which "we turn our chairs toward one another and do life together." "Focus on the Family" at TMH means a focus first of all on their own congregation and especially Home Church. This emphasis on "church family" is not an uncommon practise in evangelical culture (Ault 2004).

15 In a tweet on 26 December 2017, Cavey wrote, "As a pacifist who's [sic] favourite Christmas movie is *Die Hard*, I could post a long, introspective blog on the subject of my own contradictory nature, theological questioning, and inner struggle. Or, I could just post this picture." The photo below the tweet features a sweatshirt that appeared in the film *Die Hard* with the blood-red words "Now I have a machine gun ho-ho-ho." Cavey lets the irony rest rather than explain it away.

16 When I pressed Cavey on the blood-and-gore issue in one of our interviews, he said some people may have sensitivities to it, but for him "fantasy is fantasy" and he compartmentalizes it in his head. He grew up playing with his camera and experimenting with special effects,

such as making someone's head appear to blow up on film. He finds it simply entertaining. The reality of violence, however, deeply upsets Cavey; he recalled seeing the clip of JFK being shot, and while there was no gore, his "stomach was in knots." "The Bible contains violence, too," he added on a less subjective note. Significant for this chapter's focus, concerning the teaching series on pacifism and its violent film clips, Cavey remarked, "Sometimes we aim to be disturbing."

17 The Christian mass media are saturated with prosperity theologians. Lee (2005, 103) writes, "Today it would be very difficult to find an African-American church with members unaffected by prosperity teaching." Joel Osteen represents one TV prosperity influence that crosses most racial barriers (Lee and Sinitiere 2009; Lehmann 2016).

18 Hillsong receives a lot of attention and academic scrutiny as a megachurch movement and musical industry (e.g., Connel 2005; Goh 2008; Riches and Wagner 2012; Maddox 2012, 2013; Hynes and Wade 2013; Marti 2018). For a journalistic take on its music, see Schuurman (2018).

19 On the fourth Sunday of the series Cavey directly compares the advice given in *The Secret* to randomly open its pages for immediate guidance with the evangelical practice of opening the Bible at random to receive guidance from God. "It's just silly," he concludes. "Immaturity and self-centredness."

20 In chapter 6 I note how Cavey is admired for his modest lifestyle. He seems to resemble the Weberian charismatic leader who "shuns the possession of money" and "all rational economic conduct" (Weber 1968, 21). The luxurious lifestyle of other megachurch leaders (Nigerian pastor David Oyedepo is reported to be worth $150 million, according to the *Economist*, "Celebrity Priests," 7 July 2012, 48) may be compared alongside Weber's charismatic "pirate genius" and his gold, as well as the glamour of celebrity (Rojek 2001, 73–5).

21 Cavey preaches against easy miracles, insisting people take responsibility for their difficult circumstances: "You are God's Plan A." "Sometimes we say [*in preacher's voice*], 'God is still in the miracle-working business!' as if that were his full-time job. But its not. He is not in the miracle-working business; he is in the relationship-building business, the partnership business" (14 February 2010).

22 Cavey steers away from God's wrath as the cause of Jesus's crucifixion. He avoids substitutionary atonement theory and places the death of Jesus firmly on the violence of the crowds (see teaching entitled "Why Did Jesus Die?" 8 April 2012).

23 Cavey can also approach the issue from a more jocular perspective. A tweet on 5 March 2017 has a portrait of Confucius overlaid with a proverb: "It is only when a mosquito lands on your testicles that you realize there is always a way to solve problems without using violence." The scatological and religious boundary crossing further distance Cavey from the prim and proper conservative evangelical.

24 Hunter translates this as resentment, but with a combination of anger, envy, hate, rage, and revenge motivating any political action that arises from it. It is most visible among those who perceive themselves as weak or aggrieved (2010, 107).

CHAPTER FIVE

1 There are no systematic studies on the global prevalence of prosperity theology megachurches, but some experts estimate that 80–95 per cent of megachurches around the world feature some degree of prosperity gospel culture, with about 35 per cent being significantly weighted towards prosperity theology and the rest being more or less amenable to it, with a small leftover percentage actively resisting it (from correspondence with Scott Thumma and Warren Bird). James (2015) includes prosperity teaching as one of the seminal characteristics of megachurches in the Global South. This is in contradistinction to the United States, where approximately only 10–20 per cent of American megachurches embrace prosperity theology themes (Bowler 2013, 239; see also Lee 2005; Lee and Sinitiere 2009; Sinitiere 2015). The Meeting House is a global anomaly, fitting in more closely with a minority of the American megachurch portrait, promoting a gospel of downward mobility rather than individual prosperity. Springs Church, a megachurch in Winnipeg, Manitoba, fits the global pattern of Pentecostal prosperity theology more closely (Bowler 2013).

2 Cavey actually wrote a blog post entitled "Fighting the Monster" on 21 October 2017. In this blog, he writes, "*The monsters of The Meeting House are BAD IDEAS about the GOOD NEWS.*" He briefly mentions religion as one of the "strongholds" of bad ideas, such as "God is male," and "avoiding hell is our primary motivation for preaching and accepting Christ."

3 John Ralston Saul (2008) offers one articulation of this character of Canadian culture, positing its origins in Aboriginal civilization, especially a "Metis mindset" that embraces difference and social complexity. The official multicultural policy of Canadian society since 1971 has

cultivated values of tolerance, diversity, and accommodation. Cavey's antipathy for loud right-wing evangelicals and even his recent distancing from his controversial colleague Greg Boyd (a megachurch pastor in Minneapolis with similar Anabaptist leanings) suggest a less polemicized religious vision consonant with Canadian evangelicalism (Reimer 2003).

4 Histories of the Jesus People Movement began early with some initial coverage (Plowman 1971; Streiker 1971; Moody 1971; Enroth, 1972; Ortega 1972; Ellwood 1973) followed by a few dissertations (Heinz 1976; Young 2011) and continue today in historical studies (Shires 2007; Schafer 2011; Eskridge 2013; Bustraan 2014). Douville (2007) focuses specifically on Toronto. Most of these accounts begin with charismatic characters who have a passion to reach out to the hippies and begin by evangelizing youth right on the street and beach. Prominent figures include Ted Wise in the Haight-Ashbury district of San Francisco, Don Williams and Arthur Blessitt in Hollywood, Jack Sparks at Berkeley, Chuck Smith and John Higgins in Costa Mesa, and Linda Meissner in Seattle (Guffin 1999, 195–215). Some JPM missions disappeared as quickly as they were started, but specific ministries, such as John Higgin's Shiloh commune in Oregon, spawned Youth Revival Centers across thirty states. Groups such as Jesus People USA and Chuck Smith's Calvary Chapel movement also grew and flourished well into the 1980s and beyond. For connections to the Emerging Church, see Olson (2014).

5 On average, Canadian large church budgets are 30 per cent smaller than American large church budgets (Bird 2014). The TMH budget hovers around ten million dollars and typically, to name a few budget items from their annual spring reports (2011–13), 6–8 per cent goes to communications, 13–14 per cent funds compassion agencies (local and African charities), 11–13 per cent pays for children's programs, and 14–22 per cent is needed for the main facility in Oakville and movie theatre rentals (the rest is mostly staffing salaries and regional site resources). For the tax year 2013 the average weekly attendance was 4,990, and 3,000 tax donation slips were issued (of which 750 or 25 per cent were on automatic withdrawal). The total general fund donations came to $7,398,000, which comes to $1,483 per attendee or $2466 per tax receipt (this does not include the receipts for compassion fund or their growth fund). I was told that yes, there are a number of "large donors," which would skew the data, but I could not obtain the details on such giving. Reimer and Wilkinson (2015, 92) have a

chapter in their book on evangelical budgets. In summary, they say if you "follow the money" it leads to in-house items and social welfare programs rather than politics. Given TMH's Anabaptist commitments, this is certainly the case.

6 Cavey (2017) spends a chapter talking about the kingdom of God, which comes very close to being constricted to the Christian church. He distinguishes God's kingdom from the "kingdoms of culture, politics, business, media, and more" (123). "Kingdom refers to a realm of relationship with God and others that is in harmony with God's will and God's way," he explains (120). He sees himself as "more of an ambassador *to* Canadians than I am a Canadian," and thus the Meeting House is portrayed as "a little embassy in a foreign land, where the culture of the kingdom of Christ can be cultivated and experienced by anyone who visits" (121). In good Anabaptist fashion, the kingdom of God is in the world, but not of the world or produced by the world, and the focus is on church community–based neighbour love and peace-making. Care for creation is mentioned (36, 99), but there is little robust creation theology or elaboration on what theologians call the "cultural mandate" (Genesis 1:28), which gives permission for a full-orbed cultural engagement in a kingdom of God beyond the church body (Hunter 2010, 174).

7 In a 2012 teaching on same-sex marriage given at Woodland Hills megachurch in St Paul, Minnesota, Cavey explains that the state, as a secular kingdom, will do what it thinks prudent. But Christians, as "visitors or tourists" in this land, are called to a different standard. He sees his church as accidentally located within a nation, dedicated to evangelism and acts of service but not investing energies in organizing rallies, policy change, or political leadership. This is not the traditional evangelicalism of prohibition days, but it is typical of Canadian evangelical congregations today (Reimer and Wilkinson 2015).

8 Cavey has a chapter in his first book (2007) entitled "Chamber of Horrors" in which he gives an inventory of the great evils of the church, including the Crusades, the Inquisition, witch hunts, and constant infighting. He concludes the chapter by saying the reason conservative Christians refrain from killing today is they lack the political power to do so. By identifying with the Anabaptists, Cavey dissociates from this history.

9 A growing movement of Anabaptist advocates called the Anabaptist Network consists of leaders originally from outside the tradition (like Cavey) who champion the Anabaptist separation from the state as a

model for all Christian denominations to follow (Murray 2010; Shenk 2011). As the Christian establishment continues to fade in the West – what some have called the end of Christendom or post-Constantinianism (Hauerwas and Willimon 1989) – these advocates promote a form of "naked" Anabaptism as the natural alternative (*naked* meaning "stripped of its cultural/ethnic traditions"). The movement simultaneously capitalizes on urban nostalgia for a simpler life (Kraybill 2003; Weaver-Zercher 2013). Historically, Anabaptists drew converts from the other churches into their fold because membership was not dependant on birth or national ties, although ethnic and family ties eventually became part of the community fabric, at times even impregnable to potential converts (Weaver 1987). Now, as ethnic and family affinities fade inside their congregations and shadow establishment denominations weaken in Canada, Anabaptists are structurally poised to be a competitive option in the spiritual marketplace once again (Driedger 2000). As Cavey declared in one teaching, "Plain is the new cool" – offering Anabaptism for those not into Anabaptism.

10 Such books are ubiquitous in evangelical circles. Cavey is not alone in his anti-religious message (Arterburn and Felton 2000; Boyd 2004; Bell 2006; James 2007; Kimball 2007; Schmelzer 2008; Bickel and Jantz 2008; Driscoll 2009; Farley 2011).

11 This kind of intimacy is basic to Cavey's teaching. In *(Re)union* Cavey writes about how in community we can be priests to one another, "come clean," and confess our sins to a trusted Christian brother or sister, in "real relationships that are relationally 'naked and unashamed.'" He concludes, "That person's acceptance and embrace become the tangible expression of God's acceptance and embrace" (2017, 115–16).

12 Such transparency with relative strangers requires vulnerability and entails risk, and sometimes confidentiality is broken through gossip, or persons feel judged by a clumsy remark. In a Roundtable podcast in the summer of 2014 Cavey and Day dealt with some of these concerns, suggesting people test the waters of their group first, establish some ground rules. Cavey insists, however, "We can't let that be used against us somehow to buffer us from intimate, honest, genuine biblical community. We need it." He emphasizes that this is "biblical fellowship" and the highlight of any Home Church.

13 The language of "script" relates to the dramaturgical metaphor and is used by social scientists such as Davidman and Greil (2007), who describe religious defectors as "characters in search of a new script." See also Harding (2001).

14 This Home Church narrative is a composite of three evenings I attended over three weeks on the same series.
15 This emphasis on stories suggests a wider "narrative turn" in scholarship, and not only in the humanities but the social sciences and other sciences as well (Fulford 1999; Phelan 2008; Spector-Mersel 2010; Rymes 2010). Some sociologists are part of this shift, drawing attention to how people order their world via story (Berger and Quinney 2005; Ammerman 2013). Subdisciplines of sociology have experienced a similar turn, such as social movement studies (Polletta 2009; Meyer 2009; Davis 2012), celebrity studies (Gabler 2001, 2009; Goodman 2010), and sociology of religion, specifically in such areas as conversion, healing, and congregational identity (Ammerman 2013). Coincidentally, as performance theorists turn to narrative, narrative research has experienced "the performative turn" (Peterson and Langellier 2006; Puroila 2013). The interdisciplinary nexus of performance and narrative has become quite wide and convoluted, as the meanings of narrative and performance are often quite varied and technical (Madison and Hamera 2006; Fenske 2007; Rosile et al. 2013; Dreyer 2014).

Stories and storytelling have been recognized to play a significant role in organizational management (Clark 1975; Gabriel 2000; Boje 2001), social movements (Davis 2012; Polletta 2009; Meyer 2009; Johnston 2009; Reed 2014), and congregational studies (Ammerman et al. 1998, 2013).

CHAPTER SIX

1 Former megachurch pastor Meredith Wheeler studied the succession process of three megachurches for his PhD dissertation. With regards to the claim of "team leadership" from all his case studies interviews he argued, "Although interviews in each of the three churches included explicit statements that the churches were not personality-centred nor built around a person, clearly in each church the senior pastoral role has enormous influence. The reported responses of various segments of the congregation and the launch of key initiatives following the transitions would indicate the influence of the role. Even in the case of [one of the megachurches] which claimed a more team orientation to the senior leadership, a point person – a directional leader of exceptional skill – was considered essential to the continued effectiveness of the church" (2008, 344).

2 Cavey downplays his role in TMH, modestly emphasizing his great team and pointing to the teaching ability of other Meeting House pastors. He has written that he teaches for only 60 per cent of the Sunday services (Cavey and Carrington-Phillips 2012), which is true for 2011. My statistics for other years, derived from counting podcasts in the archives, shows he preached 75 per cent in 2003–07, 80 per cent in 2008, 77 per cent in 2010, 75 per cent in 2012, 65 per cent in 2013, and 83 per cent in 2014. If one were to include the Drive Home and Roundtable podcasts, the percentages would rise, as he speaks on almost all of them, the latter podcasts generally including other speakers along with Cavey.
3 At the end of my data collection phase, Tim Day stepped aside as senior pastor of TMH (as of 2015). The announcement emphasized that he is not leaving the MH but merely going to take up a different role. There have not been any significant shifts in attendance numbers accompanying his departure. Day did some work for the BIC, and in 2017 his website read, "Tim Day is presently giving leadership to a new vision in Canada called 'City Movement.' This vision is to help business leaders, para-church ministries, and churches work together to advance the gospel in their city." This venture eventually became a giant web-portal called WayBase.
4 The literature on megachurch sacred space and architecture includes some articles (Rybczynski 2005; Hoover 2005; Kilde 2006; Williams 2007; Nelson 2007; Clarke 2009; Robles-Anderson 2012), two significant books (Loveland and Wheeler 2003; Bratton 2016), with some other books touching on the subject (Kilde 2005; Thumma and Travis 2007; Hoffman 2010), and a few dissertations pursuing it as a central area of research (McKenzie 2007; Jones 2011; Petrov 2011).
5 I offered some detailed profiles of Meeting Housers in my dissertation (Schuurman 2016, appendix D).
6 "Researchers believe that WOM affects consumers' decisions more than market-created sources of information such as advertising, newspapers, and sales staff ... [C]ompared with traditional mass media communication, WOM has a greater impact on consumers because of clarification and feedback opportunities" (Ismagilova et al. 2017, 10). eWOM extends volume and reach, is faster, more persistent and anonymous than WOM, and offers standardized valences and opportunities for community engagement (20–1).
7 In her case study of a Kenyan megachurch, Gitau casually uses the term *buzz* to explain how word of an exciting new church spread through

the city and garnered larger crowds for its services, as well as how controversy generated sustained attention (Gitau 2018, 3, 24, 71, 93).

8 Cavey consistently maintains that the goal of the Meeting House is to remove any cultural barriers so people can freely encounter Jesus within its walls. Yet his appearance, while turning stereotypes of clergy on their head, has little contemporary connection and sometimes repulses people. The long-haired hippie look has more connection with the sixties and seventies than current fashions. At best he has "The Dude" look (played by Jeff Bridges) in the now classic *The Big Lebowski* (1998). The closest comparison in evangelical circles would be the late Larry Norman (1947–2008), often called the "grandfather of Christian rock and roll." A more contemporary likeness would be with a younger colleague, the Christian writer and activist Shane Claiborne (b. 1975), with whom Cavey shares not only long hair and scraggly clothes, but also an Anabaptist theological tradition. Regardless, Cavey's appearance is certainly distinctive and constitutive of his charisma, tapping into stereotypes of the Jesus People in the sixties and seventies and into deeper archetypes of the eccentric prophet (Shires 2007).

9 A number of attendees, of course, did get a tattoo just like Cavey's.

10 Media and celebrity are inseparable (Boorstin 1961; Quebedeaux 1982; Schultze 1991; Evans and Hesmondhalgh 2005; Bartholomew 2006; Rojek 2001, 2011; Ruddock 2013).

11 Cavey has not had to bear much critique in electronic media. One blog made oblique references to the Meeting House, criticizing the "pixilated pastor" (formerly at www.saptapper.com), and an Ontario Harvest Bible Chapel web page temporarily carried a video of Cavey's views on gay marriage, using it to critique the perceived liberal attitude of Cavey. In chapter 8 I will briefly examine a moment when he was declared a heretic by an HBC pastor. But compared to Mark Driscoll or Pat Robertson, he generally garners little animosity. Interactive media, however, do certainly contribute to celebrity, whether it's approval or disapproval (Campbell 2010; Campbell and Teusner 2011; Bekkering 2015).

12 Sensationalized "cult" followings playing in the mass media at the time of Cavey's release from ministry (1995) and growing celebrity status at TMH (1996) include the Solar Temple's mass murders and suicides (1994), Aum Shinrikyo and their attacks on the Tokyo subway (1995), and the mass suicides of Heaven's Gate (1997). The televangelist scandals preceded these events, with Swaggart (1988, 1991) and Jim and

Tammy Faye Bakker (1988). Incidentally, as I wrote this in the fall of 2017, the front page of my local newspaper (Guelph, Ontario) had a story about a growing group of concerned citizens opposing Scientology setting up headquarters in town because it's a "cult" that will hurt people and take their money.

13 This video was part of a series of four in-house commercials, all of which play on stereotypes of evangelical churches or "cults." Beyond these, two other videos are worth noting. A very short animation created in 2002 takes sound clips from a real media interview with Cavey and dubs them over a cartoon of him. The Cavey figure explains to a female interviewer that people must "jump through hoops" in order to please him. The audio clip was no doubt taken from a random sermon of Cavey's. Another piece features a cut-and-spliced interview of Cavey from a Christian TV show called *Chuck and Jenni* from the early 2000s. In this edited video Cavey keeps repeating, no matter what the question from the host, "I'm at the top of the pyramid of power and you better do what I say" and "Please don't question us ... we don't want to connect with anyone." I found these spoofs on their website – the latter still online until 2013. All understood as ironic, they were also shown during the twenty-fifth anniversary celebration ceremonies in 2011.

14 There is another older commercial entitled "What is the worst that could happen?" and it features a couple visiting TMH for the first time. As they approach the church they are worried about being singled out, and again the male character asks, "What is the worst that could happen?" Inside, as the service opens, they are forced to come up to the stage and dance in front of the whole congregation. The entire commercial is satire, intending to communicate that TMH is informal, non-invasive, and casual with its visitors. The fact is, you can be as anonymous as you want to be with the crowds on Sunday morning.

15 Press agents, marketers, and paparazzi gather stories of celebrities, then distribute them through a variety of modern media. An audience further spreads their fame through word of mouth and by posting and sending them through their personal electronic networks – a form of modern gossip (Hellmueller and Aeschbacher 2010). People consume celebrity gossip in order to connect with something beyond themselves, as resources for casual conversation, or even to learn such things as how to dress. It is significant to note that people are not just consumers of celebrity. By telling the stories of their celebrity – especially today through the use of social media – they are contributing producers of

celebrity. Neologisms such as *citizen paparazzi* and *stalkerazzi* point towards the productive potential of anyone with a cell phone (Burns 2009, 13). One study shows that fans who post webpages about their favourite celebrity not only gather information on celebrities, but they interpret the texts in new ways and provide forums for discussion of celebrity lives (Soukup 2006, 332). Celebrity gossip is comparable to the inestimable value of word of mouth marketing; it increases exposure and solidifies visibility.

16 In February 2016, Cavey's five-minute video "Anabaptist Response to Attacks in Paris and Beruit" has almost 20,000 hits on YouTube. Ironic that a direct address to political issues gives the avowed apolitical Cavey one of his largest audiences.

CHAPTER SEVEN

1 This literature was surveyed in some detail in note 12, chapter one.
2 These commercial explanations for megachurch growth are distinguished by what aspect of the market situation they consider most seminal and how that aspect affects the development of religious institutions. In my evaluation, an approach that recognizes multiple effects of and reactions to the market is most helpful, as each assessment highlights some significant variable in what is ultimately an open system. And different megachurches "buy into" commercial culture in different ways.
3 Iannaconne (1994) built on Kelley's theory by explaining that the intense commitment required in a strict church causes free riders to self-select out, and thus the vitality of the church increases as its consistently active membership contribute time, talent, and money to the over-all experience. Again, it is the strictness of the church that causes it to grow and flourish. Thus when it comes to the burgeoning phenomenon of megachurches, one would expect that strictness would be a defining factor. But strictness need not require solemnity.
4 Rodney Stark (2008) used part of his 2007 Baylor Survey to investigate this apparent contradiction in megachurches. He maintains that his statistics unequivocally support the claims of strict church theory. Those who attend megachurches have stronger convictions about heaven and hell, attend services more often, volunteer more inside and outside the church, have a higher incidence of mystical experience, have more friends in the congregation, and are more likely to share their faith with friends and strangers than those in smaller churches.

Stark concludes that nostalgia for small intimate chapels clouds perceptions of the megachurch, which clearly provides a "better product" (34, 51) and whose growth is "mainly a result of their members' outreach efforts" (49). A study in Toronto found similar results: orthodox churches in the mainline tradition are the congregations that thrive (Haskell, Flatt, and Burgoyne 2016). This evidence does reinforce the claims of strict church theory, but Stark's survey approach, while recording conservative opinions and vibrant religious activity, does not touch on more than strictness, participation, and loyalty. The databases (Megachurch Study 2005 and Faith Communities Today 2005) examined by Thumma and Travis (2007) reveal similar conclusions about megachurch member participation, showing that in terms of prayer, evangelism, study groups, support groups, social service, and fundraising activities, megachurches garner significantly more commitment on average than other churches (103). They maintain that megachurches grow because of their consistent emphasis on evangelism, outreach, and follow-up (155). Again, strictness and commitment do not require sombreness or preclude a festival atmosphere.

5 Megachurch leaders are highly conscious of this reality. Rick Warren at Saddleback, for example, has a scheme that promises to take people "around the bases" from membership to maturity, ministry, and then home plate: missions. Another alliteration he uses to describe this trajectory is a movement from community to crowd, congregation, committed, and finally the core (of his church). Similarly, Bill Hybels at Willowcreek has the motto "Making unchurched Harry and Sally into fully devoted followers of Jesus Christ." Willow Creek recently did an assessment of this promise, called "Reveal," which showed 25 per cent of their 20,000-odd members feel "spiritually stagnant." The reverse of that, however, indicates that 75 per cent of their membership believe they are spiritually growing to varying degrees (Hawkins, Parkinson, Arnson 2007).

6 Sargeant (2000) documents how Disney has been an inspiration for pastors like Dr W. Edwin Young of Houston's Second Baptist, for, as Young, explains "church ought to be fun." Sargeant also names Pastor Walt Kallestad, author of *Entertainment Evangelism* (Abingdon 1996), who enthusiastically commends Disney's "Imagineering," explaining that it means "unearthing new and innovate ways to worship" (2000, 54). "Willow Creek works hard to incorporate humor into its drama and services," he reports, citing a program coordinator on staff who explains, "'Humor is the key for non-churched people. It shows that

Christianity is not totally serious'" (69). While Sargeant agrees that people are attracted to the church services "because they are more entertaining and less demanding," this is for him a secular compromise, a conforming to the medium of consumer culture (31).

7 Other megachurch research confirms this finding. Protestantism is undergoing a new Reformation, declared Miller (1997), and his data include charismatic megachurches in California. While he does not list play as one of the twelve characteristics of what he calls the *new paradigm* churches, he does remark, "I contemplated the relaxed and joyous style of the people. They seemed to be having fun! Their religion might be filled with commitment, but it was not at the expense of having fun" (39). Near the end he says more comprehensively, "One of the draws of the new paradigm church is that it is fun!"

Joseph Tamney (2002) does ethnographic work on four congregations, and the one that is by far the largest is where he notes "the importance of fun," the enjoyment of their activities, the jokes and humour of the pastor, and the ethic of evangelism, which is not to be seen as a duty, but as "great fun" (88, 89, 115).

8 Another scholar who offers an angle beyond the obvious "entertainment" observation is anthropologist Tanya Luhrmann (2012). Luhrmann examined Vineyard churches, a more recent charismatic-style tradition that includes some megachurches. She notices Christians in a pluralistic society can playfully layer their consciousness with different epistemological frames. When evangelicals pretend to experience God giggling alongside them, as she observes them doing, she says they understand this both in a play frame and in a real frame – an "epistemological double register" (378). God is an imaginary companion – but engaged if he were "real but not real, not real but more than real, absolutely real for all time but just not real in that moment" (378). Such play transforms identity; it is not merely escape.

9 I facetiously asked a former Overseer if TMH board was "for people not into boards." Her reply: "Don't mistake the casual style of things for any lack of seriousness in intent."

10 I am riffing on Cowan's notion of the "good, moral, decent fallacy" in religion here (2008, 8).

11 Umberto Eco gives credence to this truncated formula in his historical murder mystery *The Name of the Rose* (1986) when he puts the subversive power of laughter – and fear of such – at the heart of the incremental terror that has captivated a medieval monastery and library. Good humour is perceived as a threat to the true nature of religion.

12 Throughout his career, Peter Berger (1970, 1997) has sustained a keen interest in the connection between play, humour, and religion. He has long suggested, from what he calls an "empirical" standpoint (which I would argue betrays a more basic theological commitment), that there is a signal of transcendence or a "rumour of angels" in the comic expression that arises in the midst of the mundane or tragic. He explains in more detail: "The comic conjures up *a separate world*, different from the world of ordinary reality, operating by different rules. It is also a world in which the limitations of the human condition are miraculously overcome. The experience of the comic is, finally, a promise of redemption. Religious faith is the intuition (some lucky people would say the conviction) that the promise will be kept" (1999, x).

Berger sees close parallels between the shift in consciousness in play with religion's shift of attention to another world.

13 André Droogers (2011) not only sees play as fundamental to constructions of the sacred, but also as integral to the researcher's study, an approach he calls "methodological ludism." Thus play is built directly into his definition of religion, which includes both researcher and researched: "Religion is the field of experiencing the sacred in the body – a field in which both believers and scholars act, each category applying the human capacity for play, within the constraints of power mechanisms, to articulate basic human dichotomies, thus adding an extra dimension to their view of reality" (26). For Droogers, power offers restraining social structures on play's possibilities.

14 Fletcher is approving quoting Sir Christopher Musgrave. *Dictionary of National Biography,* edited by Leslie Stephen and Sidney Lee (Smith, Elder, 1892), 31:295.

15 On being a blurring of secular/sacred styles and institutions, see Powell 2004; Brown 2012; Vega 2012; Chang and Lim 2009.

16 While Cavey is a champion of parody and allusion to popular culture, I sense he is less committed to the Christianized pop music distributed by his church. My inquiries confirmed this: "That part was more initiated by Tim Day," said a staff member. DJ Cavey prefers his Top 40.

17 Although held in contempt by more elitist Christian musicologists as "junk for Jesus" or even a form of fraud distributed by large secular corporations (Linton 2000), Howard and Steck (1999) argue Christian Contemporary Music (CCM, or what others have more disdainfully called "C-Pop") "represents a microcosm of the contemporary evangelical experience" (6). Others call it "a window on American piety" (Powell 2004, 131).

18 Bekkering (2015) writes of "parody religions" and "recreational Christianity" as manifest in anti-megachurch fan clubs, but those realities exist beyond the boundaries of mainstream evangelicalism.
19 Cavey is often self-deprecating about his body. A fifty-six-year-old male attendee who worked as a crisis counsellor confronted Cavey on his physical condition. "Bruxy always answers questions in a funny way," he said. "Like I asked him once, 'How come it's not OK for a gay person to speak or marry as a minister, but it's OK to do it if you're a glutton?'" Apparently, Cavey thrust out his stomach and said, "Who are you calling a glutton?" He does not hide this fault. "Gluttony," he once said one Sunday morning, "is unfortunately the one sin that you wear for everyone to see."

CHAPTER EIGHT

1 Josh Packard suggested this proposal for Emerging Churches in personal conversation with me in November 2013.
2 I was asked once if Goffman didn't really mean "dramatic trouble" – trouble with the performance, the impressions a social actor is trying to make to the audience. I have kept his term *dramaturgical trouble* because I believe he meant the trouble was not simply a "bad performance" but in fact a break or breech in the entire plot, a failure to successfully perform so that the drama is believed and accepted.
3 Schultze (2013) specifically distinguishes his use of the term *personality cult* from the popular notion of "a close-knit group that recruits unwitting members, employs mind control, and promotes false beliefs." He gives the term his own particular sociological definition, as "a group of devoted followers of a particular person whom the group believes has a special relationship with God and is thereby worthy of following" (145). He focuses on evangelists known primarily through radio, television, and other media.
4 Charismatic leaders are a risk on various fronts; they can get obsessed with one idea and ignore the brutal facts (Collins 2001,70); employees may come to rely so much on the charisma, they lose their own sense of entrepreneurialism and focus more on what the leader wants than what circumstances suggest (72); and "larger-than-life heroes" can leave a management void that sets their successors up for failure (26). Collins's notion of charisma seems limited to a trait theory, and many of his examples of charisma are negative, describing either self-aggrandizing or narcissistic behaviours. He is more positive when

describing the antics of Sam Walton, the charismatic founder of Wal-Mart, who he insists uses his personality to advance the company rather than the other way around. He quotes Walton, who remarked, "Underneath that personality, I have always had the soul of an operator, somebody who wants to make things work well" (Collins and Porras 2002, 36). The "big hairy audacious goals" (BHAGS) of the company are really the driving mechanism of growth and success, which live on past the tenure of the CEO (105). It is visionary companies that become great and last, not necessarily visionary leaders. I suggest a similar assessment pertains to megachurches.

5 W.A. Creswell, the megachurch pastor at First Baptist, Dallas, reportedly had four offices, all of which were luxuriously furnished (Gregory 1994).

6 This is not uncommon with Emerging Church pastors. Marti and Ganiel write, "Some leaders even exude a guru-like quality in attracting followers" (2014, 118).

7 Goffman states, "Performers tend to give the impression, or tend not to contradict the impression, that the role they are playing at the time is their most important role and that the attributes claimed by or imputed to them are the most essential and characteristic attributes" (1959, 136). Cavey disrupts that expectation.

8 His secretary told me she saw him angry only once, and it involved a dispute with his daughter. He apparently gets very quiet when he is annoyed. In my interviews with Cavey, he has always been civil, if not mildly friendly to me, and on one occasion where we met in a coffee shop, he greeted me with a hug. On another occasion at his home, he offered me a beer as we talked. But his demeanour was always fairly distant and never familiar or jocular.

9 When Mark Driscoll was at his peak as a megachurch pastor, I sensed Cavey saw him as an antithesis to his own aspirations as a leader. I recall subtle references from Cavey and Day to Driscoll and his ministry, which they critiqued for its theology, ethics, and the authoritarian attitude of Driscoll. Driscoll had a significantly larger audience than Cavey and may not have even known of Cavey's existence. Nevertheless, Driscoll makes a good foil for the gentler, Anabaptist Canadian megachurch leader.

10 Jacob Reaume blog, "Not By the Hair of My Chinny Chin Chin! Or, What Not to Do with Wolves," 18 July 2018. https://trinitybiblechapel.ca/not-by-the-hair-of-my-chinny-chin-chin-or-what-not-to-do-with-wolves/.

11 Jacob Reaume, "Bruxy Cavey Should Apologize," 3 February 2017. https://trinitybiblechapel.ca/bruxy-cavey-apologize/.
12 Jacob Reaume, "Bruxy Cavey and the Cross," 10 March 2017. https://trinitybiblechapel.ca/gospel-according-bruxy-cavey-christianity-bruxyianity/.
13 Eric Schneider, "Why Is Bruxy Cavey Teaching at Tyndale?" 23 April 2017. https://onceforalldelivered.wordpress.com/2017/04/23/why-is-bruxy-cavey-teaching-at-tyndale/.
14 Randall Rauser, "Who Is Eric Schneider and Why Is He defaming Bruxy Cavey?" 29 April 2017. https://randalrauser.com/2017/04/eric-schneider-defaming-bruxy-cavey/.
15 Bruxy Cavey, "Understanding Atonement," 13 April 2017. http://www.bruxy.com/other/understanding-atonement/.
16 Bruxy Cavey, "Radical Christians and the Word of God," 4 July 2018. http://www.bruxy.com/theology/the-word-of-god-part-1-authority/.
17 Eric Schneider has a running list of those critiquing Cavey (with links), which in October 2018 includes the Rebel Alliance Podcast #72, Tim Barnett, Dean Lentini, Tim Challies, John Neufeld, Rich Davis (Tyndale professor), Wyatt Graham, Carl Muller, Sean Sheeran, and Don Horban. See https://onceforalldelivered.wordpress.com/other-material-on-bruxy-cavey/.
18 Paul Carter, "Seeking Clarity with Bruxy Cavey," 25 September 2018. https://ca.thegospelcoalition.org/columns/ad-fontes/seeking-clarity-with-bruxy-cavey-analysis-and-recommendations/.
19 Bruxy Cavey, "Unwelcome," 15 July 2018 (Sunday teaching). http://www.themeetinghouse.com/teaching/archives/2018/faithful-one-the-bread-and-the-blood/unwelcome-6108.
20 Jacob Reaume, "Defining the Evangelical Fault Line: The Bruxy Cavey Controversy," 17 July 2018, https://trinitybiblechapel.ca/defining-the-evangelical-fault-line-the-bruxy-cavey-controversy/.
21 Numerous other books are available on pastoral succession intended as practical aids for smaller church pastors and boards (Umidi 2000; Russell and Bucher 2010; Weese and Crabtree 2012; Mead 2012; Mullins 2015). Most succession processes involve some disruption and organizational instability and are "messy, complex, and dynamic" (Wheeler 2008, 4), although megachurches are more visible and affect a larger population. Vanderbloemen and Bird (2014) recommend pastors and boards look at some business literature that also deals with succession from a practical standpoint (Carey and Ogden 2000; Oswald, Heath, and Heath 2003; Cionca 2004; Wiersema et al. 2009; Rothwell 2010; Goldsmith 2013).

22 This typology is filled out in much more detail in my dissertation (Schuurman 2016, 181).
23 In another study, Hogan and Hogan (2001) surveyed over ten thousand working adults and developed eleven dimensions associated with management incompetence, summarized into three large factors: tendencies to blow up, show off, or conform when under pressure.
24 These statistics were brought to my attention by Scott Thumma, Hartford Institute for Religion Research.
25 Leadership failure in larger organizations is also costlier. Hogan, Hogan, and Kaiser (2011) cite studies that estimate costs resulting from a derailed senior corporate executive will range from $500,000 to $2.7 million.
26 Other historical examples would include the antics, divorces, and public mischief trials of Aimee Semple McPherson (Angelus Temple, Lost Angeles) (Sutton 2007) and the murder trial of J. Frank Norris (First Baptist Church, Fort Worth, Texas) (Stokes 2011). Both were acquitted or found not guilty, and the popularity of neither seemed diminished by their scandalous publicity; rather, in some ways the scandals magnified their notoriety and public influence.
27 Randal Balmer has a chapter on a visit to Jimmy Swaggart's church long after the scandals (entitled "Prime Time") (2014). He reports small crowds.
28 Grant, who was originally Archie Leach, often struggled with the dichotomy between his persona and his veridical self (Rojek 2001, 11, 178).

CHAPTER NINE

1 For one example, Cavey writes that the Old Testament and New Testament are two "radically different ways," the Old Testament being about "the old way of religion" and the New Testament focused on "the new way of Jesus." He champions the word *obsolete* from Hebrews 8:13, emphasizing the old covenant is "former, over, worn out, in the past … the story of what doesn't work" (Cavey 2017).
2 Sim (2002) claims postmodernism as the new cultural paradigm, whose advocates "look back with irony on older paradigms, and their opponents accuse them instead of an unwarranted flippancy and destructive iconoclasm" (5). Lemert (2003) claims the charisma of Muhammad Ali as the epitome of the "trickster in a culture of irony." "Surprise, if not irony is the trickster's potion" he explains, quoting a longer definition from Lewis Hyde, which ends by saying, "Trickster is the mythic embodiment of ambiguity and ambivalence, doubleness and

duplicity, contradiction and paradox" (38). Cavey is not fully the trickster, but Ali's claim "I don't have to be what you want me to be" fits very well on Cavey.

3 I interviewed a significant anomaly: Harold Albrecht, former dentist and BIC pastor, who became member of Parliament for Kitchener-Conestoga in 2006. He recognizes the tension of his role with his faith tradition, but the region he represents has a large contingent of Anabaptists, and they support him. He continued to serve as MP through the 2015 election.

4 "Missional church" writing, stemming out of the work of Lesslie Newbigin (1936–1974) was launched by a collective reflection on his vision (Guder 1998; chronicled in Goheen 2010).

5 Ironically, Cavey used the James Smith book mentioned above in a sermon series in November 2016, even calling one of the teachings "Liturgy of Love." The sharp contradiction of this endorsement of ritual and ceremony with his "irreligious" vision did not surface during the series. On life and theology as drama, see Vanhoozer (2014).

6 After my fieldwork was complete, some more direct attention to the issue developed. An event called "Ears to Hear" took place at the Oakville site on Sunday, 16 November 2017, subtitled "Learning from Diverse Voices among Us." The intention was to give space for visible minorities to voice any concerns or comments and possibly develop some policy or practice from the feedback. A Meeting House Roundtable podcast entitled "White Blokes and White Supremacy – with Jarrod McKenna" aired 14 February 2018. For research on how white congregations strategize for a multi-ethnic community, see Marti (2012), for example, who investigates churches that use ethnic minorities as worship leaders to leverage for racial diversity in their congregation.

7 Beyond 2016 this changed considerably as more women were hired as site pastors. I counted seven from the website listings in 2018.

APPENDIX

1 The disproportion in my sampling reflects staff gender imbalances: seventeen of my twenty-one staff interviewees were male. In 2013 there were ten times as many male pastors as female pastors (and no female pastors at the time of my interviews). Associate pastors (who generally worked in the head office), consisted of more females than males. All but one of the executive leaders were male as well at this

time. I interviewed many regional pastors, because while their interviews sometimes reflected the "promotional" rhetoric of TMH, some of these leaders I would classify as "key informants" and became quite valuable to my work – for data, news, and references (Reimer and Wilkinson 2015, 11). Of my interviews with attendees, the gender imbalance is significantly decreased – thirty-five interviewees were male and twenty-five were female.
2 There is one academic article co-written with Cavey on "the house church model" (Cavey and Carrington-Phillips 2012). The endorsement blurbs for Cavey's *(Re)Union* (2017) claim the book is as humorous and "irreligious" as his first book. The book is, in fact, much more positively Christian in many ways, as it affirms more Christian theology than his previous book, which was more of a critique of the concept of religion, a *via negativa*. Irony operates best when for a season.
3 For example, Cavey describes Anabaptism as a revolutionary force, and a pet phrase of TMH is "hitting the reset button." In contrast, the Reformed Kuyperian tradition has held that "unlike revolution, Christianity aims to restore and not to destroy" (Bartholomew 2017, xi, 34). While the revolution in question is the Enlightenment for Bartholomew, revolution in general has been viewed in the Reformed tradition as overlooking God's providence and common grace. A carefully discerned re-forming of community life – including religious life – suggests a validation of history and an alternative to revolutionary dreams.

References

Aasland, Merethe Schanke, Anders Skogstad, Guy Notelaers, Morten Birkeland Nielsen, and Stale Einarsen. 2010. "The Prevalence of Destructive Leadership Behaviour." *British Journal of Management* 21 (2): 438–52.

Aberbach, David. 1996. *Charisma in Politics, Religion and the Media: Private Trauma, Public Ideals*. London: Palgrave Macmillan.

Abrams, M.H., and Geoffrey Harpham. 2008. *A Glossary of Literary Terms*. 9th ed. Boston, MA: Wadsworth Publishing.

Adams, Jim. 2011. "Pastor Bill Bohline: His Lifetime Investment." *Star Tribune*, 24 December. http://www.startribune.com/local/south/136036258.html.

Agadjanian, Alexander. 2012. "Evangelical, Pentecostal and Charismatic Churches in Latin America and Eastern Europe: An Introduction." *Religion, State and Society* 40 (1): 3–10.

Agnew, Robert. 1992. "Foundation for a General Strain Theory of Crime and Delinquency." *Criminology* 30 (1): 47–88.

Aicken, Allen John. 2004. "Synergy in Ministry: A Study of One Congregation's Experience of 'Team Ministry' over the Course of Three Decades." DMin diss., Vancouver School of Theology.

Albanese, Catherine L. 2008. *A Republic of Mind and Spirit: A Cultural History of American Metaphysical Religion*. New Haven, CT: Yale University Press.

Alessandra, Tony. 2000. *Charisma: Seven Keys to Developing the Magnetism That Leads to Success*. New York: Warner.

Alexander, Jeffrey C. 2004. "Cultural Pragmatics: Social Performance between Ritual and Strategy." *Sociological Theory* 22 (4): 527–73.

- 2006. "Cultural Pragmatics: Social Performance between Ritual and Strategy." In *Social Performance: Symbolic Action, Cultural Pragmatics, and Ritual*, edited by Jeffrey C. Alexander, Bernhard Giesen, and Jason L. Mast, 26–41. Cambridge: Cambridge University Press.
- 2010a. "Barack Obama Meets Celebrity Metaphor." *Society* 47 (5): 410–18.
- 2010b. "The Celebrity-Icon." *Cultural Sociology* 4 (3): 323–36.

Alexander, Jeffrey C., Ronald N. Jacobs, and Philip Smith. 2012. "Introduction: Cultural Sociology Today." In *The Oxford Handbook of Cultural Sociology*, edited by Jeffrey C. Alexander, Ronald N. Jacobs, and Philip Smith, 3–26. New York: Oxford University Press.

Algranti, Joaquín. 2012. "Megachurches and the Problem of Leadership: An Analysis of the Encounter between the Evangelical World and Politics in Argentina." *Religion, State and Society* 40 (1): 49–68.

Ammerman, Nancy, Jackson Carroll, Carl Dudley, and William McKinney, eds. 1998. *Studying Congregations: A New Handbook*. Nashville, TN: Abingdon.

Ammerman, Nancy Tatom. 1987. *Bible Believers: Fundamentalists in the Modern World*. New Brunswick, NJ: Rutgers University Press.
- 1994. "Telling Congregational Stories." *Review of Religious Research* 35 (4): 289–301.
- 1996. *Congregation and Community*. New Brunswick, NJ: Rutgers University Press.
- 2005. *Pillars of Faith: American Congregations and Their Partners*. Berkeley: University of California Press.
- 2013. *Sacred Stories, Spiritual Tribes: Finding Religion in Everyday Life*. New York: Oxford University Press.

Ammerman, Nancy Tatom, and Carl S. Dudley. 2002. *Congregations in Transition: A Guide for Analyzing, Assessing, and Adapting in Changing Communities*. San Francisco: Jossey-Bass.

Applegate, Debby. 2007. *The Most Famous Man in America: The Biography of Henry Ward Beecher*. New York: Image.

Archer, Margaret S. 2009. *Conversations about Reflexivity*. New York: Routledge.

Arterburn, Stephen, and Jack Felton. 2000. *More Jesus, Less Religion: Moving from Rules to Relationship*. Colorado Springs, CO: WaterBrook.

Asamoah-Gyadu, J. Kwabena. 2010. "'Unwanted Sectarians': Spirit, Migration and Mission in an African-Led Mega-Size Church in Eastern Europe." *Evangelical Review of Theology* 34, no. 1 (January 1): 71–8.

Asay, Paul, and Meredith Whitmore. 2014. "The Walking Dead." Plugged In, 12 October. http://www.pluggedin.ca/tv/vwxyz/walkingdead.aspx.

Ault, James M., Jr. 2004. *Spirit and Flesh: Life in a Fundamentalist Baptist Church*. New York: Alfred A. Knopf.

Aycock, Ryan. 2003. "Megachurches: How the Individual's Search for Meaning Led to the Disneyfication of the Church." Unpublished manuscript.

Bac, Jo. 2013. *Charisma: Visionary Leadership*. Bloomington, IN: Trafford Publishers.

Bacon, Douglas Arthur. 1982. "The Impact of a Study of Christian Worship (with Special Reference to the Sacrament of the Lord's Supper) on a Congregation of the United Church of Canada (Ontario)." DMin, Drew University.

Bader, Michael. 2009. "Mega-Churches, Psychology, and Social Change." *Psychology Today*, 28 April. http://www.psychologytoday.com/blog/what-is-he-thinking/200904/mega-churches-psychology-and-social-change.

Bahktin, Mikhail. 2009. *Rabelais and His World*. Bloomington: Indiana University Press.

Bailey, Sarah Pulliam. 2018. "In an Age of Trump and Stormy Daniels, Evangelical Leaders Face Sex Scandals of Their Own." *Washington Post*, 30 March. https://goo.gl/vtBEBF.

Balmer, Randall. 2014. *Mine Eyes Have Seen the Glory: A Journey into the Evangelical Subculture in America*. 25th anniversary ed. New York: Oxford University Press.

Balmer, Randall Herbert. 1999. *Blessed Assurance: A History of Evangelicalism in America*. Boston: Beacon.

Barber, Benjamin. 1996. *Jihad vs McWorld: Terrorism's Challenge to Democracy*. New York: Ballantine Books.

Barber, Kendra. 2011. "What Happened to All the Protests? Black Megachurches' Responses to Racism in a Colorblind Era." *Journal of African American Studies* 15 (2): 218–35.

– 2012. "The Black Megachurch: Theology, Gender, and the Politics of Public Engagement." *Sociology of Religion* 73 (1): 102–3.

Barker, Eileen. 1993. "Charismatization: The Social Production of 'An Ethos Propitious to the Mobilisation of Sentiments.'" In *Secularization, Rationalism, and Sectarianism: Essays in Honour of Bryan R. Wilson*, edited by Bryan R. Wilson, James A. Beckford, Karel Dobbelaere, and Eileen Barker, 181–207. New York: Oxford Press.

Barna, George. 1988. *Marketing the Church*. Colorado Springs: NavPress.

– 1992. *A Step-by-Step Guide to Church Marketing Breaking Ground for the Harvest*. Ventura, CA: Regal Books.
Barnes, Douglas F. 1978. "Charisma and Religious Leadership: An Historical Analysis." *Journal for the Scientific Study of Religion* 17 (1): 1–18.
Barnes, Julian. 2008. *Nothing to Be Frightened Of*. New York: Knopf.
Barnes, Sandra L. 2010. *Black Megachurch Culture: Models for Education and Empowerment*. New York: Peter Lang International Academic Publishers.
– 2012. *Live Long and Prosper: How Black Megachurches Address HIV/AIDS and Poverty in the Age of Prosperity Theology*. New York: Fordham University Press.
Barnes, Sandra Lynn. 2012. "Chinese Megachurch Persecution: Application of an Indigenous Resource Framework." *International Journal of Social Science Studies* 1 (1): 22–36.
Bartholomew, Craig G. *Contours of the Kuyperian Tradition: A Systematic Introduction*. Downers Grove, IL: InterVarsity Press.
Bartholomew, Craig G., and Michael W. Goheen. 2014. *The Drama of Scripture: Finding Our Place in the Biblical Story*. Grand Rapids, MI: Baker Academic.
Bartholomew, Richard. 2006. "Publishing, Celebrity, and the Globalisation of Conservative Protestantism." *Journal of Contemporary Religion* 21 (1): 1–13.
Bass, Diane Butler. 2012. *Christianity after Religion: The End of Church and the Birth of a New Spiritual Awakening*. New York: HarperOne.
Bass, Bernard M., and Bruce J. Avolio. 1994. *Improving Organizational Effectiveness through Transformational Leadership*. New York: Sage.
Bates, Matthew David. 2005. "Growing the Church, Resisting the Powers, Reforming the World: A Theological Analysis of Three Options for Ecclesial Faithfulness in North American Protestantism." PhD diss., Union Theological Seminary & Presbyterian School of Christian Education.
Beaman, Lori G. 2003. "The Myth of Pluralism, Diversity, and Vigor: The Constitutional Privilege of Protestantism in the United States and Canada." *Journal for the Scientific Study of Religion* 42 (3): 311–25.
Bean, Lydia. 2014. *The Politics of Evangelical Identity: Local Churches and Partisan Divides in the United States and Canada*. Princeton, NJ: Princeton University Press.
Bean, Lydia Nan. 2009. "The Politics of Evangelical Identity in the United States and Canada." Cambridge, MA: Harvard University Press.

Beaumont, Justin, and Christopher Baker. 2011. *Postsecular Cities: Space, Theory and Practice*. New York: Continuum.

Bebbington, David W. 1989. *Evangelicalism in Modern Britain: A History from the 1730s to the 1980s*. New York: Routledge.

Beck, Ulrich. 2010. *A God of One's Own: Religion's Capacity for Peace and Potential for Violence*. Translated by Rodney Livingstone. Cambridge: Polity.

Becker, Penny Edgell. 1999. *Congregations in Conflict: Cultural Models of Local Religious Life*. Cambridge: Cambridge University Press.

Becker, Penny Edgell, and Nancy L. Eiesland. 1997. *Contemporary American Religion: An Ethnographic Reader*. Lanham, MD: Rowman Altamira.

Bekkering, Denis J. 2015. "Drag Queens and Farting Preachers: American Televangelism, Participatory Media, and Unfaithful Fandoms." Waterloo, ON: University of Waterloo Press.

Bell, Rob. 2006. *Velvet Elvis: Repainting the Christian Faith*. Grand Rapids, MI: Zondervan.

– 2012. *Love Wins*. New York: HarperOne.

Bellah, Robert N. 2011. *Religion in Human Evolution: From the Paleolithic to the Axial Age*. Cambridge, MA: Belknap Press of Harvard University Press.

Bender, Sue. 1991. *Plain and Simple*. San Francisco: HarperOne.

Bensman, Joseph, and Michael Givant. 1975. "Charisma and Modernity: The Use and Abuse of a Concept." *Social Research* 42 (4): 570–614.

Benson, Delvon. 2011. "Black Religiosity: An Analysis of the Emergence and Growth of Black Megachurches." Toledo, OH: University of Toledo Press.

Benton, D.A. 2005. *Executive Charisma: Six Steps to Mastering the Art of Leadership*. New York: McGraw Hill Professional.

Berenson, Edward and Eva Giloi, eds. 2012. *Constructing Charisma: Celebrity, Fame, and Power in Nineteenth-Century Europe*. New York: Berghahn Books.

Berger, Peter L. 1963. "Charisma and Religious Innovation: The Social Location of Israelite Prophecy." *American Sociological Review* 28 (6): 940–50.

– 1967. *The Sacred Canopy: Elements of a Sociological Theory of Religion*. Norwell, MA: Anchor Books.

– 1970. *A Rumor of Angels: Modern Society and the Rediscovery of the Supernatural*. Norwell, MA: Anchor.

– 1976. *A Precarious Vision: A Sociologist Looks at Social Fictions and Christian Faith*. Santa Barbara, CA: Praeger.

- 1997. *Redeeming Laughter: The Comic Dimension of Human Experience*. Berlin: Walter de Gruyter.
- 1999. *The Desecularization of the World: Resurgent Religion and World Politics*. Grand Rapids, MI: Wm B. Eerdmans Publishing.

Berger, Peter L., Brigitte Berger, and Hansfried Kellner. 1973. *The Homeless Mind: Modernization and Consciousness*. New York: Vintage.

Berger, Peter L., and Thomas Luckmann. 1967. *The Social Construction of Reality: A Treatise in the Sociology of Knowledge*. Norwell, MA: Anchor.

Berger, Peter L., and Richard John Neuhaus. 1977. *To Empower People: The Role of Mediating Structures in Public Policy*. Washington: American Enterprise Institute for Public Policy Research.

Berger, Ronald J., and Richard Quinney. 2005. *Storytelling Sociology: Narrative as Social Inquiry*. London: Lynne Rienner Publishers.

Beyer, Peter. 2013. "Deprivileging Religion in a Post-Westphalian State: Shadow Establishment, Organization, Spirituality and Freedom in Canada." In *Varieties of Religious Establishment*, edited by Winnifred Fallers Sullivan and Lori G. Beaman, 75–91. Ashgate AHRC/ESRC Religion and Society Series. Farnham, Surrey: Ashgate.

Bibby, Reginald Wayne. 1987. *Fragmented Gods*. Toronto: Irwin Publishing.
- 1993. *Unknown Gods: The Ongoing Story of Religion in Canada*. Toronto: Stoddart.
- 2003. "The Circulation of the Saints: One Final Look at How Conservative Churches Grow." Paper presented at the Annual Meeting of the Pacific Sociological Association, Pasadena, CA, April. http://www.reginaldbibby.com/images/circofsaints03.pdf.
- 2004. *Restless Gods: The Renaissance of Religion in Canada*. Toronto: Stoddart.
- 2009. "Restless Gods and Restless Youth." Paper presented to the Annual Meeting of the Canadian Sociological Association. Ottawa.
- 2011. *Beyond the Gods & Back: Religion's Demise and Rise and Why It Matters*. Lethbridge, AB: Project Canada Books.

Bickel, Bruce, and Stan Jantz. 2008. *I'm Fine with God ... It's Christians I Can't Stand: Getting Past the Religious Garbage in the Search for Spiritual Truth*. Eugene, OR: Harvest House Publishers.

Bicksler, Harriet Sider. 2002. *Living Our Faith*. Nappanee, IN: Evangel Publishing House.

Biehl-Missal, Brigitte. 2010. "Hero Takes a Fall: A Lesson from Theatre for Leadership." *Leadership* 6 (3): 279–94.

Bielo, James. 2009. *Words upon the Word: An Ethnography of Evangelical Group Bible Study*. New York: New York University Press.
— 2011. *Emerging Evangelicals: Faith, Modernity, and the Desire for Authenticity*. New York: New York University Press.
Billington, Dallas F. 1972. *God Is Real*. Akron, OH: David McKay.
Birch, Rich. 2014. "Bruxy Cavey on the Misunderstood Leadership Traits of Jesus." Unseminary.com, 18 December. https://unseminary.com/bruxycavey/.
Bird, Warren. 2009. "Teacher First: Leadership Network's 2009 Large-Church Senior Pastor Survey." Leadership Network, 14 July. http://leadnet.org/teacher_first_2009_survey_large_church_senior_pastors/ (page discontinued).
— 2012. "How Many Megachurches?" Leadership Network. http://leadnet.org/how_many_megachurches/.
— 2014a. "Leadership Network/Vanderbloemen 2014 Large Church Salary Report: An Executive Summary of Research Trends in Compensation and Staffing." Leadership Network (page discontinued).
— 2014b. "Multisite Church Scorecard: Faster Growth, More New Believers and Greater Lay Participation." Leadership Network/Generis. http://leadnet.org/wp-content/uploads/2014/03/2014_LN_Generis_Multisite_Church_Scorecard_Report_v2.pdf (page discontinued).
— 2015. "Large Canadian Churches Draw an Estimated 300,000 Worshippers Each Week: Findings from a National Study." Leadership Network. http://leadnet.org/canada/.
Bird, Warren, and Kristin Walters. 2009. "Multi-Site Is Multiplying: Survey Identifies Leading Practices and Confirms New Developments in the Movement's Expansion." Leadership Network. http://www.willmancini.com/wp-content/uploads/2011/01/LN_multi-site_report.pdf.
Bishop, Bill. 2009. *The Big Sort: Why the Clustering of Like-Minded Americans Is Tearing Us Apart*. Boston: Houghton Mifflin Harcourt.
Bissonette, Melissa Bloom. 2010. "Teaching the Monster: Frankenstein and Critical Thinking." *College Literature* 37 (3): 106–20.
Black, Gary, Jr. 2013. *The Theology of Dallas Willard: Discovering Protoevangelical Faith*. Eugene, OR: Pickwick Publications.
Boje, David M. 2001. *Narrative Methods for Organizational & Communication Research*. New York: Sage.
Bolt, John. 1984. *Christian and Reformed Today*. Jordan Station, ON: Paideia.
Booker, Christopher. 2004. *The Seven Basic Plots: Why We Tell Stories*. London: Bloomsbury Academic.

Boorstin, Daniel J. 1961. *The Image: A Guide to Pseudo-Events in America*. New York: Vintage Books.
– 1988. "Beware of Charisma." *News and World Report*, 20 June.
Bordalo, Pedro, Nicola Gennaioli, and Andrei Shleifer. 2014. *Stereotypes*. Cambridge, MA: National Bureau of Economic Research.
Bork, Brian. 2018. "Dark Corners." *Christian Courier*, 10 September. http://www.christiancourier.ca/columns-op-ed/entry/dark-corners.
Bourdieu, Pierre. 1987. "Legitimation and Structured Interests in Weber's Sociology of Religion." In *Max Weber, Rationality and Modernity*, edited by Scott Lash and Sam Whimster, 119–36. Boston: Allen and Unwin.
Bowen, Kurt. 2004. *Christians in a Secular World: The Canadian Experience*. Montreal and Kingston: McGill-Queen's University Press.
Bowler, Kate. 2013. *Blessed: A History of the American Prosperity Gospel*. New York: Oxford University Press.
Boyd, Gregory A. 2000. *God of the Possible: A Biblical Introduction to the Open View of God*. Grand Rapids, MI: Baker Books.
– 2004. *Repenting of Religion: Turning from Judgment to the Love of God*. Grand Rapids, MI: Baker Books.
– 2007. *The Myth of a Christian Nation: How the Quest for Political Power Is Destroying the Church*. Grand Rapids, MI: Zondervan.
– 2009. *The Myth of a Christian Religion: Losing Your Religion for the Beauty of a Revolution*. Grand Rapids, MI: Zondervan.
– 2013. "Can You Have an Anabaptist Mega-Church?" ReKnew, 8 October. http://reknew.org/2013/10/can-you-have-an-anabaptist-mega-church/.
Boyd, K.C. 2012. *Being Christian: A Novel*. Los Angeles, CA: Rebel Island.
Bramadat, Paul. 2000. *The Church on the World's Turf: An Evangelical Christian Group at a Secular University*. New York: Oxford University Press.
– 2009. "Beyond Christian Canada: Religion and Ethnicity in a Multicultural Society." In *Religion and Ethnicity in Canada*, edited by Paul Bramadat and David Seljak, 1–29. Toronto: University of Toronto Press.
Bramadat, Paul, and David Seljak. 2008. *Christianity and Ethnicity in Canada*. Toronto: University of Toronto Press.
Bratton, Susan Power. 2016. *ChurchScape: Megachurches and the Iconography of Environment*. Waco, TX: Baylor University Press.
Braudy, Leo. 1997. *The Frenzy of Renown: Fame and Its History*. New York: Vintage Books.
Brecht, Bertolt. 1964. *Brecht on Theatre: The Development of an Aesthetic*. New York: Hill and Wang.

Brende, Eric. 2009. *Better Off*. New York: HarperCollins.
Brenneman, Todd M. 2014. *Homespun Gospel: The Triumph of Sentimentality in Contemporary American Evangelicalism*. New York: Oxford University Press.
Brierley, Justin. 2017. "Bruxy Cavey: Creating Church for People Who Don't Do Church." Podbean, 30 December. https://goo.gl/QjbgZz.
Bro, Harmon Hartzell. 1955. *The Charisma of the Seer: A Study in the Phenomenology of Religious Leadership*. Chicago: University of Chicago Press.
Bronwell, Claire. 2014. "The Sermon on the Monitor: The New Wave of Evangelists Who've Turned Preaching into a Multimedia Endeavour." *Financial Post*, 20 December.
Brooker, Peter. 1994. "Key Words in Brecht's Theory and Practice of Theatre." In *The Cambridge Companion to Brecht*, edited by Peter Thomson and Glendyr Sacks, 185–200. Cambridge: Cambridge University Press.
Brooks, David. 2000. *Bobos in Paradise: The New Upper Class and How They Got There*. New York: Simon and Schuster.
– 2004. *On Paradise Drive: How We Live Now (and Always Have) in the Future Tense*. New York: Simon and Schuster.
Brown, Charles. 2012. "Selling Faith: Marketing Christian Popular Culture to Christian and Non-Christian Audiences." *Journal of Religion and Popular Culture* 24 (1): 113–29.
Bruce, Steve. 2000. *Choice and Religion: A Critique of Rational Choice Theory*. New York: Oxford University Press.
– 2002. *God Is Dead: Secularization in the West*. Hoboken, NJ: Wiley-Blackwell.
Brueggemann, Walter. 2001. *The Prophetic Imagination*. Minneapolis, MI: Fortress.
Bryman, Alan. 1992. *Charisma and Leadership in Organizations*. New York: Sage Publications.
– 2004. *The Disneyization of Society*. New York: Sage Publications.
Buddenbaum, Judith M. 2013. "Scandalous Evangelicals: Sex, Greed, Politics, and the Arts." In *Evangelical Christians and Popular Culture: Pop Goes the Gospel*, edited by Robert Woods, 110–27. Santa Barbara, CA: Praeger.
Burke, Kathryn L., and Merlin B. Brinkerhoff. 1981. "Capturing Charisma: Notes on an Elusive Concept." *Journal for the Scientific Study of Religion* 20 (3): 274–84.
Burke, Spencer. 2003. *Making Sense of Church: Eavesdropping on Emerging Conversations about God, Community, and Culture*. Grand Rapids, MI: Zondervan/Youth Specialties.

— 2007. *Out of the Ooze: Unlikely Love Letters to the Church from beyond the Pew*. Colorado Springs, CO: NavPress.

Burns, Kelli S. 2009. *Celeb 2.0: How Social Media Foster Our Fascination with Popular Culture*. Santa Barbara, CA: Praeger/ABC-CLIO.

Burwell, Ron. 2006. "BIC Church Member Profile Survey." Mechanicsburg, PA: Messiah College.

Busman, Joshua Kalin. 2015. "(Re)Sounding Passion: Listening to American Evangelical Worship Music, 1997–2015." PhD diss., University of North Carolina at Chapel Hill.

Bussie, Jacqueline. 2016. *Outlaw Christian: Finding Authentic Faith by Breaking the "Rules."* Nashville, TN: Nelson Books.

Bustraan, Richard A. 2014. *The Jesus People Movement: A Story of Spiritual Revolution among the Hippies*. Eugene, OR: Pickwick Publications.

Butler, Judith. 1988. "Performative Acts and Gender Constitution: An Essay in Phenomenology and Feminist Theory." *Theatre Journal* 40 (4): 519–31.

Cabane, Olivia Fox. 2012. *The Charisma Myth: How Anyone Can Master the Art and Science of Personal Magnetism*. New York: Penguin.

Cable, Pamela King. 2012. *Televenge*. Hardwick, MA: Satya House Publications.

Cady, Linell Elizabeth, and Delwin Brown. 2002. *Religious Studies, Theology, and the University: Conflicting Maps, Changing Terrain*. Albany, NY: State University of New York Press.

Cain, Susan. 2013. *Quiet: The Power of Introverts in a World That Can't Stop Talking*. New York: Broadway Paperbacks.

Caistor, Nick. 2010. *Che Guevara: A Life*. Northampton, MA: Interlink Books.

Campbell, Charles L., and Johan H. Cilliers. *Preaching Fools: The Gospel as a Rhetoric of Folly*. Waco, TX: Baylor University Press.

Campbell, Heidi. 2010. *When Religion Meets New Media*. London: Routledge.

Campbell, Heidi, and Paul Emerson Teusner. 2011. "Religious Authority in the Age of the Internet." *Christian Reflection* 38:59–68.

Campolo, Tony, and Shane Claiborne. 2016. "The Evangelicalism of Old White Men Is Dead." *New York Times*, 29 November. https://www.nytimes.com/2016/11/29/opinion/the-evangelicalism-of-old-white-men-is-dead.html.

Carey, Dennis C., and Dayton Ogden. 2000. *CEO Succession*. New York: Oxford University Press.

Carlyle, Thomas. 1840. *On Heroes, Hero-Worship and the Heroic in History*. London: Chapman and Hall.

Carnegie, Dale. 2010. *How to Win Friends and Influence People*. New York: Simon and Schuster.

Carroll, Caitlan. 2011. "Crystal Cathedral Shows Mega-Sized Megachurches May Be a Thing of the Past." Southern California Public Radio, 20 August. http://www.scpr.org/news/2011/08/20/28339/crystal-cathedral-shows-mega-sized-megachurches-ma/.

Carroll, John. 2010. "The Tragicomedy of Celebrity." *Society* 47 (6): 489–92.

Carroll, Marilyn Florence, and Joan Mae Jarvis. 1997. "Being: The Essence and Vitality of Rural Congregational Life and Ministry." MTS thesis, St Stephen's College.

Carter, Craig. 2014. "Is There Such a Thing as a 'Third Way' on Homosexuality?" Bayview Review, 3 November. https://thebayviewreview.com/2014/11/03.

Carter, Lewis F. 2010. *Charisma and Control in Rajneeshpuram: A Community without Shared Values*. Cambridge: Cambridge University Press.

Casanova, Jose. 1994. *Public Religions in the Modern World*. Chicago: University of Chicago Press.

– 2012. "Are We Still Secular? Exploration on the Secular and the Post-Secular." In *Post-Secular Society*, edited by Peter Nynas, Mika Lassander, and Terhi Utriainen, 27–46. New York: Transaction Publishers.

Cavey, Bruxy. 2007. *The End of Religion: Encountering the Subversive Spirituality of Jesus*. Colorado Springs, CO: NavPress.

– 2017a. "The Good News in a Tattoo." Bruxy Cavey. 28 February. http://www.bruxy.com/book/the-good-news-in-a-tattoo/.

– 2017b. *(Re)union: The Good News of Jesus for Seekers, Saints, and Sinners*. Harrisburg, PA: Herald.

Cavey, Bruxy, and Wendy Carrington-Phillips. 2012. "Adapting the House Church Model." In *The Church, Then and Now*, edited by Stanley E. Porter and Cynthia Long Westfall, 151–77. Eugene, OR: Wipf and Stock Publishers.

Cavicchi, Daniel. 1998. *Tramps Like Us Music & Meaning among Springsteen Fans*. New York: Oxford University Press.

Chandler, Siobhan. 2008. "The Social Ethic of Religiously Unaffiliated Spirituality." *Religion Compass* 2 (2): 240–56.

Chang, Paul W., and Dale J. Lim. 2009. "Renegotiating the Sacred-Secular Binary: IX Saves and Contemporary Christian Music." *Review of Religious Research* 50 (4): 392–412.

Chapman, Mark Denis. 2004. "No Longer Crying in the Wilderness: Canadian Evangelical Organizations and Their Networks." PhD diss., University of Toronto.
Chaves, Mark. 2004. *Congregations in America*. Cambridge, MA: Harvard University Press.
– 2006. "All Creatures Great and Small: Megachurches in Context." *Review of Religious Research* 47 (4): 329–46.
– 2011. *American Religion: Contemporary Trends*. Princeton, NJ: Princeton University Press.
Chesterton, G.K. 2004. *Orthodoxy*. Mineola, NY: Dover Publications.
Chia, Lloyd. 2010. "Emerging Faith Boundaries: Bridge-Building, Inclusion, and the Emerging Church Movement in America." PhD diss., University of Missouri.
Chidester, David. 2005. *Authentic Fakes: Religion and American Popular Culture*. Berkeley: University of California Press.
Chong, Terence. 2018. *Pentecostal Megachurches in Southeast Asia: Negotiating Class, Consumption and the Nation*. Singapore: Institute of Southeast Asian Studies – Yusof Ishak Institute.
Chriss, James J. 1995. "Habermas, Goffman, and Communicative Action: Implications for Professional Practice." *American Sociological Review* 60 (4): 545–65.
Christians, Clifford G. 2013. "Evangelical Perspectives on Technology." In *Evangelical Christians and Popular Culture: Pop Goes the Gospel*, edited by Robert Woods, 323–40. Santa Barbara, CA: Praeger.
Cimino, Richard. 1999. "Choosing My Religion." *American Demographics* 21 (4): 60–5.
Cimino, Richard, and Don Lattin. 1998. *Shopping for Faith: American Religion in the New Millennium*. Hoboken, NJ: Wiley.
Cionca, John R. 2004. *Before You Move: A Guide to Making Transitions in Ministry*. Grand Rapids, MI: Kregel Publications.
Claiborne, Shane. 2006. *The Irresistible Revolution: Living as an Ordinary Radical*. Grand Rapids, MI: Zondervan.
– 2011. "The Emerging Church Brand: The Good, the Bad, and the Messy." Red Letter Christians, 1 June. http://www.redletterchristians.org/the-emerging-church-brand-the-good-the-bad-and-the-messy/.
Clark, B.R. 1975. "The Organizational Saga in Higher Education." *Administrative Science Quarterly* 17 (2): 178–84.
Clark, Brian, and Stuart MacDonald. 2017. *Leaving Christianity: Changing Allegiances in Canada since 1945*. Montreal and Kingston: McGill-Queen's University Press.

Clark, Lynn Schofield, ed. 2007. *Religion, Media, and the Marketplace.* New Brunswick, NJ: Rutgers University Press.

Clark, William. 2007. *Academic Charisma and the Origins of the Research University.* Chicago: University of Chicago Press.

Clarke, Joseph. 2009. "Infrastructure for Souls." *Triple Canopy* 6 (June). https://www.canopycanopycanopy.com/issues/6/contents/infrastructure_for_souls.

Clutterbuck, David. 2012. *The Talent Wave: Why Succession Planning Fails and What to Do about It.* Philadelphia: Kogan Page Publishers.

Coates, Ta-Nehisi. 2010. "Long Odds." *Atlantic*, 27 September. http://www.theatlantic.com/national/archive/2010/09/long-odds/63583/.

Cohen, Robert. 2004. "Role Distance: On Stage and on the Merry-Go-Round." *Journal of Dramatic Theory and Criticism* (Fall): 115–24.

Coleman, Simon. 2000. *The Globalisation of Charismatic Christianity.* Cambridge: Cambridge University Press.

Collins, James Charles. 2001. *Good to Great: Why Some Companies Make the Leap ... and Others Don't.* New York: Random House Business.

Collins, Jim, and Jerry I. Porras. 2002. *Built to Last: Successful Habits of Visionary Companies.* New York: Harper Collins.

Conger, Jay A. 1989. *The Charismatic Leader: Behind the Mystique of Exceptional Leadership.* San Francisco: Jossey-Bass.

Conger, Jay A., and Rabindra N. Kanungo. 1988. *Charismatic Leadership: The Elusive Factor in Organizational Effectiveness.* San Francisco: Jossey-Bass.

Conn, Harvie M. 1977. *Theological Perspectives on Church Growth.* Nutley, NJ: Presbyterian and Reformed Publishing.

Connel, J. 2005. "Hillsong: A Megachurch in the Sydney Suburbs." *Australian Geographer* 36 (3): 315–32.

Cooke, Phil. 2008. *Branding Faith: Why Some Churches and Nonprofits Impact Culture and Others Don't.* Ventura, CA: Regal.

Cordero, Rodrigo. 2008. "Performing Cultural Sociology." *European Journal of Social Theory* 11 (4): 523–42.

Corrigan, Tom. 2010. "Rockin' to His Own Religious Beat: EastLake Pastor, Churchgoers Congregate in Bothell." *Bothell/Kenmore Reporter*, 8 September.

Corsi, Jerome R. 2008. *The Obama Nation.* New York: Simon and Schuster.

Coser, Lewis A. 1974. *Greedy Institutions: Patterns of Undivided Commitment.* New York: Free Press.

Cowan, Douglas Edward. 2008. *Sacred Terror: Religion and Horror on the Silver Screen.* Waco, TX: Baylor University Press.

Cox, Harvey. 1969. *The Feast of Fools.* New York: Harper.

– 2001. *Fire from Heaven: The Rise of Pentecostal Spirituality and the Reshaping of Religion in the 21st Century.* Boston: Da Capo.

Creswell, John W. 2006. *Qualitative Inquiry and Research Design: Choosing among Five Approaches.* 2nd ed. New York: Sage Publications.

Cron, Ian Morgan. 2013. *Chasing Francis: A Pilgrim's Tale.* Grand Rapids, MI: Zondervan.

Crouch, Andy. 2018. "It's Time to Reckon with Celebrity Power." Gospel Coalition, 24 March. https://www.thegospelcoalition.org/article/time-reckon-celebrity-power/.

Crowe, Justin, Susan McWilliams, and Sean Beienburg. 2010. "A Pilgrimage to the Disneyland of Faith." *Political Science and Politics* 43 (2): 359–61.

Csordas, Thomas J. 1997. *Language, Charisma, and Creativity: The Ritual Life of a Religious Movement.* Berkeley: University of California Press.

Cullen, Lisa Takeuchi. 2013. *Pastors' Wives: A Novel.* New York: Plume.

Cummergen, Paul A. 1997. "Preaching and Other Verbal Performance in a United Church of Canada Congregation: Speaking of Experience." PhD diss., University of Ottawa.

Daft, Richard L. 2014. *The Leadership Experience.* 6th ed. Stamford, CT: South-Western College Publishing.

Dark, David. 2016. *Life's Too Short to Pretend You're Not Religious.* Downers Grove, IL: InterVarsity.

Dauer, Tysen. 2014. "The Place of Power: The Christian Acquisition of the Roman Basilica." *Journal of Undergraduate Research* 6 (1). https://cornerstone.lib.mnsu.edu/jur/vol6/iss1/3/.

Davidman, Lynn, and Arthur L. Greil. 2007. "Characters in Search of a Script: The Exit Narratives of Formerly Ultra-Orthodox Jews." *Journal for the Scientific Study of Religion* 46 (2): 201–16.

Davis, Charles, and Nicholas Mills. 2014. "Innovation and Toronto's Cognitive Cultural Economy." In *Innovation and Knowledge Flows in Canadian City-Regions*, edited by David Wolfe, 59–91. Toronto: University of Toronto Press.

Davis, Joseph E. 2012. *Stories of Change: Narrative and Social Movements.* New York: SUNY Press.

Dawkins, Richard. 2008. *The God Delusion.* Boston: Houghton Mifflin Harcourt.

Dawn, Marva J. 1995. *Reaching Out without Dumbing Down: A Theology of Worship for This Urgent Time.* Grand Rapids, MI: Wm B. Eerdmans Publishing.

Dawson, Lorne. 2006. *Comprehending Cults: The Sociology of New Religious Movements.* New York: Oxford University Press.

– 2011. "Charismatic Leadership in Millennial Movements." In *The Oxford Handbook of Millennialism,* edited by Catherine Wessinger, 113–33. New York: Oxford University Press.

Day, Barry Bruce. 1982. "Helping a Congregation to Explore and Renew the Meaning of Membership." DMin diss., Drew University.

Day, Tim. 2014. *Plot Twist: God Enters Stage Left.* Oakville, ON: Meeting House.

de Botton, Alain. 2004. *Status Anxiety.* Toronto: Penguin.

de Certeau, Michel. 1984. *The Practice of Everyday Life.* Berkeley: University of California Press.

deChant, Dell. 2002. *The Sacred Santa: Religious Dimensions of Consumer Culture.* New York: Pilgrim.

Deflem, Mathieu. 1991. "Ritual, Anti-Structure, and Religion: A Discussion of Victor Turner's Processual Symbolic Analysis." *Journal for the Scientific Study of Religion* 30 (1): 1–25.

Demerath, Jay III. 2007. "Secularization and Sacralization Deconstructed and Reconstructed." In *The SAGE Handbook of the Sociology of Religion,* edited by James A. Beckford and Jay Demerath III, 57–73. New York: Sage.

Denzin, Norman K., and Yvonna S. Lincoln. 2011. *The Sage Handbook of Qualitative Research.* 4th ed. Thousand Oaks, CA: Sage.

Dias, Elizabeth. 2015. "A Change of Heart: Inside the Evangelical War over Gay Marriage." *Time,* 15 January.

Dixit, Rajkumar. 2010. *Branded Faith: Contextualizing the Gospel in a Post-Christian Era.* Eugene, OR: Wipf and Stock Publishers.

Dollar, Creflo. 2015. *Why I Hate Religion: 10 Reasons to Break Free from the Bondage of Religious Tradition.* New York: Faith Words.

Douglas, Kelly Brown. 2018. "How Evangelicals Became White." *Sojourners.* April, 19–22.

Donnelly, Christopher M. 2011. "Kickin' It with God: Clerical Behavior, Denominational Meaning, and the Expression of Emotion in Ritual." MA thesis, University of Connecticut.

Douville, Bruce Michael. 2007. "'And We've Got to Get Ourselves Back to the Garden': The Jesus People Movement in Toronto." *Canadian Society* of Church History. https://historicalpapers.journals.yorku.ca/index.php/historicalpapers/article/view/39186/35528.

Downton, James V. 1973. *Rebel Leadership: Commitment and Charisma in the Revolutionary Process*. New York: Free Press.

Drane, John. 2001. *The McDonaldization of the Church: Consumer Culture and the Church's Future*. Macon, GA: Smyth & Helwys Publishing.

– 2009. "From Creeds to Burgers: Religious Control, Spiritual Search, and the Future of Work." In *McDonaldization: The Reader*, 3rd ed., edited by George Ritzer, 222–28. New York: Sage Publications.

Draper, Scott. 2014. "Effervescence and Solidarity in Religious Organizations." *Journal for the Scientific Study of Religion* 53 (2): 229–48.

Dreher, Rod. 2006. *Crunchy Cons How Birkenstocked Burkeans, Gun-Loving Organic Gardeners, Evangelical Free-Range Farmers, Hip Homeschooling Mamas, Right-Wing Nature Lovers and Their Diverse Tribe of Countercultural Conservatives Plan to Save America (or at Least the Republican Party)*. New York: Crown Forum.

Drescher, Elizabeth. 2016. *Choosing Our Religion: The Spiritual Lives of America's Nones*. New York: Oxford.

Drewery, Malcolm P. 2008. "Black Megachurches and Social Services." PhD diss., American University.

Dreyer, Jaco S. 2014. "The Narrative Turn in Practical Theology: A Discussion of Julian Muller's Narrative Approach." *Verbum et Ecclesia* 35 (2). http://www.scielo.org.za/scielo.php?script=sci_arttext&pid=S2074-77052014000200006.

Driedger, Leo. 2000. *Mennonites in the Global Village*. Toronto: University of Toronto Press, Scholarly Publishing Division.

Driscoll, Mark. 2009. *Religion Saves: And Nine Other Misconceptions*. Wheaton, IL: Crossway Books.

Droogers, André. 2011. *Play and Power in Religion: Collected Essays*. Berlin: de Gruyter.

Drucker, Peter F. 1998. "Management's New Paradigms." *Forbes*, October, 152–77.

Duncan, Carol B. 2008. *This Spot of Ground: Spiritual Baptists in Toronto*. Waterloo, ON: Wilfrid Laurier University Press.

Duncan, John Alan. 2011. "A Critical Analysis of Preaching in the Emerging Church." PhD diss., Southern Baptist Theological Seminary.

Dunn, James D.G. 1975. *Jesus and the Spirit*. London: SCM-Canterbury.

Durkheim, Emile. 1995. *The Elementary Forms of Religious Life*. Translated by K.E. Fields. New York: Free Press.

Dyer, Jennifer Eaton. 2007. "The Core Beliefs of Southern Evangelicals: A Psycho-Social Investigation of the Evangelical Megachurch Phenomenon." PhD diss., Vanderbilt University.

Dyer, Richard. 1987. *Heavenly Bodies: Film Stars and Society*. 2nd ed. New York: Routledge.

Dyer, Richard, and Paul McDonald. 2002. *Stars*. London: British Film Institute Publications.

Eagle, David E. 2015. "Historicizing the Megachurch." *Journal of Social History* 48 (3): 589–604.

Eco, Umberto. 1986. *The Name of the Rose*. San Diego, CA: Harcourt.

Edgell, Penny. 2012. "A Cultural Sociology of Religion: New Directions." *Annual Review of Sociology* 38 (1): 247–65.

Eiesland, Nancy L. 1997. "Contending with a Giant: The Impact of a Megachurch on Exurban Religious Institutions." In *Contemporary American Religion: An Ethnographic Reader*, edited by Penny Edgell and Nancy Eiesland, 191–219. Walnut Creek, CA: Altamira.

– 1999. *A Particular Place: Urban Restructuring and Religious Ecology in a Southern Exurb*. New Brunswick, NJ: Rutgers University Press.

Einstein, Mara. 2007. *Brands of Faith: Marketing Religion in a Commercial Age*. New York: Routledge.

Eisenstadt, S.N. 1968. "Introduction." In *On Charisma and Institution Building: Selected Papers*, edited by S.N. Eisenstadt, xi–lv. Chicago: University of Chicago Press.

Ekelund, Robert B., Jr, Robert F. Hébert, and Robert Tollison. 2008. *The Marketplace of Christianity*. Cambridge, MA: MIT Press.

Elisha, Omri. 2011. *Moral Ambition: Mobilization and Social Outreach in Evangelical Megachurches*. Berkeley: University of California Press.

Ellingson, Stephen. 2007. *The Megachurch and the Mainline: Remaking Religious Tradition in the Twenty-First Century*. Chicago: University of Chicago Press.

– 2010. "The New Megachurch: Non-Denominationalism and Sectarianism." In *The New Blackwell Companion to the Sociology of Religion*, edited by Bryan S. Turner, 447–66. Malden, MA: Wiley-Blackwell.

Ellwood, Robert S. 1973. *One Way: The Jesus Movement and Its Meaning*. Englewood Cliffs, NJ: Prentice Hall.

Emberley, Peter. 2002. *Divine Hunger: Canadians on Spiritual Walkabout*. New York: HarperCollins Publishers.

Enroth, Ronald M. 1972. *The Story of the Jesus People; A Factual Survey*. Exeter: Paternoster.

Eskridge, Larry. 2013. *God's Forever Family: The Jesus People Movement in America*. New York: Oxford University Press.

Evans, Jessica, and David Hesmondhalgh. 2005. *Understanding Media: Inside Celebrity*. Maidenhead, Berkshire: Open University Press.

Evensen, Bruce J. 2003. *God's Man for the Gilded Age: D.L. Moody and the Rise of Modern Mass Evangelism*. Oxford: Oxford University Press.

Faccio, Elena, Norberto Costa. 2013. "The Presentation of Self in Everyday Prison Life: Reading Interactions in Prison from a Dramaturgic Point of View." *Global Crime* 14 (4): 386–403.

Falco, Raphael. 2011. *Charisma and Myth*. London: A&C Black.

Falwell, Macel. 2008. *Jerry Falwell: His Life and Legacy*. New York: Howard Books.

Farley, Andrew. 2011. *God without Religion: Can It Really Be This Simple?* Grand Rapids, MI: Baker Books.

Fath, Sébastien. 2005. "Evangelical Protestantism in France: An Example of Denominational Recomposition?" *Sociology of Religion* 66 (4): 399–418.

– 2008. *Dieu XXL: La Révolution des Megachurches*. Paris: Éditions Autrement.

Feltmate, David. 2017. *Drawn to the Gods: Religion and Humor in the Simpsons, South Park, and Family Guy*. New York: New York University Press.

Fenske, Mindy. 2007. "Interdisciplinary Terrains of Performance Studies." *Text and Performance Quarterly* 27 (4): 351–68.

Ferris, Kerry. 2010. "The Next Big Thing: Local Celebrity." *Society* 47 (5): 392–5.

Ferris, Kerry O. 2007. "The Sociology of Celebrity." *Sociology Compass* 1 (1): 371–84.

Feuchtwang, Stephan. 2008. "Suggestions for a Redefinition of Charisma." *Nova Religio* 12 (2): 90–105.

Finger, Thomas N. 2004. *A Contemporary Anabaptist Theology: Biblical, Historical, Constructive*. Downers Grove, IL: InterVarsity Press.

Fiol, C. Marlene, Drew Harris, and Robert House. 1999. "Charismatic Leadership: Strategies for Effecting Social Change." *Leadership Quarterly* 10 (3): 449–82.

First, Sara Babcox. 2009. "The Mechanics of Renown; Or, the Rise of a Celebrity Culture in Early America." PhD diss., University of Michigan.

Flatt, Kevin N. 2014. *After Evangelicalism: The Sixties and the United Church of Canada*. Montreal and Kingston: McGill-Queen's University Press.

Fletcher, John. 2013. *Preaching to Convert: Evangelical Outreach and Performance Activism in a Secular Age*. Ann Arbor: University of Michigan Press.

Florida, Richard. 2014. "The Creative Class and Economic Development." *Economic Development Quarterly* 28 (3): 196–205.

Foltz, Richard. 2007. "The Religion of the Market: Reflections on a Decade of Discussion." *Worldviews: Global Religions, Culture, and Ecology* 11 (2): 135–54.

Ford, David F., Ben Quash, and Janet Martin Soskice. 2005. *Fields of Faith: Theology and Religious Studies for the Twenty-First Century*. Cambridge: Cambridge University Press.

Foucault, Michel. 1973. *Birth of the Clinic: An Archaeology of Medical Perception*. Translated by A.M. Sheridan Smith. New York: Pantheon.

– 1977. *Discipline and Punish: The Birth of the Prison*. Translated by Alan Sheridan. 1st American ed. New York: Pantheon Books.

Fowler, Doug. 2012. "God as a Drug: The Rise of American Megachurches." American Sociological Association. https://www.eurekalert.org/pub_releases/2012-08/asa-gaa081412.php.

Fowler, James W. 1995. *Stages of Faith: The Psychology of Human Development and the Quest for Meaning*. New York: HarperOne.

Frank, Thomas. 1997. *The Conquest of Cool: Business Culture, Counterculture, and the Rise of Hip Consumerism*. Chicago: University of Chicago Press.

Freedman, Samuel G. 2007. "An Unlikely Megachurch Lesson." *New York Times*, 3 November. http://www.nytimes.com/2007/11/03/us/03religion.html.

Friedland, William W. 1964. "For a Sociological Concept of Charisma." *Social Forces* 43 (1): 18–26.

Friedman, Lawrence Meir. 1990. *The Republic of Choice: Law, Authority, and Culture*. Cambridge, MA: Harvard University Press.

Frye, Northrop. 1957. *Anatomy of Criticism: Four Essays*. Princeton, NJ: Princeton University Press.

Fuist, Todd Nicholas. 2014. "The Dramatization of Beliefs, Values, and Allegiances: Ideological Performances among Social Movement Groups and Religious Organizations." *Social Movement Studies* 13 (4): 427–42.

Fulford, Robert. 1999. *The Triumph of Narrative: Storytelling in the Age of Mass Culture*. Toronto: House of Anansi.

Fulkerson, Mary McClintock. 2007. *Places of Redemption: Theology for a Worldly Church*. Oxford: Oxford University Press.

Fuller, Robert C. 2001. *Spiritual, but Not Religious: Understanding Unchurched America*. New York: Oxford University Press.

Furedi, Frank. 2010. "Celebrity Culture." *Society* 47 (6): 493–7.

Furman, Lou. 1988. "Theatre as Therapy: The Distancing Effect Applied to Audience." *Arts in Psychotherapy* 15 (3): 245–9.

Furseth, Inger, and Pal Repstad. 2006. *An Introduction to the Sociology of Religion: Classical and Contemporary Perspectives*. Farnham, UK: Ashgate Publishing.

Gabler, Neal. 2001. "Toward a New Definition of Celebrity." Norman Lear Centre, University of Southern California. https://learcenter.org/pdf/Gabler.pdf.

– 2009. "Tiger-Stalking: In Defense of Our Tabloid Culture." *Newsweek*, 11 December.

Gabriel, Yiannis. 2000. *Storytelling in Organizations: Facts, Fictions, and Fantasies*. New York: Oxford University Press.

Gamson, Joshua. 1994. *Claims to Fame: Celebrity in Contemporary America*. Berkeley, CA: University of California Press.

Gardner, William L., and Bruce J. Avolio. 1998. "The Charismatic Relationship: A Dramaturgical Perspective." *Academy of Management Review* 23 (1): 32–58.

Garfinkel, Harold. 1976. *Studies in Ethnomethodology*. Cambridge: Polity.

Gassner, John. 1966. *The Theatre in Our Times: A Survey of the Men, Materials and Movements in the Modern Theatre*. New York: Crown.

Gauthier, François, and Tuomas Martikainen. 2013. *Religion in Consumer Society: Brands, Consumers and Markets*. Burlington, VT: Ashgate.

Gauvreau, Michael. 1991. *The Evangelical Century: College and Creed in English Canada from the Great Revival to the Great Depression*. Montreal and Kingston: McGill-Queen's University Press.

Geertz, Clifford. 1977. *The Interpretation of Cultures*. New York: Basic Books.

Georgescu, P. 2013. "Exchange Religion for Faith." *Huffington Post*, 14 November.

Gerson, Michael. 2018. "The Last Temptation." *Atlantic*, April, 43–52.

Gibbs, Eddie, and Ryan K. Bolger. 2005. *Emerging Churches: Creating Christian Community in Postmodern Cultures*. Grand Rapids, MI: Baker Academic.

Giddens, Anthony. 1991. *Modernity and Self-Identity: Self and Society in the Late Modern Age*. Hoboken, NJ: John Wiley & Sons.

– 1992. *The Transformation of Intimacy: Sexuality, Love and Eroticism in Modern Societies*. Hoboken, NJ: John Wiley & Sons.

— 2003. *Runaway World: How Globalization Is Reshaping Our Lives.* New York: Routledge.
— 2009. "On Rereading 'The Presentation of Self': Some Reflections." In "50th Anniversary of 'The Presentation of Self in Everyday Life,'" special issue, *Social Psychology Quarterly* 72 (4): 290–95.
Gilley, Gary. 2002. *This Little Church Went to Market: The Church in the Age of Modern Entertainment.* Maitland, FL: Xulon.
Gilmore, James W., and B. Joseph Pine II. 2007. *Authenticity: What Consumers Really Want.* Boston, MA: Harvard Business School Press.
Giroux, Henry A. 2011. *Zombie Politics and Culture in the Age of Casino Capitalism.* New York: Peter Lang.
Gitau, Wanjiru M. 2018. *Megachurch Christianity Reconsidered: Millennials and Social Change in African Perspective.* Downers Grove, IL: InterVarsity Press.
Gladwell, Malcolm. 2005. "The Cellular Church." *New Yorker*, 12 September. http://www.newyorker.com/magazine/2005/09/12/the-cellular-church.
Glasser, Arthur F. 1986. "Church Growth at Fuller." *Missiology: An International Review* 14 (4): 401–20.
Glassman, Ronald M. 1975. "Legitimacy and Manufactured Charisma." *Social Research* 42 (4): 615–36.
Glassman, Ronald M., and William W. Swatos. 1986. *Charisma, History, and Social Structure.* New York: Greenwood.
Gledhill, Christine, ed. 1991. *Stardom: Industry of Desire.* London: Routledge.
Glover, Voyle A. 1990. *Fundamental Seduction: The Jack Hyles Case.* Merrillville, IN: Brevia Publishing.
Goffman, Erving. 1959. *The Presentation of Self in Everyday Life.* Norwell, MA: Anchor.
— 1961a. *Asylums: Essays on the Social Situation of Mental Patients and Other Inmates.* Norwell, MA: Anchor Books.
— 1961b. *Encounters; Two Studies in the Sociology of Interaction.* Eastford, CT: Martino Fine Books.
— 1963. *Stigma: Notes on the Management of Spoiled Identity.* New York: Prentice Hall.
— 1967. *Interaction Ritual: Essays in Face to Face Behavior.* Piscataway, NJ: Aldine Transaction.
— 1981. *Forms of Talk.* Philadelphia: University of Pennsylvania Press.
— 1986. *Frame Analysis: An Essay on the Organization of Experience.* Boston: Northeastern.

Goh, Robbie B.W. 2008. "Hillsong and 'Megachurch' Practice: Semiotics, Spatial Logic and the Embodiment of Contemporary Evangelical Protestantism." *Material Religion* 4 (3): 284–304.

Goheen, Michael W. 2010. "Historical Perspectives on the Missional Church Movement: Probing Lesslie Newbigin's Formative Influence." *Trinity Journal for Theology and Ministry* 4 (2): 62–84.

Gold, Raymond L. 1958. "Roles in Sociological Field Observations." *Social Forces* 36 (3): 217–23.

Goldsmith, Marshall. 2013. *Succession: Are You Ready?* Cambridge, MA: Harvard Business Press.

Goodbrand, Grant. 2010. *Therafields: The Rise and Fall of Lea Hindley-Smith's Psychoanalytic Commune*. Toronto: ECW.

Goodman, Lenn. 2010. "Supernovas: The Dialectic of Celebrity in Society." *Society* 47 (6): 510–15.

Goodman, William R., and James J.W. Price. 1981. *Jerry Falwell: An Unauthorized Profile*. Lynchburg, VA: Paris & Associates.

Goodstein, Laurie. 2006. "Disowning Conservative Politics, Evangelical Pastor Rattles Flock." *New York Times*, 30 July. http://www.nytimes.com/2006/07/30/us/30pastor.html.

Goodstein, Laurie. 2018. "'This Is Not of God': When Anti-Trump Evangelicals Confront Their Brethren." *New York Times*, 23 May. https://www.nytimes.com/2018/05/23/us/anti-trump-evangelicals-lynchburg.html.

Gooren, Henri. 2010. *Religious Conversion and Disaffiliation: Tracing Patterns of Change in Faith Practices*. New York: Palgrave Macmillan.

– 2011. "Deconversion: Qualitative and Quantitative Results from Cross-Cultural Research in Germany and the United States: A Review Essay." *Pastoral Psychology* 60 (4): 609–17.

Gordon, Ian. 2002. "Satire." *Literary Encyclopedia*. http://www.litencyc.com/php/stopics.php?rec=true&UID=984.

Gorski, Philip, David Kyuman Kim, John Torpey, and Jonathan VanAntwerpen, eds. 2012. *The Post-Secular in Question: Religion in Contemporary Society*. New York: New York University Press.

Gouldner, Alvin W. 1970. *The Coming Crisis of Western Sociology*. New York: Basic Books.

Goulet, Jean-Guy A. 1998. *Ways of Knowing: Experience, Knowledge, and Power among the Dene Tha*. Illustrated ed. Omaha, NB: University of Nebraska Press.

Gowing, Wesley Thomas. 2003. "Filling the Void: A Spiritual Urban Intervention." M.A. thesis, Dalhousie University.

Graham, Ruth. 2014. "How a Megachurch Melts Down," *Atlantic*, 7 November. https://www.theatlantic.com/national/archive/2014/11/houston-mark-driscoll-megachurch-meltdown/382487/.
Grant, John Webster. 1998. *The Church in the Canadian Era*. Updated and expanded ed. Vancouver: Regent College Publishing.
Gregory, Joel. 1994. *Too Great a Temptation: The Seductive Power of America's Super Church*. Fort Worth, TX: Summit Publishing Group – Lega.
Griffin, Mark L. 2010. *Pastor, CEO*. Maitland, FL: Xulon.
Griffith, R. Marie. 2000. *God's Daughters: Evangelical Women and the Power of Submission*. Berkeley: University of California Press.
Griswold, Wendy. 2008. *Cultures and Societies in a Changing World*. 3rd ed. Thousand Oaks, CA: Pine Forge.
Grusky, O. 1960. "Administrative Succession in Formal Organizations." *Social Forces* 39: 105–15.
Guder, Darrell L. 1998. *Missional Church: A Vision for the Sending of the Church in North America*. Grand Rapids, MI: Wm B. Eerdmans Publishing.
Guffin, Scott Lee. 1999. "An Examination of Key Foundational Influences on the Megachurch Movement in America, 1960–1978." PhD diss., Southern Baptist Theological Seminary.
Guhin, Jeffrey. 2013. "Is Irony Good for America? The Threat of Nihilism, the Importance of Romance, and the Power of Cultural Forms." *Cultural Sociology* 7 (1): 23–38.
Guinness, Os. 1993. *Dining with the Devil: The Megachurch Movement Flirts with Modernity*. Grand Rapids, MI: Baker Books.
Gustafsson, Maria. 2005. "Workers for Christ: A Study of Young People in a Costa Rican Mega Church." *Svensk Missionstidskrift* 93 (4): 505–34.
Gutierrez, Gustavo. 1988. *A Theology of Liberation: History, Politics, and Salvation*. Rev. ed. Maryknoll, NY: Orbis Books.
Habermas, Jürgen. 1985. *The Theory of Communicative Action*. Vol. 1, *Reason and the Rationalization of Society*. Translated by Thomas McCarthy. Boston: Beacon.
– 2005. "The Public Role of Religion in Secular Context." In The Holberg Prize Seminar. University of San Diego's Kyoto Symposium, 5 March.
– 2010. *An Awareness of What Is Missing: Faith and Reason in a Post-Secular Age*. Boston: Polity.
Hadaway, Kirk C. 2011. "FACTs on Growth: 2010." Faith Communities Today, Hartford Institute for the Study of Religion. http://faith

communitiestoday.org/sites/default/files/FACTs%20on%20Growth%20 2010.pdf.

Hambrick-Stowe, Charles E. 1996. *Charles G. Finney and the Spirit of American Evangelicalism*. Grand Rapids, MI: Wm B. Eerdmans Publishing.

Hale, Grace Elizabeth. 2011. *A Nation of Outsiders: How the White Middle Class Fell in Love with Rebellion in Postwar America*. New York: Oxford University Press.

Hall, David D. 1997. *Lived Religion in America: Toward a History of Practice*. Princeton, NJ: Princeton University Press.

Hall, John R., Laura Grindstaff, and Lo Ming-Cheng. 2010. *Handbook of Cultural Sociology*. London: Routledge.

Harding, Kimberly L. 1998. "St Philip's African Orthodox Church a Case Study of a Unique Religious Institution." MA thesis, Acadia University.

Harding, Susan Friend. 1991. "Representing Fundamentalism: The Problem of the Repugnant Cultural Other." *Social Research* 58 (2): 373–93.

– 2001. *The Book of Jerry Falwell: Fundamentalist Language and Politics*. Princeton, NJ: Princeton University Press.

Harris, Hamil R. 2012. "Some Are Swapping Mega-Churches for Tiny Ones." *Washington Post*, 29 February.

Harris, Lisa Ohlen. 2015. "Against Sentimentality." *Books and Culture* 21 (1): 14.

Harrison, Jim. 2003. *Paul's Language of Grace in Its Graeco-Roman Context*. Tübingen: Mohr Siebeck.

Harrison, Paul M. 1977. "Toward a Dramaturgical Interpretation of Religion." *Sociology of Religion* 38 (4): 389–96.

Harrison, William H. 2014. *In Praise of Mixed Religion: The Syncretism Solution in a Multifaith World*. Montreal and Kingston: McGill-Queen's University Press.

Harrold, Philip. 2006. "Deconversion in the Emerging Church." *International Journal for the Study of the Christian Church* 6 (1): 79–90.

Hart, Darryl G. 2004. *Deconstructing Evangelicalism: Conservative Protestantism in the Age of Billy Graham*. Grand Rapids, MI: Baker Academic.

Haskell, David M. 2009. *Through a Lens Darkly: How the News Media Perceive and Portray Evangelicals*. Toronto: Clements Publishing Group.

Haskell, David Millard, Kevin Flatt, and Stephanie Burgoyne. 2016. "Theology Matters: Comparing the Traits of Growing and Declining

Mainline Protestant Church Attendees and Clergy." *Review of Religious Research* 58 (4): 515–41.

Hatch, Nathan O. 1989. *The Democratization of American Christianity.* New Haven, CT: Yale University Press.

Hauerwas, Stanley, and William H. Willimon. 1989. *Resident Aliens: A Provocative Christian Assessment of Culture and Ministry for People Who Know That Something Is Wrong.* Nashville, TN: Abingdon.

Hava, Dayan, and Chan Kwok-bun. 2012. *Charismatic Leadership in Singapore: Three Extraordinary People.* New York: Springer.

Hawkins, Greg L., Cally Parkinson, and Eric Arnson. 2007. *Reveal: Where Are You?* Chicago: Willow Creek Association.

Hay, C., M. O'Brien, and Susan Penna. 1997. "Giddens, Modernity and Self-Identity: The 'Hollowing Out' of Social Theory." In *Anthony Giddens: Critical Assessments*, edited by Christopher G.A. Bryant and David Jary, 85–112. Milton Park, UK: Taylor & Francis.

Haynes, Naomi. 2013. "Evangelicals and Moral Ambition." *Books and Culture*, September/October, 17.

Heath, Joseph, and Andrew Potter. 2005. *Nation of Rebels: Why Counterculture Became Consumer Culture.* New York: Harper Paperbacks.

Heelas, Paul. 2008. *Spiritualities of Life: New Age Romanticism and Consumptive Capitalism.* Hoboken, NJ: Wiley-Blackwell.

Heelas, Paul, and Linda Woodhead. 2005. *The Spiritual Revolution: Why Religion Is Giving Way to Spirituality.* Hoboken, NJ: Wiley-Blackwell.

Heifetz, Ronald A. 1994. *Leadership without Easy Answers.* Cambridge, MA: Harvard University Press.

Heinz, Donald John. 1976. "Jesus in Berkeley." PhD diss., Graduate Theological Union.

Hellmueller, Lea C., and Nina Aeschbacher. 2010. "Media and Celebrity: Production and Consumption of 'Well-Knownness.'" *Communication Research Trends* 29 (4): 3–33.

Henderson, Jim, and Doug Murren. 2015. *Question Mark: Why the Church Welcomes Bullies and How to Stop It.* Edmonds, WA: 90-Day Books.

Herrick, James A. 2006. *The Making of the New Spirituality: The Eclipse of the Western Religious Tradition.* Downers Grove, IL: InterVarsity.

Heschel, Abraham. 2001. *The Prophets.* New York: Harper.

Hey, Sam. 2013. *Megachurches: Origins, Ministry, and Prospects.* Eugene, OR: Wipf & Stock.

Hinch, Jim. 2013. "Where Are All the People?" *American Scholar*, December.

Hindmarsh, D. Bruce. 2005. *The Evangelical Conversion Narrative: Spiritual Autobiography in Early Modern England*. Oxford: Oxford University Press.

Hinds, Sonia Sandra Juanita. 2013. "A Perspective on Cultural Diversity in an Anglican Setting." DMin diss., University of Trinity College Faculty of Divinity and University of Toronto.

Hitchens, Christopher. 2009. *God Is Not Great: How Religion Poisons Everything*. New York: Hatchette Book Group.

Hoffman, Douglas R. 2010. *Seeking the Sacred in Contemporary Religious Architecture*. Kent, OH: Kent State University Press.

Hofmann, David C., and Lorne L. Dawson. 2014. "The Neglected Role of Charismatic Authority in the Study of Terrorist Groups and Radicalization." *Studies in Conflict & Terrorism* 37 (4): 348–68.

Hogan, Joyce, Robert Hogan, and Robert B. Kaiser. 2011. "Management Derailment: Personality Assessment and Mitigation." In *American Psychological Association Handbook of Industrial and Organizational Psychology*. Vol 3, *Maintaining, Expanding, and Contracting the Organization*, 555–75. APA Handbooks in Psychology. Washington, DC: American Psychological Association.

Hogan, Robert, and Joyce Hogan. 2001. "Assessing Leadership: A View from the Dark Side." *International Journal of Selection and Assessment* 9 (1–2): 40–51.

Hoge, Dean R., ed. 1979. *Understanding Church Growth and Decline, 1950–1978*. New York: Pilgrim.

Hong, Young-gi. 2000a. "The Backgrounds and Characteristics of the Charismatic Mega-Churches in Korea." *Asian Journal of Pentecostal Studies* 3 (1): 99–118.

– 2000b. "The Charisma of Cho Yonggi and Its Routinization in the Yoido Full Gospel Church in Korea." *Journal of Asian Mission* 2 (1): 65–90.

– 2003. "Encounter with Modernity: The 'Mcdonaldization' and 'Charismatization' of Korean Mega-Churches." *International Review of Mission* 92 (365): 239–55.

Hoover, Stewart M. 2005. "The Cross at Willow Creek: Seeker Religion and the Contemporary Marketplace." In *Religion and Popular Culture in America*, edited by Bruce D. Forbes and Jeffrey H. Mahan, 145–59. Berkeley: University of California Press.

Hopper, Tristan. 2014. "'Gods of Our Own Making': How Hardcore Fans Are Turning Dead Celebrities into the New Sainthood." *National Post*, 1 June. http://news.nationalpost.com/news/canada/

gods-of-our-own-making-how-hardcore-fans-are-turning-dead-celebrities-into-the-new-sainthood.

Horn, Eva. 2011. "Introduction [to Issue on Narrating Charisma]." *New German Critique* 114 (October): 1–16.

Horton, Michael. 2008. *Christless Christianity: The Alternative Gospel of the American Church*. Grand Rapids, MI: Baker Books.

– 2014. *Ordinary: Sustainable Faith in a Radical, Restless World*. Grand Rapids, MI: Zondervan.

Horvath, Agnes. 2013. *Modernism and Charisma*. Houndmills, Basingstoke, Hampshire: Palgrave Macmillan.

House, Robert J., William D. Spangler, and James Woycke. 1991. "Personality and Charisma in the U.S. Presidency: A Psychological Theory of Leader Effectiveness." *Administrative Science Quarterly* 36 (3): 364–96.

Houston, Brian. 2000. *You Need More Money: Discovering God's Amazing Financial Plan for Your Life*. Sydney, AUS: Trust Media Distribution.

Howard, Jay R., and John M. Streck. 1999. *Apostles of Rock: The Splintered World of Contemporary Christian Music*. Lexington, KY: University of Kentucky Press.

Hughes, Mark. 2008. *Buzzmarketing: Get People to Talk about Your Stuff*. New York: Penguin Group.

Hughes, Michael. 2000. "Country Music as Impression Management: A Meditation on Fabricating Authenticity." *Poetics* 28 (2–3): 185–205.

Hughes, Richard T. 2013. "A Theological Coat of Many Colors: The Extraordinary Journey of the Brethren in Christ." *Brethren in Christ History and Life* 36 (3): 361–91, 408–11.

Huizinga, Johan. 1950. *Homo Ludens: A Study of the Play-Element in Culture*. Boston: Beacon.

Hunt, Allen. 2010. *Confessions of a Mega Church Pastor: How I Discovered the Hidden Treasures of the Catholic Church*. Cincinnati, OH: Beacon Publishing.

Hunter, James Davison. 1992. *Culture Wars: The Struggle to Control the Family, Art, Education, Law, and Politics in America*. New York: Basic Books.

– 2010. *To Change the World: The Irony, Tragedy, and Possibility of Christianity in the Late Modern World*. New York: Oxford University Press.

Hunter, Mark. 2013. "Bethany Church Grows from House to Multiple Campuses in 50 Years." *Advocate*, 15 November. http://theadvocate.com/features/people/7138503-123/it-is-baton-rouge.

Hurston, Karen. 1994. *Growing the World's Largest Church*. Springfield, MO: Gospel Publishing House.
Hutchins, Bob, and Greg Stielstra. 2009. *Faith-Based Marketing: The Guide to Reaching 140 Million Christian Customers*. Hoboken, NJ: Wiley.
Hybels, Lynne, and Bill Hybels. 1995. *Rediscovering Church: The Story and Vision of Willow Creek Community Church*. Grand Rapids, MI: Zondervan Publishing House.
Hynes, Maria, and Matthew Wade. 2013. "Worshipping Bodies: Affective Labour in the Hillsong Church." *Geographical Research* 51 (2): 173–9.
Iannaccone, Laurence R. 1994. "Why Strict Churches Are Strong." *American Journal of Sociology* 99 (5): 1180–1211.
Imber, Jonathan, ed. 2007. *Markets, Morals, and Religion*. New Brunswick, NJ: Transaction Publishers.
Inglis, Fred. 2010. *A Short History of Celebrity*. Princeton, NJ: Princeton University Press.
Ingold, John. 2009. "Rev. Blair, 88, Was Megachurch Pioneer." *Denver Post*, 23 August. http://www.denverpost.com/headlines/ci_13186157.
Ingram, Haroro J. 2014. *The Charismatic Leadership Phenomenon in Radical and Militant Islamism*. Farnham, UK: Ashgate.
Ingram, Larry C. 1982. "Underlife in a Baptist Church." *Review of Religious Research* 24 (2): 138–52.
– 1986. "In the Crawlspace of the Organization." *Human Relations* 39 (5): 467–86.
– 1989. "Evangelism as Frame Intrusion: Observations on Witnessing in Public Places." *Journal for the Scientific Study of Religion* 28 (1): 17–26.
Inskeep, Kenneth W. 1993. "A Short History of Church Growth Research." In *Church and Denominational Growth: What Does (and Does Not) Cause Growth and Decline*, edited by David A. Roozen and C. Kirk Hadaway, 135–48. Nashville, TN: Abingdon.
Ismagilova, Elvira, Yogesh K. Dwivedi, Emma Slade, and Michael Williams. 2017. *Electronic Word of Mouth (eWOM) in the Marketing Context*. Cham, Switzerland: Springer.
Ivanov, Sergey A. 2006. *Holy Fools in Byzantium and Beyond*. New York: Oxford University Press.
Jackson, John. 2011. *Pastorpreneur: Creative Ideas for Birthing Spiritual Life in Your Community*. Nashville, TN: InterVarsity.
Jacobs, Janet. 1987. "Deconversion from Religious Movements: An Analysis of Charismatic Bonding and Spiritual Commitment." *Journal for the Scientific Study of Religion* 26 (3): 294–308.

Jacobs, Mark, and Nancy Weiss Hanrahan. 2005. *The Blackwell Companion to the Sociology of Culture*. Malden, MA: Wiley-Blackwell.

Jacobsen, Chanoch, and Robert J. House. 2001. "Dynamics of Charismatic Leadership: A Process Theory, Simulation Model, and Tests." *Leadership Quarterly* 12 (1): 75–112.

Jacobsen, Michael Hviid, and Soren Kristiansen. 2015. *The Social Thought of Erving Goffman*. Los Angeles: Sage Publications.

James, Aaron. 2013. "Rehabilitating Willow Creek: Megachurches, De Certeau, and the Tactics of Navigating Consumer Culture." *Christian Scholar's Review* 43 (1): 21–40.

James, Jonathan D. 2015. "Introduction." In *A Moving Faith: Mega Churches Go South*, edited by Jonathan D. James, 1–18. Thousand Oaks, CA: Sage Publications.

James, Rick. 2007. *Jesus without Religion: What Did He Say? What Did He Do? What's the Point?* Nashville, TN: InterVarsity.

James, William Closson. 2006. "Dimorphs and Cobblers: Ways of Being Religious in Canada." In *Religion and Canadian Society: Traditions, Transitions, and Innovations*, edited by Lori G. Beaman, 119–31. Toronto: Canadian Scholars' Press.

– 2011. *God's Plenty: Religious Diversity in Kingston*. Montreal and Kingston: McGill-Queen's University Press.

Jamieson, Alan. 2006. "Post-Church Groups and Their Place as Emergent Forms of Church." *International Journal for the Study of the Christian Church* 6 (1): 65–78.

Janes, Dominic. 2008. *Shopping for Jesus: Faith in Marketing in the USA*. Washington, DC: New Academia Publishing.

Jay, Martin. 1993. *Downcast Eyes: The Denigration of Vision in Twentieth-Century French Thought*. Berkeley: University of California Press.

Jelen, Ted G., ed. 2003. *Sacred Markets, Sacred Canopies: Essays on Religious Markets and Religious Pluralism*. Lanham, MD: Rowman & Littlefield Publishers.

Jemielity, Thomas J. 2006. "Ancient Biblical Satire." In *A Companion to Satire: Ancient and Modern*, edited by Ruben Quintero, 15–30. Malden, MA: Wiley-Blackwell.

Jenson, Joli. 1992. "Fandom as Pathology: The Consequences of Characterization." In *The Adoring Audience: Fan Culture and Popular Media*, edited by Lisa A. Lewis, 9–29. London: Routledge.

Jethani, Skye. 2011. "Megachurches: When Will the Bubble Burst?" *Huffington Post*, 8 November. http://www.huffingtonpost.com/skye-jethani/the-coming-megachurch-bub_b_1075999.html.

– 2012. "The Evangelical Industrial Complex and the Rise of Celebrity Pastors." *Christianity Today*, 20 February.
– 2014. "How Churches Became Cruise Ships." Blog. 30 June. http://skyejethani.com/how-churches-became-cruise-ships-3/.
Jindra, M. 2000. "Star Trek Fandom as a Religious Phenomenon." *Sociology of Religion* 55:27–51.
Joas, Hans. 1996. *The Creativity of Action*. Cambridge: Polity.
Johnson, Benton. 1992. "On Founders and Followers: Some Factors in the Development of New Religious Movements." *Sociological Analysis* 53:1–13.
Johnson, Birgitta Joelisa. 2008. "'Oh, for a Thousand Tongues to Sing': Music and Worship in African American Megachurches of Los Angeles, California." PhD diss., University of California.
Johnson, Jessica. 2018. *Biblical Porn: Affect, Labor, and Pastor Mark Driscoll's Evangelical Empire*. Durham, NC: Duke University Press.
Johnston, Hank. 2009. *Culture, Social Movements, and Protest*. Farnham, UK: Ashgate.
Jones, Laurie Beth. 1996. *Jesus CEO: Using Ancient Wisdom for Visionary Leadership*. New York: Hachette Books.
Jones, Tony. 2008. *The New Christians: Dispatches from the Emergent Frontier*. San Francisco: Jossey-Bass.
– 2011. *The Church Is Flat: The Relational Ecclesiology of the Emerging Church Movement*. Minneapolis, MN: JoPa Productions.
Jones, Trestae M. 2011. "Christian Church Architecture across the United States: How the Rhetoric of the Building and Its Appointments Speak to the Doctrine and Practices of a Church." MA thesis, California State University, Long Beach.
Joosse, Paul. 2006. "Silence, Charisma and Power: The Case of John de Ruiter." *Journal of Contemporary Religion* 21 (3): 355–71.
– 2012. "The Presentation of the Charismatic Self in Everyday Life: Reflections on a Canadian New Religious Movement." *Sociology of Religion* 73 (2): 174–99.
– 2014. "Becoming a God: Max Weber and the Social Construction of Charisma." *Journal of Classical Sociology* 14 (3): 266–83.
– 2017. "Max Weber's Disciples: Theorizing the Charismatic Aristocracy." *Sociological Theory* 35 (4): 334–58.
– 2018. "Countering Trump: Toward a Theory of Charismatic Counter-Roles." *Social Forces*, 9 May, 1–24.
Kaifetz, Jerry D. 2012. *Profaned Pulpit: The Jack Schaap Story*. Seattle, WA: CreateSpace Independent Publishing Platform.

Kallestad, Walt. 1996. *Entertainment Evangelism*. Nashville, TN: Abingdon.
Kao, Yi Feng Everest. 2009. "Inclusivity and Traditional, First-Generation, Elderly, Chinese Christians." DMin, Vancouver School of Theology.
Kay, William K. 2013. "Empirical and Historical Perspectives on the Growth of Pentecostal-Style Churches in Malaysia, Singapore and Hong Kong." *Journal of Beliefs & Values* 34 (1): 14–25.
Kee, Kevin. 2006. *Revivalists: Marketing the Gospel in English Canada, 1884–1957*. Montreal and Kingston: McGill-Queen's University Press.
Keefer, Luke L., Jr. 2005. "Three Streams in Our Heritage: Separate or Parts of a Whole?" In *Reflections on a Heritage: Defining the Brethren in Christ*, edited by E. Morris Sider, 31–47. Grantham, PA: Evangel Publishing House.
Keith, Bill. 2011. *W.A. Criswell: The Authorized Biography*. London: StoneGate Publishing.
Keller, Timothy. 2013. *Jesus the King: Understanding the Life and Death of the Son of God*. New York: Riverhead Books.
Kelley, Dean M. 1972. *Why Conservative Churches Are Growing*. New York: Harper & Brown.
Kenneson, Philip D., and James L. Street. 1997. *Selling Out the Church: The Dangers of Church Marketing*. Nashville, TN: Abingdon.
Khurana, Rakesh. 2002. *Searching for a Corporate Savior: The Irrational Quest for Charismatic CEOs*. Princeton, NJ: Princeton University Press.
Kilde, Jeanne Halgren. 2005. *When Church Became Theatre: The Transformation of Evangelical Architecture and Worship in Nineteenth-Century America*. New York: Oxford University Press.
– 2006. "Reading Megachurches: Investigating the Religious and Cultural Work of Church Architecture." In *American Sanctuary: Understanding Sacred Spaces*, edited by Louis P. Nelson, 225–50. Bloomington: Indiana University Press.
Kim, Jung Yeal. 2001. "An Analysis of Church Design in Korea: A Comparative Study of Five Mega-Churches." DMin, Regent University.
Kim, Kirsteen. 2007. "Ethereal Christianity: Reading Korean Mega-Church Websites." *Studies in World Christianity* 13 (3): 208–24.
Kim, Young Jong. 2011. "Megachurch Growth in Korea: With Special Reference to Gwacheon Presbyterian Church." DMiss diss., Fuller Theological Seminary, School of Intercultural Studies.
Kimball, Dan. 2003. *The Emerging Church: Vintage Christianity for New Generations*. Grand Rapids, MI: Zondervan/Youth Specialties.
– 2007. *They Like Jesus but Not the Church: Insights from Emerging Generations*. Grand Rapids, MI: Zondervan.

Kinnaman, David, and Gabe Lyons. 2007. *unChristian: What a New Generation Really Thinks about Christianity ... and Why It Matters*. Grand Rapids, MI: Baker Books.

Kitiarsa, Pattana. 2008. *Religious Commodifications in Asia: Marketing Gods*. New York: Routledge.

– 2010. "Toward a Sociology of Religious Commodification." In *The New Blackwell Companion to the Sociology of Religion*, edited by Bryan S. Turner, 563–83. Hoboken, NJ: Wiley-Blackwell.

Knauss, Stefanie, and Alexander D. Ornella, eds. 2007. *Reconfigurations: Interdisciplinary Perspectives on Religion in a Post-Secular Society*. Munster, Austria: LIT Verlag.

Ko, Young Do. 2008. "Exploring a New Leadership Approach for Ottawa Korean Methodist Church." DMin, Drew University.

Kotter, John P. 1999. *John P. Kotter on What Leaders Really Do*. Boston: Harvard Business Review.

Kraybill, Donald B. 2003. *The Amish: Why They Enchant Us*. Harrisburg, PA: Herald.

Kunin, Seth, and Francesca Murphy. 2003. *Religious Studies and Theology: An Introduction*. New York: New York University Press.

Kurzman, Charles, Chelise Anderson, Clinton Key, Youn Ok Lee, Mairead Moloney, Alexis Silver, and Maria W. Van Ryn. 2007. "Celebrity Status." *Sociological Theory* 25 (4): 347–67.

Kuykendall, Jim. 2011. "Rapid Growth Pastors on a Wild Ride." Leadership Network. http://leadnet.org/docs/11for11-2011-FEB-Pastors_Wild_Ride-Kuykendall.pdf (page discontinued).

Kwon, Lillian. 2010. "Rick Warren Tells Passive, Fake Christians to Find Another Church." *Christian Post*, 24 May.

Kyle, Richard G. 2006. *Evangelicalism: An Americanized Christianity*. New Brunswick, NJ: Transaction Publishers.

Labanow, Cory E. 2009. *Evangelicalism and the Emerging Church*. Farnham, UK: Ashgate.

Labberton, Mark. 2018. *Still Evangelical? Insiders Reconsider Political, Social, and Theological Meaning*. Downers Grove, IL: InterVarsity.

Laderman, Gary. 2009. *Sacred Matters: Celebrity Worship, Sexual Ecstasies, the Living Dead and Other Signs of Religious Life in the United States*. New York: New Press.

Ladkin, Donna Marie. 2010. *Rethinking Leadership: A New Look at Old Leadership Questions*. Cheltenham, UK: Edward Elgar.

Lampman, Jane. 2006. "Megachurches' Way of Worship Is on the Rise." *Christian Science Monitor*, 6 February.

Lawler, Peter A. 2010. "Celebrity Studies Today." *Society* 47:419–23.
Lebo, Layne Alan. 2001. *Identity or Mission: Which Will Guide the Brethren in Christ into the Twenty-First Century?* Wilmore, KY: Ashbury Theological Seminary.
Lee, Morgan. 2014. "Megachurch Pastor David Yonggi Cho Convicted of Embezzling $12M Says 'Suffering' Taught Him Individuals 'Shouldn't Possess Anything.'" *Christian Post*, 25 February.
Lee, Shayne. 2005. *T.D. Jakes: America's New Preacher*. New York: New York University Press.
Lee, Shayne, and Phillip Sinitiere. 2009. *Holy Mavericks: Evangelical Innovators and the Spiritual Marketplace*. New York: New York University Press.
Lehmann, Chris. 2016. *Money Cult: Capitalism, Christianity, and the Unmaking of the American Dream*. Brooklyn: Melville House.
Lemert, Charles. 2003. *Muhammad Ali: Trickster in the Culture of Irony*. Malden, MA: Polity.
Leslie, D., M. Hunt, and S. Brail. 2014. "Attracting and Retaining Artistic Talent in Toronto: Cosmopolitanism, Cultural Diversity and Inclusion." In *Seeking Talent for Creative Cities: The Social Dynamics of Innovation*, edited by J. Grant, 59–76. Toronto: University of Toronto Press.
Lewin, Simon, and Scott Reeves. 2011. "Enacting 'Team' and 'Teamwork': Using Goffman's Theory of Impression Management to Illuminate Interprofessional Practice on Hospital Wards." *Social Science & Medicine* 72 (10): 1595–1602.
Lewis, Beverly. 2008. *The Shunning*. Minneapolis: Bethany House Publishers.
Lewis, Lisa A., ed. 1992. *The Adoring Audience: Fan Culture and Popular Media*. London: Routledge.
Lewis, Sinclair. 1927. *Elmer Gantry: A Novel*. New York: J. Cape.
Lindholm, Charles. 1990. *Charisma*. Cambridge, MA: Blackwell.
– 2013. *The Anthropology of Religious Charisma: Ecstasies and Institutions*. London: Palgrave Macmillan.
Linton, Michael. 2000. "Apostles of Rock: An Insider's Look at the Past, Present, and Future of Contemporary Christian Music." *First Things*, February. https://www.firstthings.com/article/2000/02/apostles-of-rock.
Lloyd, Vincent. 2018. *In Defense of Charisma*. New York: Columbia University Press.
Lofland, John, and Rodney Stark. 1965. "Becoming a World-Saver: A Theory of Conversion to a Deviant Perspective." *American Sociological Review* 30 (6): 862–75.

Lofton, Kathryn. 2011. *Oprah: The Gospel of an Icon*. Berkeley: University of California Press.
Long, James. 2014. "Into the Neighborhood: Randy Frazee and Oak Hills Church." *Outreach Magazine*, 19 June. http://www.outreachmagazine.com/features/5800-into-the-neighborhood-randy-frazee-and-oak-hills-church.html.
Longacre, Doris. 1976. *More-with-Less Cookbook*. Updated. Scottdale, PA: Herald.
Loveland, Anne C., and Otis B. Wheeler. 2003. *From Meetinghouse to Megachurch: A Material and Cultural History*. Illustrated. Kansas City, MO: University of Missouri Press.
Luhr, Eileen. 2009. *Witnessing Suburbia: Conservatives and Christian Youth Culture*. Berkeley: University of California Press.
Luhrmann, T.M. 2012. *When God Talks Back: Understanding the American Evangelical Relationship with God*. New York: Knopf.
Lyon, David. 1995. *Living Stones: St James' Church, Kingston, 1845–1995: From Stuartville to Queen's Campus*. Kingston, ON: Quarry.
– 2000. *Jesus in Disneyland: Religion in Postmodern Times*. Illustrated. Boston: Polity.
– 2007. *Surveillance Studies: An Overview*. Boston: Polity.
– 2018. "God's Eye: A Reason for Hope." *Surveillance and Society* 16 (4). https://ojs.library.queensu.ca/index.php/surveillance-and-society/article/view/12858.
MacArthur, John. 2010. *Ashamed of the Gospel: When the Church Becomes Like the World*. 3rd ed. Wheaton, IL: Crossway.
MacDonald, G. Jeffrey. 2010. *Thieves in the Temple: The Christian Church and the Selling of the American Soul*. New York: Basic Books.
MacDonald, Marci. 2010. *The Armageddon Factor: The Rise of Christian Nationalism in Canada*. Toronto: Random House Canada.
MacNair, Wilmer. 2009. *Unraveling the Mega-Church: True Faith or False Promises?* Westport, CT: Praeger.
Maddox, Marion. 2012. "'In the Goofy Parking Lot': Growth Churches as a Novel Religious Form for Late Capitalism." *Social Compass* 59 (2): 146–58.
– 2013. "Prosper, Consume and Be Saved." *Critical Research on Religion* 1 (1): 108–15.
Madison, D. Soyini, and Judith Hamera. 2006. "Performance Studies at the Intersections." In *The SAGE Handbook of Performance Studies*, edited by Judith Hamera and D. Soyini Madison, xi–xxv. Thousand Oaks, CA: Sage.

Madsen, Douglas, and Peter G. Snow. 1991. *The Charismatic Bond: Political Behavior in Time of Crisis*. Cambridge, MA: Harvard University Press.

Malick, Joan Bradner. 1996. "The Sex-Role Self-Perception of Megachurch Pastors and the Attributes of Leadership." PhD diss., Union Institute.

Manning, Philip. 1992. *Erving Goffman and Modern Sociology*. Stanford, CA: Stanford University Press.

Manzullo-Thomas, Devin C. 2013. "Beyond 'Indianapolis 50': The Brethren in Christ Church in an Age of Evangelicalism." *Brethren in Christ History and Life* 36 (3): 433–63.

Mardis, Matthew. 2003. "Niche Congregations and the Problem of Institutional Isomorphism: A Study of the Church as Institution." *Quodlibet Journal* 5 (23). http://www.quodlibet.net/articles/mardis-institution.shtml (page discontinued).

Markofski, Wes. 2015. *New Monasticism and the Transformation of American Evangelicalism*. New York: Oxford University Press.

Marsden, George M. 1991. *Understanding Fundamentalism and Evangelicalism*. Grand Rapids, MI: Wm B. Eerdmans Publishing.

– 2008. *A Short Life of Jonathan Edwards*. Grand Rapids, MI: Wm B. Eerdmans Publishing.

Marshall, P. David. 1997. *Celebrity and Power: Fame in Contemporary Culture*. Minneapolis: University of Minnesota Press.

Marshall, Paul, Lela Gilbert, and Roberta Green-Ahmanson. 2008. *Blind Spot: When Journalists Don't Get Religion*. New York: Oxford University Press.

Marti, Gerardo. 2005. *A Mosaic of Believers: Diversity and Innovation in a Multiethnic Church*. Bloomington, IN: Indiana University Press.

– 2008. *Hollywood Faith: Holiness, Prosperity, and Ambition in a Los Angeles Church*. New Brunswick, NJ: Rutgers University Press.

– 2009. *A Mosaic of Believers: Diversity and Innovation in a Multiethnic Church*. Bloomington, IN: Indiana University Press.

– 2012. *Worship across the Racial Divide: Religious Music and the Multiracial Congregation*. New York: Oxford University Press.

– 2018. "The Global Phenomenon of Hillsong Church: An Initial Assessment." *Sociology of Religion* 78 (4): 377–86.

Marti, Gerardo, and Gladys Ganiel. 2014. *The Deconstructed Church: The Religious Identity and Negotiated Practices of Emerging Christianity*. New York: Oxford University Press.

Martin, Robert F. 2002. *Hero of the Heartland: Billy Sunday and the Transformation of America*. Bloomington, IN: Indiana University Press.

Marty, Martin E. 1995. "Sic Transit Mega." *Christian Century* 112 (5): 191.

– 2010. "Decline in the Megachurches." *Sightings*, 7 June.

Masters, Matthew. 2007. "Melting the Matrices: Structure, Anti-Structure, and the Emerging Conversation." MA thesis, Brock University.

May, John Alexander. 1989. "Developing Possibilities for Ministry with the Aging." DMin diss., Drew University.

McCarthy-Brown, Karen McCarthy. 1991. *Mama Lola: A Vodou Priestess in Brooklyn*. Berkeley, CA: University of California Press.

McClung, Grant. 1985. "From BRIDGES (McGavran 1955) to WAVES (Wagner 1983): Pentecostals and the Church Growth Movement." *Pneuma* 7 (1): 5–18.

McCoy, Seth. 2011. "ThirdWay Community: From Megachurch to Mennonite." In *Widening the Circle: Experiments in Christian Discipleship*, edited by Joanna Shenk, 173–80. Harrisonburg, VA: Herald.

McDonald, Marci. 2010. *The Armageddon Factor: The Rise of Christian Nationalism in Canada*. Toronto: Random House Canada.

McGee, Paula L. 2012. "The Wal-Martization of African American Religion: T.D. Jakes and Woman Thou Art Loosed." PhD diss., Claremont Graduate University.

McGuire, Meredith B. 2008. *Lived Religion: Faith and Practice in Everyday Life*. Oxford: Oxford University Press.

McIntire, C. Thomas. 2012. "Protestant Christians." In *The Religions of Canadians*, edited by Jamie Scott, 75–130. Toronto: University of Toronto Press.

McIntosh, Gary, ed. 2004. *Evaluating the Church Growth Movement: 5 Views*. Grand Rapids, MI: Zondervan.

McIntosh, Gary L. 2005. "The Life and Ministry of Donald A. McGavran: A Short Overview." Unpublished.

McKeen, Leah. 2015. "Canadian Christian Nationalism? The Religiosity and Politics of the Christian Heritage Party of Canada." PhD diss., Wilfrid Laurier University.

McKenzie, Karen. 2007. "Architectural Crusades: A Comparison and Interpretation of French Cathedrals and American MegaChurches as Cultural Catalysts and Material Culture." BA thesis, Oregon State University.

McKinnon, Andrew M. 2013. "Ideology and the Market Metaphor in Rational Choice Theory of Religion: A Rhetorical Critique of 'Religious Economies.'" *Critical Sociology* 39 (4): 529–43.

McKnight, Scot. 2008. "The Ironic Faith of Emergents." *Christianity Today*, 26 September. http://www.christianitytoday.com/ct/2008/september/39.62.html.

McLaren, Brian, and Tony Campolo. 2003. *Adventures in Missing the Point: How the Culture Controlled Church Neutered the Gospel*. Grand Rapids, MI: Zondervan/Youth Specialties.

McLaren, Brian D. 2001. *A New Kind of Christian: A Tale of Two Friends on a Spiritual Journey*. San Francisco: Jossey-Bass.

– 2003. *Church on the Other Side*. Grand Rapids, MI: Zondervan.

– 2006. *A Generous Orthodoxy: Why I Am a Missional, Evangelical, Post/Protestant, Liberal/Conservative, Mystical/Poetic, Biblical, Charismatic/Contemplative, ... Emergent, Unfinished Christian*. El Cajon, CA: Zondervan/Youth Specialties.

McLuhan, Marshall. 1964. *Understanding Media: The Extensions of Man*. Milwaukee, WI: New American Library.

McLuhan, Marshall, and Quentin Fiore. 1968. *The Medium Is the Massage: An Inventory of Effects*. New York: Bantam Books.

McMenamie, Logan. 2009. "Testing the Applicability of Peter Senge's Five Disciplines of a Learning Organization, in a Church Setting." DMin diss., Vancouver School of Theology.

McNally, David. 2012. *Monsters of the Market: Zombies, Vampires and Global Capitalism*. Chicago, IL: Haymarket Books.

McTeague, James H. 1994. *Playwrights and Acting: Acting Methodologies for Brecht, Ionesco, Pinter, and Shepard*. Santa Barbara, CA: Greenwood.

Mead, George Herbert. 1934. *Mind, Self, and Society: From the Standpoint of a Social Behaviorist*. Chicago: University of Chicago Press.

Mead, Loren B. 2012. *A Change of Pastors ... and How It Affects Change in the Congregation*. Lanham, MD: Rowman & Littlefield.

Meigs, Anna S. 1995. "Ritual Language in Everyday Life: The Christian Right." *Journal of the American Academy of Religion* 63 (1): 85–103.

Melton, J. Gordon. 1991. "When Prophets Die: The Succession Crisis in New Religions." In *When Prophets Die: The Postcharismatic Fate of New Religious Movements*, edited by Timothy Miller, 1–12. New York: SUNY Press.

Mercadante, Linda A. 2014. *Belief without Borders: Inside the Minds of the Spiritual but Not Religious*. New York: Oxford University Press.

Meyer, David S. 2009. "Claiming Credit: Stories of Movement Influence as Outcomes." In *Culture, Social Movements, and Protest*, edited by Hank Johnston, 55–66. Farnham, UK: Ashgate Publishing.

Meyer, Kem. 2009. *Less Clutter. Less Noise: Beyond Bulletins, Brochures and Bake Sales.* Camby, IN: Thirty:One.
Michel, Jen Pollock. 2014. *Teach Us to Want: Longing, Ambition and the Life of Faith.* Downers Grove, IL: InterVarsity.
Middelmann, Udo W. 2004. *The Market-Driven Church: The Worldly Influence of Modern Culture on the Church in America.* Wheaton, IL: Crossway Books.
Middleton, J. Richard, and Brian J. Walsh. 1995. *Truth Is Stranger Than It Used to Be: Biblical Faith in a Postmodern Age.* Downers Grove, IL: InterVarsity Press Academic.
Middleton, Vernon James. 2011. *Donald McGavran, His Early Life and Ministry: An Apostolic Vision for Reaching the Nations.* Pasadena, CA: William Carey Library.
Middleton, Vernon James, and Donald Anderson McGavran. 1990. "The Development of a Missiologist: The Life and Thought of Donald Anderson McGavran, 1897–1965." DMin diss., Fuller Theological Seminary.
Miedema, Gary R. 2005. *For Canada's Sake: Public Religion, Centennial Celebrations, and the Re-Making of Canada in the 1960s.* Montreal and Kingston: McGill-Queen's University Press.
Miller, Donald E. 1997. *Reinventing American Protestantism: Christianity in the New Millennium.* Berkeley, CA: University of California Press.
– 2003. *Blue Like Jazz: Nonreligious Thoughts on Christian Spirituality.* Nashville, TN: Thomas Nelson.
Miller, Vincent. 2005. *Consuming Religion: Christian Faith and Practice in a Consumer Culture.* New York: Continuum.
Millin, Edward Frederick. 1988. "Growing beyond Our Traditions: A Strategy for the Renewal of Congregational Life, St Andrew's Presbyterian Church, Kimberley, British Columbia." DMin diss., Fuller Theological Seminary.
Moody, Jess C. 1971. *The Jesus Freaks.* Waco, TX: Word Books.
Moody, Katharine Sarah. 2015. *Radical Theology and Emerging Christianity: Deconstruction, Materialism and Religious Practices.* New York: Routledge.
Moon, Dawne. 2004. *God, Sex, and Politics: Homosexuality and Everyday Theologies.* Chicago: University of Chicago Press.
Moore, Ellen E. 2013. "Evangelical Churches' Use of Commerical Entertainment Media in Worship." In *Evangelical Christians and Popular Culture: Pop Goes the Gospel,* edited by Robert Woods, 246–60. Santa Barbara, CA: Praeger.

Moore, R. Laurence. 1995. *Selling God: American Religion in the Marketplace of Culture*. New York: Oxford University Press.

Morgan, Adam, and Mark Barden. 2015. *A Beautiful Constraint: How to Transform Your Limitations into Advantages, and Why It's Everyone's Business*. Hoboken, NJ: Wiley.

Morgan, Lee. 2014. "David Yonggi Cho of South Korean Megachurch Supported by American Pastor Bob Rodgers after $12M Embezzlement Conviction." *Christian Post*, 24 February. https://goo.gl/VELrpD.

Morgan, Nick. 2008. *Trust Me: Four Steps to Authenticity and Charisma*. Hoboken, NJ: John Wiley & Sons.

Morgenthaler, Sally. 2007. "Leadership in a Flattened World: Grassroots Culture and the Demise of the CEO Model." In *An Emergent Manifesto of Hope*, edited by Doug Pagitt and Tony Jones, 175–86. Grand Rapids, MI: Baker Books.

Mortensen, Kurt W. 2010. *The Laws of Charisma: How to Captivate, Inspire, and Influence for Maximum Success*. New York: AMACOM Division American Management Association.

Mouw, Richard J. 1994. *Consulting the Faithful*. Grand Rapids, MI: Wm B. Eerdmans Publishing.

Mullins, Tom. 2015. *Passing the Leadership Baton: A Winning Transition Plan for Your Ministry*. Nashville, TN: Thomas Nelson.

Murray, Stuart. 2010. *The Naked Anabaptist: The Bare Essentials of a Radical Faith*. Scottdale, PA: Herald.

Myung, Sung-Hoon, and Young-gi Hong. 2003. *Charis and Charisma: David Yonggi Cho and the Growth of Yoido Full Gospel Church*. Oxford: Regnum Books International.

Neitz, Mary Jo. 1987. *Charisma and Community: A Study of Religious Commitment within the Charismatic Renewal*. New Brunswick, NJ: Transaction Publishers.

Nelson, Louis P. 2007. "Placing the Sacred: Reflections on Contemporary American Church Architecture." *Institute of Sacred Music: Colloquium Journal* 4:69–78.

Newbigin, Lesslie. 1995. *The Open Secret: An Introduction to the Theology of Mission*. Grand Rapids, MI: Wm B. Eerdmans.

Niebuhr, Gustav. 1995. "The Minister as Marketer: Learning from Business." *New York Times*, 18 April. http://www.nytimes.com/1995/04/18/us/megachurches-second-article-series-gospels-management-minister-marketer-learning.html?pagewanted=all&src=pm.

Noll, Mark A. 1988. "Primitivism in Fundamentalism and American Biblical Scholarship." In *The American Quest for the Primitive Church*,

edited by Richard T. Hughes, 120–8. Urbana, IL: University of Illinois Press.
– 2006. "What Happened to Christian Canada?" *Church History* 75 (2): 245–73.
Nynas, Peter, Mika Lassander, and Terhi Utriainen, eds. 2012. *Post-Secular Society*. New Brunswick, NJ: Transaction Publishers.
Oakes, Len. 1997. *Prophetic Charisma: The Psychology of Revolutionary Religious Personalities*. Syracuse, NY: Syracuse University Press.
O'Dea, Thomas F., and J. Milton Yinger. 1961. "Five Dilemmas in the Institutionalization of Religion." *Journal for the Scientific Study of Religion* 1 (1): 30–41.
O'Guinn, T. 2000. "Touching Greatness: The Central Mid-West Barry Manilow Fan Club." In *The Consumer Society Reader*, edited by J. Schor and D. Holt, 155–68. New York: New Press.
Olasky, Marvin, and Warren Cole Smith. 2013. *Prodigal Press: Confronting the Anti-Christian Bias of the American News Media*. Phillipsburg, NJ: Presbyterian & Reformed Publishing.
Olson, Roger E. 2011. "Postconservative Evangelicalism." In *Four Views on the Spectrum of Evangelicalism*, edited by Andrew David Naselli and Collin Hansen, 161–87. Grand Rapids, MI: Zondervan.
– 2014. "Emerging Churches and the Jesus People Movement Compared." Patheos. http://www.patheos.com/blogs/rogereolson/2012/04/emerging-churches-and-the-jesus-people-movement-compared/.
O'Neill, Kevin Lewis. 2009. *City of God: Christian Citizenship in Postwar Guatemala*. Berkeley: University of California Press.
Ong, Walter J. 1967. *The Presence of the Word: Some Prolegomena for Cultural and Religious History*. New Haven, CT: Yale University Press.
Orsi, Robert A. 2003. "Is the Study of Lived Religion Irrelevant to the World We Live in? Special Presidential Plenary Address, Society for the Scientific Study of Religion, Salt Lake City, November 2, 2002." *Journal for the Scientific Study of Religion* 42 (2): 169–74.
Ortega, Ruben. 1972. *The Jesus People Speak Out!* Elgin, IL: D.C. Cook Publishing.
Ostwalt, Conrad. 2012. *Secular Steeple: Popular Culture and the Religious Imagination*. London: Bloomsbury.
Oswald, Roy M., James Heath, and Ann Heath. 2003. *Beginning Ministry Together: The Alban Handbook for Clergy Transitions*. Lanham, MD: Rowman & Littlefield.
Packard, Josh. 2012. *The Emerging Church: Religion at the Margins*. Boulder, CO: Lynne Rienner Publishers.

Packard, Josh, and Ashleigh Hope. 2015. *Church Refugees: Sociologists Reveal Why People Are Done with Church but Not Their Faith.* Loveland, CO: LifeTree.

Packer, George. 2008. "The Choice." *New Yorker*, 28 January. http://www.newyorker.com/magazine/2008/01/28/the-choice-6.

Packer, J.I., R.C. Sproul, Alister E. McGrath, and Charles W. Colson. 1997. *Power Religion: The Selling Out of the Evangelical Church?* Chicago: Moody.

Paddey, Patricia. 2005. "Church Uses 'Purge Sundays' to Send Non-Committed Elsewhere." *Christian Week*, April.

Paffenroth, Kim, and John W. Morehead. 2012. *The Undead and Theology.* Eugene, OR: Wipf and Stock Publishers.

Pagitt, Doug. 2004. *Reimagining Spiritual Formation: A Week in the Life of an Experimental Church.* Grand Rapids, MI: Zondervan.

– 2008. *A Christianity Worth Believing: Hope-Filled, Open-Armed, Alive-and-Well Faith for the Left Out, Left Behind, and Let Down in Us All.* San Francisco, CA: Jossey-Bass.

Pally, Marcia. 2011. *The New Evangelicals: Expanding the Vision of the Common Good.* Grand Rapids, MI: Wm B. Eerdmans Publishing.

Palmer, Jim. 2006. *Divine Nobodies: Shedding Religion to Find God.* Nashville, TN: Thomas Nelson.

Pals, Daniel L. 1987. "Is Religion a Sui Generis Phenomenon?" *Journal of the American Academy of Religion* 55 (2): 259–82.

Park, Myung-Soo. 2003. "A Study of Him and the Growth of Yoido Full Gospel Church." In *Charis and Charisma: David Yonggi Cho and the Growth of Yoido Full Gospel Church*, edited by Sung-Hoon Myung and Yŏng-gi Hong, 173–95. Oxford: Regnum Books International.

Paschen, Michael, and Erich Dihsmaier. 2013. *The Psychology of Human Leadership: How to Develop Charisma and Authority.* New York: Springer Science & Business Media.

Patterson, Paige, and Joyce Rogers. 2005. *Love Worth Finding: The Life of Adrian Rogers and His Philosophy of Preaching.* Nashville, TN: B&H Books.

Peacock, C. 2004. *At the Crossroads: Inside the Past, Present, and Future of Contemporary Christian Music.* 2nd ed. Colorado Springs, CO: Random House.

Penner, James. 1993. *Goliath: The Life of Robert Schuller.* New York: HarperPaperbacks.

Penney, Mary Paula. 1980. "A Study of the Contributions of Three Religious Congregations to the Growth of Education in the Province of Newfoundland." PhD diss., Boston College.

Peterson, Eric E., and Kristin M. Langellier. 2006. "The Performance Turn in Narrative Studies." *Narrative Inquiry* 16 (1): 173–80.

Petrov, Antonio. 2011. *Superordinary! Aesthetic and Material Transformations of Megachurch Architecture in the United States.* Cambridge, MA: Harvard University Press.

Pettit, Michael. 2011. "The Con Man as Model Organism: The Methodological Roots of Erving Goffman's Dramaturgical Self." *History of the Human Sciences* 24 (2): 138–54.

Phelan, James. 2008. "Narratives in Contest: Or, Another Twist in the Narrative Turn." *PMLA* 123 (1): 166–75.

Pinsky, Drew, and S. Mark Young. 2009. *The Mirror Effect: How Celebrity Narcissism Is Seducing America.* New York: Harper.

Pinto, Antonio Costa, and Stein Ugelvik Larsen. 2006. "Conclusion: Fascism, Dictators and Charisma." In *Charisma and Fascism in Interwar Europe*, edited by Antonio Costa Pinto, Roger Eatwell, and Stein Ugelvik Larsen, 251–7. London: Routledge.

Plamper, Jan. 2012. *The Stalin Cult: A Study in the Alchemy of Power.* New Haven, CT: Yale University Press.

Platts, Todd K. 2013. "Locating Zombies in the Sociology of Popular Culture." *Sociology Compass* 7 (7): 547–60.

Plowman, Edward E. 1971. *The Jesus Movement in America: Accounts of Christian Revolutionaries in Action.* Elgin, IL: DC Cook Publishing.

Pollard, D. 2007. *Fools' Heaven: Love, Lust and Death beyond the Pulpit.* New York: iUniverse.

Polletta, Francesca. 2009. *It Was Like a Fever: Storytelling in Protest and Politics.* Chicago: University of Chicago Press.

Poloma, Margaret M. 2003. *Main Street Mystics: The Toronto Blessing and Reviving Pentecostalism.* Lanham, MD: Altamira.

Porterfield, Amanda. 2001. *The Transformation of American Religion: The Story of a Late-Twentieth-Century Awakening.* Oxford: Oxford University Press.

Potter, Andrew. 2011. *The Authenticity Hoax: Why the "Real" Things We Seek Don't Make Us Happy.* Scranton, PA: Harper Perennial.

Potts, John. 2009. *A History of Charisma.* London: Palgrave Macmillan.

Powell, Mark Allan. 2004. "Contemporary Christian Music: A New Research Area in American Religious Studies." In *American Theological Library Association Summary of Proceedings* 58:129–41.

Preston, John. 2005. "Even I Want to Be Cary Grant." *Telegraph*, 6 March.

Purdy, Jedediah. 2000. *For Common Things: Irony, Trust and Commitment in America Today.* New York: Vintage.

Puroila, Anna-Maija. 2013. "Young Children on the Stages: Small Stories Performed in Day Care Centers." *Narrative Inquiry* 23 (2): 323–43.

Putnam, Robert D., and David E. Campbell. 2010. *American Grace: How Religion Divides and Unites Us*. New York: Simon & Schuster.

Putney, Clifford. 2003. *Muscular Christianity: Manhood and Sports in Protestant America, 1880–1920*. Cambridge, MA: Harvard University Press.

Quebedeaux, Richard. 1982. *By What Authority? The Rise of Personality Cults in American Christianity*. New York: Harper & Row, Publishers.

Raabe, Tom. 1991. *The Ultimate Church: An Irreverent Look at Church Growth, Megachurches, & Ecclesiastical "Show-Biz."* New York: HarperCollins Canada / Zondervan Carr.

Raffel, Stanley. 2013. "The Everyday Life of the Self: Reworking Early Goffman." *Journal of Classical Sociology* 13 (1): 163–78.

Rah, Soong-Chan. 2009. *The Next Evangelicalism: Freeing the Church from Western Cultural Captivity*. Downers Grove, IL: InterVarsity.

Rawlings, Kaitlyn O. 2013. *The Lord Is Not through with Me Yet: The Story of Dr John W. Rawlings*. Nashville, TN: CrossBooks.

Rawlyk, George A. 1996. *Is Jesus Your Personal Saviour? In Search of Canadian Evangelicalism in the 1990s*. Montreal and Kingston: McGill-Queen's University Press.

Reed, Isaac. 2009. "Culture as Object and Approach in Sociology." In *Meaning and Method: The Cultural Approach to Sociology*, edited by Isaac Reed and Jeffrey C. Alexander, 1–14. Boulder, CO: Paradigm Publishers.

Reed, Jean-Pierre. 2014. "Religious Storytelling and Revolutionary Outlooks." Paper presented at Society for the Scientific Study of Religion, Indianapolis, Nov. 24.

Reid, John Edgar Jr. "The Use of Christian Rock Music by Youth Group Members." *Popular Music and Society* 17 (2): 33–45.

Reimer, Samuel. 2003. *Evangelicals and the Continental Divide: The Conservative Protestant Subculture in Canada and the United States*. Montreal and Kingston: McGill-Queen's University Press.

Reimer, Sam, and Michael Wilkinson. 2015. *A Culture of Faith: Evangelical Congregations in Canada*. Montreal and Kingston: McGill-Queen's University Press.

Reising, Richard L. 2006. *Church Marketing 101: Preparing Your Church for Greater Growth*. Grand Rapids, MI: Baker Books.

Rhodes, Blair. 2015. "Trinity Western Law Students OK to Practise in Nova Scotia." CBC News, 28 January. http://www.cbc.ca/1.2935248.

Riches, Tanya, and Tom Wagner. 2012. "The Evolution of Hillsong Music: From Australian Pentecostal Congregation into Global Brand." *Australian Journal of Communication* 39 (1): 17–36.

Riddell, Kathleen. 2008. "When the Music's Over, Renew My Subscription to the Resurrection: Why Doors Fans Won't Let Jim Die." MA thesis, McMaster University.

Riddle, Douglas. 2009. "Executive Integration: Equipping Transitioning Leaders for Success." Greensboro, NC: Center for Creative Leadership.

Rieff, Philip. 2008. *Charisma: The Gift of Grace, and How It Has Been Taken Away from Us*. New York: Knopf Doubleday Publishing Group.

Riesebrodt, Martin. 1999. "Charisma in Max Weber's Sociology of Religion." *Religion* 29 (1): 1–14.

Ritzer, George. 2010. *The McDonaldization of Society*. 6th ed. Thousand Oaks, CA: Pine Forge.

Robbins, Thomas. 1998. "Charisma." In *Encyclopedia of Religion and Society*, edited by William W. Swatos, 78–80. Lanham, MD: AltaMira.

Roberts, Robert C. 1983. *Spirituality and Human Emotion*. Grand Rapids, MI: Wm B. Eerdmans Publishing.

— 2014. "Anger in the Christian Life." Institute for Faith and Learning, Baylor University. https://www.baylor.edu/content/services/document.php/235699.pdf.

Robinson, Anthony B. 2013. "Innovations in Mainline Protestant Leadership." In *Religious Leadership: A Reference Handbook*, edited by Sharon Henderson Callahan, 99–107. New York: Sage Publications.

Robinson, Ryan. 2012. "When My Church Gets Together." Anabaptist Redux: Anabaptist Faith in the Postmodern Age, 11 November. https://www.anabaptistredux.com/when-my-church-gets-together/.

Robles-Anderson, Erica. 2012. "The Crystal Cathedral: Architecture for Mediated Congregation." *Public Culture* 24 (3): 577–99.

Rojek, Chris. 2001. *Celebrity*. London: Reaktion Books.

— 2011. *Fame Attack: The Inflation of Celebrity and Its Consequences*. London: Bloomsbury Academic.

Rollins, Peter. 2006. *How (Not) to Speak of God*. Ashland, OH: Paraclete.

Roof, Wade Clark. 1993. "Religion and Narrative: The 1992 RRA Presidential Address." *Review of Religious Research* 34 (4): 297–310.

— 2001. *Spiritual Marketplace: Baby Boomers and the Remaking of American Religion*. Princeton, NJ: Princeton University Press.

Roozen, David A., and C. Kirk Hadaway. 1993. *Church and Denominational Growth*. Nashville, TN: Abingdon.

Rose, Michael S. 2009. *Ugly as Sin: Why They Changed Our Churches from Sacred Places to Meeting Spaces – and How We Can Change Them Back Again*. Manchester, NH: Sophia Institute.

Rosile, Grace Ann, David M. Boje, Donna M. Carlon, Alexis Downs, and Rohny Saylors. 2013. "Storytelling Diamond: An Antenarrative Integration of the Six Facets of Storytelling in Organization Research Design." *Organizational Research Methods* 16 (4): 557–80.

Rosin, Hanna. 1995. "Woolly Pulpit." *New Republic* 212 (11): 12.

Rothwell, William J. 2010. *Effective Succession Planning: Ensuring Leadership Continuity and Building Talent from Within*. New York: American Management Association.

Roxburgh, Alan. 2013. "What Kind of Leaders Do We Need?" In *Green Shoots out of Dry Ground: Growing a New Future for the Church in Canada*, edited by John Bowen, 183–95. Eugene, OR: Wipf & Stock.

Roxburgh, Alan, Fred Romanuk, and Eddie Gibbs. 2006. *The Missional Leader: Equipping Your Church to Reach a Changing World*. San Francisco, CA: Jossey-Bass.

Royster, Michael D. 2013. "The African American Context." In *Religious Leadership: A Reference Handbook*, edited by Sharon Henderson Callahan, 11–20. New York: Sage Publications.

Rubin, Rebecca B., and Michael P. McHugh. 1987. "Development of Parasocial Interaction Relationships." *Journal of Broadcasting and Electronic Media* 31 (3): 279–92.

Ruddock, Andy. 2013. *Youth and Media*. New York: Sage.

Russell, Bob, and Bryan Bucher. 2010. *Transition Plan: 7 Secrets Every Leader Needs to Know*. Louisville, KY: Ministers Label.

Rybczynski, Witold. 2005. "An Anatomy of Megachurches." *Slate*, 10 October.

Rymes, Betsy. 2010. "Why and Why Not? Narrative Approaches in the Social Sciences." *Narrative Inquiry* 20 (2): 371–4.

Salomonsen, Jone. 2002. *Enchanted Feminism: Ritual, Gender and Divinity among the Reclaiming Witches of San Francisco*. New York: Routledge.

Sam, Edward Rajamony. 1982. "Congregational Renewal and Community Outreach in Morven United Church." DMin diss., Drew University.

Sanders, Jack T. 2000. *Charisma, Converts, Competitors: Societal and Sociological Factors in the Success of Early Christianity*. London: SCM.

Sanders, Ryan. 2018. "The Megachurch Model Is Unsustainable." *Dallas News*, 18 November. https://goo.gl/G9S7iD.

Sandvoss, Cornel. 2005. *Fans: The Mirror of Consumption*. Malden, MA: Polity.

Sargeant, Kimon Howland. 2000. *Seeker Churches: Promoting Traditional Religion in a Nontraditional Way*. New Brunswick, NJ: Rutgers University Press.

Sargisson, Lucy. 2007. "Strange Places: Estrangement, Utopianism, and Intentional Communities." *Utopian Studies* 18 (3): 393–424.

Saul, John Ralston. 2008. *A Fair Country: Telling Truths about Canada*. Toronto: Viking.

Sawyer, Liz. 2014. "For Megachurches, Changing of the Pastoral Guard Is a Time of Risk and Opportunity." *Star Tribune*, 27 December. http://www.startribune.com/local/south/286908951.html.

Schaap, Cindy Hyles. 1998. *The Fundamental Man: An Authorized Biography of My Pastor, My Father, My Friend: Jack Frasure Hyles*. Hammond, IN: Hyles Publications.

Schafer, Axel R. 2011. *Countercultural Conservatives: American Evangelicalism from the Postwar Revival to the New Christian Right*. Madison: University of Wisconsin Press.

Schaller, Lyle E. 1996. *The New Reformation: Tomorrow Arrived Yesterday*. Nashville, TN: Abingdon.

Scharen, Christian, and Aana Marie Vigen, eds. 2011. *Ethnography as Christian Theology and Ethics*. London: Bloomsbury Academic.

Schatzmann, Siegfried S. 1987. *A Pauline Theology of Charismata*. Peabody, MA: Hendrickson Publishing.

Schechner, Richard. 1988. *Performance Theory*. New York: Routledge.

– 2013. *Performance Studies: An Introduction*. New York: Routledge.

Schickel, Richard. 2000. *Intimate Strangers: The Culture of Celebrity*. Chicago: Ivan R. Dee.

Schiffer, Irvine. 1973. *Charisma: A Psychoanalytic Look at Mass Society*. New York: Free Press.

Schlabach, Theron F. 1995. "Renewal and Modernization among American Mennonites, 1800–1980: Restorationist?" In *The Primitive Church in the Modern World*, edited by Richard T. Hughes, 197–220. Urbana, IL: University of Illinois Press.

Schmelzer, Dave. 2008. *Not the Religious Type: Confessions of a Turncoat Atheist*. Carol Stream, IL: SaltRiver.

Schmidt, Leigh. 2006. *Restless Souls: The Making of American Spirituality*. New York: HarperOne.

Schrauwers, Albert. 2002. "Sitting in Silence: Self-Emotion, and Tradition in the Genesis of a Charismatic Ministry." *Ethnos* 29 (4): 430–52.

Schultz, Jack M. 1999. *The Seminole Baptist Churches of Oklahoma: Maintaining a Traditional Community*. Civilization of the American Indian Series, vol. 233. Norman, OK: University of Oklahoma Press.

Schultze, Quentin J. 1991. *Televangelism and American Culture: The Business of Popular Religion*. Grand Rapids, MI: Baker Book House.

– 2013. "Evangelical Media Cults." In *Evangelical Christians and Popular Culture: Pop Goes the Gospel*, edited by Robert Woods, 128–48. Santa Barbara, CA: Praeger.

Schuurman, Peter John. 1995. "Spying, Peeping and Watching Over: The Beguiling Eyes of Video Surveillance." MA thesis, Queen's University.

– 2014. "The Brethren in Christ: Re-invigorating Denominational Culture." *Christian Courier*, 22 September. http://www.christiancourier.ca/news/entry/the-brethren-in-christ.

– 2016. "Bruxy Cavey and the Meeting House Megachurch: A Dramaturgical Model of Charismatic Leadership Performing 'Evangelicalism for People Not into Evangelicalism.'" PhD diss., University of Waterloo.

– 2018a. "Festival of Faith and Politics: Trump's Shadow Falls on Centre Stage at Calvin College's Writing Festival." *Christian Courier*, 14 May. http://www.christiancourier.ca/news/entry/festival-of-faith-and-politics.

– 2018b. "The Hillsong Worship Industry." *Christian Courier*, 23 April. http://www.christiancourier.ca/news/entry/the-hillsong-worship-industry.

Seerveld, Calvin. 1980. *Rainbows for a Fallen World: Aesthetic Life and Artistic Task*. Toronto: Tuppence.

Sharma, Abz, and David Grant. 2011. "Narrative, Drama and Charismatic Leadership: The Case of Apple's Steve Jobs." *Leadership* 7 (1): 3–26.

Shearing, Clifford D., and Philip C. Stenning. 1985. "From the Panopticon to Disney World: The Development of Discipline." In *Perspectives in Criminal Law*, ed. A. Doob and E. Greenspan, 335–49. Aurora, ON: Canada Law Book.

Sheler, Jeffrey L. 2009. *Prophet of Purpose: The Life of Rick Warren*. New York: Doubleday Religion.

Shelley, Bruce L., and Marshall Shelley. 1992. *The Consumer Church: Can Evangelicals Win the World without Losing Their Souls?* Downers Grove, IL: InterVarsity.

Shenk, Joanna, ed. 2011. *Widening the Circle: Experiments in Christian Discipleship*. Harrisonburg, VA: Herald.

Shenk, Wilbert R. 1983. *Exploring Church Growth*. Grand Rapids, MI: Eerdmans.

Shils, Edward. 1965. "Charisma, Order, and Status." *American Sociological Review* 30 (2): 199–213.

Shils, Edward. 1972. "Intellectuals, Tradition, and the Traditions of Intellectuals: Some Preliminary Considerations." *Daedalus* 101 (2): 21–34.

Shires, Preston. 2007. *Hippies of the Religious Right: From the Countercultures of Jerry Garcia to the Subculture of Jerry Falwell.* Waco, TX: Baylor University Press.

Shiu, Henry C.H. 2010. "Buddhism after the Seventies." In *Wild Geese: Buddhism in Canada*, edited by Victor Sogen Hori, Alexander Soucy, and John S. Harding, 84–110. Montreal and Kingston: McGill-Queen's University Press.

Shoemaker, Terry, and William Simpson. 2014. "Revisiting Sacred Metaphors: A Religious Studies Pedagogical Response to the Rise of the Nones." *Journal of Religion & Society* 16:1–16.

Sider, E. Morris. 1988. *The Brethren in Christ in Canada: Two Hundred Years of Tradition and Change.* Grantham, PA: Evangel Publishing House.

– 1999. *Reflections on a Heritage: Defining the Brethren in Christ.* Grantham, PA: Evangel Publishing House.

Sider, Ronald. 1978. *Rich Christians in an Age of Hunger: Moving from Affluence to Generosity.* Rev. ed. Nashville, TN: Thomas Nelson.

Sim, Stuart. 2002. *Irony and Crisis: A Critical History of Postmodern Culture.* Penguin: Toronto.

Sinitiere, Phillip. 2015. *Salvation with a Smile: Joel Osteen, Lakewood Church, and American Christianity.* New York: New York University Press.

Skinner, Dale S. 2009. "A Mission of People, Places and 'Altared' Spaces: From St Stephen's on-the-Hill to St Stephen's Off-the-Hill." DMin diss., Drew University.

Slagle, Amy. 2011. *The Eastern Church in the Spiritual Marketplace: American Conversions to Orthodox Christianity.* DeKalb, IL: Northern Illinois University Press.

Smith, Christian. 1998. *American Evangelicalism: Embattled and Thriving.* Chicago: University of Chicago Press.

– 2003. *Moral, Believing Animals: Human Personhood and Culture.* New York: Oxford University Press.

– 2010. *What Is a Person? Rethinking Humanity, Social Life, and the Moral Good from the Person Up.* Chicago: University of Chicago Press.

Smith, Craig R. 2000. *The Quest for Charisma: Christianity and Persuasion*. Westport, CT: Praeger.

Smith, David Norman. 1998. "Faith, Reason, and Charisma: Rudolf Sohm, Max Weber, and the Theology of Grace." *Sociological Inquiry* 68 (1): 32–60.

Smith, Greg. 2006. *Erving Goffman*. Abingdon, UK: Routledge.

Smith, James G. 2009. "Intercultural / Intercongregational Resource Sharing: Creating Space for Shared Ministry." ThM thesis, Vancouver School of Theology.

Smith, James K.A. 2009. *Desiring the Kingdom: Worship, Worldview, and Cultural Formation*. Grand Rapids, MI: Baker Academic.

– 2014. *How (Not) to Be Secular: Reading Charles Taylor*. Grand Rapids, MI: Wm B. Eerdmans Publishing.

– 2016a. "The Church as Jig: What Would It Mean to Resurrect the Idea of a 'Christian Society'?" *Comment*. Winter.

– 2016b. *You Are What You Love: The Spiritual Power of Habit*. Grand Rapids, MI: Brazos.

Smith, Leslie Dorrough. 2014. *Righteous Rhetoric: Sex Speech, and the Politics of Concerned Women for America*. New York: Oxford University Press.

Smith, P. 2000. "Culture and Charisma: Outline of a Theory." ACTA *Sociologica* 43: 101–11.

Snider, Phil, and Emily Bowen. 2010. *Toward a Hopeful Future: Why the Emergent Church Is Good News for Mainline Congregations*. New York: Pilgrim.

Snow, David A., James A. Bany, Michelle Peria, and James E. Stobaugh. 2010. "A Team Field Study of the Appeal of Megachurches: Identifying, Framing, and Solving Personal Issues." *Ethnography* 11 (1): 165–88.

Soja, Edward W. 1996. *Thirdspace: Journeys to Los Angeles and Other Real-and-Imagined Places*. Hoboken, NJ: Wiley.

Sonnenfeld, Jeffrey A. 1991. *The Hero's Farewell: What Happens When CEOs Retire*. New York: Oxford University Press.

Sorensen, Sue. 2014. *The Collar: Reading Christian Ministry in Fiction, Television, and Film*. Eugene, OR: Cascade Books.

Sosik, John J., Bruce J. Avolio, and Dong I. Jung. 2002. "Beneath the Mask: Examining the Relationship of Self-Presentation Attributes and Impression Management to Charismatic Leadership." *Leadership Quarterly* 13 (3): 217–42.

Soukup, Charles. 2006. "Hitching a Ride on a Star: Celebrity, Fandom, and Identification on the World Wide Web." *Southern Communication Journal* 71 (4): 319–37.

Sparks, Paul, Tim Soerens, and Dwight J. Friesen. 2010. *The New Parish: How Neighborhood Churches Are Transforming Mission, Discipleship and Community*. Downers Grove, IL: InterVarsity.

Spate, David James. 1996. "Gaining a Perspective and Plan for Continued Growth at Laurier Heights Baptist Church." DMin diss. Fuller Theological Seminary.

Spector-Mersel, Gabriela. 2010. "Narrative Research: Time for a Paradigm." *Narrative Inquiry* 20 (1): 204–24.

Spickard, James V. 2007. "Micro Qualitative Approaches to the Sociology of Religion: Phenomenologies, Interviews, Narratives, and Ethnographies." In *Sage Handbook of the Sociology of Religion*, edited by James A. Beckford and N.J. Demerath III, 104–27, Los Angeles: Sage.

Stackhouse, John G., Jr. 1993. *Canadian Evangelicalism in the Twentieth Century: An Introduction to Its Character*. Toronto: University of Toronto Press.

– 2005. "Who's Afraid of Evangelicals?" *Faith Today*, February.

– 2010. "Marci McDonald, 'The Armageddon Factor': Part 1: Information." Blog, 18 May. http://www.johnstackhouse.com/2010/05/18/marci-mcdonald-the-armageddon-factor-part-1-information/.

– 2011. "Canadian Evangelicals and Religious Freedom." *Policy in Public* 4 (Winter): 55–62.

Stake, Robert E. 1995. *The Art of Case Study Research*. Thousand Oaks, CA: Sage.

Stark, Rodney. 1999. "Secularization, R.I.P." *Sociology of Religion* 60 (3): 249–73.

– 2008. *What Americans Really Believe*. Waco, TX: Baylor University Press.

Stark, Rodney, and Roger Finke. 2000. *Acts of Faith: Explaining the Human Side of Religion*. Berkeley: University of California Press.

Starks, Glenn L. 2013. *Sexual Misconduct and the Future of Mega-Churches: How Large Religious Organizations Go Astray*. Santa Barbara, CA: Praeger.

Stearns, Rich. 2012. "Shedding Lethargy." *Leadership Journal* 33 (1). https://willowcreeksa.wordpress.com/2012/04/04/shedding-lethargy-by-rich-stearns/.

Steele, Terrance S. 2012. "The Missiology of the Emerging Church in Portland, Oregon." PhD diss., Trinity International University.

Steensland, Brian and Philip Goff. 2013. *The New Evangelical Social Engagement*. New York: Oxford.

Stennett, Rob. 2008. *The Almost True Story of Ryan Fisher: A Novel*. Grand Rapids, MI: Zondervan.

Stetzer, Ed. 2008. "The Evolution of Church Growth, Church Health, and the Missional Church: An Overview of the Church Growth Movement From, and Back to Its Missional Roots." Paper presented at American Society of Church Growth, Pasadena, CA, 14 November.

– 2013. "The Explosive Growth of U.S. Megachurches, Even While Many Say Their Day Is Done." Exchange, blog, 19 February. http://www.christianitytoday.com/edstetzer/2013/february/explosive-growth-of-us-megachurches-even-while-many-say.html.

– 2018. "Debunking the 81 Percent." *Christianity Today*, October, 21–4.

Stevenson, Jill. 2013. *Sensational Devotion: Evangelical Performance in Twenty-First-Century America*. Ann Arbor, MI: University of Michigan Press.

Stewart, Adam. 2015. *The New Canadian Pentecostals*. Waterloo, ON: Wilfrid Laurier University Press.

Stewart, Elizabeth. 1999. *Jesus the Holy Fool*. New York: Sheed and Ward.

Stiller, Karen. 2007. "Evangelicals: On the Way to Reclaiming a Great Name." *Faith Today*, March/April. https://bbnc.evangelicalfellowship.ca/page.aspx?pid=1324.

Stokes, David R. 2011. *The Shooting Salvationist: J. Frank Norris and the Murder Trial That Captivated America*. Hanover, NH: Steerforth.

Storr, Anthony. 1996. *Feet of Clay: Saints, Sinners, and Madmen: A Study of Gurus*. New York: Free Press.

Stout, Harry. 1991. *The Divine Dramatist: George Whitefield and the Rise of Modern Evangelicalism*. Grand Rapids, MI: Wm B. Eerdmans Publishing.

St Philip, Elizabeth. 2006. "This Little Hipster Went to Church; Where Do Downtowners Seek Spiritual Comfort? These Days, It's the Paramount Theatre." *Globe and Mail*, 11 March.

Streib, Heinz, Ralph W. Hood, Barbara Keller, Christopher F. Silver, and Rosina-Martha Csoeff. 2009. *Deconversion: Qualitative and Quantitative Results from Cross-Cultural Research in Germany and the United States of America*. Gottingen: Vandenhoeck & Ruprecht.

Streiker, Lowell D. 1971. *The Jesus Trip; Advent of the Jesus Freaks*. Nashville, TN: Abingdon.

Strine, Mary S., Beverly W. Long, and Mary Francis Hopkins. 1990. "Research in Interpretation and Performance Studies: Trends, Issues,

Priorities." In *Speech Communication: Essays to Commeemorate the 75th Anniversary of the Speech Communication Association*, edited by G.M. Phillips and J.T. Wood, 181–204. Carbondale, IL: Southern Illinois University Press.

Strobel, Lee. 2011. *The Ambition: A Novel*. Grand Rapids, MI: Zondervan.

Stromberg, Peter G. 2009. *Caught in Play: How Entertainment Works on You*. Stanford, CA: Stanford University Press.

Strong, Robert Wendell. 2013. "A Pastoral Succession Plan to Help Long-term Pastors Prepare for Inevitable Ministry Transition." DMin diss., Biola University.

Studebaker, Steven, and Lee Beach. 2012. "Emerging Churches in Post-Christian Canada." *Religions* 3 (3): 862–79.

Surratt, Sherry, and Wayne Smith. 2011. "Team Collaboration: Broadening the Church Leadership Platform." Leadership Network. http://ministryformation.com.au/attachments/article/255/Team_Collaboration.pdf.

Sutton, Matthew Avery. 2007. *Aimee Semple McPherson and the Resurrection of Christian America*. Cambridge, MA: Harvard University Press.

Swartz, David R. 2014. *Moral Minority: The Evangelical Left in an Age of Conservatism*. Philadelphia: University of Pennsylvania Press.

Swidler, Ann. 2001. *Talk of Love: How Culture Matters*. Chicago: University of Chicago Press.

Tacey, David. 2003. *The Spirituality Revolution: The Emergence of Contemporary Spirituality*. New York: Routledge.

Tamney, Joseph B. 2002. *The Resilience of Conservative Religion: The Case of Popular, Conservative Protestant Congregations*. Cambridge: Cambridge University Press.

Tanner, Marcus N., Anisa M. Zvonkovic, and Charlie Adams. 2012. "Forced Termination of American Clergy: Its Effects and Connection to Negative Well-being." *Review of Religious Research* 54 (1): 1–17.

Tataru, Ludmilla. 2012. "Celebrity Stories as a Genre of Media Culture." *Journal of Teaching and Education* 1 (6): 15–21.

Taylor, Charles. 2007. *A Secular Age*. Cambridge: Belknap.

Teel, Roy A., Jr. 2008. *Against the Grain: The American Mega Church and Its Culture of Control*. Chatsworth, CA: NarroWay.

Terry, Jonathan C. 1997. "A Liberationist Critique of the Church Growth Movement." PhD diss., Temple University.

Teusner, Paul Emerson. 2010. "Emerging Church Bloggers in Australia: Prophets, Priests and Rulers in God's Virtual World." BA thesis, RMIT University.

Thiessen, Elmer. 2011. "Review: To Change the World." *Conrad Grebel Review* 29 (2): 104–7.

Thiessen, Joel. 2015. *The Meaning of Sunday: The Practice of Belief in a Secular Age*. Montreal and Kingston: McGill-Queen's University Press.

Thomson, Peter, and Glendyr Sacks. 2007. *The Cambridge Companion to Brecht*. 2nd ed. Cambridge Companions to Literature and Classics. Cambridge: Cambridge University Press.

Thumma, Scott L. 1996. "The Kingdom, the Power, and the Glory: The Megachurch in Modern American Society." PhD diss., Emory University.

Thumma, Scott, and Warren Bird. 2008. "Changes in American Megachurches: Tracing Eight Years of Growth and Innovation in the Nation's Largest-Attendance Congregations." Leadership Network, Hartford Institute for Religion Research.

– 2009. "Not Who You Think They Are: The Real Story of People Who Attend America's Megachurches." Leadership Network, Hartford Institute for Religion Research.

– 2011. "A New Decade of Megachurches: 2011 Profile of Large Attendance Churches in the United States." Leadership Network, Hartford Institute for Religion Research.

– 2014. "Megafaith for the Megacity: The Global Megachurch Phenomenon." In *The Changing World Religion Map: Sacred Places, Identities, Practices and Politics*, edited by Stanley E. Brunn, 2331–52. The Netherlands: Springer Publishing.

– 2015. "Recent Shifts in America's Largest Protestant Churches: Megachurches 2015 Report." Leadership Network, Hartford Institute for Religion Research.

Thumma, Scott, and Dave Travis. 2007. *Beyond Megachurch Myths: What We Can Learn from America's Largest Churches*. San Francisco: Jossey-Bass.

Todd, Douglas. 2005. "U.S. Religious Right Pushing into Canada." *Vancouver Sun*, 30 July.

– 2008a. "An Interview with Douglas Todd on Canadian Evangelicalism." *Church and Faith Trends* 1 (3): 1–5.

– 2008b. "Why Stephen Harper Keeps His Evangelical Faith Very Private." *Vancouver Sun*, 10 September.

– 2011. "The State of Evangelicalism: Canada Differs from the U.S." *Vancouver Sun*, 30 October.

Tomlinson, Dave. 2003. *The Post-Evangelical*. Rev. ed. Grand Rapids, MI: Zondervan.

Tong, Joy Kooi Chin. 2008. "McDonaldization and the Megachurches: A Case Study of City Harvest Church, Singapore." In *Religious Commodification in Asia: Marketing Gods*, edited by Pattana Kitiarsa, 186–204. London: Routledge.
– 2011. "Religious Experience of a Young Megachurch Congregation in Singapore." In *Mediating Faiths: Religion and Socio-Cultural Change*, edited by Michael Bailey and Guy Redden, 159–71. Surrey, UK: Ashgate.
Toth, Michael A. 1972. "Toward a Theory of the Routinization of Charisma." *Rocky Mountain Social Science Journal* 9 (2): 93–8.
Trice, H.H., and J.M. Beyer. 1986. "Charisma and Its Routinization in Two Social Movement Organizations." *Research in Organizational Behavior* 8:113–64.
Trueheart, Charles. 1996. "Welcome to the Next Church." *Atlantic Monthly*, August, 37–58.
Tseelon, E. 1992. "Is the Presented Self Sincere? Goffman, Impression Management and the Postmodern Self." *Theory, Culture & Society* 9 (2): 115–28.
Tucker, James D., Jr. 1998. "Post-McGavran Church Growth: Divergent Streams of Development." DMin diss., Mid-America Baptist Theological Seminary.
Tucker, Robert C. 1968. "The Theory of Charismatic Leadership." *Daedalus* 97 (3): 731–56.
Tucker, Ruth A. 2006. *Left Behind in a Megachurch World: How God Works through Ordinary Churches*. Grand Rapids, MI: Baker Books.
Tucker-Worgs, Tamelyn. 2001. "Get on Board, Little Children, There's Room for Many More: The Black Megachurch Phenomenon." *Journal of the Interdenominational Theological Center* 29 (1–2): 177–203.
– 2011. *The Black Megachurch: Theology, Gender, and the Politics of Public Engagement*. Waco, TX: Baylor University Press.
Turner, Bryan S. 2010. "Religion in a Post-Secular Society." In *The New Blackwell Companion to the Sociology of Religion*, edited by Bryan S. Turner, 563–83. Hoboken, NJ: Wiley-Blackwell.
Turner, Graeme. 2004. *Understanding Celebrity*. New York: Sage.
– 2006. "The Mass Production of Celebrity." *International Journal of Cultural Studies* 9 (2): 153–65.
– 2010. "Approaching Celebrity Studies." *Celebrity Studies* 1 (1): 11–20.
Turner, S. 2003. "Charisma Reconsidered." *Journal of Classical Sociology* 3 (1): 5–26.
– 2011. "Classic Sociology: Weber as an Analyst of Charisma." *Leadership Studies: The Dialogue of Disciplines*, edited by Michael Harvey and Ron Riggio, 82–8. Northampton, MA: Edward Elgar.

Turner, Victor. 1982. *From Ritual to Theatre: The Human Seriousness of Play*. New York: Performing Arts Journal Publications.
— 1995. *Ritual Process: Structure and Anti-Structure*. New York: Routledge & Kegan Paul.
TV Tropes. n.d. "Look Both Ways." http://tvtropes.org/pmwiki/pmwiki.php/Main/LookBothWays.
Twitchell, James B. 2004. *Branded Nation: The Marketing of Megachurch, College Inc., and Museumworld*. New York: Simon and Schuster.
— 2007. *Shopping for God: How Christianity Went from In Your Heart to In Your Face*. New York: Simon & Schuster.
Umidi, Joseph L. 2000. *Confirming the Pastoral Call: A Guide to Matching Candidates and Congregations*. Grand Rapids, MI: Kregel Academic.
Usunier, Jean-Claude, and Joerg Stolz, eds. 2014. *Religions as Brands: New Perspectives on the Marketization of Religion and Spirituality*. Burlington, VT: Ashgate Publishing.
Vanderbloemen, William. 2014. "Why Mark Driscoll's Resignation Shows We're in a New Era for Pastors." *Christianity Today*, 14 October.
Vanderbloemen, William, and Warren Bird. 2014. *Next: Pastoral Succession That Works*. Grand Rapids, MI: Baker Books.
VanGronigen, Bill. 2013. "The Megachurch and Social Architecture: Realities and Questions." *Comment*, 4 October. http://www.cardus.ca/comment/article/4063/the-megachurch-and-social-architecture-realities-and-questions/.
Van Holten, Maria Christina. 2005. "Ministry without Resident Clergy: How Two Small Congregations Have Found Alternative Ways to Minister." DMin diss., Vancouver School of Theology.
Vanhoozer, Kevin J. 2014. *Faith Speaking Understanding: Performing the Drama of Doctrine*. Louisville, KY: Westminster John Knox.
Van Krieken, Robert. 2012. *Celebrity Society*. New York: Routledge.
Vaughan, John. 1993. *Megachurches and America's Cities: How Churches Grow*. Grand Rapids, MI: Baker.
Vautour, Doreen Eleanor. 1995. "Maritime Entrants to the Congregation of Notre Dame, 1880–1920: A Rise in Vocations." MA thesis, University of New Brunswick.
Vega, April. 2012. "Music Sacred and Profane: Exploring the Use of Popular Music in Evangelical Worship Services." *Journal of Religion and Popular Culture* 24 (3): 365–79.
Verchery, Lina. 2010. "The Woodenfish Program: Fo Guang Shan, Canadian Youth, and a New Generation of Buddhist Missionaries." In *Wild Geese: Buddhism in Canada*, edited by Victor Sogen Hori,

Alexander Soucy, and John S. Harding, 210–35. Montreal and Kingston: McGill-Queen's University Press.

Vick, Joyce. 2003. *Tom Malone: The Preacher from Pontiac*. Murfreesboro, TN: Sword of the Lord Publishers.

von der Ruhr, Marc, and Joseph Daniels. 2012. "Examining Megachurch Growth: Free Riding, Fit, and Faith." *International Journal of Social Economics* 39 (5): 357–72.

Vosper, Greta. 2008. *With or Without God*. New York: Harper.

Wach, Joachim. 1944. *Sociology of Religion*. Chicago: University of Chicago Press.

Wacker, Grant. 2014. *America's Pastor: Billy Graham and the Shaping of a Nation*. Cambridge, MA: Belknap.

Wade, Matthew. 2010. "The Institution, the Ethic, and the Affective: The Hillsong Church and Affinities of the Self." MA thesis, Australian National University.

Wagner, C. Peter. 1980. "Recent Developments in Church Growth Understandings." *Review & Expositor* 77 (4): 507–19.

Wallace, David Foster. 1993. "E Unibus Pluram: Television and U.S. Fiction." *Review of Contemporary Fiction* 13(2): 151–94.

Walker, Ken. 2015. "Is Buying Your Way onto the Bestseller List Wrong?" *Christianity Today*, 20 January. http://www.christianitytoday.com/ct/2015/januaryfebruary/buying-bestsellers-resultsource.html.

Wallis, Roy. 1982. "The Social Construction of Charisma." *Social Compass* 29 (1): 25–39.

– 1993. "Charisma and Explanation." In *Secularization, Rationalism, and Sectarianism: Essays in Honour of Bryan R. Wilson*, edited by Eileen Barker, James A. Beckford, and Karel Dobbelaere, 167–79. Oxford: Clarendon.

Walters, Jeffrey Kirk. 2011. "'Effective Evangelism' in the City: Donald Mcgavran's Missiology and Urban Contexts." PhD diss., Southern Baptist Theological Seminary.

Warner, R. Stephen. 1988. *New Wine in Old Wineskins: Evangelicals and Liberals in a Small-Town Church*. Berkeley: University of California Press.

– 1997. "Convergence towards the New Paradigm: A Case of Induction." In *Rational Choice Theory and Religion: Summary and Assessment*, edited by Lawrence Young, 87–103. New York: Routledge.

– 2005. *A Church of Our Own: Disestablishment and Diversity in American Religion*. New Brunswick, NJ: Rutgers University Press.

Warren, Rick. 1995. *The Purpose Driven Church: Every Church Is Big in God's Eyes*. Grand Rapids, MI: Zondervan.

— 2002. *The Purpose Driven Life: What on Earth Am I Here For? 40 Days of Purpose*. Grand Rapids, MI: Zondervan.

Warrier, Maya, and Simon Oliver. 2008. *Theology and Religious Studies: An Exploration of Disciplinary Boundaries*. London: T & T Clark International.

Watson, Stuart. 2014. "How Elevation Church, Pastor Furtick Produce 'Spontaneous' Baptisms." WCNC. http://www.wcnc.com/news/iteam/How-Elevation-Church-Pastor-Furtick-produce-spontaneous-baptism-246072001.html (page discontinued).

Wead, Douglas. 1980. *Compassionate Touch*. Minneapolis: Bethany House Publishing.

Weaver, J. Denny. 1987. *Becoming Anabaptist*. Scottdale, PA: Herald.

Weaver-Zercher, Valerie. 2013. *Thrill of the Chaste: The Allure of Amish Romance Novels*. Baltimore, MD: Johns Hopkins University Press.

Weber, Max. 1968. *On Charisma and Institution Building: Selected Papers*. Edited by S.N. Eisenstadt. Chicago: University of Chicago Press.

Webster, Douglas D. 1992. *Selling Jesus: What's Wrong with Marketing the Church*. Eugene, OR: Wipf & Stock Publishers.

Weese, Carolyn, and J. Russell Crabtree. 2012. *The Elephant in the Boardroom: Speaking the Unspoken about Pastoral Transitions*. Hoboken, NJ: John Wiley & Sons.

Wellman, James K. 1999. *The Gold Coast Church and the Ghetto: Christ and Culture in Mainline Protestantism*. Chicago: University of Illinois Press.

— 2012. *Rob Bell and a New American Christianity*. Nashville, TN: Abingdon.

Wellman, James K., and Kate Corcoran. 2014. "'God Is Like a Drug …' Explaining Interaction Ritual Chains in American Megachurches." *Sociological Forum* 29 (3): 650–72.

— 2016. "'People Forget He's Human': Charismatic Leadership in Institutionalized Religion." *Sociology of Religion* 77 (4): 309–32.

Wells, David F. 2005. *Above All Earthly Pow'rs: Christ in a Postmodern World*. Grand Rapids, MI: Wm B. Eerdmans Publishing.

— 2008. *The Courage to Be Protestant: Truth-Lovers, Marketers, and Emergents in the Postmodern World*. Grand Rapids: Wm B. Eerdmans Publishing.

Wessinger, Catherine, 2012. "Charismatic Leaders in New Religious Movements." In *Cambridge Companion to New Religious Movements*, edited by Olav Hammer and Mikael Rothstein, 80–96. Cambridge: Cambridge University Press.

Wheeler, Meredith Edward. 2008. "The Leadership Succession Process in Megachurches." PhD diss., Temple University.

White, Thomas, and John Yeats. 2009. *Franchising McChurch: Feeding Our Obsession for Easy Christianity*. Elgin, IL: David C. Cook Publishing.

Wiebe, Rudy. 1962. *Peace Shall Destroy Many*. Toronto: Vintage Canada.

Wiersema, Margarethe, Jay W. Lorsch, Rakesh Khurana, Michael E. Porter, Nitin Nohria, Dan Ciampa, Kevin P. Coyne, Edward J. Coyne Sr, Ram Charan, and Joseph L. Bower. 2009. *Harvard Business Review on CEO Succession*. Boston: Harvard Business School Publishing.

Wikipedia. n.d. "Pride Toronto." https://en.wikipedia.org/wiki/Pride_Toronto.

Wildeboer, Henry. 1983. "First Christian Reformed Church: Renewal, Its Reformed Theological Basis, Its Development, and Its Implications for Other Congregations (Canada, Calgary, Alberta)." DMin diss., Fuller Theological Seminary, School of Theology.

Wilford, Justin. 2012. *Sacred Subdivisions: The Postsuburban Transformation of American Evangelicalism*. New York: New York University Press.

Wilkinson, Michael, and Peter Althouse. 2012. "Apology and Forgiveness as an Expression of Love in a Charismatic Congregation." *PentecoStudies* 11 (1): 87–102.

Wilkinson, Michael, and Peter Schuurman. 2019. "Megachurches in Canada." In *The Brill Book of Megachurches*, edited by Stephen Hunt. Leiden: Brill.

Willard, Dallas, and Donald Simpson. 2005. *Revolution of Character: Discovering Christ's Pattern for Spiritual Transformation*. Colorado Springs, CO: NavPress.

Willey, Robin D. 2016. "Leaving Grand Rapids: Investigating the Postconservative Turn in Canadian Evangelicalism." PhD diss., University of Alberta.

Williams, Premkumar D. 2007. "Between City and Steeple: Looking at Megachurch Architecture." In *Everyday Theology: How to Read Cultural Texts and Interpret Trends*, edited by Kevin J. Vanhoozer, Charles A. Anderson, and Michael J. Sleasman, 115–32. Grand Rapids, MI: Baker Academic.

Willimon, William W. 2012. *Incorporation*. Eugene, OR: Cascade Books.

Willner, Ann Ruth. 1984. *The Spellbinders: Charismatic Political Leadership*. New Haven, CT: Yale University Press.

Wilson, Bryan R. 1975. *The Noble Savages: The Primitive Origins of Charisma and Its Contemporary Survival*. Berkeley: University of California Press.

Wilson, Jonathan R. 2007. *Why Church Matters: Worship, Ministry, and Mission in Practice*. Grand Rapids, MI: Brazos.

Winnicott, Donald Woods. 1971. *Playing and Reality*. New York: Basic Books.

Wise, Philip. 1995. "Theological Issues Raised by the Church Growth Movement." *Theological Educator* 51:95–105.

Witham, Larry. 2010. *Marketplace of the Gods: How Economics Explains Religion*. Oxford: Oxford University Press.

Wollschleger, Jason, and Jeremy R. Porter. 2011. "A 'WalMartization' of Religion? The Ecological Impact of Megachurches on the Local and Extra-Local Religious Economy." *Review of Religious Research* 53 (3): 279–99.

Wolsey, Roger. 2011. *Kissing Fish: Christianity for People Who Don't Like Christianity*. Bloomington, IN: Xlibris.

Wolterstorff, Nicholas. 1983. *Until Justice and Peace Embrace: The Kuyper Lectures for 1981 Delivered at the Free University of Amsterdam*. 2nd ed. Kampen, Netherlands: Wm B. Eerdmans Publishing.

Works, Herbert Melvin. 1974. "The Church Growth Movement to 1965: An Historical Perspective." DMin diss., Fuller Theological Seminary.

Worthen, Molly. 2014. *Apostles of Reason: The Crisis of Authority in American Evangelicalism*. New York: Oxford University Press.

Wright, Bradley R. Entner, Dina Giovanelli, Emily G. Dolan, and Mark Evan Edwards. 2011. "Explaining Deconversion from Christianity: A Study of Online Narratives." *Journal of Religion & Society* 13:2011–21.

Wright, N.T. 2012. *How God Became King: The Forgotten Story of the Gospels*. New York: HarperOne.

Wuthnow, Robert. 1998. *After Heaven: Spirituality in America since the 1950s*. Berkeley: University of California Press.

– 2001. *I Come Away Stronger*. Wm B. Eerdmans Publishing.

– 2007. *After the Baby Boomers: How Twenty- and Thirty-Somethings Are Shaping the Future of American Religion*. Princeton, NJ: Princeton University Press.

– 2010. *Boundless Faith: The Global Outreach of American Churches*. Berkeley: University of California Press.

Yoder, John Howard. 1995. "Primitivism and the Radical Reformation: Strengths and Weaknesses." In *The Primitive Church in the Modern World*, edited by Richard T. Hughes, 74–97. Urbana: University of Illinois Press.

Young, Lawrence. 1997. *Rational Choice Theory and Religion: Summary and Assessment*. New York: Routledge.

Young, Richard. 2007. *Rise of Lakewood Church and Joel Osteen*. New Kensington, PA: Whitaker House.

Young, Shawn David. 2011. "Jesus People USA, the Christian Woodstock, and Conflicting Worlds: Political, Theological, and Musical Evolution, 1972–2010." PhD diss., Michigan State University.

Young, Wm Paul. 2008. *The Shack*. Thousand Oaks, CA: Windblown Media.

Zablocki, Benjamin David. 1980. *Alienation and Charisma: A Study of Contemporary American Communes*. New York: Free Press.

Zawadzki, Diana Lea. 2008. "Fellowship as Social Capital: Student Religious Belief and Religious Organization on a Canadian University Campus." MA thesis, Queen's University.

Zilber, Tammar B., Rivka Tuval-Mashiach, and Amia Lieblich. 2008. "The Embedded Narrative Navigating through Multiple Contexts." *Qualitative Inquiry* 14 (6): 1047–69.

Index

aesthetics, xvii, 28, 35, 182, 187
affect, xvii, 25, 29, 33, 38, 70, 89–93, 114, 138, 158, 174, 184–7, 233, 242; emotional bond with Cavey, 33, 38, 72–3, 76, 86, 119, 138, 195; as emotional manipulation, 25, 69, 201; sentimentality 86. *See also* anger; play
Amish, 25, 85, 100–2
Anabaptism, Anabaptist, 88, 99, 101–4; Cavey's identity as, 211; community hermeneutic, 108; and drinking alcohol, 17; modernized, xvi, 25, 101; and pacifism, 90–1, 229; persecution of, 88, 91, 212; in politics, xiv, 56, 99–100, 108, 191, 226, 243, 276n5, 276n9, 282n16, 290n3; and popular culture, 102, 186; simplicity 87–9, 108, 141, 229, 262n4
anger, 89–93, 110, 206, 225, 240
asceticism, 88. *See* Anabaptism: simplicity
atonement, 273n22, 210–11

"bad, poisonous, violent" fallacy, 240

bait-and-switch, 137
Bell, Rob, 195, 218, 258, 262n6
Berger, Peter, 34, 48, 50, 121, 258n18, 268n8; religion and humour, 165, 183, 240, 259n24, 285n12
body, embodiment, xi, xvii, 7, 28, 71, 97, 141–2, 158, 186–7, 190–1, 223–4, 253n7, 267n2, 286n19
Boyd, Greg, 14, 140, 178, 252n6, 257n14, 275n3, 277n10
brand, branding, 7, 23, 74, 118, 135, 162, 223, 224; calcifying, 218–20; consistency, 131, 166, 175. *See* marketing
Brethren in Christ, Be In Christ (BIC denomination), 12–14, 16, 40–1, 66–7, 101–2, 105, 129, 170, 229, 239; name change, 63
buzz, xvii, 73, 128, 137–43, 151

Calvinism, Calvinist, 43, 60, 92, 102, 113–15, 209, 232, 249–50
Canada, Canadian, xvi, xix; as anti-American, xiii, 40; as Christian country, 8, 55; irenic, 78; modesty, 61, 160, 191; multicultural, 46, 50, 67, 274n3; as

poṣt-Christian, 3, 8, 22, 47–53, 237; same-sex marriage, 39–40; secular establishment, 23; tolerant, 43–4

Cavey, Bruxy: awkwardness, 201–6; biography, 58–65; buzz about, 137–43; divorce, 13, 41, 62–3, 65, 92–3, 249; DJ, xiv, xv, xviii, 6, 27, 75, 170–1, 176–7, 179–81, 187; as evangelical, 258n17; marriage, 64, 89, 178; Pentecostal past, 201; similarity to Muhammad Ali, 289n2; view of Old Testament, 223, 289n1

celebrity: audience, 137–43; charisma, 139; evangelical, 61, 87, 93; and media, 40, 42, 46, 280n10; and megachurch pastors, 10, 25; as narrative, 57, 65, 138, 140; studies, 34–9, 56; subcultural, 57, 63

charisma, charismatic: bond, 33, 76, 97, 121, 124, 138, 203, 218, 220; contrived, 35–8, 46, 143; definition, 22, 26, 30, 32; diamond, 46, 71–2, 95–6, 194; and dramatic web, 17, 28; graphic, 34; sociological/situational, 32–4; spiritual/biblical, 30–1. See also succession

choice, 167–9, 271n9

church growth movement, 23, 261n3

Christian Contemporary Music (CCM), 185–7, 285n17

communications team, 18, 38, 128, 143–8, 153–4, 162–6, 188–90; budget, 275n5

compassion activities, 99–100, 148, 176, 200, 229; in budget, 275n5

consumerism, 10, 23–4, 29, 74, 81–4, 86, 108, 158, 162, 166–9, 182, 235, 271n9; resisting, 24, 81, 84, 188, 236, 241–3

cool factor, xiv, 4, 7, 44, 118, 158, 172, 190–1, 204; in Anabaptism, 277n9; as outsider, 236

cooperative egoism, 108

cult, 79, 127, 143–7; of personality, 6, 10, 17, 25–6, 29, 74, 144–5, 147, 195–6, 206, 257n13, 286n3; in popular imagination, 195–6, 222, 280n12

cultural component, 7, 17, 24, 33, 121, 199, 246

cultural creatives, 65, 67, 147, 184

Day, Tim, 129–31, 279n3

deconversion, xiv, 60, 65, 69, 73, 78, 107, 119–20, 157, 162, 187, 191

Disney, Disneyfication, Disneyization, 69, 81, 134, 166, 210, 242, 256n12, 283n6

dramatic web, 26–9, 74, 98, 106, 187, 194, 199, 201, 219–20, 227, 239; graphic, 107; spin cycle, 123

dramaturgical trouble, 193, 286n2

dramaturgy, 96–7; just a show? 226

Driscoll, Mark, 25, 56, 146, 150, 195, 199, 209, 216, 219, 252n7, 280n11, 287n9

Droogers, Andre, 183, 285n13

effervescence, 138, 159, 162, 174

Elmer Gantry stereotype, 10, 25, 215, 231, 239–41, 249, 256n13

Emerging Church, 6, 66, 73, 75, 98, 188, 199; defined, 14–15, 253n3;

and leaderless myth, 230–2; and megachurches, 14, 236; and missional church, 231; and reflexivity, 254n5
emotions. *See* affect
entrepreneurial evangelism, 199
ethnography, 9, 39, 137, 162, 245–6
evangelical, evangelicalism: enjoyment, 159, 172, 187, 243; reflexive, xiii, xvii, 6–7, 9, 11, 15–19, 145, 159, 169, 212, 224–5, 230–1, 236, 244; stereotype, xiv, xv, 6, 19, 27, 82, 86, 89, 249

family trope, xvi, 41–2, 106–7, 111, 131, 141, 165, 171, 180, 272n14; BIC as, 229; "one family" slogan, 66, 221
fun, xii, xix, 11, 16, 146, 148, 155, 156–91, 283n6, 284n7
Furtick, Steve, 271n6

Geertz, Clifford, 28, 106, 121, 219, 255n8
Goffman, Erving, 26–7, 72, 75, 197, 205, 227, 255n8; humour, 81; interaction order, 72; role distance, 75; self, 78, 202; sidekick, 129; teams, 126; total institution, 83; underlife of institutions, 78, 197. *See also* dramaturgical trouble; dramaturgy; impression management; identity: spoiled

Harvest Bible Chapel, 43, 116, 209–12
hell, 3–5
Hillsong Church, 87, 273n18
hippie culture, 97, 275n4, 280n8
hit-by-a-bus trope, 213
"holy mavericks," 25
Home Church, xvii, 94–124; as centre of TMH, 95, 134, 152; connection to Sunday teaching, 141; dissent, 169, 197, 238; as evangelistic, 170; as fluid, fragile, failed, 115–21, 208; games, 110, 156, 169, 177, 246; as guided tutorials, 139; off-script, 111–15; on-script, 109–11; as pure relationship, 104–9; statistics on, 13, 133, 152; tattoos, 7; volunteering, 24, 110, 246
horror films, 5, 84–7, 225
Huddles, 106, 110, 123, 277nn11–12
Hybels, Bill, xiii, 25, 178, 199, 216, 283n5

identity: crisis, 54–6; management, 72, 74, 134, 145; spoiled, xiv, 7, 27, 48, 71–93, 157, 190, 224
iftobums, 165
impression management, 27, 53, 72, 80, 144–5, 196
irony, ironic, 17, 71–93, 145, 154, 225–6; charisma, xvi, 6, 7, 26, 134; and cynicism, 73, 95, 226, 243; definition, xviii; and dramatic web, 46; and Emerging Church, 74; as mainstream, 236, 289n2; and play, 159, 191, 243; as prophetic, 47; and reflexivity, 241
irreligion, irreligious, xi, xviii, 11, 15, 29, 45–93, 104, 148, 193, 219, 227, 229, 233–4, 251n1
irreligious paradox, xvii, 8, 10, 18, 29, 156–91

Jakes, T.D., 87, 96
Jesus Christ, xii, xiv, xvi, xvii, 4, 9–11, 14, 19, 98–9, 108, 122, 223
Jesus People Movement, 97, 275n4, 280n8
joke, jokes, xviii, 16, 81, 156, 159
Joosse, Paul, 31, 33, 55, 76, 128, 203

leadership, 17, 30–2, 262n6; centralized, 127, 133, 170, 191, 193, 238; development, 221; failure, 214–18; heroic, 36–8, 230, 264n12, 264n13; institutional entrepreneur, 199; leaderless myth, 230–2; missional, 230–2; shared, 200; team, 126–9. *See also* charisma; succession
liminality, 7, 157–8, 162, 176, 180, 186–8, 190–1, 228, 241
liturgy, 6, 71, 176–7, 184, 233–4, 236, 254n6, 290n5
Lloyd, Vincent, 21, 35, 133, 188, 243, 266n23
Lyon, David, 242, 268n9

mainline churches, xi, 8, 23, 51, 67, 104, 167, 173
marketing, 35, 38, 138, 143, 147–8, 150, 163, 166–7, 173, 261n3
markets, marketplace, 23, 25, 83, 161, 166–7, 172, 184, 197, 236, 256n12, 261n2
Marti, Gerardo, 66, 73, 75, 108, 182–4, 199
McDonald, Marci, 39–40, 252n5
McDonaldization, 166, 174–5, 188, 240, 242–4, 249, 249–50, 256n12

McPherson, Aimee Semple, 160–1, 198, 216, 232, 289n26
media, 35–8, 40, 46, 143–55, 144, 148–53, 188–90, 205, 247, 280n10, 281n15; Canadian, 51; as web, 218–20
Meeting House, The: budget, 100, 275n5; demographics, 65–8, 132; gender, 238, 290n7, 290n1; history, 16, 63–5, 269n12; loyalty, 208; as network for business, 197; and race and ethnicity, 237, 290n6; whiteness of, 7, 9, 13, 45, 49, 65, 112, 146, 190, 225, 237, 290n6
megachurch, megachurches, 7, 13, 161; attendees, 65, 69, 120, 269n13; and charisma, 26, 38; as commercialized, 9–10, 23, 166–7, 173, 190, 240, 256n12; defined, 78–9, 254n7; as evangelical, 168; as fun, 159, 172; as gated community, 134, 232; global, 67, 87, 96, 274n1; as "greedy institution," 83–4; as ideal type, 36; leadership, 128, 146, 152; literature, 20, 36–7, 166, 169, 172, 245, 256n11, 279n4; non-denominational, 122; as passé, 239; as play, 19; proliferation of, 23–4, 172; and prosperity theology, 169; as pseudo-church, 37; scandals, 25, 214–18; socially engaged, 229–30; as strict, 167–8; success, 230. *See also* succession
Mennonites. *See* Anabaptism
method, 9, 19–20, 39, 245–50
missional church, 230–1, 290n4
monsters, 96–101, 106–7, 121, 239

Moral Majority, xiii, 5, 38, 46, 56, 249
music, 137, 146; Christian popular music, 185–7; at dance parties, 170–2, 174, 176–81; Hillsong, 273n18; prescribed song lists, 133; as "worship," 135

narrative. *See* story
Noll, Mark, 49, 102

Old Spice parody video, 188–90
Osteen, Joel, xix, 22, 87, 273n17
Oyedepo, David, 273n20

pacifism. *See* Anabaptism, Anabaptist
paradox, 8, 11, 15, 17, 74, 92, 156–91; as ambivalence, 224; definition, 158; as insincerely sincere, 227; intensifying it, 236–7; as liminal space, 191
parody, 19, 73–4, 89, 91, 99, 103, 163, 185–6, 188, 190–1, 285n16, 286n18; definition, 185
party, parties, xv, 19, 105, 110, 169–81, 185–7, 246
performance, 7, 26–7, 33, 48, 56, 123, 227; as aesthetic, 187; counter-performances, 74, 79, 89, 93; end of 212–18; just a show 226–7; performance studies 75–6, 255n8, 278n15; regions, 193, 205; as teamwork, 126
personality cult. *See* cult: of personality
play, playfulness, xii, xvi, xviii, 15, 19, 75, 82, 155–91, 240, 243, 244, 262n8. *See also* paradox; parody; irony; satire

pluralist congregations, 66
politics. *See* Anabaptism: politics
popular culture, 46, 56, 73, 85, 102, 137, 172, 186–7, 213, 225, 241–2, 270n1, 285n16
preaching, 59, 95, 104, 127, 137, 279n2
primitivism, 95; defined, 102
prophetic, 15, 47, 56, 73–4, 147, 189, 226, 233, 239–44
prosperity gospel/theology, 23, 74, 79, 87–9, 96, 113, 169, 260n1, 273n17, 274n1
pure relationship, 96–7, 105–7, 109, 115, 123, 208, 233
Purge Sunday, xix, 26–7, 69–70, 74, 78–84

reflexive evangelicals. *See* evangelical: reflexive
reflexivity, 13, 16, 75, 78, 93, 196, 225, 244, 254n5
religion, definitions, 54–5, 232–7
religious ludism, 162, 187
revolution, 92, 99–101, 232, 244, 250, 291n3
ritual, 19, 26, 32, 78–84, 118, 121, 157, 174, 183–4, 187–8, 234–6; as negative, xii, 3, 55, 96, 104, 157, 190
Roberts, Robert C., 91, 158
romance, romantic, xix, 32, 61, 86, 93–124, 134, 190, 195, 230, 263n8
routinization of charisma. *See* Weber, Max: routinization

sacred/secular binary, 158, 160, 169, 172, 180, 184–6, 190, 285n15

sacred space, 6, 106, 134–7, 190, 279n4
same-sex marriage. *See* Canada: same-sex marriage
satire, 73–4, 91, 93, 95, 147, 189, 225
Schleitheim Confession, 17
secularization, 47–53
sentimentality. *See* affect: sentimentality
seriousness fallacy, 157, 162, 167–9, 174, 182, 184, 240, 244
Sider, Craig, 12, 16, 63, 179, 260n25
simplicity. *See* Anabaptism: simplicity
Smith, James K.A., 158, 224, 234, 236, 254n6, 290n5
social media, 96, 122, 143, 150–2, 238, 247, 264n15, 280n15
spiritual but not religious (SBNR), 11, 68, 88, 98, 191, 199, 257n14, 277n10
spoiled identity. *See* identity: spoiled
Springs Church, MB, 274n1
status anxiety, 252n4
stigmatization, xiii, 5–6, 47–53, 74, 80–2, 267n4
story, story-telling, 28, 35, 56–7, 60, 62, 80–1, 96–104, 107–8, 121–4, 138, 143, 242, 259n21, 278n15
strictness theory, 18, 157–8, 167–9
suffering, 58, 88–9, 99, 112–13, 183, 196
switching, switchers, 84, 107, 119–20, 140, 208–9
subversion, subversive, xv, 6–7, 14–16, 22, 24, 43, 56, 70, 85, 92, 98, 212, 241, 259n22, 284n11

succession: leadership, 192–222, 278n1, 288n21
Sunday, Billy, 160, 194

tattoos, xviii, 5–8, 15, 178, 219, 223–4, 241
Taylor, Charles, 8, 25, 33, 49, 176, 260n26, 262n7
team, teamwork, 18, 26, 28, 64, 125–55, 201, 218, 222, 227
televangelists, 55, 76, 82, 86–8, 113, 146, 280n12
third way, xii, xiv, 6, 19, 39–44, 74, 224–5, 244, 258n20
Trump, Donald, xiii, 53, 224, 251n3, 264n15

Wallace, David Foster, 73, 204, 223, 225–6
Warren, Rick, 33–5, 78, 82, 195, 229, 270n13, 283n5
Weber, Max, 26, 28–9, 32–8, 45, 48, 126, 140, 264n12; bureaucracy, 26, 32, 191, 219, 226, 236; charismatic aristocracy, 128; and Hitler, 264n14; rationality, 29, 159, 174–5, 191, 242, 273n20; routinization, 29, 36, 38, 126, 133, 151, 191, 193, 198–9, 222, 238, 263n10; succession 214–18; *verstehen*, 246
world religions, 5, 114; Buddha, xi; Confucius, 274n23; Judaism, 223, 289n1; Muslim, 5, 12, 51–2, 55, 90, 137

zombies, xvi, 74, 84–7, 271–3